WITHDRAWN FROM
TSC LIBRARY

A PHILOSOPHY OF RELIGION

A PHILOSOPHY
OF RELIGION

By

EDGAR SHEFFIELD BRIGHTMAN

Borden Parker Bowne Professor of Philosophy
Boston University

GREENWOOD PRESS, PUBLISHERS
WESTPORT, CONNECTICUT

Copyright © 1940 by Prentice-Hall, Inc.

Reprinted with the permission of Mrs. Edgar Brightman.

Reprinted in 1969 by Greenwood Press,
A division of Congressional Information Service, Inc.
88 Post Road West, Westport, Connecticut 06881

Library of Congress catalog card number 72-95112
ISBN 0-8371-2468-9

Printed in the United States of America

10 9 8 7 6 5 4 3 2

DEDICATED TO MY CHILDREN
HOWARD
MIRIAM
ROBERT

088703

088403

PREFACE

HIS book is a philosophy of religion. In other words, it is written for thoughtful readers who wish to examine religion in its relations to the whole life of man today. The keynote of the book is experience. My primary purpose is to interpret religious experience rather than to discuss systems of philosophy. I have a system of my own, but I am convinced that my views are not absolute truth. I present them as hypotheses to stimulate thought and as stepping stones to higher truth, rather than as the last word on any issue. The book, as I have said, is *a* philosophy of religion. Only God, or someone who confused himself with deity, could write *the* philosophy of religion.

The facts of experience are summarized in the sciences. As a philosophy of religion, this book is an interpretation of science, but is not itself science. The science of religion gives the facts of everyday religious experience as they appear to the historian, the psychologist, and the sociologist. Philosophy in all its branches relies upon science and has no organized subject matter apart from the facts set forth by science. It is the responsibility of the scientist to gather the facts for the philosopher to interpret. Some philosophers of religion deem it best to repeat the results of the sciences at length; I have chosen to condense these results into a single chapter (Chapter II), which serves the purpose of review or of orientation (depending on the reader's previous studies). This chapter is no substitute for a thorough study of the sciences themselves; likewise, the sciences of history, psychology, and sociology are no substitutes for philosophy. Yet they are essential to it. So essential are they that the ideal student will master them before undertaking philosophy and will continually go back to them for rootage in the soil of experience.

Certain aspects of religion are investigated by theology, but this book is not a theology. It is true that some modern theologians in England and America regard theology as substantially identical with philosophy of religion or as a branch of it. Yet theology, as distinguished from philosophy, starts with the faith of some particular religion—the Christian, the Jewish, or the Buddhist, for example—and expounds that faith, sometimes with philosophical objectivity, sometimes with complete acceptance of it as divine revelation. In contrast with theology, philosophy of religion treats all types of religion and religious faith as its domain, not presupposing the privileged position of any type, but seeking to discover what religious truths are implied by the history, psychology, and sociology of religion. Philosophy of religion does not include a treatment of the peculiar tenets of any faith, but seeks for the truth in all.

A·book on philosophy of religion should prove helpful in practical living, but it is not a manual of devotion or of edification. Instead, it is an objective and rational interpretation of experience, perhaps more or less "cold-blooded," as emotionalists, shy of reason, sometimes say. Yet I accept Kant's principle of the primacy of the practical reason, and believe that theoretical knowledge is and should be sought primarily for the purpose of making better persons. They are needed. Knowledge should result in a deepening of the devotional life, if there is any value in devotion, and should literally edify, that is, build up the spiritual life. But any devotion or edification that lacks a background of intelligent faith may easily be harmful to religion by creating the nervous idea that religion cannot survive honest investigation. True devotion must be a by-product of truth. Philosophy deepens and broadens life, gives it a principle of growth, disciplines its excesses, and points it toward the eternal. Men of deepest devotion—like Saint Augustine, Saint Thomas Aquinas, John Calvin, John Wesley, and, in our own day, Gandhi, Kagawa, and Rufus M. Jones—are men of profound thought. Religion without thought is like a boat without a rudder; it should be added that an excellent rudder without any boat also leaves its possessor in a predicament.

This book would have been impossible without the help of many former teachers, present colleagues, students, and other friends. Among those to whom I am chiefly indebted for valuable suggestions based on a laborious reading of my entire manuscript are Professor Arthur E. Murphy of the University of Illinois, editor of the series of which this volume is a part, Professor J. Seelye Bixler of Harvard University, Dean Emeritus Albert C. Knudson of Boston University, and Dr. Jannette E. Newhall of the Andover Harvard Theological Library. Professor Wayland F. Vaughan, of the department of psychology in Boston University, has rendered valued aid in connection with Chapter XI. Several of my students have given helpful suggestions. Without the criticisms of Mrs. M. G. Baily of Newton Center as well as of the experts associated with Prentice-Hall, Inc., the form of this book would be far less accurate, consistent, and artistic than it is. Should there be any error of form or of fact or any unfairness of argument in dealing with naturalistic and antitheistic thought, or with pragmatism, or with phenomenology or realism or theistic absolu-

tism or psychology, it is my own fault. I shall have sinned
against the light so generously furnished by specialists in
those fields. My sin be upon my own head, and not on
theirs.

Readers of this book are invited to write to the author (in
care of the publisher) any suggestions for its improvement.

EDGAR SHEFFIELD BRIGHTMAN

NEWTON CENTER, MASSACHUSETTS

TABLE OF CONTENTS

CHAPTER   PAGE

I. ORIENTATION   I
  §1. Empirical method in philosophy of religion . . .   I
  §2. Objections to empirical method by apriorists,
     logical positivists, and Barthians   I
  §3. The justification of empirical method . . .   6
  §4. Experience: nonscientific and scientific . . .   8
  §5. What is religion?   13
  §6. Science of religion   18
  §7. Philosophy   20
  §8. Philosophy of religion (and theology) . .   22
  §9. History of philosophy of religion   26

II. RELIGION AS A FACT   31
  §1. Scientific and philosophical investigation of
     religion   31
  §2. Sciences of religion   33
  §3. History of religion: primitive   36
  §4. History of religion: tribal   45
  §5. History of religion: national (priestly) . .   46
  §6. History of religion: universal (prophetic) .   56
  §7. History of religion: living religions . . .   63
  §8. Psychology of religion: psychology of con-
     version   67
  §9. Psychology of religion: psychology of mys-
     ticism   69
  §10. Psychology of religion: psychology of prayer
     and worship   70

CHAPTER   PAGE

II. Religion as a Fact (*Cont.*)

§11. Psychology of religion: psychology of individual types   72

§12. Psychology of religion and the subconscious   73

§13. Psychology of religion and social psychology   74

§14. Sociology of religion: religion and social
groups and institutions   76

§15. Sociology of religion: religion and economic
forces   78

§16. Sociology of religion: religion and social reforms   79

§17. Chief religious beliefs   81

III. Religious Values   85

§1. Religion as experience of value   85

§2. Fundamental definitions   88

§3. A table of values   94

§4. The uniqueness and the coalescence of the
intrinsic values   100

§5. The uniqueness of religious values   102

§6. The coalescence of religious values with other
values   104

§7. The relations of ideals to existence   105

IV. Religion as a Philosophical Problem . . .   108

§1. If religious values were unique and autonomous, religion might be independent of philosophy   108

§2. Even then it would be a problem for history,
psychology, and sociology   111

§3. Reasons for treating it as a philosophical problem   112

§4. What is the philosophical problem of religion?   116

§5. What is the method of philosophical interpretation?   116

CHAPTER PAGE

IV. RELIGION AS A PHILOSOPHICAL PROBLEM (*Cont.*)
§6. What is the criterion of religious truth? . . 122
§7. The problem of religious certainty 129
§8. The central beliefs of religion 131

V. CONCEPTIONS OF GOD 133
§1. Why begin with conceptions of God? . . . 133
§2. God as objective source and conserver of values 134
§3. God as personified particular value (polytheism) 137
§4. God as personified national spirit (henotheism) 138
§5. God as supreme personal creator (monotheism) 140
§6. God as the whole of reality (pantheism) . . 141
§7. God as the unknowable source of all being (agnostic realism) 142
§8. God as human aspiration for ideal values (humanism) 143
§9. God as superhuman and supernatural revealer of values (deistic supernaturalism) . 145
§10. God as the system of ideal values (impersonal idealism). 147
§11. God as the tendency of nature to support or produce values (religious naturalism) . . . 148
§12. Conceptions of God as revolutionary or evolutionary 153
§13. An evolutionary conception: God as conscious mind, immanent both in nature and in values (theism) 157

VI. WAYS OF KNOWING GOD 162
Introductory 162
§1. Immediate experience of God 168

CHAPTER   PAGE

VI. WAYS OF KNOWING GOD (*Cont.*)
     §2. Revelation 172
     §3. Faith 178
     §4. A priori principles 182
     §5. Action 186
     §6. Coherence 189
     §7. Knowing as certain or as heuristic 194

VII. THE PROBLEM OF BELIEF IN GOD 196
     §1. Why is belief in God a problem? 196
     §2. How could the problem be solved? 200
     §3. Is there no God at all? 202
     §4. Is God one or many? 203
     §5. Is God human experience only? 207
     §6. Is God a part of nature? 209
     §7. Is nature a part of God? 216
     §8. Is God all that there is? 218
     §9. Is God wholly other than nature? 220
     §10. Is God unconscious axiogenesis? 223
     §11. Is God a person? 224
     §12. Is God a superperson? 236
     §13. Religion and theory 237

VIII. THE PROBLEM OF GOOD-AND-EVIL 240
     §1. Belief in God raises the problem of good-and-
          evil 240
     §2. Goods-and-evils as intrinsic and instrumental 241
     §3. Intrinsic goods-and-evils 243
     §4. Instrumental goods-and-evils 246
     §5. The religious problem of good-and-evil . . 248
     §6. The philosophical problem of good-and-evil . 250
     §7. The dialectic of desire 251
     §8. Current solutions of the problem of evil
          examined 259
     §9. The trilemma of religion 272

CHAPTER   PAGE

IX. THEISTIC ABSOLUTISM AND FINITISM   276
     §1. Summary of possible solutions of the problem
          of good-and-evil 276
     §2. The issues at stake 277
     §3. Theistic absolutism vs. theistic finitism . . 280
     §4. Historical sketch of theistic absolutism . . 283
     §5. Historical sketch of theistic finitism . . . 286
     §6. What theistic absolutists and theistic finitists
          have in common 301

X. IS GOD FINITE? 305
     §1. Argument for theistic absolutism 305
     §2. Argument against theistic absolutism . . . 307
     §3. Argument for theistic finitism 313
     §4. Argument against theistic finitism 324
     §5. Restatement of the hypothesis of a Finite-
          Infinite Controller of The Given 336
     §6. Perfection or perfectibility? 340

XI. THE PROBLEM OF HUMAN PERSONALITY . . . 342
     §1. The importance of man for religion . . . 342
     §2. Why not then begin with man? 342
     §3. What is the problem of personality? . . . 344
     §4. Definition of personality 346
     §5. The unity and identity of personality . . . 353
     §6. Personality and its environment 358
     §7. The reality of the spiritual life 361
     §8. Personality human and divine: likenesses . 362
     §9. Personality human and divine: differences . 364

XII. THE PROBLEM OF HUMAN PURPOSE 371
     §1. Persons as purposers 371
     §2. Religion as concern about purpose 372
     §3. Teleology and mechanism: problem and defi-
          nition 373

CHAPTER   PAGE

XII. THE PROBLEM OF HUMAN PURPOSE (*Cont.*)

§4. Stages of thought about teleology and
    mechanism 375
§5. The validity of mechanism 376
§6. The limits of mechanism 377
§7. The evidence for teleology 379
§8. The problem of freedom 381
§9. Relations between mechanism and teleology 382
§10. Purpose and community 383
§11. Purpose and time 384
§12. Purpose and eternity 385

XIII. THE PROBLEM OF HUMAN IMMORTALITY . . . 387

§1. Religious belief in immortality 387
§2. Belief in immortality as extension of experi-
    ence of purpose 388
§3. Weak arguments 389
§4. Crucial argument against immortality: phys-
    iological psychology 395
§5. Crucial argument for immortality: the good-
    ness of God 400
§6. Immortality and the problem of good-and-evil 404
§7. Conditional immortality 406
§8. The religious value of belief in immortality 409

XIV. THE PROBLEM OF RELIGIOUS EXPERIENCE . . . 411

§1. Religion as experience 411
§2. The meaning of experience 412
§3. The meaning of religious experience . . . 415
§4. Foundations of religious experience . . . 417
§5. Development of religious experience . . . 423
§6. The validity of religious experience . . . 436

XV. INTERNAL CRITICISMS OF RELIGION 438

§1. Philosophy of religion as critical interpretation
    of religion 438

CHAPTER   PAGE

XV. INTERNAL CRITICISMS OF RELIGION (*Cont.*)

§2. Internal and external criticism 439
§3. History of religion as a process of internal criticism 440
§4. Religious criticism of the present as disloyal to the past 443
§5. Religious criticism of the present and past as disloyal to the ideal 444
§6. Religious criticism of the present as disloyal to spiritual growth 450
§7. Religious criticism of the tendency of religion to extremes 452

XVI. EXTERNAL CRITICISMS OF RELIGION 459

§1. The meaning and value of external criticism 459
§2. Religion as outgrowth of fear 461
§3. Religion as a rationalization of desire . . . 464
§4. Religion as a device in the class struggle . 472
§5. Origin as determining meaning and value . 476
§6. Religion as free play of imagination . . . 477
§7. Religion as inconsistent with science . . . 480
§8. Religious beliefs as unverifiable 485
§9. Religion as providing no positive value . . 487

HISTORICAL BIBLIOGRAPHY 490

GENERAL BIBLIOGRAPHY 495

INDEX AND LEXICON 523

ONE

ORIENTATION

§ 1. Empirical Method in Philosophy of Religion

UR experience consists of our entire conscious life. Religion is one phase of experience. Philosophy of religion is the experience of interpreting those experiences which we call religious and of relating them to other experiences, as well as to our conception of experience as a whole. All the problems of philosophy of religion concerning faith, worship, tradition, God, revelation, immortality, doubt, skepticism, or secularism are stresses and strains within experience. Any solution of these problems must always be a reinterpretation of experience, for all human knowledge begins, continues, and ends in experience. Science is one stage of reinterpretation of experience, philosophy another. Both science and philosophy are movements of experience from a state of confusion and contradiction toward a state of order and coherence. Science is such a movement within a limited field; philosophy aims to include and interpret all experience in a comprehensive unity.

§ 2. Objections to Empirical Method by Apriorists, Logical Positivists, and Barthians

The foregoing statements about experience, which are either fundamental truths or dangerous errors, may be regarded in the latter light by at least three groups of thinkers: (1) the apriorists; (2) the logical positivists, and (3) the

Barthians. At the very outset, therefore, it is necessary to present these three objections to the proposition that religious knowledge arises in and is tested by experience.

According to the apriorists,[1] it is necessary to distinguish between experience and reason. Experience for them consists of given data, especially those of sensation, of morality, and of religious life. Reason consists of eternal principles of validity which are not derived from experience as defined. Four apples are inferred from sense data, but the truth that $2 + 2 = 4$ is an eternal, universal, and necessary truth which is derived not from observing apples, but either from the nature of the mind or from pure logic. The religious apriorists hold that faith in God is not like the belief in four apples; it is like the truth of $2 + 2 = 4$, or, rather, like the axioms and postulates from which that truth is derived and which render it certain. Those postulates are true, and hence $2 + 2 = 4$, no matter how many apples may be visible—in short, they are true, independent of experience. The apriorist discovers numerous a priori truths in logic, in mathematics, in ethics, and in religion. He thus seems to endow religious faith with an absolute and unshakable certainty.[2]

Now, one who holds the standpoint of the first paragraph in this chapter is called an empiricist. An empiricist would reply to an apriorist somewhat as follows: It is misleading, he would say, to declare that there is anything independent

---

[1] For a discussion of their views, see A. C. Knudson, in Wilm, SPT, 93–127, and Knudson's VRE. (As a rule, references to sources are indicated in this volume by abbreviations which are explained in the Bibliography at the back of the book. The author's name should be consulted.)

[2] There are, it is true, wide differences among those who call themselves religious apriorists. The view stated in the text is that of Jakob Friedrich Fries, the Kantian, and was held by Rudolf Otto when he wrote his *Philosophy of Religion Based on Kant and Fries* (London: Williams and Norgate Ltd., 1931). Otto says explicitly that every a priori principle rests on judgments "independent of experience," the "a priori religious" among them (18). Fries and Otto thus ac-

of experience. The case of the apriorist derives its force from the indubitable fact that there is a difference in importance between four apples and $2 + 2 = 4$. The empiricist insists, however, that the process of thinking that $2 + 2 = 4$ is as truly a conscious experience as is the process of observing four McIntosh Reds. The same is true of our thought regarding any axiom or postulate. The assertion that one part of experience is independent of another part of experience may be true. But the assertion that one part of experience is independent of all experience is logically contradictory. The trouble arises from using the word experience in a restricted meaning (as confined to sensations or like content) and then forgetting the restriction. It is better to be a thoroughgoing empiricist and define experience as meaning all that is at any time present in consciousness. Thus the misunderstandings to which apriorism gives rise are largely a matter of definition of terms and illustrate the harm done by inadequate definition. The quality of being independent of experience appertains to no truth, if experience be defined inclusively. No truth can be said to be unqualifiedly a priori unless it is necessarily related to all experience in such a way that it is always valid, no matter what happens. No truth about religion can be called a priori unless it has a necessary relation to all religious experience. It is possible that some truths are universal and necessary; but this fact cannot be known prior

---

cepted Kant's logical conception of the a priori and differed from him only in asserting the metaphysical objectivity of a priori knowledge. Other apriorists, like Troeltsch and Knudson, mean by the religious a priori a native capacity of the soul for religious experience; thus they conceive it psychologically and, in a sense, empirically, rather than logically. But these writers are often led into so great an emphasis on their faith in the ideal that they sometimes may underestimate the weight of contrary empirical evidence when it raises difficulties for faith. The apriorism discussed in the text, however, is closer to historical rationalism as expressed in the ontological argument than it is to the psychological a priori.

to experiences of thinking and observing. Hence the objection of the apriorist to empiricism can be raised or tested
only by means of experience.[3]

The logical positivists comprise another group which
would regard the empirical method as dangerous in the
philosophy of religion. But their reasons are quite different from those of the apriorists. The logical positivists
agree with the apriorists in distinguishing between experience and reason, although they do not like to speak of
reason, a term which seems to them too psychological.
They would prefer to describe the distinction as one between logical propositions and factual propositions. Logical
propositions are purely formal truths regarding the principles of logical implication. They entail nothing regarding
the real world and do not even assume that there is one,
as Bertrand Russell pointed out in his *Introduction to
Mathematical Philosophy* (203). Hence, no purely logical
a priori principle can define either religion or anything else
in the real world. For all information about real experience
we must consult experience itself. Thus the logical positivist seems to be asserting substantially what was asserted in
the first paragraph of this chapter. He really is saying
something very different, however. By experience he means
exclusively the area of what we commonly call sense experiences. The logical positivist will accept as true what
can be verified in sense experience. As a matter of fact,
religious experience, as it actually occurs, always includes
not only certain sense experiences but also other experiences
which are often called religious values. The exaltation of
the spirit in worship and the experience of moral obligation
are characteristic of religion; they both contain factors
which are not verifiable in sense perception. You certainly

---

[3] This view will be considered more fully in Chap. VI, § 4.

cannot perceive by any senses either religious adoration or the consciousness of "I ought."

There is, therefore, a genuine issue between the logical positivist and the empiricist in philosophy of religion. If a thinker has reason to suppose that no fact is truly empirical unless it is a sense experience, he has by "initial predication" excluded all religious experience from the possibility of making any contribution to truth. This is one aspect of the issue. Another aspect arises from the fact that the logical positivist regards philosophy as confined to the realm of logic and science as confined to sense experience. As opposed to this, a broadly empirical philosophy aims to interpret the relations of all kinds of experience to each other, seeking for some clue to the interrelations of logic, sense experience, and value experience. If we were to accept logical positivism at the start, it would mean that we regarded the search for such a clue as meaningless and our problem would be solved negatively before we began. To do this would be as unempirical and unphilosophical as it would be to presuppose that the teachings of some particular sect or religion are true. Hence the objection of the logical positivist need not cause us to suspend investigation; it may well teach us to be precise in our conceptions of experience and of verification.[4]

The rationalistic apriorists seek to protect religion from the cruel risks of experience by elevating it into the realm of pure reason. The logical positivists seek to annihilate religion by denying it any standing in experience. Apriorists and logical positivists agree in rejecting empirical method in philosophy of religion—the former because they hold empirical method to be inadequate and the latter

---

[4] See A. J. Ayer, *Language, Truth, and Logic* (New York: Oxford University Press, 1936) for an excellent survey of logical positivism. Stuart Chase has popularized a similar standpoint in *The Tyranny of Words.*

because their empirical method discloses no religious experience. A third group of thinkers, the Barthians, are even more devastating in their attack, for they hold that neither reason nor experience can be trusted as a basis for religious faith. Continuing and elaborating the tradition of John Calvin (1509–1564), Karl Barth [5] teaches that the only source of salvation is "the Word," or divine revelation. God, he holds, is totally "other" than anything in this world, and in Barth's opinion it is sheer idolatry to trust the results of reason as being the truth. The only value of reason in religion is to make revelation clearer. But he trusts experience no more than he trusts reason. The very word religion is distasteful to him, as implying human experience and human belief rather than divine revelation and divine action. He would base his faith on God alone, not on any human thinking or experiencing.

§ 3. The Justification of Empirical Method

Here, then, are three formidable attacks on an empirical philosophy of religion. Have we, therefore, made a false start? Is it necessary to discuss and refute each of these objections before beginning an investigation of the nature of religion?

Fortunately, the very nature of empirical method renders any such skirmishes unnecessary. If a philosophy of religion were to be written from an a priori or from a Barthian point of view, it would be necessary first to dispose of all competing methods in order to leave the field clear. If a logical positivist were to write a philosophy of religion, he

---

[5] The clearest exposition of his views is in Karl Barth, *The Doctrine of the Word of God* (New York: Charles Scribner's Sons, 1936). See the Index under Theology and Philosophy. Barth, the most distinguished contemporary Christian theologian, taught for many years in Germany. He was expelled from that country in 1935 for his political opinions and has since resided in Switzerland.

would have to show at the very start that he could not possibly find any objectively valid religious data in experience, on his premises, in order to prepare for his solely negative treatment. An empirical method, on the contrary, does not require that the field be thus cleared of all opponents, for the reason that it is so inclusive and liberal in its attitude as to find a place for all points of view, all types of belief, and even all objections to itself. The empirical method demands that the mind should survey all facts that have any bearing on the subject in hand; and this would include all competing theories, too. A true empiricist will examine experience to find whether it contains or implies or presupposes any a priori principles; he will ask the precise meaning of verification and will consider all that the logical positivist has to say, in the light of the very experiences that positivism challenges; he will grant to the Barthians that some experiences claim to be revelations and he will examine their claims. In short, the method requires that all the data and points of view of rationalistic apriorism, logical positivism, and Barthianism eventually be observed and evaluated; it also requires observation and evaluation of experiences which each of these methods would reject or belittle. Accordingly, there seems to be no good reason for declining to try empirical method.

It is a fact that religion and religious knowledge (or claims to such knowledge) arise in our conscious experience and are in some way tested by it. To accept this fact is to adopt an empirical method of open-minded inquiry that commits us in advance to no conclusions. At the same time, it is obvious that the apriorist, the logical positivist, and the Barthian are committed in advance, the first to a rationalistic belief in God and religion, the second to skepticism, and the third to a supernatural religion. Is it not the part of wisdom to pursue the liberal and open-minded path of the empiricist? This is the path of genuine investigation—as John Dewey says, of "inquiry."

§ 4. EXPERIENCE: NONSCIENTIFIC AND SCIENTIFIC

Experience is the necessary starting point of any philosophy of religion. But what experience and whose experience? It would be quite in accord with the scientific temper of the age to reply to the former question by saying that the only experience worthy of serious attention is experience as investigated by scientific method, and to the latter by asserting that the experience of men of science is the only basis of philosophy of religion. Ordinary experience is so confused, inaccurate, and narrow that it is quite untrustworthy. Experience is a chaos until it has been studied scientifically.

On the other hand, a quite different answer might be given to the same question by a truly radical empiricist. He might say that it is impossible for anyone, even the greatest scientist, to start with scientific experience. Science is a development out of ordinary experience. No scientist begins by being a scientist. He begins by being born as a baby. He goes through the "blooming, buzzing confusion" which William James made famous; gradually he learns to identify objects and to use language. Thus his experience is enlarged and ordered. A long time later he develops a desire to understand and to control that experience in which hidden forces operate and hidden perils lurk— perils so great that they are certain, sooner or later, to bring to an end the very possibility of further experience in this world. The desire to understand and control experience leads to the growth of science. Science is based on controlled experiences called experiments or observations; it leads to experiences of understanding which we call laws; laws are applied to the further control of experience—the mastery of nature, the conquest of disease, the attainment of many ends desired by man.

A philosophy of religion, therefore, must take into account both scientific and nonscientific experience. By *scientific experience* is meant experience as described and explained by the sciences. The chief sciences of religion are history of religion, psychology of religion, and sociology of religion; their main results will be considered in Chapter II. It is necessary, however, for any philosophical investigation to include in its data nonscientific experience. By *nonscientific experience* is meant neither unscientific experience nor poor science, but rather all human experience which is not science. It includes all of our actual everyday consciousness, all our sense experiences, our feelings and desires, our imaginations and many of our beliefs; it includes all of our thoughts, with the exception of those which arise in the course of scientific investigation.

Nonscientific experience is both more fundamental and more inclusive than scientific experience. It is more fundamental, because it is the precondition of science. If there were no nonscientific experience—no sensations, no crude guesses about their meaning, no failures to adjust—there would be no science. Similarly, if there were no prayer, no worship, no faith, there would be no science of religion. This is what James Bissett Pratt meant [6] when he called religious experience the "goose that laid the golden egg" for the psychologists of religion. Nonscientific experience is more fundamental, also, in view of the purpose of science. One purpose, doubtless, is to systematize knowledge; knowledge for its own sake has intrinsic value and is prized by every truly scientific mind. The pure scientist who exclaims, "Thank God that I have found a truth for which

[6] Pratt, RC, 336.

there is no possible practical application," is expressing something of great importance, namely, the insight that the mere knowledge of truth is a delight to the mind, regardless of its uses. Even the most practical-minded critic of such a pure scientist will have to admit that the greatest advances of science have often occurred as a result of sheer curiosity and that discoveries which at first were regarded as pure theory were later found to be of great practical value. But after all, it must be granted that the chief purpose of science is not the blissful contemplation of the propositions of Euclid or of Riemann; its chief purpose lies in its applications to experience for the betterment of human living, by banishing disease, building bridges, railroads, aircraft, and ships, and understanding human nature in all of its manifestations in order to learn how to solve the social and psychological problems of the present. History may, it is true, be investigated out of pure objective interest in the pageant of human life; but the drive which impels humanity to study its own past is ultimately the desire to profit by the past in order to build a better future. Consequently, a large part of the aim of scientific experience is the production of better everyday nonscientific experiences for the common man.[7] In short, nonscientific experience is more fundamental than scientific, since the former is both subject matter and goal of the investigations of the latter.

It remains to show that nonscientific experience is more inclusive than scientific. At first glance this statement appears like a barren truism. It seems obvious that the field of exact knowledge is narrower than the field of everyday experience. What we know accurately is less than what we

---

[7] This idea is related to, although not identical with, Immanuel Kant's thesis of "the primacy of the pure practical reason." The speculative reason, according to Kant, deals with the world of physical phenomena, the practical reason with the moral will. Kant believed that all physical knowledge was for the sake of moral will.

know inaccurately. However, when one considers the expansion of experience by microscope, by telescope, by excavations, and by scientific means of communication and transportation, this is not so certain. Yet the significant meaning of the greater inclusiveness of nonscientific experience is not to be found in such considerations. It is to be found, rather, by inquiring into the nature of scientific experience and observing exactly what it includes and what it excludes.

The word "scientific" is often applied loosely to any and all attempts to systematize experience. Thus astrology, phrenology, and Fichtean metaphysics have been called science; logic, ethics, aesthetics, and theology are often called sciences; and there is Christian Science. So broad a use of the term is not usual in scientific circles. If we are to be precise and in harmony with scientific usage, we should define science not as any and every attempt to systematize knowledge, but rather as a description of the laws of the behavior of objects disclosed by some particular field of experience. Physics, for example, is a description of the laws of matter in motion; chemistry, a description of the laws of the composition and transformations of substances. Now, all strictly scientific experience is descriptive; it tells what the facts are and to what laws the facts conform. But human experience does more than describe the facts. It is inquisitive, and seeks to find out what the facts are good for, what they are worth, what we should do about them. This experience of good or worth or "should" is commonly called the experience of value. Psychology, anthropology, sociology, and history, as descriptive sciences, take account of the value experiences of man. They describe what this man values, what another; what is valued by this group or that group, this nation or that nation. Yet there is nothing within these sciences that would enable the scientist to say that one value or set of values is better than another. Scientific experience is purely descriptive; nonscientific experience contains many statements about better and worse. It is better to live than to die, better to enjoy beauty than to ignore it, better to live happily than unhappily, better to be honest than dishonest, better to listen to a symphony than to the tunes of a popular dance orchestra.

Nonscientific experience is accordingly more inclusive than scientific because it asks such questions as: What is better to do? What is right? What is beautiful? What is holy?—questions not merely about facts, but about the values of facts. Description specifies what the facts are; evaluation determines what they are worth. From the point of view of the descriptive sciences, all evaluation is nonscientific. Many [8] think that, on the basis of the descriptive sciences, normative sciences may be built up which yield normative laws—statements of what ought to be. Such normative sciences might be ethics (laws of how we ought to choose), aesthetics (laws of how we ought to appreciate), logic (laws of how we ought to think), and philosophy of religion (laws of how we ought to worship). Thus we should have normative sciences of the good, the beautiful, the true, and the holy. But there is considerable difference of opinion about whether a normative science should be called a science or a branch of philosophy, and also as to whether "normative" sciences (especially logic) constitute a kind of description. Perhaps the normative sciences belong in scientific experience; perhaps they belong in nonscientific experience. Wherever they are to be classified, they call attention to the value experiences about which descriptive science gives no standards for judging.

[8] Including the author. See Brightman, ML, Chap. I.

At any rate, their data—our daily evaluations—raise questions that lie beyond the field of mere description.

Everyday nonscientific experience is largely dominated by interest in values. One experience is preferred to another; certain objects are desired and others avoided. It is in this realm that all our moral choices, our aesthetic enjoyments, and our religious worship fall. The experience of goodness is nonscientific; psychology and sociology may describe phenomena of goodness and ethics may evaluate the phenomena; but an actual choice by a good will is not a part of any science—it is the reality which makes a science of goodness possible. In the field of religion, prayer is not a psychological description of something or a sociological theory or a philosophical theory; it is the actual experience of "the soul's sincere desire" directed toward what is believed to be the Supreme Being and the Supreme Value in the universe.

Nonscientific experience contains the actual life of value and raises questions about the meaning and importance of value which descriptive science does not raise. This is where religion lives. It is here that every student of nature or of religion must begin his investigations.

§ 5. What is Religion?

A philosophy of religion is itself an attempt to define religion, and an adequate definition of religion must be the product of an adequate investigation. It might, therefore, seem to be excusable (as well as conventional) to postpone any attempt to define it until the investigation is completed. But this would really be a piece of academic hypocrisy. Two facts show the value of a tentative definition at the start. (1) It is necessary to have some idea of what religion is in order to select any subject matter for investigation; if we have no idea of what we are investigating, we have no facts to investigate. (2) Every definition of a real object is an hypothesis, subject to correction. Thus, the preliminary definition of religion will be genuinely tentative; indeed, there is no such thing as a final definition of religion unless all facts about religion are known and these facts are all correctly and completely interpreted. Just as man's definition of a physical thing has changed from Democritus to Planck and Einstein, so definitions of religion change.

In approaching the task of defining religion, the student is easily duped by the seeming certainty and authority of his own personal or social experiences. In a nonscientific realm like religion, where values are at stake, where the life of emotion and desire is involved, and where the mores of family, church, synagogue, party, or clique prescribe a particular kind of faith or unfaith, it is natural to say: "Religion is what I and my group have experienced religion to be." Such experience is indeed the necessary starting point for any study of religion, but a little reflection will show why it cannot be a stopping place. No one can rightly say: "A belief is true because it is mine; contrary beliefs are false because I doubt them." Nor can anyone rightly say: "Our group belief is true because it is ours; other beliefs are false because our group rejects them." If this were done, "truth" would become a meaningless chaos. The seeming authority of the individual's own experience and that of his group must always submit to the light that is shed by a larger experience. It is only when personal and group experience has been examined in the light of the whole range of knowable experience that one has the materials at hand for estimating the meaning and value of one's own experience. In religion, as in all other fields, the observation of one person must be supplemented by the observations of countless others if truth is to be found.

The definition of religion with which philosophy may

start should, therefore, be one which notes not merely the characteristics of the definer's own religion, but rather those which are common to all persons and groups who experience what they regard as religion. This description should be purely descriptive; that is, it should be quite neutral to the normative question whether religion as it has been bears any resemblance to religion as it ought to be. A proper descriptive definition, then, is neutral to all inquiries on whether religion is true or false, helpful or harmful, illusory or veridical. It will contain solely a concept of what religion has actually been, and, like any good definition, will distinguish the *definiendum* from all other terms with which it might be confused. Thus a definition of religion will distinguish religion from science, from philosophy, from morals, from art, and from all nonreligious personal and social experiences.

Such are the qualifications of a satisfactory descriptive definition of religion. Can a definition be furnished which will conform to the specifications? It must be said at once that a bewildering variety of contradictory definitions of religion has been set forth by authorities in the field. A sample list of such definitions is found in the twenty-one-page Appendix to J. H. Leuba's *A Psychological Study of Religion,* which is analyzed and criticized in a chapter entitled, "Constructive Criticism of Current Conceptions of Religion." A textbook (Vergilius Ferm's *First Chapters in Religious Philosophy*) devotes seventy-one pages to a discussion of the definition of religion. To consider all proposed definitions would be an endless task.[9]

---

[9] Ten sample definitions are given, which the student may test for himself by applying the criteria given in the text.

Immanuel Kant: "Religion is (subjectively regarded) the recognition of all duties as divine commands." RLR, 142.

Friedrich Schleiermacher: "To take everything individual as a part of the whole, everything limited as a representation of the infinite,—that is religion."

An approach to the goal may be made by defining the field of religion as including all the experiences that are generally recognized as belonging to the great historical movements which regard themselves as religious—such as Christianity, Judaism, Mohammedanism, Buddhism, Hinduism, Confucianism, and the like—together with the earlier experiences out of which these religions have grown and the movements now developing within them. The variety of beliefs and practices thus designated as religious might seem to defy all definition. One can understand why definitions have been widely divergent. Doubtless every definition that has been proposed is either a correct description

---

Tr. from ÜR, 56. "The common element in all expressions of religion [*Frömmigkeit*], no matter how different, whereby they are distinguished from all other feelings, the permanently identical essence of religion, is that we are conscious of ourselves as absolutely dependent or, to say the same thing in other words, we are conscious of being in relation with God." Tr. from CG, I. 15, sec. 4.

Ludwig Feuerbach: "Man is the beginning of religion, man is the center of religion, man is the end of religion." Tr. from WC, Kap. 19.

Salomon Reinach: "I propose to define religion as: *A sum of scruples which impede the free exercise of our faculties.*" ORP, 3.

Harald Höffding: "That which expresses the innermost tendency of all religions is the axiom of the conservation of values." PR, 215.

William James: "Religion [means] . . . the feelings, acts, and experiences of individual men in their solitude, so far as they apprehend themselves to stand in relation to whatever they may consider the divine." VRE, 31. (Cf. A. N. Whitehead: "Religion is what the individual does with his own solitariness." RM, 16.)

V. F. Calverton: "Magic and religion evolved as (a) means whereby (man) believed he was able to acquire . . . power (over his environment) and make the universe bend to his wishes." PG, 51.

John Dewey: "Whatever introduces genuine perspective is religious." CF, 24. "The religious attitude (is) a sense of the possibilities of existence and . . . devotion to the cause of these possibilities." QC, 303.

W. E. Hocking: "Religion . . . is the present attainment in a single experience of those objects which in the course of nature are reached only at the end of infinite progression. Religion is anticipated attainment." MGHE, 31. "Religion . . . is the habitual reference of life to divine powers." TP, 26.

Vergilius Ferm: "*To be religious is to effect in some way and in some measure a vital adjustment (however tentative and incomplete) to w(W)hatever is reacted to or regarded implicitly or explicitly as worthy of serious and ulterior concern.*" FCRP, 61.

of certain aspects of religion or at least an honest evaluation of religion by the definer (even when Reinach oddly brands religion as a sum of scruples which hinder the free exercise of our powers).

If the student examines all religions empirically with a view to picking out their essential common traits, one who lives in a Judaeo-Christian civilization must be prepared to admit that some of the most essential features of Christianity (such as faith in Jesus Christ) are lacking from Judaism; and that the belief in a conscious, personal God, common to most forms of Judaism and Christianity, is lacking from Hinayana Buddhism, as well as from American religious humanism. Immortality is doubted or rejected by many religious believers. Nevertheless, all kinds of religion have in common such traits as to warrant the following definition: *Religion is concern about experiences which are regarded as of supreme value; devotion toward a power or powers believed to originate, increase, and conserve these values; and some suitable expression of this concern and devotion, whether through symbolic rites or through other individual and social conduct.* Religion, then, is a total experience which includes this concern, this devotion, and this expression. It always involves a set of beliefs about reality in addition to attitudes and practices of various sorts.

Religion differs from magic in being devotion to the power that is the source of values, whereas magic is a kind of mechanical compulsion of that power. Religion differs from science in being concerned about values, while science ignores the value of its facts and confines itself to objective description. Religion resembles morals and art in being concerned with values, but differs from them in its primary devotion to the power or powers that originate the supreme value of life, as well as in the use of ritual for its expression.

The proposed definition is to be treated solely as descrip-

tive. It is an heuristic hypothesis that will enable the
student of religion to select his data. It is not intended to
express any judgment about the truth or value of religion.
It is simply a guide to the discovery of religious facts. A
normative definition can be sought only as the outcome of
a philosophy of religion.

§ 6. Science of Religion

The definition of religion which has just been proposed
is one which a believer who is ignorant of or indifferent
to the existence and claims of other religions would not
think of proposing. In short, the definition is the result
of a systematic investigation of the facts of all religious
experience. Such investigation is called the science of
religion,[10] a form of what we have called scientific experience.

In order to make clear what is meant by the science of
religion, it is necessary to define science more precisely.
A science is, in the broadest sense, systematized knowledge
of some particular field. No science exists if mere facts
are accumulated without system or law; and no science
aims to investigate all the objects in the universe. Astronomy may include all of the heavenly bodies, but it
does not include life cells or ethical principles. No science
is all-inclusive.

There are two main kinds of science, the formal and the
empirical. The formal sciences, like logic and mathematics,
deal with the laws of implication or deduction, which are
universally valid, in the sense that they cannot be changed
or affected by any further experiences, and are true of
whatever experiences they may be applied to. It is of
this kind of science that religious apriorists and logical

---

[10] See § 4 above.

positivists [11] are thinking. In addition to the formal sciences, there are the empirical sciences, which are what most people have in mind when they speak of science. An empirical science is one that selects a particular kind of object observable in experience and attempts, by repeated observations, hypotheses, and experiments (wherever possible) to describe the laws of its phenomena. Typical empirical sciences are physics, chemistry, biology, geology, astronomy, and the like. It is evident that the laws of one science may be very different from the laws of another. The laws of biology are not applicable to physics, and the laws of physics do not account for life. Still less like physics are the sciences of psychology, anthropology, sociology, and history; and it must be granted that the laws which these sciences discover are less numerous, less precise, and (as a rule) less verifiable than the laws of physics.[12] Yet knowledge of these fields, since they concern man himself directly, is of even greater practical importance than knowledge of the inorganic world, for if man knew physics without knowing his own nature and powers he would never be able to apply physics intelligently to meet human needs. If, on the other hand, man understood himself, he would be unable to restrain his curiosity about nature.

The science of religion falls among the empirical sciences which deal with man's psychology, history, and sociology, rather than among the physicochemical or biological sciences. Hence there are three main sciences of religion: psychology of religion, which describes the conscious processes of religious experience, as well as their relations to individual

---

[11] See § 2 of this chapter.

[12] There is still great difference of opinion about the interrelations of the sciences, and some writers insist on holding that the social sciences are scientific only in proportion as they conform to the methods and principles of physics. See, for example, Jacques Rueff, *From the Physical to the Social Sciences* (Baltimore: The Johns Hopkins Press, 1929).

and social behavior and to the unconscious; history of religion and comparative religion, which describes the development of religious beliefs and practices; and sociology of religion, which investigates the laws and functions of religion as a group phenomenon. A survey of these sciences will appear in Chapter II.

§ 7. PHILOSOPHY

The goal of our investigation is not, however, a science of religion, but a philosophy of religion. What, then, is the essential difference between science and philosophy?

There is probably as much confusion among authorities about the definition of philosophy as about that of religion. But if we adopt the same general method in seeking a definition of philosophy as we previously did in seeking to define religion, we shall find that, with all their differences, philosophers have been distinguished from workers in the special sciences by their interest in the unity of experience. Every science deals with a specific, delimited field—some part or aspect of experience—or raises a specific problem, such as the measurement of motion. Philosophy, however, aims to understand experience as a whole, and to correlate all problems. Moreover, the sciences only describe necessary or probable laws of their subject matter, whereas philosophy, by its more inclusive aim, raises also the question of value and asks to what end the laws of science ought to be applied and what may be the moral, aesthetic, or religious worth of the facts. Since questions about value can be answered seriously only in the light of the unity of our whole experience, the so-called normative sciences of logic, [13] ethics, aesthetics, and philosophy of religion are sometimes called philosophical sciences (as by Fullerton),

---

[13] Many modern logicians object to regarding logic as normative. They treat it as descriptive of the laws of implication. However, these laws, when known

and sometimes are incorporated wholly into philosophy as branches of the theory of value (axiology). Philosophy, however, is not exclusively concerned with value. If it were, it could not deal with the unity of all experience. The philosopher must raise questions about the relation of value to existence, the meaning and limits of human knowledge in its entire scope, the relation of human experience to the rest of the universe, and the nature of that universe as a whole. Investigation of knowledge is called epistemology; investigation of the nature of existence, ontology; investigation of the universe as a whole, cosmology; investigation of the ultimate nature of human consciousness and its relations to body and world, rational psychology; and investigation of values and their relation to existence, axiology. The name of metaphysics is now usually given to the system of philosophy as a whole.

If we use the real as a word to indicate the whole active universe of which our experience is but a tiny fragment, then we may say that *philosophy is an attempt to discover a coherent and unified definition of the real.* Or, alternatively, *philosophy is an attempt to give a reasoned account of experience as a whole.* More simply still, *philosophy is an attempt to discover the whole truth.*

Philosophy is akin to religion in that both are dealing with ultimates. Each is an attitude toward fundamental reality. Religion penetrates, as best it can, to the source of its values and usually relates that source, as its God, to all of the real. "In the beginning God created the heavens and the earth." Philosophy also, as has already been implied, agrees with religion and differs from science in dealing with the values of life and in distinguishing higher

---

by human beings, indicate how men ought to think, not how they actually do think day by day. Hence it is still possible to regard logic as normative. See § 4 of this chapter.

from lower values. Philosophy differs from religion in that religion consists of attitudes of concern, devotion or worship, and conduct, whereas philosophy is a rational understanding. Both have the same object, the ultimate unity of reality and the source of values in the universe. Religion takes practical and emotional attitudes toward that object, while philosophy seeks to define and interpret it.

Out of this situation has arisen the fact that religion on the one hand needs philosophy in order to have an objective basis for its faith, but on the other hand it fears philosophy, lest free investigation destroy both the attitude of religious faith and also the grounds on which it rests.

§ 8. PHILOSOPHY OF RELIGION (AND THEOLOGY)

It is now possible to offer a preliminary definition of the main topic of our investigation. *Philosophy of religion is an attempt to discover by rational interpretation of religion and its relations to other types of experience, the truth of religious beliefs and the value of religious attitudes and practices.*

Philosophy of religion is a branch of metaphysics (specifically of axiology) which interprets the relations of man's experience of religious values to the rest of his experiences; thus it seeks both to contribute concrete religious values to the interpretation of experience as a whole and to criticize those values in the light of a rational view. Philosophy of religion thus has no methods, no criteria, no authorities which are not the common property of all philosophy. All experience is open to philosophical investigation without reserve or exception. Neither piety nor science is exempt from the need of being interpreted in the light of the total experience of which each is but a part.

For the sake of clarity, it is necessary to relate philosophy of religion to another branch of thought which is called theology. The word theo-logy, derived from the Greek theos (God) and logos (word), means "theory about God." Aristotle's "First Philosophy" culminated in the idea of God as Pure Form; and hence Aristotle called his metaphysics "theological." Plato's thought also led to a conception of God; his *Timaeus*, in many ways analogous to the book of Genesis, exercised a profound influence over Christian thought. A large part of the history of philosophy is an attempt to arrive at a rational definition of God. Not Plato and Aristotle only, but also the Stoics, even the Epicureans, the Neo-Platonists, the Christian Fathers, the Scholastics, the British empiricists, the Continental rationalists, Kant and the German idealists, the Scotch common sense school, and American thinkers down to Royce, Bowne, Hocking, and Whitehead, have all dealt seriously and constructively with the central theological problem. Nevertheless, it is generally recognized that philosophy should be distinguished from theology.

Historically, theology has been classified as natural or revealed. Natural theology is an investigation of the problem of God based on reason and experience, without recourse to the authority of any special revelation. Natural theology may be either rational or empirical. Revealed theology (also called dogmatic theology) is such theology as relies on a divine revelation (the Bible, the Koran, or the Book of Mormon, for example) as its ultimate religious authority.

In the main, however, this old distinction between natural and revealed theology has come to be largely ignored, especially among Protestant "modernist" theologians. With the breakdown of traditional standards of belief, resulting from the growth of science and philosophy and from the application of scientific methods to Biblical criticism, the idea of a dogmatic authority in Biblical revelation has

come to be widely challenged. Other religions than Christianity are undergoing similar developments. The result
is that the experiences recorded in the Bible and in other
sacred literatures are regarded as data for investigation just
like any other experiences; no authority attaches to them
other than the authority of experience and reason. For
theologians who take this point of view (including most
contemporary American Protestant thinkers in the field,
such as A. C. Knudson, W. A. Brown, H. N. Wieman,
John Bennett, R. L. Calhoun, W. M. Horton, and others),
theology is a branch of philosophy of religion. It differs
from philosophy of religion simply in the nature of its
starting point. For philosophy of religion, all religious beliefs and experiences, of whatever sort or kind, are considered as the primary source material for interpretation.
For theology, the historical beliefs of the theologian's own
religious community are the primary sources. Theology
thus has a more restricted field as its starting point; but the
materials of this field are studied by the same critical and
rational methods as philosophy applies in any field. If the
theologian maintains his ideal as thus set up, he is a philosopher of religion engaged in a peculiarly thorough and
critical philosophical interpretation of the subject matter
of some one religious faith. Unfortunately, it sometimes
happens that preoccupation with one tradition tends to
produce a bias in favor of that tradition which renders
objectivity all but impossible.

In addition to the type of theology just described, which
corresponds roughly to the old natural theology, there is a
contemporary counterpart of revealed theology, which often
rejects natural theology. There are still many who believe
that they can find in the Bible (or in whatever Sacred Scriptures they may possess) an authoritative revelation of God
that is above reason and to which reason must submit

exactly as it must submit to the authority of any given fact. This point of view is found among the Orthodox Jews, supported by an ancient and learned tradition. It is the standpoint of the theology of the Roman Catholic Church, the intellectual and spiritual authority of which exceeds even its extensive temporal powers. It is shared by many Lutherans and by Calvinists. It is held by those called "Fundamentalists." It is the basis of movements as different as Christian Science and the Witnesses of Jehovah. In an acute form it has recently been reasserted by the most famous living Protestant theologian, Karl Barth, and less sharply by others like Emil Brunner and Paul Tillich. For those who rest theology on authoritative revelation, theology is a very different matter from philosophy of religion, for Christian faith is said by Brunner to be "a fundamentally different thing from every philosophy," because "the complex of grounds and consequences developed by natural reason . . . has been broken into by revelation." [14] Paul Tillich builds his philosophy of religion on the antithesis between religion, which is human action, and revelation, which is divine action.[15]

It is evident from this discussion that there are different conceptions of the meaning of theology and of the importance of revelation. The student should be warned against hasty or partisan decisions, and especially against any decision at all at the outset of the investigation.

There is one further difference between philosophy of religion and theology which has not yet been mentioned. That difference is founded on the fact that theology, as the word implies, is chiefly concentrated on the definition of God and his purpose. The field of theology is summarized in the titles of two able works,[16] *The Doctrine of God* and

---

[14] Brunner, PR, 13.
[15] Tillich, RP, in Dessoir, PEG, 769.
[16] By A. C. Knudson.

The Doctrine of Redemption. Philosophy of religion, on the other hand, is an attempt to interpret not merely the idea of God, but also the meaning and value of the whole development of religion and of all phases of religious experience.

§ 9. HISTORY OF PHILOSOPHY OF RELIGION

Attention has already been called to the fact that the history of Occidental philosophy is largely a history of attempts to solve the problem of God. That history is summarized in the "Selected Historical Bibliography" at the end of this book. But the systematic investigation of the whole field of religion and religious ideas as a separate department of philosophy proper is something modern. It may be said to have begun with David Hume's works on *The Natural History of Religion* (1755) and *Dialogues Concerning Natural Religion* (published posthumously in 1799), which rigorously analyzed religious beliefs. Kant's epoch-making *Critique of Pure Reason* (1781) contained a searching and devastating attack on the traditional arguments for God, while his *Critique of Practical Reason* (1788) developed a new form of the moral argument for God. His later work, *Religion Within the Limits of Reason Alone* (1793), is a sketch of his philosophy of religion. The modern conception of the subject, however, and the popularization of the term "philosophy of religion," are due largely to Hegel's *Lectures on the Philosophy of Religion* (published posthumously, 1832ff.). Hegel held the task of philosophy of religion to be that of discovering the principles at work in its history, and so he based his treatment on a survey of the movement of religion as an historical force. His empirical method of judging each aspect of religious history by its relation to the whole is essentially the method described earlier in this chapter. Thus, Kant is an apriorist and

Hegel an empiricist. Schelling made original contributions in his *Lectures on Mythology and Revelation* (1843). Hegel's influence was long dominant among Scottish philosophers of religion (for example, Edward and John Caird and Andrew Seth Pringle-Pattison), as well as among British (F. H. Bradley, Bernard Bosanquet) and American thinkers (the St. Louis School, Josiah Royce, W. E. Hocking).

A fourth German has contributed much, namely, Lotze, whose *Microcosmus* (first published 1856–1858) contained rich empirical material, and whose small volume of lecture outlines, *Philosophy of Religion* (1882), exerted an influence disproportionate to its size. Many British and American philosophers of religion are indebted to Lotze, including such Neo-Hegelians as Bosanquet and Royce and less Hegelian writers, such as B. P. Bowne and G. T. Ladd.

During the twentieth century a profusion of important investigations has appeared, a brief chronological survey of which will suffice to furnish some picture of the development of the discipline. H. Höffding, a Danish scholar, wrote in 1901 a *Philosophy of Religion,* which has been widely translated and is famous for its conception of religion as resting on the axiom of the conservation of values. He rejected belief in the personality of God and in personal immortality. Josiah Royce delivered his Gifford Lectures in Scotland on *The World and the Individual* (1899–1900, published 1904), in which he interpreted religion in the light of his absolute idealism.[17] In 1901–1902, William James also gave Gifford Lectures, which were published at once as *The Varieties of Religious Experience.* Although primarily psychological, this work contained many philosophical ideas and did much to increase the confidence of the scholarly public in the normality and validity of re-

---

[17] He was the first American invited to this famous lectureship.

ligious experience.   J. M. E. McTaggart, the distinguished
Cambridge University professor, wrote *Some Dogmas of
Religion* (1906) as a critique of religious ideas; he rejected
the personality of God but accepted belief in immortality.

The year 1912 saw two brilliant contributions, very different from each other.   W. E. Hocking, Royce's successor
at Harvard, published *The Meaning of God in Human
Experience,* another idealistic philosophy of religion on an
empirical basis, and É. Durkheim, the French sociologist,
wrote *The Elementary Forms of Religious Life,* which interpreted all religious beliefs and practices as purely social
phenomena.   During the World War, Rudolf Otto wrote
The Idea of the Holy (1917), which has passed into many
editions, and is famous for its description of religion as an
experience which he called numinous, having the quality
of unique religious awe and mystery.   The British realist,
S. Alexander, presented a new, evolutionary idea of God and
religion in *Space, Time, and Deity* (1920).   G. H. Joyce's
Principles of Natural Theology (1923), well represents the
great scholastic tradition.   A. N. Whitehead's Gifford Lectures, *Process and Reality* (1929), offer a profound interpretation of God in the light of the modern developments
of science and philosophy.   F. R. Tennant's systematic two-
volume work on *Philosophical Theology* (1928, 1930), the
greatest product of recent British philosophy of religion, is
matched by A. C. Knudson's volumes in America, *The
Doctrine of God* (1930) and *The Doctrine of Redemption*
(1933).

The leading French philosopher, Henri Bergson, has
crowned his life's work with a brilliant contribution entitled *The Two Sources of Morality and Religion* (1932).

John Dewey, leading American philosopher, is not primarily a philosopher of religion, but his little book on
A Common Faith (1934) has aroused much discussion by

its challenge of traditional concepts, as did his Gifford Lectures on *The Quest for Certainty* (1929).

An account of the history of philosophy of religion would not be complete without reference to hostile treatments of religion by ideologists of the Communist and National Socialist groups. The most systematic work by a Marxist is probably V. F. Calverton's *The Passing of the Gods* (1934), while the best known National Socialist work is Alfred Rosenberg's *Der Mythus des 20. Jahrhunderts* (*The Myth of the Twentieth Century*) (1930). The former work regards religion as the tool of capitalism. The latter treats it as a myth to be superseded by the higher myth of "blood," that is, race.

The present state of philosophy of religion, therefore, is that of conflict, or as Hegel would say, of dialectic.

BIBLIOGRAPHICAL NOTE

The abbreviations used are explained in the bibliography at the back of the book. The purpose of the bibliographical notes is to survey the most important recent literature in the field.

The modern empirical study of religion, in a sense founded by Schleiermacher, was given its chief impetus by James in VRE(1902). Macintosh, TES(1919), raised the problem of empirical method in the field; Bixler (ed.), NRE(1937) shows diversity of opinion among those influenced by Macintosh, who himself replies to them in an article, "Empirical Theology and Some of Its Misunderstanders," in *The Review of Religion*, 3(1939), 383-399. A more pragmatic and less theistic use of empirical method is that of Wieman in Wieman and Horton, GOR(1938), and many other works. Wieman and Meland, APR(1936), contains a critique of most current views. Tennant, PT(1928), is the best British treatment. Ayer, LTL(1936), gives a logical positivist's destructive criticism of all religious experience and defines an empirical method valid only for sense data. The method of apriorism is best stated in Knudson, VRE(1937); see also England, VRE(1938), and Moore, TRE(1939). The point of view of the text is presented in Brightman, Art.(1937), and in Bertocci, EAG(1938), and in reviews of the latter in the *Journal of Philosophy* and the *Review of Religion*. Related problems are discussed in Dewey, LOG(1938), Wieman, NPR(1935), and, from a semi-Barthian point of view, in Brunner, PR(1937). An historically valuable, but somewhat one-sided, treatment of the problem is found in Walker's article, "Can Philosophy of Religion be Empirical?" in *Jour. Rel.*, 19(1939), 315-329.

TWO

RELIGION AS A FACT

§ 1. Scientific and Philosophical Investigation of Religion [1]

IN the preceding chapter there was proposed a definition of religion as essentially a concern about experiences which are supremely valued. This or any other definition must be derived from the facts of experience. Such a definition is not a faith or a belief; it is a description, intended to be as objective as a physicist's description of the properties of an electron. Only after having established what religion is can the investigator proceed to a philosophical interpretation of it. The nonscientific facts of course are the basis of science, of religion, and of philosophy of religion alike. But it would be arbitrary and wasteful for a thinker to try to build up a philosophy on his own personal, unscientific experiences without regard to the work of the sciences of religion. These sciences—the history, psychology, and sociology of religion—furnish a survey of the facts without which philosophy would be spinning cobwebs of desire or hate or of formal logic, none of which lead to any trustworthy conclusions about the real world.

The error of some philosophers of religion in disregarding the facts of religion has led others to approach the extreme of holding that philosophy of religion consists entirely of

[1] Review Chap. I, §§ 6–9.

31

a survey of its history, psychology, and sociology; in fact, each of the sciences of religion has partisans who identify it with philosophy. We read in turn that the historical, the psychological, or the sociological approach is the only one. Nevertheless, the error of identifying science with philosophy is as misleading as the error of supposing philosophy to be independent of science. The one is pseudo science as the other is pseudo philosophy. Perhaps the worst phase of the pseudoscientific error is to suppose that if we can only discover the earliest forms of primitive religion, as inferred from the practices of the Aruntas of Australia or the Ainus of Japan,[2] then we shall know what religion is. This valuation of origins is both unscientific and unphilosophical. It is unscientific because the evolutionary method is not interested in origins for their own sake, but only as one stage in a developing life process. Religion cannot be understood by a contemplation of its obscure origins in paleolithic times any more than a Judaean mustard tree can be understood by contemplating a grain of mustard seed. It is unphilosophical because the philosopher is concerned with our experiences as a whole and cannot give any more exalted rank to one experience than to another until after he has surveyed the whole. To interpret religion in terms of its earliest manifestations would be as rational as to interpret the Kantian philosophy in terms of the earliest babblings of little baby Immanuel. "Origin does not determine meaning or value."[3]

In the present chapter, the aim is to present the main facts of religion in highly condensed form, yet with sufficient detail to furnish orientation, and with guidance for supplementary reading when further information is desired. The method is purely descriptive or, as the Ger-

[2] On both, consult the Index Volumes of ERE and EB.
[3] An expression often used by Borden Parker Bowne.

mans say, *wertfrei* (free from value); no question of the ideal worth of religious values or of the truth of religious beliefs is raised in this chapter. In short, religious valuations are to be described without evaluation or criticism.

§ 2. Sciences of Religion

As has already been stated, the sciences of religion are history of religion, psychology of religion, and sociology of religion.

The sciences of religion are all relatively recent developments. In view of man's age-long experience with religion it may seem strange that neither the Greeks nor the Romans nor modern man has until recently undertaken to inquire objectively and scientifically into the facts of religion. This long delay is not, however, so strange as it appears to be. It is due (in Greece, in Rome, and in later Europe) partly to the lack of the development of an historical sense, and perhaps even more to the warfare of theology with science. A great mind like Plato's was far more concerned about the truth of religion than about its history, and he had enough of a fight on his hands when he challenged the mores of the sacred Homeric scriptures without also going into questions of the higher criticism. Throughout the Middle Ages, theology was so predominant that the objective attitude necessary for the scientific study of religion was almost unattainable. The sciences of religion can be pursued only when the scientist is able to forget for the time being his own beliefs and describe the beliefs of others without any thought of orthodoxy or heresy, edification or peril to faith.

It is not until recent times that this precondition for a history of religion could be fulfilled. The debates of the Enlightenment (the eighteenth century) about the origins of religion—whether it was monotheistic or (as Hume held) polytheistic—were still far from a history of religion. Here and there an obscure writer began to seek to bring the facts together.[4] The first serious attempt to view the history of religion as a connected whole was made by Hegel in his *Lectures on the Philosophy of Religion,* posthumously published in 1832. But the modern science of history of religion had its real inception in the work of the Orientalist and philologist, Friedrich Max Müller (1823-1900). A student of Sanskrit, he retired from a professorship at Oxford to become, in 1876, editor of *The Sacred Books of the East,* a series that is still today a standard collection of English translations of the various Oriental scriptures. Since Max Müller, countless scholars have worked in the field. Now, history of religions is a thoroughly scientific discipline. As pre-eminent achievements should be mentioned *The Golden Bough,* a massive collection of facts about primitive religions by Sir J. G. Frazer (1854-   ), a distinguished British anthropologist; the two-volume *History of Religions* by George Foot Moore (1851-1931) of Harvard; and the comprehensive *Encyclopaedia of Religion and Ethics* edited by James Hastings (1852-1922). Anthropology, philology, archaeology, and general history all contribute to the development of history of religions. *Introduction to the History of Religions* by C. H. Toy (1836-1919), although published in 1913, is still one of the most valuable surveys of comparative religions and its bibliography (pp. 585-623) shows the range of work being done in the field. Hundreds of able French, Italian, German, British, Ameri-

---

[4] See, for instance, William Ward, *All Religions and Religious Ceremonies* (Hartford: Oliver D. Cooke and Sons, 1823). Mr. Ward undertook "to exhibit an impartial view of the *Doctrines* of each Religious denomination of the present day . . . as far as practicable from their own Creeds or Confessions of faith" and "to present *statements of facts,* and without *comment."* This work included "Christianity, Mahometanism, and Judaism, . . . the religion . . . of the Hindoos" and "of other pagan nations." Here was an honest effort to be scientific, yet without adequate method or access to sources.

can, and Oriental scholars have contributed to the science.
Similarly, psychology of religion is a recent growth. It
is one of the few sciences which have had their birth in the
United States of America. The first writer to make systematic empirical observations of the psychological states
and processes involved in religious experience was Jonathan
Edwards (1703–1758), who became the third president of
Princeton University.[5] It is not surprising that the great
eighteenth-century theologian was a leader in the religious
revival of the time, known as "The Great Awakening"
(1734–1749); what is surprising is that he wrote careful
objective reports of the psychological phenomena of the
revival in *A Faithful Narrative of the Surprising Work of
God* (1737) and *A Treatise Concerning Religious Affec-
tions* (1746). Such psychological interest was not dupli-
cated until well into the next century, when revivalists began
to gather data regarding the age at which converts "experienced religion." It was found that conversion occurred
typically during adolescence. From this clue, psychology
of religion was developed. The first book in the field was
the *Psychology of Religion* (1900) by E. D. Starbuck (1866–
     ), soon to be followed by William James's (1842–1910)
classic, *The Varieties of Religious Experience* (1902), and
by numerous investigations by G. A. Coe (1862–   ), J. H.
Leuba (1868–   ), J. B. Pratt (1875–   ), F. L. Strickland
(1871–   ), and many others in America, England, France,
Germany, and Austria. But this branch of science of religion has developed less satisfactorily than has the history.
On the Continent, and to some extent in England and
America, psychology of religion has tended to become a
branch of practical theology in the service of the church,

[5] See C. H. Faust and T. H. Johnson, *Jonathan Edwards* (New York: The
American Book Company, 1935), an excellent volume of selections with notes in
the American Writers Series.

or else has turned into naturalistic propaganda. Further-more, the development of general psychology, with its ex-perimental techniques and its tendency to objective methods, has produced methods unsuited to the interpretation of the inner life. Starbuck, Coe, and Pratt are no longer working in the field, although Leuba continues productive; no out-standing new worker has appeared.

Still more recent is the growth of sociology of religion. That religion is a social phenomenon is too obvious a fact to escape attention, and the positivism of Auguste Comte (1798–1857), the founder of sociology, who regarded humanity as *le grand être* (the supreme being), directed the attention of sociologists to the religious problem from the start. It was in the special field of anthropology that modern sociology of religion was first explicitly developed, notably in the study of the totemic system by J. G. Frazer and by Émile Durkheim (1858–1917), whose *Elementary Forms of the Religious Life* (1912, English tr. 1915) has been widely influential. The greatest work yet done in the field is Max Weber's (1864–1920) *Gesammelte Aufsätze zur Religionssoziologie* (1920, 1921), a three-volume investigation which lays chief stress on the interrelation between religion and economic factors. (Marxist treatments of religion, like V. F. Calverton's *The Passing of the Gods* [1934], con-centrate on the same problem.) Joachim Wach, the chief authority in the field at present, conceives the problem from the standpoint of group life. His *Einführung in die Religionssoziologie* (1931) (*Introduction to the Sociology of Religion*) sets forth a program for future research.

§ 3. History of Religion: Primitive

The history of religion, as of any other human activity, is not a mere record of events; still less is it a selection of especially striking or sensational events. It is rather an attempt to see the development of man's religious culture as a whole and to trace the guiding principles and causes of that development. Single facts or sets of facts out of the past or present are historical in the sense that they are actual events which have happened. But they are what we have called nonscientific facts until the historian has set them in their proper relations to historical process. The footprint of Man Friday was a nonscientific fact until Robinson Crusoe discovered its relation to Friday himself; then he saw it as part of a development and it became for his insight an item in the history of both himself and Friday.

Although history is properly an interest in development, it is also an interest in beginnings. Just as Genesis starts with the words, "In the beginning," so every mind sooner or later wants to know about the beginning of everything it finds. Some carry this interest so far that they may fairly be said to be obsessed by it. The child who asks, "Who made God?" has embarked on the infinite regress of beginnings, and is no more foolish than the man who cannot distinguish a rational from an irrational question. The person who is obsessed with beginnings, however, is often too easily satisfied, and is less rational than the wondering child. Such a person supposes that the first stage of the development of any process reveals what that process really is. If he finds that the first stage of morality was the mores of the group, he is certain that morality is nothing but group mores. If he learns that the first stage of astronomy was a kind of astrology, he declares that astronomy is nothing but astrology. And if he discovers that the Christian sacrament of the Lord's Supper can be traced back through the mystery religions to the early custom of eating the totemic animal, he concludes that the Lord's Supper is nothing but a totem rite. Such a process of interpretation is fallacious in method. Yet the fallacy—which we may call the fallacy of primitivism—has been so prevalent in open or disguised form among certain thinkers about religion that it requires somewhat fuller treatment.

The fallacy of primitivism is the assertion that any process can be best understood and evaluated by knowing its primitive form. When used in the field of philosophy of religion it is a short and easy way of proving that all religion is nonsense, for the primitive forms of religion, taken by themselves and judged in the light of modern knowledge, seem largely nonsense. Yet the absurdity of judging the truth and value of fully developed religion by the beliefs and practices of the Bushmen of Australia or of the aborigines of Tierra del Fuego is no greater than the parallel absurdity of judging the merits of the Sermon on the Mount by a study of the infant psychology of Jesus at the time of the slaughter of the innocents, or of judging a college education to be worth no more than the state of mind of the educand at the moment when he decided that he would go to college.

While historical understanding must indeed include the most primitive phases of its subject matter, it must also include the development of the primitive into the mature. Knowledge of primitive religion is necessary to an understanding of religion; nevertheless, the fallacy of primitivism effectually prevents the understanding of religion or of anything else.

Thus far the word primitive has been used as if it meant earliest or first stage. This is not strictly correct. The earliest stage of a development is primitive, it is true; but the primitive stage of culture may last long after the beginning, and may survive even in the contemporary world. In fact, were this not true, we should have almost no knowledge of primitive religion, since it is from contemporary "primitives" that we infer what the first primitives may

have been. It should be noted that these inferences are
precarious. In the nature of the case, the first primitives
left no written records and not even any artifacts. Indeed,
evolutionary anthropology makes it almost impossible to
point out one stage and say: "Here is the first primitive man
in contrast with his parents, who were the last of the prehuman ancestors of man." It must, therefore, be admitted
that our knowledge of the beginnings of religion is and will
probably remain speculative. Yet speculation founded on
common traits of primitives still living as our contemporaries in parts of Australia, Asia, and Africa, is based on
authentic facts and is not mere fancy.

We have thus established two preliminaries to the study
of the history of religion, especially of primitive religion:
(1) the fallacy of primitivism is to be avoided; (2) the
relatively speculative character of our knowledge of primitive religion is to be recognized to such an extent that all
statements about it are to be accepted with caution and reserve.

What, then, was the beginning of religion? At once we
face a difference of opinion among authorities. Some,
notably Andrew Lang, hold that the earliest religious conception is that of an "All-Father," a heavenly analogue to
the headman of the tribe or clan; and there is evidence to
show that traces of this idea survive among primitives
whose present religious practices are on a much lower level,
ethically and intellectually. Other anthropologists, however, are inclined either to minimize this evidence on account of its vagueness and the neglect with which the
belief is treated, or to ascribe it to the influence of missionaries on the primitives.[6] As C. G. Seligman points out,[7]

[6] See the excellent discussion by Andrew Lang in the article, "God (Primitive
and Savage)," in ERE, VI, 243–247.
[7] In his article on Nuba, ERE, IX, 403.

the Nuba, a primitive African tribe, believe in a "high god," but this god is otiose, and in practice the spirits of the dead overshadow him. No matter how fascinating it may be to conjure up theories, on the one hand, about a primitive universal revelation of monotheism or, on the other hand, about the influence of missionaries on primitives, it is wiser to suspend judgment on problems about early belief in an All-Father or High God, and turn our attention to more certain facts.

From the start, it is certain that all life in this world has had to contend against environmental forces for its survival, and it is also certain that primitive man lacked the advantages of newspaper, radio, and college education. With no science, no literature, and only the crudest beginnings of language, he had to struggle for his survival against the forces of nature, wild beasts, and wild men. As Schopenhauer has said, the beginning of religion and philosophy may be found in the fact of death.[8] If men never died, they would neither reason nor worship. But they do die, and they seek for means to avert death, to postpone it, or at least to face it with dignity.

Man's earliest procedure for warding off death was, of course, the search for food and protection from the elements. But this search did not suffice. Man did not understand the causes of storms, of diseases, or even of the procreation of his young.[9] In the presence of the terrifying unknown with which he was surrounded, he had recourse to magic, as a means of subduing the cosmic powers and bending them to the service of his needs. Magic, then, with its taboos, spells, incantations, fetishes, secrets of "medicine

[8] See his famous essay, "Man's Need of Metaphysics."
[9] See M. F. Ashley-Montagu, *Coming into Being Among the Australian Aborigines* (New York: E. P. Dutton and Co., 1938). See Notice in *Jour. Phil.*, 35 (1938), 532.

men" or shamans, is a means of compelling the hidden powers of the universe to submit to human will and to fulfill man's desires.

But even primitive man has intelligence enough to perceive that magic does not always work. In spite of the power of superstition to assert itself against all contrary evidence, facts are facts. According to Sir J. G. Frazer and other anthropologists, religion arises at the point where magic is seen to fail; when primitive thinkers perceived (1) that magic did not reach its goal, and (2) that the goal of magic—the compulsion of the cosmic powers—was unattainable, they seemed to conclude that it would be wiser to use the methods of persuasion than of compulsion. Religion, then, from the start, is an attempt to persuade the cosmic powers to be friendly to man, and is based on the presupposition that magic is inadequate and that man's desires cannot wholly control the course of events.[10] Nevertheless, not only in primitive religion, but even in the most highly developed religions of today, remnants of magic continue; the sacred book is often treated as a fetish and prayer is often regarded as a means of compelling Deity to obey man's whims or longings. Belief in witchcraft is still potent in some parts of the United States. Investigations show that some superstitions still prevail even among the educated.

What has been said about Schopenhauer's view of the

---

[10] On this general topic see Paul Radin's two books: *Primitive Man as Philosopher* (New York: D. Appleton and Company, 1927) and *Primitive Religions* (New York: The Viking Press, 1937). Sir J. G. Frazer's *Golden Bough* is a rich mine of material. See also Read, OMS, and Lucien Lévy-Bruhl's works: *Primitive Mentality* (New York: The Macmillan Company, 1923) and *How Natives Think* (London: Allen and Unwin, 1926). Moore, BGR, Friess and Schneider, RVC, and Galloway, PR, 88–109, are illuminating. Note the references to Malinowski in the bibliography. Murdock's OPC is a recent treatment. Murdock points out (OPC, 42) that primitives ascribe the failure of magic to stronger adverse magic. Thus its power was almost unbreakable. Yet religion broke it.

function of death in man's struggle for survival must not be taken as an endorsement of Petronius's (or Statius's) oversimple formula, *primus in orbe fecit deos timor* (fear first made gods in the world),[11] or of Stefan Zweig's view that religion arose solely because man suffers. The desire for self-preservation and for the avoidance of death cannot be based on fear or suffering alone. There would be no fear of death and no hope for relief of suffering if life held no values worth keeping or striving for. Magic itself is as much a struggle for a successful, healthy, and happy life as it is a struggle against dangers. Religion, even more than magic, aims at the conservation and increase of values, as Harald Höffding, the Danish philosopher, said. Perhaps, then, Schopenhauer was not wholly right. Perhaps man would have been led to religion for the sake of the organization and creation of values, even if death did not threaten to bring them all to an end. In fact, all attempts to trace the origins of religion to a single source, including Carveth Read's view that human culture is all due to the results of a flesh diet and the consequent hunter's life,[12] are oversimplifications. Even the most primitive religion is complex.

Whatever its causes, religion actually arose and was differentiated from magic. It is possible to trace with some plausibility at least four conceptions of primitive religion, all of which have been exhaustively investigated by anthropologists and historians of religion. For present purposes it will suffice to give a very brief survey of (1) animism, (2) spiritism, (3) totemism, and (4) mana.[13]

[11] It occurs in Publius Papinius Statius, *Thebais,* III, 664, and also in Petronius, *Fragments,* No. 76. These facts are derived from B. Stevenson, *The Home Book of Quotations* (New York: Dodd, Mead and Company, 1934), 800.

[12] Read, OMS, 1. Read's work, however, is valuable on the general topic of magic and religion.

[13] All histories of religion and most philosophies of religion contain accounts of these concepts. See, for example, works by Galloway, Wright, Drake, Toy, and Carpenter, mentioned in the bibliography.

(1) *Animism.* As far back as our knowledge of man extends, we find him presupposing a kinship between himself and his world. In himself he is aware of life, the power of movement, and feeling; he takes for granted that similar life and power and feeling animate all natural objects. This vague idea, obviously based on no clear notion of life or mind or matter, is called animism. It is evident that the most primitive religion entails more respect for the life of the world than does magic; when religion persuades the unseen forces instead of compelling them, it assumes that their life has a structure and rights of its own. Thus religious animism is more objective than magic; but it is also more personal, for it treats the unseen as will.[14]

(2) *Spiritism.* Animism survived for an indefinitely long period, then gradually was superseded by a less vague and (in a sense) more empirical view, called spiritism. Animists regarded the life or soul as confined to the object which it animated—human body or tree or river. But, as Lucretius long ago observed,[15] and as the literature of religion abundantly testifies, dream experiences began at an early date to play a role in man's religion. In dreams, sons would meet their dead fathers and mothers; parents would see their dead children; chiefs would see their dead warriors alive and marching. The dreamer would find himself far away from the tent where he was sleeping, perhaps in distant lands where he had never been in the body. In dreams, the ordinary laws of matter were suspended; one could fly or vanish at will. Marvelous events and beings would

[14] Crude as magic and animism are, magic bears a rough resemblance to science and animism to philosophy (especially to idealism). But the warning against the fallacy of primitivism should suffice to prevent any attempt to evaluate science in terms of magic, or idealism in terms of animism, although a philosophical psychologist like William McDougall does not hesitate to recognize an element of truth in animism or even to use that term to describe his own thought.

[15] *De rerum natura,* V, 1171.

appear. Thus it was quite natural and apparently empirical for men to infer that their souls were not "bound" to their bodies, as animists held, but were "free" and separable. Thus spiritism was developed, and with it the beginnings of the distinction between mind and matter, the belief in immortality, perhaps ancestor worship, and certainly the belief in marvelous spiritual powers. Spiritism, let it be noted, moved even further than animism toward the belief in personal gods and away from impersonal magic.

(3) *Totemism*.[16] Animism and spiritism appear to have been substantially universal among primitives. Totemism, a much more complex system of beliefs and practices, was not equally universal, but was very widespread and socially important. The totem, an animal (or plant) of some kind, was supposed to be connected in some mysterious way with the life and well-being of the tribe. It typified, and possibly caused, the unity of the tribe as a social whole; it was often regarded as an ancestor from whom all were descended. In some tribes, such as the Arunta of Australia, the totem was eaten at ceremonial meals, which seem to have some remote historical connection with the sacraments of the Oriental Mystery Religions and of Christianity. Totemism was more social than were animism or spiritism, for it regulated not only social customs and taboos (as did magic), but also to some extent the relations of tribes to each other, as in the practice of exogamy (the rule that marriage can occur only with a person outside of one's own totem group). It thus marks the beginnings of a crude international law, as well as of group loyalty.

(4) *Mana*. Among the Melanesians a term is used which has been adopted by anthropologists to cover a primitive belief that is supposed to have been rather widely held.

[16] See Durkheim, EFRL, for information and bibliography.

Mana is a name for the power or force by virtue of which peculiar effects are exerted. This force is conceived impersonally, and thus mana is closer to magic and animism than to spiritism and totemism. However, it also bears some faint resemblance to modern notions of energy, and perhaps is a transition concept from magic to religion. Mana, then, may be the peculiar magical property of a stone, or the peculiar force that makes a hero heroic, so that cannibalism may be in part due to a desire to secure the mana of the deceased.[17]   The Algonkins use the word "manitu" for a similar concept; other tribes use other names. The reader may recall "Gitche Manito the Mighty," from Longfellow's "Song of Hiawatha," as well as the humble rabbit's foot, without having been aware that each is a possessor of mana.

§ 4. History of Religion: Tribal

Early religion was not merely primitive metaphysics, like spiritism or the concept of mana; it was, like totemism, a form of social organization.   In fact, it is probable that primitive religion was much more concerned with tribal customs, initiation rites (such as those studied by Spencer and Gillen among the Aruntas), and forms of sacrifice, than with the animistic or spiritistic beliefs underlying them.   Notions of divine powers or beings were but vaguely held; the aim of religious practices was not the achievement of some noble ideal, or the discovery of the divine will, but rather the preservation of the traditions and the identity of the tribe or clan in its struggle for survival as well as in its conflicts against other tribes. Save for totemism and for traces of the "high god," there was hardly a glimmer

---

[17] See Wright, SPR, 24–29 and bibliography; also the article "Mana" in ERE, VIII. Some scholars, like Murdock, believe that the role of mana has been exaggerated.

of an intertribal religious consciousness. Early religion was tribal rather than individual, exclusive rather than inclusive. In modern Germany we have seen a few nationalistic extremists going back quite logically to the tribal exclusiveness of primitive religion. Racialism is deeply rooted in the stage of tribal religion.

§ 5. History of Religion: National (Priestly)

Human history is a process of social change and no moment of its development is final. Although custom and ritual appeared to be rigidly static during the tribal stage, it was impossible that mankind should continue to exist divided into small, mutually exclusive and hostile clans. It was inevitable that tribes should merge into larger societies, as did the twelve tribes of Israel, and also that the new groups should seek a new and broader basis of unity, for it was impossible that the religious customs of each group should remain unchanged under the new social conditions. Thus ties of kinship or affinity brought tribes together into nations, and thus also national religions developed. By the time the Egyptian, the Babylonian, the Assyrian, the Persian, the Indian, the Chinese, the Hebrew, the Greek, or the Roman peoples had developed a national life and a corresponding national religion, civilization had attained a high level, and religion had passed through many changes.

It is not necessary or desirable for a philosophy of religion to repeat the complicated systems of belief and practice in the religions of the great nations that have just been named. It is the function of history of religion to investigate these facts, and they are readily accessible in many noteworthy manuals, such as those of G. F. Moore, G. A. Barton, C. H. Toy, E. W. Hopkins, and of Friess and Schneider; the smaller works by Allan Menzies and R. E. Hume are also instructive, but somewhat less objective and critical.

Articles on all the great national religions are readily available in ERE and general encyclopaedias. It would be superfluous to detail here what is easily found elsewhere. Since, however, philosophy of religion is an interpretation of the facts of religion, it will prove useful to recapitulate the chief traits which national religions have in common and to note the most striking peculiarities of certain ones. For this purpose eight points will be considered. (1) Particularism, (2) Social organization, (3) Shrines and temples, (4) Ritual and sacrifice, (5) Sacred writings, (6) *Mores* and morality, (7) Soul and immortality, and (8) Gods.

(1) *Particularism.* Like primitive religions, nationalistic religions—at least in their earlier forms—are particularistic, not universal. That is to say, the values which they seek to conserve are the values of a particular group, not the universal values of all humanity. The nation or the race is the religious unit, not the individual or mankind as a whole. Particularism appears in the distinction between Greek and Barbarian; in the Vedas [18] which are the scriptures of the early (about 1500 B.C.) Aryan invaders of India, who felt themselves superior to the native Dravidians; in Shinto, which traces the descent of the Japanese imperial family from the primal male and deities, Izanagi and Izanimi; [19] and in the revival of Germanic tribal deities by some groups in National Socialist Germany. The instance of particularism best known to the Western world is the Hebrew theory of a chosen race, commonly referred to as the doctrine of election. In a document dating from about 850 B.C.,[20] we read that "Jehovah said unto Abram, . . . I will make of thee a great nation . . . and I will bless them

[18] Veda means knowledge; cf. German *wissen*, English wit.
[19] See Barton, RW, 229–232.
[20] Commonly referred to as J, because of its preference for Jahve (Jehovah) as a divine name, and its origin in the tribe of Judah.

that bless thee and him that curseth thee will I curse." (Gen.
12:1–3) Particularism is well illustrated in a message from
Jephthah to the Ammonites reported in Judges 11:15–27,
where Jephthah says: "Wilt thou not possess that which
Chemosh thy god giveth thee to possess? So whomsoever
Jehovah our God hath dispossessed from before us, them
will we possess." Chemosh and Jehovah appear here in
a role almost as provincial and patriotic as Uncle Sam or
John Bull. The doctrine of a chosen nation was reflected
in the New Testament idea of the "saved" as "the elect,"
and echoes of it may be detected in modern allusions to
America as "God's country." Particularism appears in the
national stage of the development of religion whenever that
stage may occur chronologically. The Japanese trace back
their Shinto and its combination of nature-worship with
Mikado-worship to 660 B.C.

(2) *Social organization.* The very particularism of national religion implies that it is a form of social organization.
Religion was a social phenomenon before it was an individual
experience. C. H. Toy years ago pointed out that religious
development goes hand in hand with social organization.
The few tribal groups that had been shown to have little
social organization (like the Rock Veddahs of Ceylon and
the Yahgans of Tierra del Fuego) also have little if any
religion.[21] By the time tribes have been merged to form
nations, religion universally accompanies the higher social
organization and prescribes much of the structure of that
organization. Words for the sacred in various languages
refer both to that which is socially forbidden (compare
taboo) or ritually defiling, and also to that which is a
source of strength and is socially approved. Religion thus
sets up the categories of sacred and profane to govern customs, rites, and the very days of the week or month. On

[21] Toy, IHR, 7.

the sacred days, special rites are performed, ordinary activities suspended. The priestly class develops as a phase of national religion and acquires social prestige and wealth. The fame of Egyptian priests, their scholarship and their social influence, was widespread in the ancient world, and they were often mentioned by Greek writers, notably Plato. In Greek religion, important social undertakings were governed by religious motives, and the Sibylline oracles of Graeco-Roman religion were so authoritative that Jewish and Christian writers produced "Sibylline" oracles predicting the rise of those religions.

The caste system of Hinduism (with its division of society into the Brahman or priestly class, the warrior class, the agricultural class, the serfs, and the outcasts) dominates the entire organization of social, economic, and cultural life in India. The gods of the Roman religion well illustrate the social character of religion: Mars is god of war, Venus goddess of love; Saturn governs the sowing of crops, Ceres their growth, Consus and Ops the harvest, Flora the blossoming of fruit trees, and Pomona the ripening fruit. Janus is the deity for the door of the house, Vesta for the hearth, Lares for the fields, Fons for the springs of water.[22] Diana is the goddess of the hunt. In short, the gods of the Romans were largely names for social activities or for the bases of social processes in nature, and thus the forms of religion permeated all aspects of their social life. In most religions, the very laws of the state were regarded as divinely commanded or sanctioned. The famous Babylonian Code of Hammurabi (2104–2061 B.C.) is inscribed on a block of black dionite, with Hammurabi pictured as receiving the laws from the sun-god.[23] The laws of Israel are commands

[22] See Moore, HR, I, Chap. XXI.
[23] For the text of this code see Hastings, DB, Extra Volume, or Barton, AB, 377–405.

of God to Moses. The church in most forms of national religion was almost a department of the state, and church officials were government officials. The stage of national religion is still reflected in the existence of "established" churches, receiving governmental recognition and support, and in the membership of bishops in the British House of Lords.

(3) *Shrines and temples.* Tribal religion had already recognized many sacred places—trees, groves, rivers, hills (the Biblical "high places" of Canaanitic religion), stones, pillars, and the like—where rites were performed and certain "taboos" respected. National religion usually continued to respect the traditions of these shrines, although the religion of Israel was, by exception, intolerant of them, both because of the exclusiveness of its theory of election and because of the religious prostitution and other immoral features connected with the Canaanitic shrines. But small local shrines do not embody the spirit of national religion. To typify national unity, great temples and a certain centralization of worship are required. The Parthenon in Athens, the great temples of the Assyrian religion in Nineveh, and of the Babylonian in the city of Babylon, are examples. The greatest temples were thus usually in the capital cities. The temple in Jerusalem, in which all the worship of the Israelitic religion was centralized by law under King Josiah in 621 B.C. in accordance with the provisions of Deuteronomy, was perhaps the most famous of all the temples erected by religion in its national phase. Discoveries of papyri in Egypt, however, show that at least one temple to Jahve existed outside of Jerusalem, namely, at Elephantine from 494–400 B.C.[24] But in general, the places of local Jewish religious gatherings are synagogues, not temples, down to the present day. This architectural phase

[24] Barton, AB, Chap. XXI.

of national religion survives in such a patriotic shrine as
Westminster Abbey. The building of temples requires
great wealth and both expresses and increases the power of
the priestly class.

(4) *Ritual and sacrifice.* Because religion is a social expression handed down from generation to generation, it is
invariably accompanied by certain rites. Sacraments are
ancient and widespread. The rite of circumcision was practised among Egyptians, Semites, Africans, Australasians,
Polynesians and others. Many religious rites are occasions
for public prayer either by the community in unison or by
the priests on its behalf.[25] Religious songs, chants, psalms,
and hymns are also common to all stages of religion, but
reached full expression first in the national stage.

The rites of most national religions include dances and
processions. The religious dance is said to have found its
highest development among certain North American In-
dians, yet it is found in the religion of Israel,[26] as well as in
the Chinese, Japanese, Hindu, Greek, and Roman religions.[27]
It is interesting to note that the custom of sacred dances led
by bishops survived in early Christianity even after its prohibition by a Council in A.D. 692. For aesthetic reasons, symbolic and religious dances are now being revived in some
American churches.

Even more universal than dances or processions is sacrifice. The invisible powers regarded as the sources of value
could not be approached readily and easily. They were busy
about their own affairs, and made many demands. Even
in the early stages of primitive and tribal religion there was
a universal custom of offering gifts to the spirits of the

[25] See Heiler, PRA.
[26] "David danced before the Lord," 2 Sam. 6:14. See also Psalms 149:3 and
150:4.
[27] See Moore, HR, I, Index, s.v. "Dance." See also the rather inadequate
article, "Processions and Dances," in Hastings, ERE, X, and Ellis, DL.

dead.[28]   Also, it very early became customary to offer food
and other articles of value to the gods.   The best of the
fruits and grains and the best, or first-born, of all animals
in the herds of the people were offered as sacrifice.   From
early times, it was also common to offer human beings,
especially first-born children, to the gods.   Human sacrifice is known to have existed in most of the Semitic religions, among the Hindus and the Chinese, in the Germanic religion, in Mexico, and in Africa.   The story of the
sacrifice of Isaac (Gen. 22) and Micah's question, "Shall
I give my first-born for my transgression, the fruit of my
body for the sin of my soul?" (Micah 6:7), are signs of the
existence of the practice among the Hebrews and of its
abandonment for religious reasons.   The Christian concep=
tion of the death of Christ is the highest historical sublima
tion of the idea of sacrifice.[29]   With the decline of national religion, the practice of sacrifice as means of appeas-
ing the gods or of securing divine favor dies out with it.

(5) *Sacred writings.*   Culture is at so low a level at the
primitive-tribal stage that literature is nonexistent and tradition is transmitted orally.   But national religion is coinci-
dent with the development of language and of learning.
Very early, the priests of all national religions committed
the usages and beliefs of their faith to writing, some on
papyrus, some on stone or marble or clay bricks.   Kings and
temples accumulated great libraries and thus many of the
sacred writings of the national religions have been preserved.   One of the oldest such writings is the *Egyptian
Book of the Dead,* a collection that accumulated between
1580 and 1000 B.C.,[30] which is remarkable for its social ethics
and the high level of its faith in personal immortality.   Al-

---

[28] See Toy, IHR, Chap. X.
[29] See the book of Hebrews.
[30] See the translation by E. A. W. Budge.

most contemporary with the *Book of the Dead* were the *Vedas* of India (1500 B.C. to 800 B.C.). Many other scriptures were produced by later Brahmanism and Hinduism. In Israel, the ancient religious laws and songs began to be written down in the time of Moses (about 1250 B.C.), and the last writings of the Old Testament, the book of Esther and some of the Psalms, may have been composed as late as 135 B.C. From the Babylonian religion, we have actual tablets of part of the *Epic of the Creation,* found in the library of Ashurbanipal (668–626 B.C.), as well as later more complete versions, and also the *Epic of Gilgamesh* (a flood story) from the same library. But both go back to much earlier sources, and in the case of the latter we have parts of an early version from the period 2232–1933 B.C. The Homeric poems, *The Iliad* and *The Odyssey* (assigned by Herodotus to the ninth century before Christ), were the scriptures of the Greek national religion; it required courage for Plato to challenge them on moral grounds in the *Republic* (about 380 B.C.). Much more recent are the scriptures of Shinto, the *Ko-ji-ki* ("Records of Ancient Matters") and the *Nihon-gi* ("Chronicles of Japan"). The former was written A.D. 712 and the latter A.D. 720, although the religion itself was much older.

The writings named constitute an incomplete but fairly typical list of the scriptures of national religions. The custom of preserving religious standards in scriptural writings continues among religions that have transcended the national level. The Bible contains documents of both national and universal religion. These writings include prose, poetry, myth, legend, history, prophecy, and legislation. Modern scholarship has contributed much to the analysis and interpretation of these valuable records.

(6) *Mores and morality.* All religion, especially on the national level, is to some extent a social phenomenon and

reflects the development of the society in which it functions. Religion gives a certain expression and sanction to the mores of the group. National religion, with its political affiliation, its priestly class, and its rigid traditions, tends to be conservative and to act on the assumption that its values are ultimate and eternal. There is, therefore, some ground for W. K. Wright's repeated assertion that religion is an "endeavor to secure the conservation of socially recognized values." [31] In general, this is true of national religion. Yet even on this level, the scriptures of all religions contain moral ideals which are far ahead of the approved practices of the times. There is a tendency in religion to criticize the socially recognized values and to substitute higher ones. We have already had occasion to notice this fact in connection with the substitution of animal sacrifice for human sacrifice; and we shall find that prophetic religion substitutes spiritual idealism for animal sacrifice. The rise of moral conceptions in Egypt higher than the mores is discussed in Breasted's excellent work, *The Dawn of Conscience*. As religion moves from the national-priestly stage to the universal-prophetic, the description of it as conserver of socially approved values or mores becomes more and more inadequate. Religion then becomes the critic of social custom, as is illustrated in the defiance of King Ahab by Micaiah ben Imlah (1 Kings 22), the attacks of Isaiah and other prophets on the mores of their day, and in the rejection of the caste system by Buddha.

(7) *Soul and immortality*. The belief in the survival of bodily death is present in most religions. Its earliest form, as reflected, for instance, in Greek conceptions of the underworld or in the Biblical story of the witch of Endor, represents the life after death as being pale, wretched, and undesirable. So true is this that in some religions, like that

[31] Wright, SPR, 41.

of Israel, the life of the soul after death played substantially
no part at all, and interest was centered on the survival of
the national or religious group in this world.   But notably
in the Egyptian, and to some extent in other national
religions, the idea of a blessed immortality (based on the
"free" soul of spiritism) came to occupy a central place in
religion.   In the future life, it was thought, those who had
lived good lives in this world would enjoy the favor of the
gods and eternal bliss.   The belief in immortality has had
its fullest development on the universal-prophetic level.

(8) *Gods.*   Most religions above the primitive level express their faith in the value of existence through belief in
gods.   National religion is almost always polytheistic—
that is, it recognizes many gods.   These gods often are
thought of as in one family; the Greek Zeus is "father of
gods and men."   The early stages of Hebrew religion were
certainly polytheistic, as is implied in the allusion to sons
of God (or of the gods) who married daughters of men
(Gen. 6:1–2).   In most national religions there were male
and female deities: Zeus and Hera of Greece, Jupiter and
Juno of Rome, Osiris and Isis of Egypt.   Often, too, there
were groups of gods constituting a trinity, as Isis, Osiris, and
their son Horus; or Agni (fire), Varuna (rain), and Mitra
(the sun), in India.   On the one hand, there was almost
everywhere a tendency to the endless multiplication of
minor deities in the pantheon; on the other hand, there
was an opposing tendency among thoughtful priests and
religious leaders in Egypt, in India, in Babylonia, and Greece
not only to regard the gods as closely related, but to hold
that the different gods were simply names for one God.
Thus there was a gradual movement from polytheism toward monotheism, a belief in one God as the sole deity.
One stage of this movement is called henotheism, the belief
that although there are many gods, only one is to be wor-

shiped; or if the many gods are worshiped one at a time, we have kathenotheism. In Israel the movement from polytheism through henotheism to monotheism was more rapid than in any other religion.

§ 6.   HISTORY OF RELIGION: UNIVERSAL (PROPHETIC)

The survey of religion in its primitive-tribal and in its national-priestly stages has shown, on the one hand, that religion is a world-wide phenomenon that everywhere exhibits similar traits, and, on the other hand, that it is not static but is in process of constant development. One of the most remarkable phases of its evolution is to be found in the rise of universal prophetic religion in the period from the eighth through the fourth centuries before Christ, which witnessed, as George Foot Moore has said, "a maximum in the tides of religion." [32]

Broadly speaking, the previous stage of religion had been under the guidance of priests, particularistic, national, ritualistic, and formal. During the five centuries from 750 B.C. there prevailed a new movement under the guidance of prophets, universal in outlook, individualistic rather than nationalistic, ethical rather than ritualistic, and intellectual and mystical rather than formal. The new movement also turned away from polytheism toward a monotheistic or (in some cases) an atheistic religion, although the atheistic phase was temporary in every case. The table shown on the following page will bring out the world-wide nature of the prophetic movement.

The educated reader will be familiar with most of the names appearing in this table, and he is referred for full details to the standard histories of religion and of philosophy.

---

[32] Moore, HR, I, ix.   Galloway discusses the same point in PR, 131–138.   See Knudson, BLP, Leslie, PTS, Cohon, PRO, and McDonald, HPG, for the Hebrew contribution.

	ISRAEL	GREECE	PERSIA	INDIA	CHINA
8th cent.	Amos 750 Hosea 750 E 750 Isaiah 735	Hesiod (850)			
7th cent.	D 650 Jeremiah 620		Zoroaster 630		
6th cent.	Ezekiel 600 II Is. (40–55) 550	Orphic Mysteries 550 Pythagoras 550 Xenophanes 550 Heraclitus 514		Mahavira 569 Buddha 530	Lao-tse 574 Confucius 520
5th cent.	III Is. (56–66) 450 P 500	Empedocles 460 Socrates 430		Upanishads 500 on	Moh Ti 470
4th cent.		Plato 397 Aristotle 354			

(Note: dates indicate approximately when the man reached the age of 30.)

A brief explanation of the main traits of the movement will suffice for the purposes of philosophy of religion.

(1) *Prophetic*. The movement is prophetic. The word prophet means one who speaks forth; the notion of a prophet as a foreteller of future events is secondary and unessential. A prophet, then, is one who declares on his own responsibility what he believes to be a divine truth, derived primarily from his own experience and reflection. Because that experience often came to the prophet with overwhelming force and was above the level of life as he knew it, he often regarded it as the voice of God, a divine revelation. Whether the prophet was or was not right in this assumption is one of the problems of philosophy of religion. But whether his experience came through reflection on social and political injustice (as with Amos), or through domestic affliction (as with Hosea), or through war and disaster (as with Isaiah), or through ecstasy (as with the Orphics), or through reason (as with the Greek philosophers, the writers of the Upanishads, and Lao-tse), or through psychological

analysis of the experience of desire (as with Buddha), or through moral theory (as with Confucius), or through observation of the conflict of good and evil in nature (as with Zoroaster), all prophets were firmly convinced that they were spokesmen of divine truth.

(2) *Universal.* The truths which they perceived were almost without exception on a broad, international, super-racial level. The first literary prophet, Amos, begins his message by declaring that nations which behave unjustly will suffer for it, his own nation, the Israelitic, most of all, because of its opportunity for better living. God, he teaches, guides the Philistines and the Ethiopians as well as the Hebrews. Mahavira (founder of the Jainist sect of India) and Buddha both opposed the oppressive caste system of Brahmanism. The Greek appeal to reason was an appeal to what is universally human, the exclusive property of no race or nation. The problems with which the prophets deal are universal human problems—problems of social justice and means of conquering selfishness, ignorance, and the fear of insecurity and death.

(3) *Individualistic.* At the same time that the prophetic movement was universal it was also individualistic. Primitive man was important only as a member of his clan or tribe. The individual counted for almost nothing. In national religion the worshiper was the group rather than the solitary soul; the individual was tied to the group and the group was tied to the soil. *"Blut und Boden,"* the blood and soil of National Socialism, were in the thought of the exiled Psalmist who wrote, "How shall we sing Jehovah's song in a foreign land?" But the universal religion of prophetism was a direct relation of the individual to his God, not dependent on priest or temple or rite. This aspect of the prophetic movement is especially exemplified by Jeremiah. Nationalistic religion had glorified the tem-

ple. But Jeremiah said, "Trust ye not in lying words, saying, The temple of Jehovah, the temple of Jehovah, the
temple of Jehovah are these. For if ye thoroughly amend
your ways and your doings . . . then will I cause you to
dwell in this place." (Jer. 7:4–7) He declared that God gave
no command about sacrifices, but asked only obedience to
the divine voice (Jer. 7:22, 23). Religion for him was the
inner life; "I will put my law in their inward parts, and in
their heart will I write it" (Jer. 31:33). This individualism
is akin to the Socratic appeal to reason, and to the teaching
of Plato that it is better to suffer wrong than to do wrong.
The Hebrew Ezekiel and the Indian Buddha both teach
that "the reward a man reaps accords with his deeds." The
teachings of the prophetic movement thus appeal to universal
humanity.

(4) *Ethical.* As has already been implied, the prophetic
movement turns away from forms and ceremonies as the
essence of religion to the ethical. Prophetism universally
teaches kindness, altruism, and social justice. The Golden
Rule of Jesus is anticipated by Buddha who taught that one
should treat others as he treats himself.[33] Confucius often
said, "What you do not want done to yourself, do not do
to others." Lao-tse taught, "Recompense injury with kindness." Zoroaster declared, "Whatever thou dost not approve for thyself, do not approve for anyone else." Respect for the rights of others, coöperation rather than competition, economic and political justice, are the world-wide
themes of the prophetic movement.

(5) *Intellectual.* Instead of relying on tradition, the
prophetic movement respects and encourages the thought
of the individual. In Mahavira and Buddha the prophetic
movement is even more intellectual than it is religious. So
indifferent were these two prophets to ordinary religious con-

[33] For this and other parallels, with their sources, see Hume, WLR, 265–266.

ventions that they both founded an atheistic type of religion, and the scriptures of early Buddhism are replete with intellectual analysis of psychological, moral, and epistemological[34] problems. Likewise, the anonymous writers of the Upanishads, more metaphysical[35] than Buddha, develop a highly intellectual conception of religion. Lao-tse and Confucius, while more respectful of tradition, are critical, creative, and open-minded in their thinking. Greek philosophers, especially Socrates, Plato, and Aristotle, attack traditional beliefs and subject all religious concepts to the test of reason.

Less well known is the fact that the Hebrew prophets turned away from tradition in the interest of intellectual independence. Amos (750 b.c.) makes God say, "I hate, I despise your feasts" (5:21). Isaiah (29:13, about 705 b.c.), according to the improved rendering of the American Standard Version, has God declare, with scorn, "Their fear of me is a commandment of men which hath been taught them." Wisdom that consists of knowledge of tradition is rejected by Isaiah for a wisdom that consists of a reasonable interpretation of religious and other social experience. Indeed, God's own attitude is represented as an appeal to reason, "Come now, and let us reason together, saith Jehovah" (1:18, about 701 b.c.). If these words should be rendered, as some think, "Come now, and let us accuse one another," the atmosphere of free discussion is even more evident than in the dignified older translation. Jeremiah goes so far (in 7:8, about 608 b.c.) as to appear to denounce the teaching, or at least the application of the teaching of the book of Deuteronomy as "lying words." The whole body of prophetic thought, while poetic and sometimes ecstatic in form, is intellectual and antitraditional in con-

---

[34] Epistemology is that branch of philosophy which deals with the nature and limits of knowledge.

[35] Metaphysics is the attempt to give a coherent and rational description of the real. The belief in God is a metaphysical belief.

tent.[36] So, too, the thought of Zoroaster in Persia, attended though it is by imaginative aspects, is a genuine intellectual wrestle with the problem of good and evil. Ahura-Mazda, the god of light, is approached by truth and goodness. In the old Zoroastrian confession of faith (Yasna XII), the intellectual attitude is expressed in the vow, "I promise well-thought thought, well-spoken word, well-done deed."

It cannot be denied that the national-priestly stage of religion had also developed a high type of intellectual life. But the learning of the priests was mostly historical and traditional; independent thought was chiefly esoteric (as with Pythagoras). In contrast to this, the intellectual life of the prophetic movement was free and open, critical of tradition, and relevant to actual life.

(6) *Mystical.* It is no contradiction to say that the prophetic movement was both intellectual and mystical at the same time. After all, the intellectual and the mystical experience of God are both forms of the inner life in contrast with the external forms and group ceremonies which were almost the whole of primitive and national religion. Mysticism is illustrated by the greater development of the individual experience of prayer (Jeremiah and Socrates illustrate this phase); in the vision of inner enlightenment and the consequent sense of mission, such as was experienced by Isaiah in the temple at Jerusalem (6:1–5, 740 B.C.), by Jeremiah, apparently in early youth (1:4–10, about 626 B.C.), by Amos when tending his sheep (7:15, before 750 B.C.), by Buddha under the famous "Bo" or "Bodhi" tree (about 530 B.C.; see Carus, GB, 29–34), by Zoroaster at the age of thirty, when he received the vision thrice on one day (about 630 B.C.; see Barton, RW, 123).

The goal of the prophetic religion was, it is true, pre-

[36] To quote Jeremiah, "The false pen of the scribes hath wrought falsely" (8:8). See McDonald, HPG, and Knudson, BLP.

dominantly moral and social rather than mystical. The extreme mysticism which forgets the world entirely in a rapturous vision of God is characteristic of other aspects of religion more related to the priestly. Extreme mysticism is often a refuge of souls to whom the formalism of priestly religion has been unendurable; it is also cultivated, as we have seen, in the sacramental aspect of priestly religion. Nevertheless, the most intellectual and antiformal representatives of the prophetic, men like Plato and Lao-tse, are led by their reflections to a view of the universe which eventuates in an exalted mystical consciousness of unity. Socrates was warned by his "daimonion" when he was about to do wrong. Early phases of the prophetic movement in Israel appeared to identify the Spirit of God with involuntary psychological phenomena, as when Saul joined a band of prophets in their "prophesying" (1 Sam. 10:10–13, about 1030 B.C.); and Ezekiel experienced certain abnormal psychic states (as 4:4–8, about 593 B.C.). In general, however, the mystical experiences of the prophets were not of the extreme or abnormal type, but were an emotional support or exemplification of the ethical aims of the prophets.

(7) *Monotheistic.* The prophetic movement was unanimous in rejecting the traditional polytheism of the priestly stage. Although Socrates and Plato still used the terminology of the Greek pantheon, their belief in one God was evident from their teaching. The charge against Socrates that he was "guilty of rejecting the gods acknowledged by the state" [37] was literally correct; he had a better god than any in the state creed: one, instead of many; good, instead of licentious; rational, instead of traditional. Aristotle hardly deigned even to mention the names of Apollo and Zeus in his serious discussions of God; he regarded theology as a branch of metaphysics, not of priestly lore, and his

[37] Xenophon, *Memorabilia,* I, 1, 1.

logic permitted only one god.[38]   It is interesting to note that
spiritual monotheism, expressing itself in ridicule of the
anthropomorphic symbols of idolatry, was formulated con-
temporaneously (about 550 B.C.) by Xenophanes in Greece
and by the exiled Israelitic prophet, Second Isaiah in Babylon.[39] Polytheism was rejected because it was immoral,
irrational, and unspiritual. The Way of Lao-tse, the
Shang-ti or heaven of Confucius, the Ahura-Mazda of Zoroaster, and the Jehovah of the prophets of Israel all represented the concept of one supreme, spiritual deity. It is true
that Zoroaster also believed in an evil power, Ahriman, who
was opposed by Ahura-Mazda and his followers, and that
Mahavira and Buddha were themselves atheists. But Zoroaster's idea was hardly less compatible with monotheism
than the traditional Christian devil, and the Jainists and
Buddhists soon rejected the atheism of the founders of
their sects by elevating Mahavira and Buddha themselves to
the position of monotheistic deities.

§ 7.   History of Religion: Living Religions

(1) *Continued existence of several older religions.* Since
the purpose of this book is philosophical rather than historical, our interest in the history of religions is not in the minute
details of each religion but rather in those facts which express or imply beliefs about the nature of the real and
therefore are of philosophical importance. The priestly

---

[38] Jaeger calls attention to the special problem raised in Aristotle's *Metaphysics*,
Book Lambda, Chap. VIII, where there is a hint that he may have returned to
polytheism on astronomical grounds. See Jaeger, ARI, 342–367. (The reader
should not rely on the inaccurate exposition in Fuller, HP, I, 153.) Jaeger points
out that Aristotle's polytheistic line of thought "involved him in inextricable contradictions" (351).

[39] Compare Is. 41 with the fragments of Xenophanes. Note, however, that
the first clear case of monotheism in history (aside from the "high gods" of primitive times) was in Egypt, when Ikhn-Aton (Amenhotep IV) became a monotheistic reformer (1375–1358 B.C.). Thus the first religion with a personal founder
was monotheistic.

and prophetic stages saw the founding of several religions that are still in existence. There remains for our purpose only a brief consideration of the great religions which have arisen since the prophetic movement—and obviously as a continuation of it—namely Christianity and Mohammedanism. The relation of the world's living religions to the development of religion as we have studied it is illustrated by the following table: [40]

Animism (primitive)	135,650,000
Hinduism (1500 B.C., first Vedas)	230,150,000
Judaism (Moses, 1275 B.C.)	15,315,359
Shinto (founded 660 B.C.?)	25,000,000
Buddhism (Buddha, 560 B.C.)	150,180,000
Taoism (Lao-tse, 604 B.C.) and Confucianism (Confucius, 550 B.C.)	350,600,000
Christianity (Jesus, 6 B.C.?)	682,400,000
Mohammedanism (Mohammed, 570 A.D.)	209,020,000

(2) *Christianity*. The Christian religion, the one which is best known to most readers of this book, was founded by Jesus, called Christ (the Greek word for the Hebrew Messiah, meaning "anointed"), about 30 A.D. Jesus thought of his religion as continuous with the Hebrew religion of the Old Testament priests and prophets, although he was much closer to the prophetic than to the priestly type, and all the main characteristics of prophetic religion appear in his teaching. The main traits of his thought were: (a) rejection of political, military, particularistic, and nationalistic views of religion, and acceptance of himself as a spiritual Messiah (see the temptation narratives in Mt. and Lk.); (b) monotheism regarded as the universal fatherhood of God (he thought of himself as "Son of God"); (c) the ideal of love and unselfish sacrifice, commonly called the brotherhood of man (hence he also thought of himself as

[40] The list of living religions and the number of their adherents is derived from *The World Almanac* for 1938. The reader should consult the table in Hume, WLR. It will be noted that all the living religions except Animism show the influence of both priestly and prophetic elements. Dates show the birth of the founder, unless otherwise noted.

"Son of Man"); (d) belief in his own "second coming" within a generation (it being disputed whether he thought of this as a physical or a purely spiritual coming).

Miracles ascribed to him and the account of his resurrection have caused problems for many modern thinkers. With Harnack, we must distinguish "the gospel of Jesus" from "the gospel about Jesus." The gospel of Jesus, as just stated, is to be found in those parts of Matthew, Mark, Luke, and John which criticism regards as most authentic; the historical evidence proves him to have been a man of extraordinary simplicity and integrity of character, a religious and moral personality unequalled in history, regardless of any special religious valuation that faith has set on him. But Christianity does not consist entirely of the gospel of Jesus. "The gospel about Jesus" is the teaching of Paul of Tarsus and of other Christian thinkers, who saw in Jesus not merely a wise and good teacher and spiritual Messiah, but also a divine redeemer. Paul thought pictorially of man as a captive of sin, needing to be ransomed; and the death of Christ was that ransom. By it, man was redeemed. These and other figures of speech were used to convey the thought that in Jesus was expressed the divine initiative in saving man from his "lost" condition, and through him was given the guarantee of divine love, forgiveness, and cooperation. Not personal success in attaining perfection (works), but faith in God is made the condition of salvation. Paul also laid stress on the church organization.

The history of Christianity has seen many developments of the thought of redemption or atonement for sin, and also of the idea of incarnation (the view that in Jesus, God was made flesh); [41] there have been varying emphases on the gospel of Jesus and the gospel about him. All Christians have been united in a sense of loyalty to Jesus and in ac-

[41] Incarnation is a common concept in the Orient, especially in Hinduism.

ceptance of his spiritual leadership, although there have
been increasing differences in other respects. The contrasts between Mark and John or between James and Paul
in the New Testament are obvious. Gnostic and Montanist heresies plagued the second century. The great
struggle between Arius and Athanasius (Council of Nice,
325 A.D.), and that between Pelagius and Augustine (a century later), evidence conflict of opinion about Pauline ideas.
The pantheism of Erigena, the searching questions of Abelard, the mysticism of Eckhart, and the divergences between
Duns Scotus and Thomas Aquinas on intellect and will,
show the continued independence of Christian thought.
Since the Reformation (Martin Luther at Worms, 1521),
ecclesiastical divisions within Christianity have increased,
although the twentieth century has seen new movements
toward "ecumenical" unity.

(3) *Mohammedanism*. In the year 622 A.D. there occurred the Hegira of Mohammed, his flight from Mecca as
a result of the persecutions to which he was subjected. His
followers, the Moslems, date their time reckoning from this
year. The teachings of Mohammed were based on knowledge of and respect for Judaism and Christianity (every
Moslem when he mentions Jesus says, "Blessed be his
name") and on opposition to the gross idolatry of the
Arabia of his day. His chief doctrines were: (a) strict
monotheism ("Allah is Allah"), which rejected Christian
ideas that there was a Trinity and that God has a Son, (b)
Mohammed as the prophet through whom the final revelation comes ("Mohammed is his prophet"), (c) absolute
submission to the will of God (Islam), (d) regularity in
prayer at stated times, with the face toward Mecca, (e) pil-
grimage to Mecca, (f) abstinence from alcohol, and (g)
belief in the reward of the faithful in a very physical heaven.
Although the prophet lived but ten years after the Hegira,

he had won the allegiance of all Arabia in that period. Under his successors, the Caliphs, the Moslem religion became associated with military conquests ("Islam or the sword") and with a high culture based not merely on the sacred "revelation" in the Koran, but also on the heritage of Hellenism. Al-Ghazali (1059–1109) was the greatest philosopher of Islam, having traits in common with men as different as Saint Augustine and David Hume. Every student of history knows the influence of the "Saracens." Islam, always a missionary religion, retained the Caliphate until March 3, 1924, when the new Turkey deposed Abdul Mejid from the office and left him without a successor. The varieties of thought within Mohammedanism almost equal those of Christianity, but since the Middle Ages Islam has been less open to the influences of science and philosophy and less liberal in its thought than has Christianity.

§ 8. Psychology of Religion: Psychology of Conversion

In our search for the facts about religion, we turn now from the historical to the psychological approach. We have seen how religion has developed and expressed itself concretely in institutions, beliefs, and practices. In recent times, as we saw in § 2 of this chapter, there has developed the science of psychology of religion. The first topic to be investigated was the experience of "conversion"—the transition from an irreligious or nonreligious life to a religious one. In the eighteenth century Jonathan Edwards had written careful descriptions of his own conversion and of similar experiences of many others. Toward the middle of the nineteenth century, Horace Bushnell (1802–1876) raised questions about the necessity of definite conversion, as that ascribed to Saint Paul in the Book of Acts. About the same time, evangelists were asking when the conversion of their hearers occurred, and results showed considerable uniformity in dating it between the ages of twelve and twenty—that is, roughly, during adolescence. The first systematic work in psychology of religion, by E. D. Starbuck (1900), dealt largely with conversion. He found three main types of conversion: (1) positive or volitional, (2) negative or self-surrender, and (3) spontaneous. G. A. Coe (1900 on) showed the influence of individual temperament and of social forces on conversion. William James (1902) proved vividly that the "healthy-minded" soul, as he called it, experiences religion without a conversion crisis, while the "sick soul" is a divided self that needs a radical conversion crisis to achieve integration. G. M. Stratton (1911) also laid stress on the importance of experiences of conflict. The number of conversion experiences has been declining in recent years. Elmer T. Clark [42] has shown that out of 2,174 instances of religious awakening, 66.1 per cent are cases of gradual growth and only 6.7 per cent clearly crisis conversions. When it occurs, conversion involves, as Coe pointed out,[43] the adoption of a more satisfactory scale of values, a step in the creation of a self, generally also a step in the creation of a society, and acquaintance with God which is closely related to the social experience. There is, accordingly, a discrepancy between the early studies, which termed conversion a normal adolescent phenomenon, and the later, for which it is exceptional. Clark thinks that "stern theological and faulty religious education tend to produce the Definite Crisis experience." [44] Others believe that the drop in the curve of conversions is due to social causes which should be opposed by religion. Psychologists agree, however, that religion appears normally both as a natural growth and as a crisis experience.

[42] See Clark, PRA, 34–51, esp. 47–48. See Stolz, PRL, 219–223 for a practical interpretation of the facts.

[43] See Coe, PR, 171–174. See Thouless, IPR, 187–204.

[44] Clark, PRA, 147.

§ 9. Psychology of Religion: Psychology of Mysticism

By mysticism is meant the direct experience of what is believed to be divine reality, as contrasted with intellectual belief in religion or moral devotion to religious causes. In most religions, as we found in our study of the prophetic movement, there is a mystical element. Many scriptures record mystical experiences (see Is. 6:1–13 and 2 Cor. 12:1–5, for examples); the classics of religious literature, such as Lao-tse's writings, the Bhagavad Gita, Saint Augustine's *Confessions,* Thomas à Kempis's *Imitatio Christi,* the *Theologia Germanica,* and the modern writings of Tagore and Gandhi, are all permeated with a sense of the actual presence of the divine in human experience. It is natural that psychology of religion should early turn its attention toward mysticism—both on account of the abundance of source material and on account of the inherent religious importance of the experience.

James's Gifford Lectures in 1901 and 1902 are largely devoted to a study of mysticism, which he called "the vital chapter." His list of the traits of mystical experience is so famous that it should be given. These traits are: (1) Ineffability (it cannot be imparted in words; in this, we may add, it is like sense qualities, such as yellow, sweet, loud); (2) Noetic quality (it is a state of knowledge, affirming insight or illumination); (3) Transiency (it can be sustained at most for an hour or two; resentment against this inevitable transiency is expressed in Mark 9:5–9); (4) Passivity (the mystic may prepare for the experience, but when it comes he feels as if grasped by a superior power; this contrasts the mystic state with religious belief and religious action).[45] James's description is accepted by most psychologists.

However, there are few psychologists who are satisfied to leave philosophical problems to philosophers. James H.

[45] For James's own account, see VRE, 379–382.

Leuba, a lifelong student of psychology of religion, is perhaps even more concerned to expose fallacious religious philosophies than he is to describe the actual psychological facts. James has been charged with a predisposition in favor of belief. Leuba appears to have a predisposition toward doubt. He is especially famous for Chapter II of his *The Psychology of Religious Mysticism,* in which he shows that a mystical ecstasy produced by certain drugs gives an impression of enlarged and perfected life, similar to that of religious mysticism proper. But it is on philosophical rather than psychological grounds that this fact must be interpreted; otherwise psychologists could infer that there is no real world merely because there are hallucinations.[46]

§ 10.   PSYCHOLOGY OF RELIGION: PSYCHOLOGY OF PRAYER AND WORSHIP

Practically speaking, the mystical experience is usually gained (or sought) in the experiences of prayer and worship. For various reasons, psychologists have not examined the facts of ordinary prayer and worship so carefully as they have the more striking phases of mystical experience. The only first-class book on prayer is Friedrich Heiler's *Das Gebet,* translated as *Prayer* by Samuel McComb and J. Edgar Park. Readers of this chapter will find the book especially interesting because of its combination of the historical and the psychological, and its treatment of primitive prayer, ritual prayer, prayer in mysticism, in prophetic religion, and in worship. As W. K. Wright points out, prayer is psychologically in the "conversational" form [47]—a dialogue between one's self and a "thou" who is addressed. As in all conversation, real or imaginary, the entire prayer is a psychological

[46] Leuba, PRM, Chap. XII, "Religion, Science, and Philosophy," is an attempt to cope with philosophical interpretations of the facts of mystical experience.

[47] Wright, SPR, Chap. XVI. "Monologues" are to be regarded as meditation rather than prayer.

process. Prayer often enhances the psychological well-being of the one who prays, adds to his energies and gives him hope and a feeling of the purpose of life. It often also results in improved bodily health. Whether prayer is divinely "answered" and whether the effects of prayer are due to "subjective" or to "objective" causes—to our subconscious or to God or to God's using subjective means—are questions for philosophy, not for psychology to deal with. The psychological fact is that prayer exists, that it takes the form of dialogue, the "thou-form"; also, that it may appear as petition (predominantly so in early religions), as communion, as intercession, or as praise.

Worship is an experience which usually includes prayer, but adds other factors such as silent meditation, ritual, music (both instrumental and vocal), reading and interpretation of religious literature, and sometimes the religious dance. Elsewhere the present writer has analyzed worship as consisting of four attitudes, namely, contemplation (meditation on the divine), revelation (insight into truth believed to be divinely imparted), communion (the consciousness of a personal relation to God), and fruition (the new life which grows out of the worship experience).[48]

The study of worship thus far has been carried on chiefly by philosophers of religion and by those ecclesiastically interested in the practical improvement of worship.[49] The chief exception is the philosopher-psychologist, J. B. Pratt, whose great work, *The Religious Consciousness,* makes a distinction between subjective and objective worship. The former is chiefly concerned with the effect of worship on the individual, the latter with a relation to God. Protestant worship, centering in the sermon, is said to be chiefly sub-

[48] Brightman, RV, 173–237, esp. 179–184.
[49] See, however, Dresser, PR, Chap. III, for a survey of the problem, and Thouless, IPR, 159–186.

jective; Catholic worship, centering in the mass, chiefly objective.

§ 11. PSYCHOLOGY OF RELIGION: PSYCHOLOGY OF INDIVIDUAL TYPES

It is not until recently that psychology has concerned itself intensively with the individual. "General" psychology was too general to consider individual differences; practical and theoretical considerations have recently combined to force attention, not only on differences of temperament, which have been known since antiquity, but also on the unique traits of each individual.[50] One result of the modern investigation of individual psychology has been various attempts to classify individuals by types. The investigators have, however, arrived at little agreement. Individuals are too individual to fit neatly into any scheme of typology. Yet if the "types" be not taken rigidly, they may often serve as guides to the understanding of religious experiences. James's healthy-minded and sick souls, and Pratt's objective and subjective worshipers are examples of this. Individual psychology has done much to liberate modern religion from a feeling of being constrained to experience one type of conversion—the Pauline-crisis type. Carl G. Jung's classification into extroverts (those chiefly interested in others or in things), introverts (those chiefly interested in themselves or in thought processes), and ambiverts (those in whom both interests are strong) affords a background for understanding "the varieties of religious experience." The existence of individuals of widely varying types leads us to expect widely varying religious experiences. We find introverts who are predominantly intellectual, extroverts predominantly ethical and practical, and ambiverts who seek a synthesis in their religion.

[50] See Allport, PER.

§ 12. PSYCHOLOGY OF RELIGION AND THE SUBCONSCIOUS

The so-called "New Psychology," under the influence of such men as Freud, Adler, and Jung, has been largely concerned with exploring the subconscious. The mind has been compared to an iceberg, one-eighth (the field of consciousness) visible, seven-eighths (the subconscious) submerged under water. The life of feeling, desire, emotion, and action are often thought of as chiefly the result of subconscious processes, "suppressed desires" (as Freud thinks), longings for superiority (as Adler believes), or the inherited experience of the race (according to Jung). The differing views of the subconscious held by great authorities should not lead to the conclusion that there is no such reality. Experiments with subjects under hypnosis, interpretation of dreams, as well as many religious experiences, show conclusively that there are conscious processes going on in connection with our organism of which our normal consciousness cannot be directly aware, but which it has every right to infer from their effects. Such conscious processes may be called the subconscious or the unconscious.[51]

While the exploration of the subconscious is valuable for all the light it can shed on prayer, conversion, mysticism, and other experiences, yet three points of caution need to be borne in mind by the student. (1) The psychology of the subconscious (psychoanalysis) is a realm in which fact and theory, description and evaluation, are not clearly distinguished in the minds of its interpreters. It is one thing to say that there is a subconscious relation between love to God and love to one's father; it is quite another to say that belief in God is only a father-complex and hence is false. The latter statement is an evaluation, a purely philosophical

[51] For a brief account of the problem, see Thouless, IPR, Chap. VIII, or Selbie, PR, Chaps. III and XV.

theory, having no place in psychology. (2) The data of the New Psychology have been largely derived from pathological subjects who have selected themselves for attention by their need for treatment from psychiatrists. What may be true of Dr. Freud's patients (usually troubled with sex-complexes) may not be true of Dr. Jung's patients, simply because the latter were suffering from a somewhat different type of mental ailment. (3) The tendency of this psychology is to reduce all religious thinking to rationalizing; that is, it often regards religious beliefs as consisting of arguments devised to support the fulfillment of our subconscious wishes rather than as honest objective thinking about reality. But after all, no thinking can be judged to be objectively true or false on purely psychological grounds. Here is another confusion between psychology and philosophy. Psychology cannot usurp the place of logic or philosophy of religion any more than it can usurp the place of physics by its study of sensations.

§ 13. Psychology of Religion and Social Psychology

The complexity of religion is illustrated by the many psychological approaches necessary to comprehend it. Important as are individual psychology and psychology of the subconscious, they fail to describe all the facts of religion unless supplemented by social psychology, another young science which is a product of the nineteenth and twentieth centuries.[52] Social psychology is an investigation of those conscious processes which arise as a result of the interaction of two or more persons. Since all historical religions are social phenomena, it might appear that psychology of religion is but a branch of social psychology. Every conversion experience is social in the sense that it is a readjustment of

[52] See Karpf, ASP, for an account of its development.

the life to the social situation; mysticism emphasizes the individual, yet different types of mysticism arise in different social situations; prayer is originally for the group, and is so truly social that in analyzing many of the Biblical Psalms, scholars are unable to determine whether the one praying is an individual or the community. Intercessory prayer is, of course, socially directed. Every individual is acted on by his social environment and is partly defined by his reaction to that environment. The subconscious is not only affected by present social relations, but is believed by Freud to be largely determined by parental influences in infancy, and by Jung to be the carrier of the past experience of the race. So important is the social aspect that many, like Comte and certain American religious humanists, as well as others like E. Scribner Ames, interpret religion as exclusively a phenomenon of social psychology. Every social experience, it has been said, is religious, even the cheering at a football game. Exponents of this view have compared God to Uncle Sam—both being social symbols.

Over against this exclusively social view, it needs to be pointed out that man's life is not wholly determined by social-psychological influences. Other sciences point out man's biological heredity, his random acts, his relations to physical nature, his individual inventiveness and initiative (what Tarde calls invention, as distinguished from imitation), his intellectual love of objective truth, his mathematics and his logic—and all of these indicate both causes and purposes operative in experience which cannot be defined as products of social psychology. In the higher religions, especially those under the influence of the prophetic movement, the relation of the individual to his God and to his religious community is thought of as in some sense a voluntary choice, not a social compulsion. Likewise, the higher religions agree in viewing social approval as being often

something to be criticized rather than to be sought.[53]   Hence
the view of religion as a fact of social psychology, while
true, is not the whole truth.

§ 14. Sociology of Religion: Religion and Social Groups
and Institutions

The French founder of sociology, Auguste Comte (1798–
1857), was at the same time the founder of sociology of religion; for in the latter part of his life he devoted himself to
an interpretation of religion from a sociological point of
view.   He went so far as to hold that all religious beliefs
about gods or God were really beliefs about social groups,
and that the true God, "le grand être" and the object of real
religious devotion, is not an eternal being, creator of the
world, but rather is to be identified with humanity.   Humanity alone is God, and is alone to be worshiped.   It is
evident that the views of Comte, and the somewhat similar
ones of the German, Ludwig Feuerbach (1804–1872), are
not purely scientific, but are a mingling of sociological and
philosophical ideas.   Comte was a positivist, holding that all
metaphysical theories are false; Feuerbach was a metaphysical materialist, perhaps best remembered today by Karl
Marx's "theses" in criticism of him.

Émile Durkheim (1858–1917), an independent French
follower of Comte, wrote the first great modern work in
sociology of religion; it appeared in French in 1912 and in
English translation in 1915, under the title, *The Elementary
Forms of the Religious Life*.   He used the results of anthropological investigation (regarding totemism in particular) to show the social origin and function of religious
beliefs.   He holds, rather dogmatically, that the genetic
method is the only method for the study of religion; this

[53] See Waterhouse, PRE, 7, and Thouless, IPR, Chap. XI.

procedure, he maintains, leads to the conclusion that "religious force" is *only* "the sentiment inspired by the group in its members" (229). He holds not only to the social origin of religion, but also to the religious origin of all our categories of thought. In his rejection of "divine reason" as an hypothesis not subject to experimental verification (15), he follows Comte and Feuerbach. All three pointed out important facts about the social function of religion and all three were right in their view that sociology could not verify belief in a real God. Nevertheless, all three committed a common error in failing to distinguish the sociological science of religion from the philosophy of religion, which must use methods and consider data foreign to sociology. Even Max. Weber, Joachim Wach, and John Dewey, the chief recent workers in the field, have been unable wholly to divest themselves of the prejudice which regards the social approach as the one and only key to all problems.

Some of the chief results of sociology of religion may be summarized in the following propositions: (1) Many of the chief terms of religions are plainly derived from social and institutional relations: Father, King of kings, Lord, gods of various crafts and professions, ransom, sacrament, and the like. (2) The form which religion takes reflects or at least is profoundly influenced by the social culture in which it exists. Not very long ago we heard of the divine right of kings. Today religion, in some countries, must be democratic; in others, racial; in still others both tsar and God are forbidden for essentially the same social reasons. (3) Religious officials, from primitive times until recently, have been regarded also as tribal or national officials.[54] (4) The origin of most ancient and great social institutions and practices is believed to be religious by thinkers as different as Durkheim and Hocking. Birth, marriage, family, planting,

[54] On this see Dewey, CF, 60, and 6.

reaping, war, art, and death were all attended by religious sanctions and rituals; man's view of social life has always been colored by his religious feelings.[55]   (5) The interaction between society and religion, without exclusive causation on the part of either, is emphasized by Joachim Wach (ERS). (6) Religion has been a social phenomenon as far back in the evolution of the race as evidence is accessible. A further important point is discussed in the following section.

§ 15. Sociology of Religion: Religion and Economic Forces

The development of economics, and especially the so-called "materialistic interpretation of history" by Karl Marx and his followers, has led sociologists of religion to consider the relations between economic conditions and religion. Marx's view is that religion is a product of economic forces and is used by the exploiting class to keep the proletariat submissive. It is "the opium of the people," at best a refuge from the realities of material existence, at worst an enslavement to them.[56] The influence of this standpoint in the U.S.S.R. is epoch-making in modern history, and illustrates in itself the sociological importance of religion. But objective sociologists, while admitting the importance of economic conditions in their influence on religion, incline to agree with Wach's view (stated above) that religion influences as well as is influenced by social and economic conditions. Such a standpoint was expressed in Max Weber's great work, *The Protestant Ethic and the Spirit of Capital-*

[55] See Durkheim, EFRL, 418–419. Note Hocking's famous description of religion as "the mother of the Arts" (MGHE, 14); also his very frank statement that "religion has fostered everything valuable to man and has obstructed everything" (MGHE, 11).

[56] The reader of German will find the chief utterances of Marx and Engels on this subject collected in a handy little volume, Marx-Engels, ROV. The best English exposition of the view is in Calverton, PG.

ism.[57] This is generally regarded as the most important contribution to sociology of religion yet made. It is an attempt to show that Protestantism was more favorable to the development of modern capitalism than was Catholicism, and within Protestantism, Calvinism more so than other forms of belief.[58] A philosophy of religion will give full weight to the economic factor, but it would not be philosophy if it confined its attention to any one factor in experience to the exclusion of others. Economic forces are a datum, but not the only datum, of philosophy of religion.[59]

§ 16. Sociology of Religion: Religion and Social Reforms

Sociologists have not made adequate investigation into the history of social reforms. Such investigation as has been made, however, shows that religion at its best has very often concerned itself with the reforming of social abuses. We have seen how Buddha opposed the caste system and how the Hebrew prophets attacked the oppressors of the poor. The Hebrew religion in particular has emphasized philanthropy and alleviation of the state of the less favored classes, and has opposed usury and other abuses. The Christian religion has given woman a higher place in society, has done much toward the undermining of slavery as an institution, has opposed the social abuse of alcohol, has repeatedly initiated movements for world peace, and has been the source

[57] It appeared in German in 1904–1905 and in English translation in 1920 (PESC).

[58] The late G. C. Cell made an able investigation of the same problem in connection with John Wesley. See the chapter on "The Decay of Religion" in his RJW, 363–441. MacArthur, EEJW, is also illuminating. A critique of Weber's view is found in Robertson, REI. See Dewey, CF, 79–80.

[59] Even an extremist like Rosa Luxemburg wrote to Franz Mehring that "your brilliant pen has taught our workers that socialism is not a bread and butter problem, but a cultural movement." Mehring, KM, ix.

of many socialistic or quasi-socialistic experiments, from the
first Christian community (Acts 2:43-45) to Brook Farm
and the contemporary world-wide Christian interest in co-
operatives,[60] as well as repeated movements under the name
of Christian socialism. All universal religions rise above
the nationalistic standpoint and favor some form of internationalism.[61] Hence the modern struggle between the
state and religion, as illustrated by totalitarian conflicts with
Judaism and Christianity, and the conflicts of a different
kind in countries like China and India where a sense of nationalism is just arising. Passive resistance, nonjuring, con-
scientious objecting, and the like are forms of religious
protest against political injustice. Religion has founded
universities and hospitals, and has often promoted the arts,
science, and philosophy.

No complete account of the relation of religion to social
reforms can be written without considering the frequent opposition of priests and churches to social advance. Religion
has often sought to crush scientific thought, has opposed
philosophical freedom, has stood with the vested economic
interests against the needy, has conducted cruel Crusades,
and has sanctified political wars. It is problematic whether
these phenomena reveal the true nature of religion or
whether they show that the religious consciousness is often
unable or unwilling to assert itself against the pressure of
the secular environment, although saints and martyrs have
been shining exceptions. The former view is accepted by
Communistic and other critics of religion; the latter is held
by many thinkers more friendly to religious belief. The
question amounts to this: Who were more truly religious,
the Medicis or the Quakers?

[60] One of the few investigations of this topic is the C.O.P.E.C. Commission Re-
port, *Historical Illustrations of the Social Effects of Christianity*. For a critical
treatment, see Westermarck, CM.
[61] See Bentwich, RFI.

§ 17. CHIEF RELIGIOUS BELIEFS

Having completed a very hasty survey of religion as a fact, we have now to summarize the results of this survey for the purposes of philosophy of religion. Such a summary must take the form of a statement of essential religious beliefs. Rites and ceremonies as such are neither true nor false, right nor wrong, but are merely more or less effective means for producing or mediating what religious belief holds to be true and right. The following list indicates the chief religious beliefs which we have found:

(1) *The belief that there are experiences of great and permanent value.* This belief is summed up in what Höffding has taken to be the basis of all religion, namely, the axiom of the conservation of values.

(2) *The belief in gods or God.* Most religions from the start rest on belief in divine beings, or a divine being, viewed as a source of value, if not the source of all value. We have found that even those religions, like Jainism, Buddhism, and Communism, which begin with atheism tend to develop a belief in some objective source of value, that is to say, a god.

(3) *The belief that there is evil as well as value.* All religions recognize that there is something in the universe to be opposed and feared. In primitive religion, it is hard to distinguish good from evil in the taboo; but the belief in demons, Satan, Ahriman, sin, the need of redemption, longing for individual conversion and social reform all imply recognition of something evil. Even a religion like Christian Science, which denies the reality of evil, recognizes it in the fact of "error of mortal mind" and in "malicious animal magnetism."

(4) *The belief that man is a soul or spiritual being, not merely a physical organism.* All religions have found the chief meaning of existence in man's spiritual nature and

attitude, rather than in any purely material condition or possession. The most crude idolatry is always regarded as a relation of the human spirit to a divine spirit.

(5) *The belief that there is purpose in human existence.* This purpose is thought of as being for the group, and in higher religions, also for the individual; it is not merely man's purpose, but also God's. Thus religion is always a relation of man to the whole of existence or at least to the whole which he believes to be supremely important and worthy of his purposive devotion. Even when belief in purpose is faint or absent, its effects abide in the form of belief in man's membership in a larger whole on which he depends.

(6) *The belief that the human soul is immortal.* This belief is not shared by all religious individuals and groups, as we have seen, but it is so nearly universal that it must be considered characteristic of religion.

(7) *The belief in valid religious experience.* This is the conviction that there are experiences, such as sacraments, conversion, worship, mystical moments, and prayer, when the religious person comes into actual and immediate relation with the divine being. Sacred scriptures are largely records of supposedly normative religious experiences.

(8) *The belief in religious action.* This appears in the believer's faith that his religion should, either partially or wholly, regulate his conduct both individual and social. So important is this that religion may well be called primarily practical, rather than primarily emotional or intellectual.

It is clear that these eight religious beliefs all imply that philosophical propositions of certain sorts are true. The belief in great and permanent value implies a distinction between true and false values. The belief in God implies a metaphysical theory of reality as a whole, since God is thought of as the ground of existence and of value. The belief in evil presupposes a theory of value and raises the question of dualism. The belief in man's soul or spirit involves philosophical psychology. The belief in purpose, human or divine, is inseparable from the philosophical problem of mechanism and teleology. The belief in immortality is incompatible with materialistic philosophy or psychology, but is consistent with certain forms of realism, dualism, pluralism, and idealism. The belief in religious experience requires criteria to distinguish valid religious experience from error and illusion. The belief in religious action presupposes a metaphysics and an ethics in order to define the arena and the aims of action.

The remainder of this book will be an endeavor to explore the chief philosophical problems occasioned by the facts of religious belief. No philosophical investigation could show that religion is not a fact, for it is empirically given. No theory can refute any fact. Neither can any philosophy hope to achieve demonstrative proof of the truth or the error of any religious belief. Such proof must wait for complete knowledge of all the evidence and a mind able to grasp and compare all possible hypotheses, eliminating all save the one most inclusive and most coherent with experience and with logical principles. Even such a mind with such evidence would be somewhat embarrassed by the fact that further experience would be sure to arise, complicating the picture.

What we can hope for and all that we can hope for, whether in philosophy of religion or in philosophy of science, not to mention philosophy of art and social philosophy, is to discover grounds for holding or rejecting a given belief with a high degree of probability. It is the inevitable absence of absolute intellectual or empirical certainty that makes postulates and hypotheses fundamental in science, as faith is fundamental in religion. But postulate, hypothesis, or faith, held without regard to reasons and evidence, must fall equally under the condemnation of a Paul who said, "Prove all things," and a Socrates who taught that "the unexamined life is not worth living."

BIBLIOGRAPHICAL NOTE

Since the chief sources have been stated rather fully in the course of the chapter, only a few introductory texts need be noted here.

For history of religion, Toy, IHR(1913), G. F. Moore, HR(1913, 1919), Hopkins, OER(1923), Barton, RW(1929), and Friess and Schneider, RVC(1932), present the main facts and refer to an extensive literature. Bevan, SAB(1938), interprets ably many of the chief symbolic concepts appearing in the history of religion. Ballou, Spiegelberg, and Friess, BOW(1939), is an excellent selection of sources.

Of special value for psychology of religion are Starbuck, PR(1900), James, VRE(1902), Leuba, PSR(1912), Coe, PR(1916), Pratt, RC(1920), Strickland, PRE(1924), and Stolz, PRL(1937). Hocking, HNR(1918, 1923), is illuminating. There are numerous other texts; but the field has not been developed satisfactorily in recent years.

The chief works in sociology of religion are Weber, PESC(1904–05), Durkheim, EFRL(1912), Wach, ERS(1931), and Dewey, CF(1934).

THREE

RELIGIOUS VALUES

§ 1. RELIGION AS EXPERIENCE OF VALUE

THE survey of the facts of religion (its phenomenology, as such a survey is called) has revealed the fundamental fact that every religious experience is an experience of value. No matter how tragic a religious experience may be, like that of Jesus in Gethsemane or on the Cross, it is not the tragedy that makes it religious; the value for the sake of which the tragedy is borne is its religious meaning. The sufferings of Jesus would have been meaningless pain had it not been for his religious valuation of God and man.

Science is objective, disinterested description. Religion is never merely disinterested description, however objective it may be. It is "interested," that is, it takes sides for value as against disvalue. Religion is definitely for the good and against the evil, whereas science is interested only in knowing the facts of good and evil, their causes and their effects. At no stage can a scientist, in his function as such, ever say of anything, "This is good, this is evil." But the scientist is not always functioning as a scientist; and if, as a human being, he has religious faith he will be, like all religious persons, a partisan of good. Religion is a choice of value, a commitment to it. There is no logical or psychological contradiction between the "value-free" [1] attitude of science and the valuing attitude of religion. It is un-

[1] A term derived from the German *wertfrei*, often used in this connection.

reasonable for a believer to say that because his religious interest is in value, therefore everyone should be interested in value at all times. It is equally unreasonable for a scientist to say that because his scientific interest is in being disinterested and in ignoring value in the laboratory, no one should ever value anything. Each extreme is absurd and neither is held by responsible leaders of either religious or scientific thought. Such genuine problems as arise in the relations between science and religion do not grow out of the nature of the one as descriptive and the other as normative.

In two senses, religion is an experience of value. In the first place, as has been said, it is a choice of value, an appreciation or adoration of value, or the source of value. But in the second place, it is also a faith in the friendliness of the universe to value. The first point means that value experience can be created by human enjoyment, choice, or appreciation; the second means that value experience will somehow be preserved in the universe, because there is in the very nature of things an unfailing source of value. These two facts of religious experience justify Höffding's oft-quoted saying that religion rests on the axiom of the conservation of value. Religion may be challenged only in so far as it can be shown that value experience is non-existent or that it lacks "cosmic support." Problems have usually arisen chiefly from the latter source. To deny that value experience exists flies in the face of experience; but it is debatable what the future of value experience in the cosmos will be. A philosophy of religion investigates questions arising from this possibility of doubt.

In order to make clearer the nature of religion as experience of value, a few illustrations will be cited. Let the reader take up the Bible and turn to the book of Psalms. There he will read at the start "Blessed is the man . . . ."

in other words, "Valuable is the experience of the man" under consideration. A little later he will read, "Why do the nations rage?" This sounds like a scientific question seeking a scientific answer; but the only answer given is, "He that sitteth in the heavens shall laugh." Thus the Psalm means: "No matter how much evil there is, good will triumph laughingly." Thus it can be shown that every verse of every Psalm is a value judgment.

Or if the reader will turn to the Gospels of the New Testament he will find further confirmation of the interest of religion in value. Here we have writings which set forth history, and one of them, the Gospel according to Luke, begins with an objective statement about the author's use of sources. But it will soon be found that the Gospels are quite unlike any scientific history. Every event is reported for the sake of the religious value which it conveys or leads to. "Jesus wept" is not meant as an objective psychological observation, but as a valuation of the sympathy of Jesus. In particular, investigation shows that Jesus very rarely, if ever, is recorded to have mentioned any fact as a bare fact; he gives advice and commands about how to attain value or blessedness, he speaks of sin, repentance, righteousness, love, service—all value terms. His interest is not in what actually is so much as in what ought to be and can be.

A similar preoccupation with value pervades the Hindu classic, the Bhagavad Gita. In Chapter XVIII we find the inquiry, "O you of mighty arms . . . I wish to know the truth about renunciation and abandonment distinctly." "The truth" is not scientific truth here; it is truth about the achievement of value. Likewise, if we turn to Buddhist scriptures we find indifference to all discussion that has not to do with the attaining of Nirvana, the supreme value experience, and a typical utterance of Buddha's is, "Hatred

is not appeased by hatred, but by love." In all religions of
the world, a religious man is recognized by his devotion
to value. The essence of this devotion is expressed in the
book of Deuteronomy: "Behold, I have set before thee this
day life and good, and death and evil; in that I command
thee to love the Lord thy God, to walk in his ways."
(30:15-16)

§ 2. FUNDAMENTAL DEFINITIONS

Thus far the words "value" and "good" have been used
without definitions. Before definitions are proposed, it
should be made clear that all definitions are attempts to
describe or point out fundamental facts of experience or
fundamental theoretical concepts. They are therefore to
be regarded as hypotheses subject to correction. Facts of
experience may be observed more accurately, or fundamental
concepts thought more correctly than hitherto. Definitions
are not dogmas or embalmed truths. They are guides to
investigation. With this in mind, we proceed.

Value means whatever is actually liked, prized, esteemed,
desired, approved, or enjoyed by anyone at any time.[2] It
is the actual experience of enjoying a desired object or
activity. Hence, value is an existing realization of desire.
A desired object not yet experienced, like a painting I have
not seen but wish to see, or a mass that I have not heard
but long to hear, is a *potential value*. *Actual value* is the
presence in experience of the painting or the mass. *Good* is
synonymous with *value,* except that the former is applied
chiefly to moral values, while the latter applies also to the
moral, the aesthetic, the logical, and the religious alike.
However, we use the adjective form freely as equivalent
to valuable: "this symphony is good," "that argument is

---

[2] Ralph Barton Perry's definition of value as "any object of any interest" has become famous. See his GTV, Chap. V.

good," "the prayer was good," are almost as common as the moral judgment, "his character is good." Worth is another synonym. The opposite of value is *disvalue* or *evil* or *worthlessness*.

Values may be *intrinsic* (immediate, consummatory, *ends,* or *instrumental* (contributory, mediate, causal, *means*).[3] By *intrinsic value* is meant whatever is desired or enjoyed for its own sake, as an end in itself. We desire to be respectably dressed partly as a means to being socially acceptable, and also because the feeling of being well dressed is inherently satisfactory regardless of results; as a humorist has said, it gives a peace which religion can neither give nor take away. Thus the consciousness of being well dressed is an intrinsic value; so is the enjoyment of a meal, of a conversation with a friend, or of the discovery of a new idea. They are immediate and consummatory; they are ends. *Instrumental value* is any fact whatever, whether in my experience or out of it, which tends to produce the experience of intrinsic value. If man's love for God is regarded as an intrinsic value, then any experience or event, however distasteful it may be intrinsically, is an instrumental value if it contributes to or causes or arouses the love of God.

It is not to be supposed that values are to be divided into two groups, one of which is purely intrinsic and the other instrumental. As a matter of experienced fact, all intrinsic values are also instrumental, for the simple reason that every experienced value must be the cause of some effects; more specifically, religious value is instrumental to moral value; moral value is instrumental to aesthetic and intellectual; intellectual value is instrumental to all the

---

[3] The terms intrinsic and instrumental, like ends and means, are common coin. Maurice Picard has popularized the terms immediate and contributory, while John Dewey speaks frequently of the consummatory experience.

others. There is no contradiction in saying that one and the same value is both intrinsic and instrumental; in fact, if art for art's sake is severed from instrumental relations to life as a whole, its very intrinsic value tends to deteriorate. But from the fact that all intrinsic values are instrumental it does not follow that all instrumental values are intrinsic. This formally illogical conversion [4] is also materially false. The labor of mining coal would never be indulged in were it not for the resultant human comfort; such labor is purely instrumental for almost any miner and lacks all intrinsic value. So, too, with the mechanic who lies on his back in dirt and grime under a car to repair it; his values are purely instrumental and may be a series of intrinsic disvalues. Yet if they lead to the enjoyment of the desired functioning of the car, they are truly instrumental values. The work of the dentist and the surgeon, of the ditch digger, and the laborer at the speeding belt in the automobile factory consists of instrumental values, in contrast with the abundance of intrinsic values in the life of the lawyer, the clergyman, and the teacher.

Ideals constitute a special class of instrumental values. An ideal is a general concept of a type of experience which we value.[5] To have such a concept is a very different fact from having the actual experience to which the concept refers. Let us suppose that the religious man values obedience to the moral teachings of his religion. Then the concept that it would be valuable to obey those teachings is an ideal, whether it is acted on or not. There is no intrinsic value in entertaining an ideal. The value of an ideal is purely instrumental in that it may serve as cause of or means to the actual intrinsic value. Only the actual attainment of the value defined by the ideal is an intrinsic value.

---

[4] See any text in logic for the explanation of this fallacy.
[5] See Brightman, POI, Chap. III on "Ideals."

An ideal is a definition of value; the value is the reality defined. A definition can never be substituted for the real thing. Thomas à Kempis had this in mind when he declared that he desired to feel compunction rather than to know its definition. Knowledge of an ideal may be an intrinsic intellectual value, but this value is far from being identical with the value of which the ideal is a definition.

Ideals have at least two different functions, one causal, the other logical. The causal function we have just called their instrumental character. Their logical function is quite different, however. Once we have a value experience —for example, the enjoyment of a sonata or a comic opera, or the sense of religious devotion after a worshipful church service—we often are in doubt whether we approve our own feelings of the moment. Were we swept away by emotions? Do we regard the value as expressive of our mature judgment? What we do in such circumstances is to consult our ideals and use them to judge our values. If our values of the moment contradict our ideal definition, then either we have made an error in valuing or we have made an error in defining. This function of ideals in judging actual or potential experiences of value is their logical function, and may be called into play whether or not the ideals were consciously present as instrumental to the production of the value. An ideal regarded from the point of view of this logical function is called a *norm*. The bare psychological existence of values is often called *valuation*. The application of ideals or norms to values (valuations) is called *evaluation*.

From another point of view, valuations may be called *empirical values, value-claims,* or *apparent values*. The first of these terms expresses the fact that values actually occur in experience. The second expresses the further fact that accompanying every value there is the explicit or implicit claim that the value now felt is a true value. A value not only contains the assertion "I like prayer," but, as an over-tone, "You all ought to like it," and anyway, "I have a right to like it whether you do or not." When such a claim is made, there arises the question: Is it true that all ought to like it? Is it true that I have a right to like it whether others do or not? The third term, *apparent value,* emphasizes the possibility of doubt about our value-claims and the need of investigating them.[6]

This leaves us with the most difficult of all our terms, namely, *true value* or *real value.* There are some, especially some logical positivists, who hold that it is absurd to call values true or false, real or apparent. "There's no disputing about tastes, as the woman said when she kissed the cow." The logical positivists, like the woman, point out that the only way to determine truth or error is by verifica-tion in experience. Statements about physical nature may be judged true or false in so far as they are verified or refuted by the results of experiment. There is no way of verifying with any similar exactness whether I ought to love my neighbor or worship my God. Hence, they argue, the category of truth doesn't apply to values at all, and no value can be said to be truly better than any other. Ap-parent values are the last word, if this be true.

But there are many others, realists and pragmatists as well as idealists, who think that the logical positivists are too narrow in their view of verification, and that the differ-ence between truth and error can never be determined by reference to a single experience. Verification is a process of relating experiences and of building up a coherent, rational system of thought and experience. Realists would achieve this by emphasis on logical analysis, pragmatists by emphasis on practical consequences and adjustments, ideal-

[6] See Brightman, RV, Chap. III, "Truth and Value in Religion."

ists by emphasis on the wholeness of experience. Each one of these methods sheds light on truth and each is applicable, as logical positivism is not, to the process of distinguishing true from apparent or false values. When value-claims conflict with other value-claims, error about value is present. When value-claims are consistent and coherent with each other and with the other facts of experience, then the claims are verified; such value-claims are true values. A *true value,* then, is what we still value after the testing of our empirical values by rational norms (rational meaning logically consistent and coherent), and after the tests of analysis, practical consequences, and coherent wholeness have been applied to the experience.

It is not to be supposed that the word true is used here with any greater absoluteness than in any other field of inquiry. All assertions of truth are subject to further investigation; but rational assertions of truth are distinguished from mere opinion by the processes of inquiry and testing to which they have been subjected. With two further warnings against common misunderstandings, we may close the discussion of definitions. The first is that *true value* is not to be confused with *intrinsic value.* An intrinsic value-claim may be false; the fact that I like an experience for its own sake, intrinsically, does not entail the proposition that the experience is a true value. If it did, then every experience of alcoholic intoxication, doubtless an intrinsic value, would be a true value—a conclusion open to more than a little doubt. The second warning is against supposing that value categories necessarily apply to all experience. While most experiences are more or less valuable or disvaluable to us, nevertheless there may be neutral experiences to which we are indifferent, neither liking nor disliking them. The experience of disinterestedness, or devotion to the ideal of impartiality, is, however, not an instance of neutral experience, for it is a moral and intellectual value of rare beauty. Impartiality is loyalty to justice and objectivity rather than neutral indifference to values.

§ 3. A TABLE OF VALUES

Thus far it has been shown that religion is an experience of value and some fundamental terms of value theory have been defined. It is now our task to give a brief account of the fundamental types of valuation to be found in experience. It is almost self-evident that the variety of experiences of value is so great that no one classification of them would be final and hardly any classification, except a very formal one, would be inclusive.

Traditionally, the values, or at least what we have called the true values, have been grouped as the good, the true, and the beautiful. Here "good" is used in the special sense of the morally good, and is not synonymous with all value. The three values might be called the ethical, the logical, and the aesthetic. Many have thought that this triad was a complete list of values.[7] But in the nineteenth century Fries and Windelband and other German philosophers advanced the view that religion, while including goodness, truth, and beauty, added a new quality, namely, holiness.[8] The tendency among writers on the psychology and philosophy of value has been to recognize increasingly the variety of value experiences. Some, indeed, have made no attempt to frame a table of values; yet the attempt can scarcely be abandoned by one who desires a philosophical survey of value experience.

W. G. Everett proposed in 1918 (in his *Moral Values*) a table of values well grounded in empirical observation and

---

[7] In recent times, A. Clutton-Brock took this view in his little book, *The Ultimate Belief*.

[8] For a recent discussion of this concept see Rudolf Otto, *The Idea of the Holy*.

generalization. His table names eight groups: economic values, bodily values, values of recreation, values of association, character values, aesthetic values, intellectual values, and religious values. These are roughly arranged in ascending order of intrinsic importance, although no absolute order is possible. But the table is not based on a consistent principle, for the economic values are purely instrumental, while all the others are both intrinsic and instrumental. Hence a revised table is proposed, with a minimum explanation of details.

1. *Purely Instrumental Values.*
   a. *Natural values.* The forces of nature—life, gravity, light, and so forth—in so far as they operate causally and are accessible to all. Such forces are instrumental to intrinsic value experience. The intrinsic values to which natural values give rise apart from control by purpose are usually bodily or aesthetic.
   b. *Economic values.* Physical things, processes (like power), human labor, or services, in so far as their possession is a socially recognized property right, acquired or surrendered by exchange for equivalents or supposed equivalents. Economic value is exchange value. No economic possession is an intrinsic value for the normal person; one who regards economic values as intrinsic is a miser. But abundance or deficiency of economic wealth has a profound effect on both the quantity and quality of realizable intrinsic values, as has been emphasized perhaps too strongly by the historical materialism of Karl Marx and his followers. Since economic values presuppose labor, they are more personal than natural values. Money, the symbol of exchange, has been called "coined life."

2. *The Lower Intrinsic Values.* (This group is called "lower" because its values are narrower, more partial than

the "higher" ones; they include a smaller area of value experience, and are more dependent on other values for their own worth.)

a. *Bodily values*. These are not to be confused with the natural instrumental values, which are purely causal. Bodily values do not include the actual state of the body as a physiological organism, but only the enjoyment in consciousness of the well-being resulting from satisfactory bodily functioning. The feeling of being in good health, the joy of living, the pleasures of sex, the delight of successful athletic endeavor all belong in this group. Bodily values constitute only one limited realm of intrinsic value experience, but they are instrumental to an incalculable amount of weal and woe among the higher intrinsic values. In practices such as fasting and penance religion has sometimes overemphasized this instrumental function of bodily values at the cost of intrinsic enjoyment.

b. *Recreational values*. The satisfactions that come from play, humor, or mere amusement. These are the chief values of childhood, but are essential to the healthy mind at every age. Since their instrumental value is great, some regard them as exclusively instrumental; but one who takes his game or his swim or his joke merely as a means to business efficiency or to moral character will never really enjoy his recreation. The very instrumental value of recreation is lost on one who does not enjoy it as intrinsic. Yet recreation is not the serious business of life and covers a relatively narrow range of experience.

c. *Work values*. Just as play is joyful, so work should be. The mere fact of being employed is itself a satisfaction. The production of instrumental values is itself an intrinsic value, or would be in a reasonably just economic order. Yet satisfaction in usefulness is a very slender value by itself; its justification lies chiefly beyond itself in the intrinsic worth of what is being produced. The work values enjoyed in a munitions plant are hardly comparable to those enjoyed by a cast of actors rehearsing Hamlet.

3. *The Higher Intrinsic Values.* (This group is called "higher" because its values are broader, more inclusive of experience as a whole, more independent, and more coherent. It is impossible to group these higher values in a scale of increasing excellence, except that social values are intrinsically lower than the others.)

a. *Social values.* This term does not refer to all values which may be experienced in society, but rather to the special value that is experienced through the consciousness of association, coöperation, or sharing. It is clear that many of life's most highly prized values can be experienced only thus; and social values should be called "higher" if only because they embody the worth of personality. Every true value is enhanced when experienced as a social value. Nevertheless, social values are classified as the lowest of the higher values, because mere association with others is almost utterly devoid of worth unless some other value besides the social is being sought. Social relations depend for their value very largely on the presence of truth, goodness, beauty, or religion. Without these, social value itself vanishes. Yet with them, it adds a luster that they could never have as experiences of an isolated individual.[9]

b. *Character values.* This somewhat unsatisfactory term designates the experience of a good will, the conscious choice of what is believed right and best. The word moral is avoided because the moral life is not merely the good will, but actual organization of the whole experience of value by the will. Thus morality is the experience of the whole

[9] The reader who cares to note a change in the author's view is referred to Brightman, ITP, 146.

table of values, while character values refer exclusively to the act of choosing. They are the experiences which Kant regarded as the only intrinsic value; in the first section of *Fundamental Principles of the Metaphysic of Morals,* he begins by saying: "Nothing can possibly be conceived in the world, or even out of it, which can be called good without qualification, except a Good Will." But critics generally hold that, high as is our justified esteem for a loyal will, the causes to which that will is loyal—the other values of truth and beauty, for instance—are also as "good without qualification" as is a good will. A loyal, consistent will that willed nothing worth willing would be good with some qualification, most of us believe; and a large part of the problem of religion arises from the need of worthy ends for human choosing. A good character is indeed a jewel that shines by its own light and is respected by every rational mind; but it is not the only higher value. Yet it is so necessary that without the control by good will all the other values soon become disorganized, incoherent, and self-destructive.

c. *Aesthetic values.* The values of aesthetic satisfaction include not only the beautiful, but the sublime, the tragic, the comic, and many other gradations. The aesthetic, whether in nature or in art, is an experience in which there is, or at least appears to be, an adequate expression of purpose in such a way as to stir feeling and achieve harmony. Art may be defined as the conformity of expression to purpose. Character value is independent of success in achieving what is chosen; aesthetic value depends entirely on such success. What does not embody the intended meaning is not aesthetically adequate. That aesthetic values are intrinsically satisfactory is the universal testimony of mankind. Like character values, aesthetic values are experiences in which the whole of life is mirrored or organized from a special point of view.

d. *Intellectual values.* The intellectual values are the experiences of truth-loving and truth-finding. Some writers object to calling truth a value; they believe that value is irrelevant to truth and that much truth is so painful or indifferent as to be devoid of value. Granting both of these contentions, it remains an empirical fact that much truth is valued and that all truth is valued by the noblest spirits, no matter how uncomfortable the truth may be. Others object to regarding truth as an intrinsic value; it is, they say, purely instrumental to the control and remaking of experience; and a whole school of philosophers are called instrumentalists partly for this reason. No one, in fact, could deny that the truths of science and philosophy are instrumental to the control of inner and outer experiences; it is a familiar observation that intrinsic values are also instrumental. The joy of knowing, the mere satisfaction of curiosity, the "wonder" which according to Plato and Aristotle is the beginning of philosophy, are experiences common to every human being. These constitute the intrinsic aspects of the intellectual values.

e. *Religious values.* Religious values are experienced when man takes an attitude toward value experience as a whole and toward its dependence on powers beyond man. Insight into this dependence elicits feelings of reverence and acts of worship. The special quality of the whole which is deemed worthy of worship is called holiness. Like all of the other higher values, religious values are an organization of the total value experience from a special standpoint. Social values organize the whole from the standpoint of sharing; character values, from the standpoint of control by will; aesthetic values, from the standpoint of appreciative feeling; intellectual values, from the standpoint of knowledge; and religious values from the standpoint of worship of and coöperation with the objective cosmic source of values.

§ 4. The Uniqueness and the Coalescence of the Intrinsic Values

The explanations just given in connection with the Table of Values suffice to establish the dual character of each of the intrinsic values: each has a unique quality of its own to contribute to the total value experience and yet each tends to coalesce with the others. Without the unique contribution of each of the values, our value experience would have no variety and would even have no content at all, or at best a monotonous one. Without variety, sweetness palls and value loses value. On the other hand, no single value can be defined or be experienced without some reference to all the other values. The one intrinsic value of which this statement appears to be false is bodily value; the glow of good health or the joy of exercise seems to be what it is altogether apart from a person's aesthetic taste, mastery of logic, or religious reverence. Yet, in some indefinable way, even the bodily satisfactions of the broadly cultured man seem to have a slightly different quality from those of the ignorant and brutish. All of the other values, however, are plainly interdependent. They "interpenetrate" (as W. G. Everett said) and tend to coalesce. In play, all the values of real life are mimicked; and without intellectual values (rules of the game), character values (playing fair), and aesthetic values (skill) no recreation is fully successful. Even more plainly do social values coalesce with the others; unless we have play, or work, or knowledge, or beauty, or religion, there is nothing to share. Again, if knowledge is to have complete content, it must include in its subject matter not only all knowable facts, but also all knowable values. The application of this same principle to aesthetic and religious values is obvious. If one could subtract from religious values all that could be called recreational, or social, or character, or intellectual, or aesthetic, what would be left?

In fact, the fusion and coalescence of values with each other is such that one might be inclined to deny that there are any separate and distinct values at all. In that case, no uniqueness pertains to any one value; and it must be granted that no rational being would be satisfied with any value in the entire table, were it stripped of the content coming to it from the other values. How empty would the value of knowledge be if there were nothing to know except the mere form of knowing! How blasphemous and worthless religion would be if it could not include either goodness or truth or beauty in either the worshiper or his God! This line of thought points toward the conclusion that there is really only one value, namely, the systematic whole of our value experience. No value has sovereignty in its national territory; only the league of values is sovereign.

Yet, as has been previously intimated, it will not do to leave the matter here and assert that system is the only value. We must ask, System of what? And we have to answer, System of various unique value experiences. But in the coalescence of the system, the values listed in the table are more like whirlpools or eddies than like fish swimming in the sea. They are centers of organization or points of view for approaching value, rather than separate and distinct entities, each more or less valuable than the other. Hence, in estimating the importance of a value, "we must give up the idea of a scale for that of a system." [10] Within the system, degrees of value would be measured by the extent to

[10] Sorley, MVIG, 51.

which the particular value in question—the symphony, the poem, the principle, the virtue—mirrors or expresses the nature of the whole system of value.

The normative and philosophical account of the coalescence of values just given should not blind our eyes to the empirical fact that historically and psychologically the coalescence is often far from perfect. While early stages of culture were homogeneous, without any clear differentiation of religion, art, science, and morality, nevertheless there arose long ago a separation among these values; the special caste or class to which the cultivation of a value was assigned came to regard it as the be-all and end-all of existence. Priests lived for God alone; artists cultivated art for art's sake; scientists loved truth regardless of its value or its application; and moralists made duty the one .and only supreme law of life. So too, the tendency of the mind to generate psychologically "water-tight compartments" (as James said), the lack of innate ability in certain fields of value experience, and defective education, may result in the omission of whole areas of potential value from an individual or a group, in complexes which lead to fanatical devotion or fanatical hatred toward some value or set of values, or in a life in which the relations of values are never clearly seen. Thus the coalescence of values is a normative ideal rather than a universal experience.

§ 5. THE UNIQUENESS OF RELIGIOUS VALUES

In view of the coalescence of values, it is easy to see how arduous is the task of showing precisely of what the unique contribution of religious value consists. If religion is an application of the axiom of the conservation of (other) values, then it consists only of what is entailed by the statements, "Good will be conserved, beauty will be conserved, truth will be conserved." Hence some have held that religion is simply an interest in the permanence of value experience in general. Others have identified it with some one other value; Spinoza, for instance, regarded it as intellectual value (knowledge of God); Kant identified it with character values ("duties as divine commands"); Oscar Wilde saw in it only aesthetic value. Modern humanists sometimes identify religious values with social values; for them every social experience and only social experience is religious. All of these efforts are one-sided if the account given of coalescence is correct.

On the other hand, in an effort to assert the autonomy of religious values, erroneous attempts have been made to define their uniqueness. It has often been said, for instance, that a value experience is religious if it has God as its object. But this definition is confronted by the existence of atheistic religions like Hinayana Buddhism, modern religious humanism, and Communism; and even if these be called irreligious by grace of definition, the definition is still unsatisfactory, for it fails to distinguish an intellectual or an aesthetic interest in God from a religious one. Hence Rudolf Otto has proposed [11] the idea that religious value is a single unique quality, called the numinous, totally different from any profane or secular experience in a peculiar kind of mysterious and fascinating awe. Certain mystics have felt religious value to consist in release from all the restrictions of other values, rational or moral; the gospel song says, "Freed from the law, Oh, happy condition." But most minds find a religion that is utterly antinomian also utterly meaningless.

If many attempts to identify the unique contribution of religion to the realm of value have failed, it is still possible to point out numerous marks of religious value that distinguish it from other types. These may be summarized as follows: a unique sense of dependence (unique, because

[11] See his work, *The Idea of the Holy.*

the sense of dependence on the ground of the universe is radically different from our dependence on particular local conditions in our environment); a mystical experience of worship and prayer; awareness of illumination or revelation; a consciousness of divine aid (cosmic support, salvation, atonement); acknowledgment that God does for man what man cannot do for himself (divine initiative, grace); consciousness of coöperation with or submission to cosmic purpose (the will of God). Belief in the uniqueness of religious value is one of the most potent factors in man's religious consciousness: "To whom then will ye liken me, that I should be equal to him? saith the Holy One." (Is. 40:25)

§ 6. THE COALESCENCE OF RELIGIOUS VALUES WITH OTHER VALUES

In what has already been said, the meaning of the coalescence of all intrinsic values with each other has been made clear.   But the religious consciousness as such has almost always been more interested in the uniqueness of its values than in their coalescence. Believers think that the sacred importance of religion is imperiled if it be regarded as integrally related to all the other values of culture. Yet the curious fact is that whatever means religion uses to emphasize its lack of relation to other values really emphasizes that relation. Monasteries are built; and the monks painfully write out the pre-Christian classics. Faith finds expression in art, in painting, music, and architecture; and the forms and media of art are determined at least in part by secular tradition and economic conditions. The unique power of almost every religion is attested by magic or miracle, which often takes the form of the healing of disease; thus religious values coalesce with natural and bodily values. When this uniqueness is defined, whether among Jews,

Hindus, Mohammedans, or Christians, it is by means of a theology inevitably influenced by nonreligious science and philosophy. Religion, except in its magical and fanatical aberrations, coalesces with character values to such an extent that the chief teachings of many religions are moral maxims. Religion cannot maintain its uniqueness apart from the interpenetration of the other values with it.

Here we seem to confront an ultimate truth about religious values: that our experience of religion makes a genuine contribution to the total experience of value, which, however, can be adequately appreciated and understood only in a living interrelation of all the values to each other, coalescing in a living whole.

§ 7. THE RELATIONS OF IDEALS TO EXISTENCE

The fact that religious values exist and have existed throughout history is one of the most certain facts known to man. The problem of philosophy of religion arises when we attempt to think through the relations of the ideals implicit in value experience to what we know, or think we know, about the facts of existence.

Man experiences ideal aspirations toward goodness, truth beauty, and holiness. These ideals are implicit in moral intellectual, aesthetic, and religious experience. Yet very few persons are able to fulfill the demands of these ideals in their own daily living. Physical health, economic conditions the shortness and the complexity of life conspire to make the task of the fulfillment of the ideal a difficult one for the noblest spirits whose wills are entirely bent on ideal goals how much more difficult is it for the less gifted, not to mention the less loyal! Subjectively considered, then, ideals are precarious.

The problem is much more serious when viewed objectively. Religious ideals are not merely definitions of possibl value experience; as religious, they are also assertions about the future continuation [12] of value experience, and about ideal attitudes toward the source of cosmic value, thought of as a God. But the facts of experience, as interpreted by the sciences, seem to reveal impersonal laws and forces rather than a God concerned about ideal values. The same facts of experience, as they come day by day to the ordinary person, do not seem to be intended to encourage and help undivided loyalty to ideal values. In fact, the very experience of religion grows out of the contrast between ideal demands and natural facts. Religious individuals are often acutely conscious of this contrast, and call on God to alter it. An amusing instance is found in the New England history of 1856, when a Boston clergyman, who was depressed by the heretical and radical ideas of Theodore Parker, is recorded to have prayed thus: "O Lord, what shall be done for Boston if thou dost not take this and some other matters in hand?" [13] Now, the problem of philosophy of religion is essentially this: If the universe is such as religious ideals define it to be, why does it appear to be so indifferent, even so hostile, to those ideals? What is the actual relation between religious ideals and actual existence? Are they illusions? Are they correct programs of action but incorrect descriptions of existence? Or is existence actually what religious ideals, truly understood, imply that it is?

BIBLIOGRAPHICAL NOTE

The problem of value (now called axiology) has been investigated by philosophers ever since Plato and his theory of Forms or

---

[12] As we have previously noted, Höffding speaks of the conservation of values as the religious axiom. But values are not fixed entities or things; they are conscious fulfillments of ideals. Therefore it is more empirical to speak of "continuation" of value experience, with Peter A. Bertocci (EAG, 165), rather than of conservation.

[13] Commager, TP, 270–271.

Ideas. Plato's *Euthyphro* was one of the first investigations of the nature of religious values.

Urban, VAL(1909), summarizes general theory of value as it existed when he wrote. A more recent account is Laird, IV(1929). Perry, GTV(1926), is the most important contribution by an American. Picard, VIC(1920), is useful; Reid, TOV(1939), expounds rather dogmatically a naturalistic theory of value. Excellent in relation to ethics is Everett, MV(1918).

Special treatments of religious values are found in Höffding, PR(tr. 1906), Hocking, MGHE(1912), and R. Otto, IH(1917, tr. 1926). Brightman, RV(1925), emphasizes the values of worship.

FOUR

RELIGION AS A
PHILOSOPHICAL PROBLEM

HE topic of the present chapter is: Religion as
a philosophical problem. Fortunately, there is
always a contradiction to any assertion. Religion a philosophical problem? Maybe it isn't!
Not only do ordinary religious believers worship without
any thought of a philosophical problem, but some religious
leaders, such as Albrecht Ritschl, have asserted that religious
faith is quite independent of metaphysics. Can it be that
our judgments about the truth of religion are actually independent of our judgments about the nature of experience
and reality as a whole? Why should anyone suppose that
religious beliefs are exempt from the scrutiny to which our
other beliefs about mind, matter, society, and history are
subjected?

Perhaps the chief actual cause for the supposed independence of religious beliefs is a deep-rooted conviction that life's
supreme values are at stake in religion, that they ought not
to be imperiled by rational investigation. Doubtless every
reader of this book has met persons holding this conviction.
But however widespread its effects may be, it is a cause and
not a reason. There is no rational ground for supposing
that a truth is more clearly grasped if it is not clearly defined

and related to other truths; there is not even ground for supposing that it is good strategy to safeguard a truth by protecting it from investigation. Such protection, instead of strengthening the belief that is protected, tends to arouse the suspicion that something is rotten in Denmark. Indeed, it is quite possible that unwillingness to subject a belief to philosophic investigation may be an overcompensation for suppressed doubts. In it may lurk the hidden fear that religious beliefs, if scrutinized closely, will turn out to be false. Wisdom would take the contrary course. If life's supreme values are really at stake in religion, it is then of the utmost importance that they be rigorously defined and criticized. If they are true, their truth will then stand out more clearly; if our conception of them can be improved, it should be; if they are false, it is essential not to treat error as supreme value.

There is, however, a different line of thought which affords a more plausible basis for the proposition that religion is independent of philosophy. Items of immediate experience are so certain that no philosophy can possibly deny them, and every philosophy must build on them. No error is possible about the fact that I now experience what I now experience. Now, if religious values are immediate experiences which are experienced without any "creed" or "theology," there is no doubt that they are independent of philosophy, at least in the sense that they are real, whatever philosophy one may hold. The awe felt by Immanuel Kant in the presence of the starry heavens and the moral law may be regarded as a religious mood which is independent of metaphysics, although a blind man could not experience the one or a disbeliever in moral law the other. But if one can see and does believe in moral law, the awe that he feels is a unique and undeniable fact, to be shaken by no philosophizing. It would be as unshakable by any later reasoning as are the experiences: "I am hungry, I am tired, I see colors."

Those who assert the uniqueness of religious values to the exclusion of their coalescence with other values, and who believe that religion is wholly incommensurable with any other dimension of life (such men as Sören Kierkegaard) are able to declare that religion is independent of philosophy. They rely on some divine revelation or mystical moment to impart an absolute quality to the whole of experience. But they do it at a very high price. The price they have to pay is either extreme subjectivism or objective irrationalism.

Subjectivism calls on them to assert the religious experience, as we saw, unaccompanied by any interpretation or beliefs; no creed or theology is possible if religion is only the immediate feeling of awe or adoration. Subjectivism, however, is a price so high that only the hopeless sophisticate will pay it and he only in a passing mood. One who feels awe, if he also feels normal curiosity, will ask why he feels it. And he is embarked on the quest in which, if he be like Saint Augustine, his soul will be restless until it finds rest in God. If he adores, whom or what does he adore? If he loves, what is the person or the cause he is loving? Subjectivism requires feelings without ideas, emotions without thought or belief. Some interpretation of feeling is necessary to the integrity of the feeling mind, and so a purely subjective religion without theology is in the long run impossible. It is a state of unstable mental equilibrium.

If few will pay the price of subjectivism, more will seek to protect the autonomy of religious values by objective irrationalism. According to this view, the ultimate religious object is so far above man as to be utterly unknowable. Herbert Spencer thought of religion as man's relation to The Unknowable. Buddhists and Brahmans made Nirvana their religious goal. Nirvana, although positive in nature, nevertheless was the negation of all desire, all knowledge, and all individual experience. Now, if The Unknowable or Nirvana be the essence of religion, then philosophy, which is rational thought about experience, can neither give nor take away any religious value or truth. Religion is then immune to all known or conceivable truth and value. At the same time, it may be questioned whether such religion is worth the protection it receives if its sole revelation is The Unknowable.

As experiences, we may conclude, religious values are not dependent on any theory or philosophy. They are given facts. But religious values are not merely subjective experiences; they involve beliefs—beliefs about right and wrong, about beauty, about man's destiny and divine power and will. If these beliefs are not blank assertions that reality is unknowable, or that all categories of knowledge are transcended in the Nirvana of religious passivity, then they are propositions which entail something about the real world. In so far as religious values assert or imply anything about the source of value or the future of value, and in so far as they coalesce to any degree with moral, intellectual, aesthetic, social, recreational, or bodily values, the demand for philosophical investigation of religion becomes urgent.

§ 2. Even Then It Would Be a Problem for History, Psychology, and Sociology

Suppose, however, the most extreme claims of Herbert Spencer and the Hindus are conceded, and religion is viewed as a unique relation to the inconceivable, or suppose on any ground whatever religion is granted to be so autonomous within its own sphere as to be independent of all philosophical investigation, it would still remain true that the unique and autonomous experiences of religious value had arisen in a historical, sociological, and psychological context. Hence, even if religion is independent of philosophical investigation it cannot be independent of history, sociology, or psychology. These sciences must investigate its rise and development, its institutional forms, its psychological structure and function. After they have done their work, another task remains—that of relating the results of these various investigations to each other; and this is the task of philosophy. Thus philosophy, by its perverse dialectic that Hegel calls "the guile of reason," when thrown out of the door comes back in through the window. It would seem that religious experience cannot be at all without falling under the eye of philosophy.

§ 3.   Reasons for Treating It as a Philosophical Problem

Arguments adduced in favor of the doctrine of the secession of religion from the republic of reason have already been examined and found insufficient. We are now ready to summarize the main grounds for treating religious value as a philosophical problem. Although it is often supposed that religion by its very nature precludes philosophical investigation, the fact is that almost all great religious thinkers of all branches of Christendom, Judaism, Islam, Brahmanism, and other religions have been far more than dogmatic expounders of an uncriticized faith; they have also been philosophers who related their tenets to experience as a whole and subjected them to radical criticism. It is a source of distress to the irreligious that many of the philosophers treated in any history of philosophy are also theologians; but, pleasant or unpleasant, it is a fact, and a fact that shows clearly the need of religion for intellectual interpretation. No matter how many may wish to believe or disbelieve in religion without thinking about it, the point of our present remarks is that it is not normal or usual for an intelligent mind to accept religion without thought. Why should this be true? Why not simply "enjoy" religion without critical analysis?

(1) *Coalescence of values.* As was shown in the previous chapter, religious values, like all others, coalesce with other types of value and become meaningless and worthless without such coalescence. But if religious, moral, and intellectual values do coalesce, the question arises as to how this happens. What intellectual values support and sustain religion? Or are the ideas with which religion is fused not values but disvalues, not truths but errors? Again, what moral values interpenetrate with the religious? In the presence of what competing values, if any, does religion wane or perish? In order to cope with such questions, philosophical method is necessary.

(2) *Relations of ideals to existence.* It has already been pointed out that religion is not concerned primarily about abstract ideals, but rather about the production, preservation, and increase of actually existing values. It is not enough for the believer to know that there is an ideal of peace which it would be excellent to attain; but he hears a divine voice say, "Peace *be* unto you"—in short, let the ideal exist in actual, empirical form. As G. E. Moore remarks in his *Principia Ethica,* "Though God may be admitted to be a more perfect object than any actual human being, the love of God may yet be inferior to human love, *if* God does not exist." [1] Religion is not abstract idealism, it is concrete and practical. It asserts that ideals are not only abstractly valid in the Platonic kingdom of Ideas, but also that they are to some extent realizable and realized in the world of actual existence. The belief that ideals are valid but are not potent in actuality is the position of an idealistic pessimist. Such a view however bravely moral it may be, is not religious,

[1] Moore, PE, 200.

because it denies the basic axiom of the conservation of values. The axiom of the eternal validity of ideals is logical, but not religious; religion requires the conservation of values. Religion, therefore, can be understood only when the philosophical problem of the relation of ideals to existence is thought through.

(3) *Religion, science, and philosophy refer to the same world.* This statement may seem to contradict the views of those who hold that science and philosophy refer to the realm of nature and religion to the realm of grace, or that the former relate to this world and the latter to a superworld. Let it be granted that some religion is predominantly otherworldly. It remains true that such religion implies a judgment on this world. Either this world is a divine creation which has fallen from grace and is under a curse; or this world is an obstacle and temptation to be overcome; or it is the scene of a conflict between the God of light and the God of darkness; or it is a gymnasium or a prison house. In any case, religion means something about the present and visible world; and in this respect its judgments are directed toward the same world that science and philosophy investigate. The relations of these various judgments to each other must be considered, if religion is to be found true or false. Furthermore, if in addition to this world, there is a superworld, it is necessary to consider the evidence in this world for belief in the other, and also to make coherent statements about the relations between the two.

(4) *There are contradictory religious value-claims and beliefs.* This indubitable fact of religious history makes it impossible to believe all religion to be true. A value-claim of one religion is that the merciful are blessed. A value-claim of another religion is that the first-born should be killed as a sacrifice. It is possible that either one of these value-claims may be valid, but not that both are at the same

time, unless the aim of religion on the second assumption is to avoid being blessed. Some believe that there are many gods; others, that there is only one. Some hold that the gods have bodily form, others assert that God is a conscious spirit without bodily form, and still others think that the divine is a force, principle, or law with no personal consciousness. Some hold that salvation is by Christ alone; some, by Buddha alone. There is no doubt that systems of belief as different as Judaism, Christian Science, Confucianism, and Roman Catholicism have all produced religious values and noble characters; but it is impossible that all the beliefs of all of them can be true at the same time. Catholicism affirms the reality of material substance; Christian Science denies it; Judaism and Confucianism do not regard any view on the subject as essential to religion. The facts reveal the presence of conflicting beliefs about religion.

From this conflict the philosophers of ancient Rome inferred, according to Gibbon, that "the various modes of worship were all equally false." [2] But a conflict of opinion about the world or the nearest route to the Indies did not, in the days before Columbus, prove the nonexistence of America or that the world had no shape. Conflicting opinions about the future do not imply that there will be no future, any more than different theories of money show that there is no money. Neither does conflict of opinion prove that all religious opinions are equally valuable, as amiable tolerance often says, when it forgets the claims of logic. All that conflict of opinion proves is that there is need for rational inquiry, unless religion is to degenerate either into the cat-and-dog fight of a war of all against all, or else into a purely subjective emotion that allows itself no rational or social expression.

[2] *Decline and Fall of the Roman Empire,* Chap. II.

§ 4. What Is the Philosophical Problem of Religion?

In view of the claims and counterclaims, the conflicting values and contradicting beliefs entertained by religious men and women, the philosophical problem of religion may be stated very briefly. It is obviously impossible that all religious beliefs can be true or all religious value-claims be true values. The question: Is religion true? would therefore be undiscriminating. The rational problem of philosophy of religion would take the form: Are any religious beliefs true? If so, which ones, and why? Are any religious value-claims truly objective? If so, which ones, and why? The best possible answer to these questions is the best possible philosophy of religion. If no religious beliefs or value-claims are true, then religion is shown to be of no metaphysical importance, and of primary importance only to phenomenologists or psychiatrists.

§ 5. What Is the Method of Philosophical
Interpretation?

If religion is to be investigated philosophically, what we mean by philosophical investigation must be made clear. There are some whose notion of philosophical method is rather crude. It consists in arriving at a system of philosophical conclusions without regard to the empirical facts of religion, and then accepting or rejecting religious beliefs according to their consistency or inconsistency with that system. Such a method is not an interpretation of religion; it is sheer dogmatism. It is to be condemned regardless of whether the system is piously theistic or impiously atheistic. The philosophical interpreter should apply methods of internal criticism rather than these crudely external ones. Internal criticism starts with the empirical subject matter to be criticized, discovers its meaning and structure, and then relates it to other areas of experience and thought. In the process of interpretation by internal criticism, there are five fairly distinct stages: (1) preliminary synopsis, (2) scientific analyses and syntheses, (3) synoptic hypotheses, (4) verification, and (5) reinterpretation. (See Chapters XV–XVI.)

(1) *Preliminary synopsis.* Interpretation must begin with something to interpret; yet the first grasp of the material must necessarily be most inadequate. It is a mere orientation (see Chapter I), a sweeping glance with the aim of getting what we call "the hang" or "the feel" of the whole. It is observation on what J. Loewenberg calls the preanalytic stage, and consists of a tentative intuition of the general field of facts to be studied.

(2) *Scientific analyses and syntheses.* The more or less shadowy and foggy whole of the preliminary synopsis acquires firm outlines and definite content only by processes of scientific analysis and synthesis. First of all, the various portions of the field are isolated and broken up into their constituent parts. Ideally, this analysis proceeds until simple elements have been found that can be analyzed no further. Then these elements are seen synthetically in their relations to each other. In Chapter II the results of such analyses and syntheses of religion were summarized. Philosophical interpretation is purely formal and empty of real content unless it rests on the firm ground of the scientific analysis and synthesis of experience.

(3) *Synoptic hypotheses.* The third stage is the most distinctly philosophical one in the process of interpretation. It is that of what Kant called the *Gedankenexperiment* (experiment of thought) or what we may call the synoptic hypothesis. All thought, scientific or philosophical, proceeds by the invention of hypotheses intended to explain the observed data. Without hypotheses, not even analysis can advance; the methods and the goal of analysis would both

be blind unless thus guided. Experiment is meaningless unless it either is made for the purpose of testing some hypothesis or else results in a new hypothesis. Facts without hypotheses are mere piles of bricks; facts ordered by hypotheses are buildings fit to dwell in.

Scientific hypotheses, however, differ from philosophical ones. A scientific hypothesis is restricted to the ordering of the limited subject matter under investigation—let us say the radiation of light or the religion of the Algonkins. A philosophical hypothesis, on the other hand, has a far wider scope and is synoptic in a very special sense, for it aims to relate the subject matter under investigation to a view of experience as a whole. The word synopsis, meaning a seeing together, has been used since Plato to denote a comprehensive view of experience, which relates the parts revealed by analysis and the relations established by synthesis to the whole structure of which they are aspects. Synopsis lays stress on the properties of wholes which their parts do not have.[3] This principle is of importance in the field of religion, for any value or ideal may be made to appear petty and worthless if it be analyzed into its simplest elements and attention fixed on those elements. To say that the ideal of worship is nothing but a complex of feelings, sensations, and thoughts, quite disregards the nature of the worship experience as a whole and its function in the ordering and elevation of life. A living whole is always more than the sum of its parts, just as a human body is more than a sum of electrons and protons. Without synoptic hypotheses, the value and function of religion would forever escape us.

An additional word is needed about the nature of a philosophical hypothesis. In being philosophical, an hypoth-

---

[3] Such properties have been discovered and interpreted most frequently by idealists; but many realists, such as G. E. Moore (in his *Principia Ethica*), E. G. Spaulding, and R. W. Sellars, recognize the reality and importance of these properties.

esis relates the particular to the universal, the present to
the eternal, the part to the whole. It seems most presumptuous for man, with his fragmentary knowledge, to make
any statements, however hypothetical, about the whole which
must forever exceed his grasp. Yet it is no more presumptuous to think of the whole than to think of the part,
for the part necessarily implies a whole to which it belongs.
In fact, the nature of reason is such that it is impossible to
avoid using universals which apply to the whole; we cannot
think time without thinking eternity; we cannot think this
space without thinking all space; and we cannot think of
man's dependence without thinking of something on which
he depends. It is futile to try to choke off philosophical
thinking by calling it presumptuous. It is more presumptuous to take any attitude without thought than it is after
thoughtful consideration. Just as the individual needs integration for his psychological health, so also he needs synoptic hypotheses for his mental health. Yet such hypotheses
are not to be tested by their value for health; on the contrary,
their value for health is tested by their truth. Religion always includes synoptic hypotheses as its very life; faith is the
religious attitude toward them.

(4) *Verification.* The fourth stage of philosophical interpretation is verification. Given a synoptic hypothesis,
faith in the goodness of God, for example, some means of
testing it must be devised, or else there is no way of knowing
whether it points to fact or to fancy.

There is difference of opinion about what constitutes verification. This is at least partly due to the different types of
object toward which our hypotheses are directed. There are
at least three such types: observable natural processes, mathematical and logical systems, and minds. It is fairly simple
to verify an hypothesis about an observable natural process;
define your hypothesis exactly, perform an experiment and

observe its results exactly, compare the results, and the verification (or falsification) of the hypothesis has taken place. Likewise in logic and mathematics, verification is a simple matter. The consistency or inconsistency of the hypothesis may be shown by repeated deductive operations that can be carried out by any rational mind and will be carried out so that the conclusion will be the same if the premises are the same. But if you ask how the existence of other minds is verified, you find yourself in a muddle. Everyone is sure that there are other minds besides his own and almost everyone thinks he knows how he verifies the hypothesis that they exist. One does it by direct intuition; another, by analogy from behavior; another, by extrasensory perception; another by communication through language.[4] However we do it, it is surely not in the same way that we verify natural processes, for other minds are not observable by the senses; nor in the same way that we verify a logical or mathematical result, because other minds are not abstract terms and relations.

What, then, happens to make us so sure that we have verified the presence of another mind which we cannot see physically or prove deductively? Social objects force us to see what is implicit in physical and logical objects, but less patent—namely, that all verification rests on postulates.[5] Unless we presuppose the unity of the verifying self, the presence of data within self-experience, the purpose of verification, the validity of reason, the trustworthiness of memory (when tested by reason), the reality of time, and the reality of an objective world which is there when not observed or verified, no verification can occur. If it is to be shared it also

---

[4] See the valuable article by H. H. Price on "Our Evidence for the Existence of Other Minds," in *Philosophy*, 13(1938), 425–456, and H. Dingle's criticism of it in the same journal, 14(1939), 457–467.

[5] See Brightman, Art.(1938).

presupposes other minds. None of these presuppositions can be verified either by sense perception or by mathematical proof; yet all of them must be granted if any verification of any kind of hypothesis is to go on. Are these presuppositions merely arbitrary? Or is there some ground for them? Surely they are not wild fancies. They are basic truths. How do we know they are truths? Simply by the fact that they are beliefs which form a system consistent with itself and consistent (as far as we know) with every phase and type of experience.

If the reader inquires what all this has to do with religion, he has a right to an answer. Religion is not an observable physical process; it is not a syllogism or a mathematical formula; it is a conscious experience that includes reference to other minds,[6] human and divine. It is therefore unreasonable to expect a religious belief to be verified or falsified by sense observations or by formal logico-mathematical operations. Religious verification or falsification must take place as all our social knowledge does, and in the light of the presuppositions of verification. A religious belief can be verified only by its relation to the system of our beliefs as a whole which have the marks of consistency with one another and with experience. No verification can hope for more than this in principle. As Dickinson S. Miller has said, the problem can be solved only in "the forum of the individual mind." [7]

(5) *Reinterpretation.* When thought has reached the stage of verification, is it then at the end of its journey? May it finally rest? No; neither in science nor in religion is there an end. No verification is completely inclusive. There is no test that does not need retesting. Nothing is

---

[6] Mind is here used as synonymous with person.
[7] For a contradictory view of verification, that of logical positivism, see Ayer, LTL.

absolute short of The Absolute—the all-inclusive whole of being. Every stage of insight may lead to deeper insight. Every interpretation requires reinterpretation. The Psalmist's word, "He that sitteth in the heavens shall laugh," must have been written for men who believe that human knowledge can completely compass the infinite. We cannot reach the end; but as long as we live and use sound method, we may grow endlessly.

Reinterpretation does not imply that when it goes on, every belief we now hold will be found to be false. It does not require groundless rejection of any faith. It requires, rather, the recognition of incomplete proof, incomplete understanding, and incomplete information, together with insight into the method of philosophical interpretation which constantly corrects and supplements, but never absolutely completes man's fragmentary but growing grasp of reality.

§ 6. What Is the Criterion of Religious Truth?

The question about the criterion of religious truth has already been given a preliminary answer, namely, that the consistency of our beliefs with each other and with experience is the test of the truth of religious beliefs.

The suggested criterion is obviously the same criterion that is applied in science and in daily life to detect the presence of error and to measure our approximation to truth. Should a different criterion be applied in religious matters? If a different criterion were proposed, let it be what it will, could it be such as to allow truth to be inconsistent? Could contradictory propositions be true in religion? Or could religious truth be of such a nature as to be irrelevant to experience? Could belief in God be entertained, for example, without regard to its relation to the facts of experience? If a totally different criterion were applied, we should indeed have a "double truth." [8] One kind of truth would be based on a rational interpretation of experience; the other kind would be based on its own criterion and would be exempt from any criticism arising in reason or experience (except the privileged experience of its own criterion). To raise such questions is to answer them. All truth accepted by any mind is subject to the jurisdiction of that mind's reason and experience.

But there is implicit in the apparent absurdity of the frequent appeal for a separate criterion for religious truth, one factor of real importance, namely, the justified demand on the part of religion that its claims shall be judged on the basis neither of abstract a priori considerations alone nor of nonreligious experiences alone. In seeking for religious truth, all that a priori logic can offer must be considered; all secular experience must be weighed; but the vital question of the truth and value of religion cannot be said to have been approached until the actual evidence of religious experience is interpreted. Neither physics nor psychology nor philosophy is competent to pass any judgment, favorable or unfavorable, on religion until religious values have been considered; one cannot know whether one is confirming or refuting religion until one knows what religion is.

The patent necessity of considering data before judging them establishes, however, no unique criterion. Yet the human mind has always struggled against the demands of reason, or (to take a more historical view) has come very slowly to a recognition of its universal claims, especially in the field of religion.[9] Not rational interpretation of experience, but *instinct,* or *custom,* or *tradition,* is the criterion

[8] Gilson, RRMA, gives reasons for maintaining that this view was not held even in the Middle Ages.
[9] See the discussion of the problem in Brightman, ITP, 31–66, and Montague, WK.

appealed to by great masses. The first is often cited by the clergy and is also the support of totalitarian views which found religion on "race and blood"; but the lack of any clear definition of instinct renders the concept useless as a criterion. Conflicting customs and traditions furnish no criterion for choice among them. Others, holding that religion is universal (a questionable proposition in itself), insist that universal agreement (*consensus gentium*) is a test of truth. But there is no universal agreement on any matter of importance; many reject evolution, medicine, and the calculations of astronomy, not to mention God, freedom, and immortality; and even if there were universal agreement on a proposition, the truth of the proposition would not be tested by the agreement (for there was once agreement on animism and a flat earth), but rather by the reasons which led to the agreement. Others have appealed to *feeling* as a test of truth; but the notoriously varying moods of feeling contain no principle for determining which of two equally strong, but conflicting, feelings is true. Hence no religious feeling, either of belief or of doubt, is to be regarded as true because of its intensity.

The five criteria just examined are plainly unacceptable. At least five other criteria have been proposed. *Sense experience,* it is often said, is the one means of access to objective reality. No philosopher would deny that it is a source of real knowledge. But something more than sense experience is needed to test whether a dream, an illusion, an hallucination, or a mirage is a veridical perception; and sense experience is not all of experience. The fundamental problems of philosophy of religion turn about the relation of value experience to sense experience. It is purely arbitrary to elevate sense experience to a preferred position while ignoring the fact that values are as truly present in consciousness as are sense data. To select sense data as being normative without considering the claims of value experience is to be dogmatic. Sense data must be seen in the light of the rest of experience and must be rationally interpreted.

Intuition is a principle often appealed to as criterion. By intuition is meant immediate knowledge, that is, awareness of a content (a quality or a principle) as given in experience and not derived from reasoning. Sense experience, for instance, is one example of intuition; value experience is another; experience of space and time is intuitional. That intuitions lie at the basis of all our knowledge is certain, and that many intuitions are true is at least highly probable. But it is not possible to distinguish a genuine intuition from a disguised appeal to feeling (a rationalization of desire) without consulting some criterion other than intuition itself. Particularly is this true of religious intuitions when they come in the form of belief in revelation. It is characteristic of religions, as we have seen, to make revelation-claims. When God has spoken, it seems irreverent to ask for further evidence, much more so to raise questions. But the fact is that the intuition, "I am now hearing the voice of God," accompanies contradictory beliefs, even within the scriptures of one religion, such as the Judaeo-Christian. Therefore all intuitions, including all religious ones, need to be tested by some criterion that is not merely one more intuition. In common with all of the criteria thus far proposed, intuition, however inadequate as a test of truth, is of the utmost importance as a source of truth. Even instinct, custom, and tradition may suggest some truths to us; what is very widely accepted may be accepted for good reasons, what is strongly felt may also be true; and sense data are certainly sources of truth. Yet in every instance some test must be applied to sift the truth from the error.

In philosophical discussion, *correspondence* often appears as a candidate for criterion in chief. Correspondence is, in fact, the definition of truth; a proposition is true if what it asserts corresponds to the object about which the assertion is made, and we should naturally expect a definition to serve as criterion of the presence or absence of what is defined. Correspondence, however, fails us in this respect; it is not a criterion of truth nor even a source of truth. It is not a criterion of truth for the simple reason that it can never be applied. Propositions are about the past, the present, the future, the timeless, or some combination of them. It is clear that it is now, at this present moment, always impossible to compare a present proposition with a past, a future, or an eternal object; such comparison would require the past, the future, or eternity to be now present for comparison, a plain impossibility. Even propositions about the present are incapable of being tested by correspondence; for the process of comparison would take time and ere it had occurred the present object would have become past. It is equally difficult to doubt that correspondence is what we mean by truth and to believe that it is a usable criterion or a source of truth.[10]

There remain two criteria which are the ones chiefly used at the present time by philosophers. They are *practical results* and *coherence*. Those who regard practical results as being the test of truth are called pragmatists. Pragmatism [11] is one of the few original contributions which American philosophy has made, and it has exerted a wide influence on all fields including philosophy of religion. The empirical method of the present work owes much to both James and Dewey. Pragmatism, however, is a broad phase of the

[10] See Pratt, PR, 74–97.

[11] The literature of pragmatism is so extensive that no attempt will be made here to do more than mention four notable works: William James's *Pragmatism*, John Dewey's *Logic*, W. P. Montague's *The Ways of Knowing* (this last contains one of the best criticisms of pragmatism), and Ralph Barton Perry's *The Thought and Character of William James*, a gem of American philosophy.

empirical movement rather than a precise system. A pragmatist, as is well known, is one who says that an idea is
true if it works, or has practical consequences. This makes
an immediate appeal to the religious mind, which cares
more for the actual religious experience than for the philosophy or theology which interprets or validates it. "By their
fruits ye shall know them"; "if any man willeth to do his
will, he shall know of the teaching." Jesus seems to be pragmatic, and the religious thinkers of India are even more so.[12]
Furthermore, pragmatism brings religion and science close
together. Each uses the test of consequences; indeed each
speaks of experiment—or at least eighteenth- and nineteenth-
century Christians often referred to "experimental Christianity," an empirical testing of religion.

That all practical consequences of ideas are facts which
must be considered; that a belief that is not tested in experience is blind and useless; and that pragmatism is a sane,
radical challenge to dogmatism cannot well be denied. Yet
there is one central difficulty in pragmatism which makes it
very difficult to apply. That difficulty is the ambiguity of
its fundamental criterion of practical results. What, exactly, is meant by practical? What is meant by saying that
an idea works? In one sense, every idea that we can fool
ourselves or others with may be said to work to that extent.
Belief in transubstantiation works among Catholics; it does
not work among Methodists or Quakers; it is utter nonsense
to Mohammedans or Shintoists. The belief in the omnipotence of God may work for the purpose of elevating the
spirit, yet not work at all for the purpose of explaining concrete evils in the world. Belief in the efficacy of the bones

---

[12] For the quotations from Jesus see Mt. 7:16 and Jn. 7:17. See also the sar-
castically pragmatic remark of the man born blind: "Why, herein is the marvel, that
ye know not whence he is, and yet he opened mine eyes" (Jn. 9:30). For Indian
religion see Glasenapp, Art.(1927).

of a saint may work until it is found that his skull is on ex-
hibition at several different shrines.

This ambiguity of terms and of their application is so
great that pragmatists have not been able to arrive at any
clear agreement on definitions. If "practical" and "work"
are not defined exactly, the use of them as criteria only adds
to the confusion of thought and belief. But if they are
defined exactly and used thoroughly, they turn into a mandate to examine all the evidence, especially all of the consequences of action, in the light of the mind's total experience.
In other words, when taken thoroughly, the pragmatist's
criterion turns into coherence.

Coherence is essentially the method of verification described earlier in this chapter. To restate it: according to
the criterion of coherence, a proposition is to be treated as
true if (1) it is self-consistent, (2) it is consistent with all of
the known facts of experience, (3) it is consistent with all
other propositions held as true by the mind that is applying
this criterion, (4) it establishes explanatory and interpretative
relations between various parts of experience, (5) these relations include all known aspects of experience and all known
problems about experience in its details and as a whole. It
is to be noted that coherence is more than mere consistency;
the latter is absence of contradiction, whereas the former
requires the presence of the empirical relations mentioned
under points (4) and (5); thus consistency is necessary to
coherence, but consistency is not sufficient.

Two very important additional points about coherence
should be noted. (1) Since coherence requires a reference
to the whole of experience, some hypothesis about the nature
of the whole is essential to the working of this criterion.
(2) Since experience and science are constantly growing,
the application of coherence cannot arrive at fixed and static
results. It is a principle of constant reorganization, a law

of criticism and growth, rather than a closed system. Coherence can never be fully applied until all thinking about all possible experience has been finished; however, in this it is no worse off than pragmatism, which requires all practical results. This does not mean that all our present beliefs are erroneous and that no truth can be known until we know all truth. In fact, it may be a very coherent hypothesis to assume that some truths (such as the validity of coherence and the need of consulting experience) will always be true no matter what else is true. Nevertheless, the criterion of coherence implies that no truth can be completely tested or proved until all truth is known; perhaps just the facts which we do not yet know may be required for the modification or rejection of any known truth. On the other hand, all of the results offered by all other proposed tests, revelations, or insights must come before the tribunal of the whole mind and its grasp on experience as a whole. This, and this only, justifies or "verifies" a scientific hypothesis or a religious faith.[18]

§ 7. THE PROBLEM OF RELIGIOUS CERTAINTY

The author's view of the criterion of coherence just presented has been subjected to criticism on the ground that it fails to afford the certainty that is needed if religion is to be a vital factor in life. The attack has come both from the right and from the left. The right-winger, Edwin Lewis, speaks of "the right to be certain," and to say to an opposing view "quietly, but finally, even dogmatically, *it is wrong.*" To hold (as the present writer does) that our highest religious affirmations are, from the logical standpoint, at most only probable is said by Lewis to introduce "a fatal and quite

---

[18] For a fuller discussion of coherence see Brightman, ITP, 58–66, 368–369, and the literature there referred to. Coherence as criterion is to be distinguished from the so-called coherence theory of truth, which is a doctrine of metaphysical absolutism.

unnecessary skepticism into the very heart of existence." [14]
On the other hand, the left-winger, Henry Nelson Wieman,
opposes the proposed use of the coherence criterion on the
ground that it would justify beliefs that have only a speculative probability, whereas we need to build, he thinks, on
more certain and stable foundations.[15] Wieman would
accordingly restrict religious beliefs to propositions about
the structure of nature which have assured scientific certainty.   John Dewey, however, in his *The Quest for Certainty* (1929) takes a position differing from that of both
Lewis and Wieman.   He holds, in substance, that the great
error of both philosophy and religion has been to claim or
even to seek certainty.   In the nature of the case, we cannot
get it without deceiving ourselves.   What we can get, and
all we can get, is an exploration of the possibilities of experience.   Dewey's view, which has much to commend it,
was in some respects anticipated by F. J. McConnell's little
book on *Religious Certainty* (1910).

Additional light on this vexed problem was shed by the
German psychologist and philosopher, Karl Groos, in an
essay entitled "The Problem of Relativism." [16]   He points
out (p. 471) that there is no way of securing objective truth
except "by the way of subjective conviction."   Now, Groos
holds that, although "it is one of our beliefs that objective,
overindividual validity attaches to many of our subjective
intuitions and experiences," it is impossible to prove this
strictly.   Thus, while theoretically all proof is relative and
not absolute, practically it is rational to believe that some
propositions are really true.   For instance, who can doubt

---

[14] See Lewis, GO, 19–46.
[15] These views have been expressed in personal correspondence.
[16] This essay appeared in both German and English in the short-lived *Forum Philosophicum*, 1(1930–1931), 461–473.   The view is developed in a pamphlet, *Die Sicherung der Erkenntnis: theoretischer Relativismus und praktischer Absolutismus* (Tübingen: Osiander, 1927).

that there are other minds than his own; but who can prove it with absolute certainty? Thus "theoretical relativism is united with 'practical absolutism." There seems little objection to this procedure, and much value in it, as long as we follow Groos's demand "that we treat our beliefs, whenever they persist in the face of cool reflection on the situation, as absolute truths, at least 'pending further developments.' " We cannot justify our commonest beliefs about the' past or the future without recourse to Groos's postulates; with them, an exploration of the possibilities of religious value experience becomes more rational than on Lewis's assumptions, and more experimental and constructive than on Wieman's.

§ 8. THE CENTRAL BELIEFS OF RELIGION

In this chapter some attempt has been made to show that religion is a philosophical problem, and to indicate by what methods and criteria philosophy may deal with religion. In order to prepare the reader for the following chapters, this chapter will be brought to a close by a statement of the fundamental religious beliefs summarizing our study of religion as a, fact. It is these beliefs that give rise to the problem of philosophy of religion and it is to them that we shall turn our attention. They are the beliefs: (1) That *there is an objective source of value* expressing itself in the cosmos (the Divine, the object of worship; gods or God; called by J. B. Pratt "the Determiner of Destiny"); (2) That *human individuals experience values* (whether alone—in "solitariness"—or in group relations); and (3) That *religious value is experienced as a relation of the human individual to the Divine.* It remains to examine these beliefs and their implications for thought and for experience: (1) in Chapters V–X; (2) in Chapters XI–XIII; and (3) in Chapter XIV.

Bibliographical Note

Elementary surveys of the problem of the chapter are found in many texts. See, for instance, Schiller, ROS(1891, 1910), 3–14; Drake, PR(1916), Chap. XVI; Wright, SPR(1935), 1–7; Burtt, TRP(1938), 1–13. The chapter on "Mistaken Notions" in Ferm, FCRP(1937), 33–55, is clarifying. See also Brightman, ITP (1925), 22–66.

Excellent and penetrating discussions are in Galloway, PR(1914), 1–53; Tennant, PT(1928), I, 333–365; Knudson, DG(1930), 19–64 (on Religion and Theology); Lyman, MTR(1933), 151–225 (on Religious Knowledge); Wieman and Horton, GOR(1938), 396–419. The discussion in German (not translated) by Tillich, RP, 769–788, is especially challenging. The view of the Hegelians and Troeltsch is expounded critically by Mackintosh in TMT(1937), 101–137, 181–217. Opposition to "rationalism" in Ritschl, Kierkegaard, and Barth is treated in Mackintosh, TMT (1937), 138–180, 218–319; consult also Brunner, PR(1937), 55–98.

An illuminating essay on method is Beck, Art.(1939). Schilpp (ed.), PJD(1939), should be consulted by advanced students, especially E. L. Schaub's contribution on "Dewey's Interpretation of Religion," in PJD, 391–416.

FIVE

CONCEPTIONS OF GOD

§ 1. Why Begin with Conceptions of God?

P to this present point, our interest in religion has been on the level of a preliminary synopsis of the whole field. After a chapter of orientation, we surveyed religion as an historical, psychological, and sociological fact (Chapter II). We were then able to view it as a value phenomenon (Chapter III), after which its setting as a philosophical problem was pointed out (Chapter IV). We are now ready to begin with a more analytic investigation of special problems and we choose to begin with the problem of God.

Why is this starting point preferable to any other? In one sense, it makes no difference where we start thinking, as long as we think. On the other hand, the conception of God is a complex one about which opinions differ widely. There are, nevertheless, three good reasons for facing at once this fundamental problem. In the first place, the idea of God is uniquely essential to religion. All religion is in some sense a form of worship, and without an object (or at least an objective) of worship, religion would not be at all. Religion is not unique in being a social phenomenon or even in being an interest in values; it is the worshipful attitude, the attitude of reverent devotion to something divine, that marks it off from other experiences. This attitude would be impossible without an object toward which it was directed. The definition of the religious

object is therefore the fundamental problem of religion.
Until it is dealt with we do not know whether or not we
have a religious phenomenon before us. In the second
place, the idea of God is a good empirical starting point.
The religious conception of God is not a mere theological
theory; it is a summation of the highest aspirations of religious experience, a shorthand account of the value-claims
of the worshipers. It therefore affords a fruitful starting
point for philosophical investigation of experience. In the
third place, ideas of God vary so widely in different religions, and even among believers in the same religion, as
to make it rationally impossible that all of them can be
true and therefore to challenge philosophical investigation.

It may be thought that the existence of atheistic religion,
such as Jainism in its earliest form, or humanism, may
refute the statement that the idea of God is uniquely essential to religion. However, for our present purpose,
which includes all religions and all ideas of God, the atheistic
religions are to be viewed as atheistic only in the sense of
denying a cosmic objective spirit; yet even early Jainism and
Buddhism and (much more) modern humanism all point
toward a supreme value toward which they assume a worshipful attitude. Even where God is taboo, the most
atheistic religion assumes some objective which is worthy
of worship and devotion, and this objective is actually
its god. A religion, then, can be atheistic in the sense
of denying some particular idea of God; it cannot be a
religion at all if it denies that there is anything in the
universe worthy of human reverence and devotion.

§ 2.   God as Objective Source and Conserver of Values

Whatever else may or may not be said about God, religion at every stage has been worship, together with striving toward what was believed to be the source and the

guarantee of the highest values—at least of what the worshiper valued most highly. Ritual, prayer, church, priest, hymns of praise, moral teachings, faith in immortality—all were directed toward an assertion of or a search for the power on which value depends. The statement, "God is the creator of the universe," or "the source of all being," is an irreligious statement, if it means that whatever may be thought of as the source of all being is therefore to be regarded as God. When the creative power is thought of as evil or as indifferent to value, it is blasphemous to call such a creator God. Only the source of value is God; if the source of value is also the redeemer, as Irenaeus held, so much the better; and this better has been the faith of most religion on the highest level of its development. But much religion has been dualistic; and such religion has excluded from God "the world," "the flesh," "Satan," "Ahriman," "Maya," or whatever by its nature opposes or conceals or is indifferent to value. On the other hand, no religion has ever thought of God except in terms of the highest values accessible to it; and it has always thought of its God as something assuring or symbolizing the permanence of those values.

Noteworthy is the wide range of values symbolized in conceptions of the divine. Among the Todas of Southern India, it is the milk supply; among the Bagunda of Central Africa, health, plenty, and success in war;[1] in Persian and Canaanitic religions, agricultural fertility; among Buddhists, conquest of desire; among the Hebrew and Christian prophets, justice and love; among the Mohammedans, mercy; among the Brahmans, cosmic unity; among the Aristotelians, complete actuality. Whether referring to milk or to complete actuality, the idea of God at all stages and levels is consistently an idea about value. Aristotle[2] treats

[1] See Wright, SPR, 19, 31–32.   [2] In Met., XII (Lambda), 9.

"theiotaton" and "timiotaton" as synonyms: "most divine" is the same as "most valuable." Here the philosopher agrees with the humblest believer; if we are to have a God at all, we must have a being that is a trustworthy source of value. When Spinoza sought for God, he sought something by means of which "continua ac summa in aeternum fruerer laetitia" [3] ("I may enjoy continuous and supreme joy forever"). *Ens perfectissimum* (most perfect being) is a synonym for God among the scholastics. Kant calls God "the moral lawgiver," or "the highest good." Jacobi, "das Allerhöchste" (the Highest of all); Fries says, "God is the one who alone is holy" and "the reality of the ideal of the eternal good." [4] William James speaks of God as the "higher part of the universe"; [5] for W. E. Hocking, God is "an Other whose relation to me is not subject to evil through its own defect." [6] H. N. Wieman identifies God with "that process of existence which carries the possibilities of the highest value." [7] Although Matthew Arnold's famous definition of God as "the power not ourselves that makes for righteousness" has often been criticized, it is historically justifiable as what may be called a minimum definition of God. [8] Such a definition does not disclose whether God is a mind, a group of minds, a drinking bout on Mt. Olympus, an ideal, a Platonic idea, or unconscious energy; it reveals only what all religion has experienced, namely, that faith in God is faith in something better than ourselves which leads us to a higher level of living. God, then, is, as Eduard von Hartmann puts it, "the ground of

---

[3] Spinoza, *De intellectus emendatione tractatus*, first paragraph.

[4] Fries, WGA, 310, 309.

[5] James, VRE, 516.

[6] Hocking, MGHE, 223.

[7] Wieman in Macintosh (ed.), RR, 159.

[8] H. N. Wieman is especially well known for his approach to the problem through his own minimum definition just stated.

love between individuals" [9]—if by love is meant devotion to the mutual realization of the highest values.

Whatever further differences of opinion we may discover about the definition of God, and whatever doubts we may entertain about the truth of any particular idea of God, there can be no well-grounded difference or doubt about the empirical fact that whenever men have taken a religious attitude toward a God they have entered into a relation to the highest value known to them, and that in some sense this relation has always been an objective one. God is always beyond the present achievement of man and is objective, either as a reality to be known and appropriated or as a goal to be sought. God is never used as a name for man as he now is. God means that toward which man moves when he rises in the scale of value, viewed as a source of that movement.

§ 3. God as Personified Particular Value (Polytheism)

When we first find gods in the clear light of history, there are many of them. The vague tradition of belief in one High God may reflect a primitive monotheism of some kind. If so, the very word "High" as applied to God evidences the exalted value attached to the divine; but our knowledge of this stage of belief is too dim to warrant many inferences. What we are sure of is that we find man for a long time in his history believing in many gods, each god regarded as a vaguely personal (or impersonal-mana) spirit which is the source of some energy which brings value to man. There are gods of rivers, springs, trees, rains; of fertility, of motherhood, of fatherhood, of love; of peace, war, hunting, planting, trades, and professions; of wisdom, of music, and of truth. It is believed that even when man

---

[9] Hartmann, KGTR, in AW, I, 640.

sees disaster, some one of these gods is at work or may be called on. It thunders, but Zeus is the source of the thunder, and he is father of gods and men. We are ill, but proper rites in the temple of Aesculapius may bring healing. Polytheism, the belief in many gods, entails incoherent views of the operation of the laws of nature and of the relations of the contending values and gods to each other.

Polytheism is, however, religiously important as a phenomenon which has continued for centuries and still persists n some sections of Asia and Africa, to say nothing of its sporadic revival among civilized peoples (as in old Teutonic cults in modern Germany). Its religious importance is twofold: it illustrates (1) the uniform connection of the idea of God with value experience, as well as the wealth and variety of that experience, and also (2) a tendency to think of god or gods as conscious persons. Philosophical interpretations of this second point vary widely; some put it down merely to "anthropomorphism" and regard it as man's tendency to create a God in his own image; others see in it a necessary implication of value experience, since all value is by its very nature the fulfillment of an ideal purpose by some conscious being. According to the former view, the personification of values in many gods is a manifestation of man's arrogance or narcissism; according to the latter, it is a crude and inadequate, yet rightly directed, manifestation of man's intelligence in grasping the true nature of value experience. This problem is one of the central ones in philosophy of religion and will be treated at some length in Chapter VII.

§ 4. GOD AS PERSONIFIED NATIONAL SPIRIT (HENOTHEISM)

As civilization advances, men become more intelligently conscious of the coalescence of their various values, and polytheism tends toward some sort of unity. What men find empirically is that their values are largely expressions of the traditiohs, the culture, and the geographical environment of their racial and national life. As the national life becomes more closely organized under one supreme monarch, so the pantheon (the hierarchy of all the gods) becomes more closely organized under one supreme god (or two, like Isis and Osiris, thought of as substantially one). Where the national unity is loose, as in Greece, the supreme god, Zeus, has a rebellious group of undergods on his hands; but where the national unity is closely knit, the supreme god tends to be regarded as absolute ruler, and (at least among the thoughtful priests) the one god of the nation. Among the Hebrews, Jahve is less dependent on national unity and more on ethical idealism.

On the level of national religion, the supreme god is rarely thought of as the only god. Even among the early Hebrews, the gods of other nations were recognized as having a certain status, and Chemosh of Moab or Dagon of Philistia was acknowledged in international relations. The point of regarding God as personified national spirit was that the highest aspirations of the national group were thus objectified. The term henotheism is often used to describe belief in and worship of one god as supreme, accompanied by recognition that others exist.[10] The situation of henotheism was rendered embarrassing by the fact that creation myths (connecting the source of value with the source of existence) arose in connection with the various national gods; it gradually became necessary to decide whether the creator of the universe was an Egyptian, a

[10] The Vedic practice of treating each god in succession as the only one while it is being worshiped had better be called kathenotheism (one-at-a-time-theism), as Menzies suggests, rather than henotheism, as Max Müller proposed.

Greek, a Hebrew, or a Babylonian.[11] Henotheism was an impossible stopping place for religious development.

§ 5. GOD AS SUPREME PERSONAL CREATOR (MONOTHEISM)

The usual development of the idea of God in most civilizations has therefore been from henotheism to monotheism. As the social, the political, the ethical, and the intellectual horizons of men widened, the similarity of the highest spiritual values for which every nation was striving came to be appreciated; the unity of the laws of cosmic nature and of human nature was realized; the religious man, like Saint Paul, could say, "He left not himself without witness" (Acts 14:17), and a religious philosopher, like the Emperor Marcus Aurelius, no longer made national success his criterion, but asked of every experience "what value it has for the whole universe." [12] The inevitable inference from all this was that there is only one God. Such was the outcome of the highest religious thought of Egypt, of Israel, of India, of Greece, and of Rome. More or less independently, there grew up the idea of one supreme personal spirit, the source of all value and the creator of all that exists other than himself. Spiritual, personalistic monotheism expresses the faith of most actual religions at what they regard as their highest point. Therefore philosophy of religion must largely concern itself with the question whether this belief is a true one.[13] Inquiry has for the most part centered about the concept of creation.

[11] Robert Munson Grey, *I, Yahweh* (Chicago: Willett, Clark and Company, 1937), is a vivid, fictional account of the development of God from the national to the universal level. See also Roark Bradford, *Ol' Man Adam an' his Chillun* (New York: Harper and Brothers, 1928).

[12] M. Aurelius, *Meditations,* III, 11.

[13] The empirical fact of monotheistic faith gives an importance to the problem of the personality of God which it might not deserve in the abstract. A well-known philosopher of religion once expressed some resentment over the inquiry into personal and impersonal views of God; he went so far as to imply that it is no more important

That a unified view must be sought is generally granted; but there is difficulty both in understanding creation and in thinking of a good God as voluntarily creating all the evil things and persons in the world.

§ 6. GOD AS THE WHOLE OF REALITY (PANTHEISM)

The difficulty about creation, the logical demand for complete unity, and the experience of mystical oneness with God have combined to lead some religious thinkers, especially in India, to the view that God is not a spirit separate from nature and man, who creates them and imparts value to them. Rather, these thinkers hold, God is the whole of which nature and man are parts. Evil appears to exist because we have an incomplete view of the whole. No part of a symphony or a painting is satisfactory by itself; it is the whole that provides true satisfaction and true beauty. And everything that is, is but a part of the whole. The partial view may be confusing, deceptive, and seemingly evil; the whole is clear as crystal, and perfect. In Greece, this view appeared in Parmenides and later in Plotinus; in India it came to classic expression in the Upanishads and the brilliant Sankara (788?–820? A.D.).[14] Although thinkers like Hegel and Royce objected to being called pantheists, their idealistic absolutism, which makes all experience the development of the one, all-inclusive cosmic spirit, is religiously pantheism. Pantheism has assumed many forms. Sometimes, as in Hegel and Royce, it has been plainly personalistic, that is, has defined the All

to question whether God is impersonal than to inquire whether he is nonturnip. But this attitude manifests a marked indifference to the empirical fact that no one thinks he has experienced God as turnip, whereas many think they have experienced him as person.

[14] On Sankara see S. Radhakrishnan, *Indian Philosophy* (New York: The Macmillan Company, 1927), Vol. II, Chap. VIII, and Rudolf Otto, *West-Östliche Mystik* (Gotha: Leopold Klotz Verlag, 1927), translated as *Mysticism East and West*.

as one conscious spirit. Sometimes it has viewed the energy
of nature as the One of which all individuals are partial
manifestations. But all types of pantheism agree in finding
the source of religious value to lie in the nature of the
whole, and religious experience to consist in the realization
of membership in or identity with the whole. The intellectual difficulties of pantheism center around the attempts
to define the precise nature of the whole, and also in the
doubt about what happens to the value and freedom of the
individual when he is thus merged with the whole.

§ 7. God as the Unknowable Source of All Being
(Agnostic Realism)

The difficulty of asserting that anyone possesses sufficient
knowledge about the universe as a whole to base the value
of his life and the validity of his religion on such a view
has led some religious thinkers to abandon both monotheism
and pantheism in favor of agnostic realism. Those who
hold such a view point out that religion does not pretend
to be a matter of human knowledge, scientific or philosophical. It is rather an aspiration toward the infinite but
unknown source of our experience of values, and of nature.
Religion is humble, and religion moves in the atmosphere
of mystery. God, therefore, is not any knowable or definable being; God is the unknowable source of the known.
This somewhat sophisticated view came to its classical expression in Herbert Spencer's (1820–1903) *First Principles*
(1862).[15] The view is called sophisticated because, although very learned, it does what sophistication usually
does, namely, it fails to see the implications of its own position. Sophistication is generally unsophisticated. After
all, if one can say no more about God than that the divine
is the unknowable, then one does not know whether God

[15] For a criticism of Spencer's thought, see Bowne, KS.

is good or bad, wise or foolish, noble or ignoble, spiritual or material. If one does not know any of these things, then one does not know whether religious experience is "Maya and illusion" or insight into the nature of the real. One who took Spencer's view seriously would very soon see that no positive religious attitude was reasonable; and he would find it hard to distinguish a mystery founded on nothing but ignorance from sheer mumbo jumbo.

§ 8. God as Human Aspiration for Ideal Values (Humanism)

Groping in ignorance among unknowables does not commend itself to the modern mind as a useful approach to the divine. Unknowables are unknowable and had better be left alone; but (according to an influential modern mood) there is something we do know, namely, that man has aspirations for a nobler world, a more ideal society, a better way of living. Auguste Comte (1798–1857), founder of modern sociology, rejected all speculation about the ultimate nature of reality, whether theological (personal gods) or metaphysical (forces and energies), and held that knowledge was confined to the "positive" sciences of experience. Hence his view was called positivism. Nevertheless, he was devoted to ideal values and his religion consisted in reverence for human personality and in altruistic endeavors to better man's condition. God, for him, was humanity itself, which he called "le grande être."

The German, Ludwig Feuerbach (1804–1872), a so-called left-wing Hegelian criticized by Engels [16] and Marx, differed from Comte in that he believed metaphysical knowledge to be possible. He was a materialist, holding that man is what he eats ("Der Mensch ist, was er isst"). As regards religion, however, his view was close to that of Comte. God

[16] See Engels, *Feuerbach.*

for him is only man's idealized consciousness, and has only a psychological existence in man's mind; no cosmic existence, and certainly no physiological organism.[17]

In America, more or less independently of Comte and Feuerbach, there has arisen a movement known as religious humanism, the essence of which is the view that God is to be found in man's highest social experiences, not in any reality beyond man. Among the most thoughtful leaders of this movement are M. C. Otto, R. W. Sellars, J. A. C. Fagginger Auer, and John Dewey. Dewey defines God as "the unity of all ideal ends arousing us to desire and actions." [18] This is put in explicit opposition to the view that there is a God other than our pursuit of a unified ideal; such a view, he thinks, would make God nonideal. God, then, for Dewey and for most humanists is an "active relation between ideal and actual." [19] Communists, refusing to use the name of God, practically treat their cause as divine in accordance with humanistic principles.

The members of this last group have so much in common with Comte and Feuerbach that all may well be called humanists. While humanism represents a radical break with almost the entire history of religion, except for certain aspects of primitive Buddhism, it cannot be rejected offhand. It is thoroughly in harmony with the empirical spirit; it shares the religious interest in values, and finds values concretely in personal and social experience; and it is devoted

---

[17] See Feuerbach, WC, 413.

[18] Dewey, CF, 42.

[19] Dewey, CF, 51. In Santayana's conception of religion as a play in the realm of essence, we have a humanism with almost no relation to the actual. Santayana's well-known quip that "there is no God and the Virgin Mary is his mother" well illustrates his feeling for religion as beautiful, but as concerned with the nonexistent. A very different type of humanism, much more dubiously religious in character, is that psychoanalytic view which regards "God" as a rationalization of the suppressed father-complex. Such a view completely evades the historical and philosophical problems.

to the active creation of that progress which some monotheists submissively leave to the will of God. Humanism is right in its insistence that religion must find its evidence in the facts of human experience. Nevertheless, there are some who question whether the facts of human experience can be understood or the highest human values achieved without the adjustment of human experience to an objective reality beyond it which is the source of its experience of values. Humanism wants to be certain in its foundations and to be modest in its claims; but perhaps if it is certain, it cannot be modest and if it is modest it will have to give up the quest for certainty in the interests of the quest for higher value.

§ 9. GOD AS SUPERHUMAN AND SUPERNATURAL REVEALER OF VALUES (DEISTIC SUPERNATURALISM)

There is at the present time among a large group of Christians a marked revolt against humanism and in favor of a radically objective attitude toward God. According to this view, God is not found in human experience at all except in so far as he chooses to reveal himself; when he reveals himself it is not as the highest man can think, but rather as something "totally other" than everything human, of a radically different quality from human hopes and strivings—as different from our best as eternity is from time. Sören Kierkegaard (1813–1855),[20] a Danish theologian, was largely responsible for initiating this line of thought in the nineteenth century, although it also has much in common with the system of John Calvin (1509–1564),[21] as well as with some of the beliefs of Martin Luther (1483–1546).

The phenomenal rise of this tendency in the world of modern religious thought is to be traced to Karl Barth

[20] See the chapter on Kierkegaard in Mackintosh, TMT.
[21] See Harkness, JC.

(1886–   ), a Swiss theologian, who, under the influence of the experiences of the World War, rethought his whole conception of God. Modern "liberalism," if not humanistic in the technical sense, has relied on human experience, human science, and human philosophy, but the War was the collapse of human wisdom. Human values were used for the destruction of human values and thus their hollowness was exposed. Man's only hope, Barth believes, is in ceasing to trust in himself, his science, and his reason. Man must trust in God or be doomed to ruin. God has revealed his Word in the Bible, although it is presumptuous for any man to say that his interpretation of that Word is final. God himself, not man, must speak; he is the judge and the controller of life, not man. Since the element of judgment is so prominent, Barth's thought is often called the crisis theology (crisis being the Greek word for judgment). Since Barth emphasizes the contrast and contradiction between God and the world, his system is also called dialectical theology. The world says, Yes, and God says, No; the world says, No, and God says, Yes.[22]   Barth's popularity has increased since he became a hero by incurring exile from Nazi Germany for his refusal to retract a statement that Christians might be of two opinions about the cause of the burning of the Reichstag in 1933.

The Barthian conception of God may be called deism because it holds so emphatically that God is other than the world, and totally distinct from it. For the same reason it may be called supernaturalism, or neosupernaturalism.[23]

This deistic supernaturalism is a wholesome emphasis on the incompleteness of a purely subjective humanism, but there are many critics who think that Barthianism goes as

---

[22] The chapter on Barth in Mackintosh, TMT, is a sympathetic introduction to Barthian thought and literature.

[23] For a related view see the account of neosupernaturalism in Wieman and Meland, APR.

far toward an unreasonable objectivism without subjective roots as humanism does toward an unreasonable subjectivism without objective roots. In any case it rests on presuppositions which are all but unintelligible to one who has any confidence in rational empiricism as the proper approach to truth.[24]

§ 10. God as the System of Ideal Values (Impersonal Idealism)

There are those who cannot accept the personal God of monotheism, and yet are dissatisfied with all of the alternative definitions hitherto proposed. Pantheism and Absolutism are for them too all-inclusive; God is not the All, but the Best. To call God unknowable is to divest him of meaning. To identify God with human aspiration is to deny the objective reference of religious experience. To say that God is utterly superhuman and supernatural is to leave us without any adequate evidence in experience on which to build the idea of God. Hence this group defines God as the system of ideal values. Its members go back to Plato, and think of God as the eternal Forms (or Ideas) of Justice, Truth, and Love, although Plato himself never identified God with the Forms. Since the Forms are thought of as eternally valid ideals or principles, God is not a person or a conscious mind for members of this group, and their view may well be called impersonal idealism.[25] Fichte's conception of God as "the moral order of the universe" is close to this view. It has had its most explicit modern formulation in the brief treatment of religion in E. G. Spaulding's *The New Rationalism,* but intimations

[24] The best criticism of Barth is found in A. C. Knudson, "The Theology of Crisis," *Meth. Rev.,* 111(1928), 329–343, 549–560. Barth is equally objectionable to rationalists and to empiricists.

[25] Many "pantheists" are also impersonal idealists.

of it appear in J. S. Bixler's Ingersoll Lecture on *Immortality and the Present Mood*.

The merit of this view is its intellectual clarity and honesty; its defect lies in its incomplete metaphysics. One who believes in eternal objective ideals must sooner or later ask himself what the relation is between those ideals and the world of brute empirical fact. The thinker cannot permanently keep the world of ideals and the world of facts in watertight compartments. He must relate them or else his thinking will be subject to the same criticism as is Barthianism—that its God and its world are so far apart that the two stand in no intelligible relation to each other.

§ 11. GOD AS THE TENDENCY OF NATURE TO SUPPORT OR PRODUCE VALUES (RELIGIOUS NATURALISM)

The reader will recall that in § 2 above it was said that all conceptions of God have in common the reference to a source or conserver of values. It is evident by this time that the word "conserver" must be taken to mean "he (or those) who, or that which, conserves," and that much of the purpose of modern thought about God has been to explore alternatives to the monotheistic idea of a personal creator (§ 5). All of the conceptions treated in § 6 through § 10 (except that in § 9, which is an alternative to the rational and empirical approaches to God) are obviously intended as such alternatives. Yet none of them has been fully satisfactory. They suffer either from vagueness or from abstractness or from a lack of coherent interpretation. Yet they have in common a ruggedly honest determination to believe no more than the evidence requires them to believe, and to indulge in no unwarranted speculations.

Since the death of the great philosopher Hegel in 1831, many thinkers have turned in the direction of what is now commonly called naturalism, a form of materialism.

Materialism, as its name implies, holds that everything is reducible to matter; matter is really the only substantial reality, and anything else, such as mind, is not really "else," but is only a special form or an unsubstantial effect of matter—its "epiphenomenon," as is often said. The older materialism (prior to the nineteenth century) tended to follow Democritus (460? to 370? B.C.) and Lucretius (96–55 B.C.) in holding that everything including mind is reducible to moving atoms which differ only in size, shape, and motion. This early view was a brilliant anticipation of certain aspects of modern science but was philosophically unsatisfactory, because the more we came to know about physical reality the clearer it became (to Descartes [1596–1650] for example) that mind is not matter, and that consciousness has no physical size or shape or motion. Further, the rise of evolutionary theory in the nineteenth century proved that matter was more complicated than the early materialists had thought.

Hence modern materialists have tended to abandon the older word and to call their theory naturalism. The chief traits of naturalism are: (1) a tendency to accept the object of the physicochemical sciences (nature) as the unbegun and unending source of all cosmic process; (2) a recognition that nature is not merely a collection of atoms, but a creative process; and (3) that in the process of its creative advance new properties arise which could not have been foreseen until they actually appeared. These new properties are called emergents. If nature is fundamentally physicochemical, it first gives rise to an emergent which we call life; then after long ages, life gives rise to an emergent known as mind or consciousness. Thus the processes of nature are an "emergent evolution" (Lloyd Morgan), and naturalism has overcome the wooden and mechanical view of the universe as a cloud of atom-dust. This modern naturalism is not dissimilar to the so-called dialectical materialism of the Communists, which emphasizes the evolutionary movement of nature.

It has been necessary to give this brief explanation in order to introduce religious naturalism or naturalistic theism, as it is sometimes called. It is an interesting phenomenon for students of religion that even materialists have usually had some conception of God. But the gods of Democritus and Lucretius were of no importance to either theory or practice. They were otiose creatures, themselves products of matter, and taking care not to influence or be influenced by human affairs or the ongoing of nature. Such a view of the gods was purely mythical and of no philosophical or religious import, for such gods explained nothing either in nature or in the experience of value. By contrast with such materialists (who have a certain analogue in Hobbes) and also with the atheistic materialists of the eighteenth century in France, modern naturalists are frequently much more comprehending in their attitude toward religion. They see religious experience as a natural phenomenon, rooted in nature, born, as W. G. Everett used to say, "in the womb of nature," and consequently as a fact to be included in naturalism, not to be cast aside as trivial or false.

The view of Herbert Spencer (§ 7), who defined God as the Unknowable, is a case in point. He was a naturalist, rejecting all traditional ideas of God, yet sympathetic with the quest of religious experience for the source and conserver of values. Humanism (§ 8) offered another naturalistic approach to the divine. Barthianism (§ 9) and Platonism (§ 10), however, were plainly revolts against naturalism, the former in the interest of supernatural revelation, and the latter in the interest of rational ideals independent of nature.

Meanwhile, naturalists have been at work seeking a

better expression of their own understanding of religion. Thinkers of this sort would agree in defining God as the tendency of nature to support or produce values. Two influential members of this group are the late Samuel Alexander (1859–1938), and Henry Nelson Wieman (1884–)—the former a British philosopher (born in Australia) and the latter an American—each a strikingly typical product of his cultural background, yet agreeing in fundamental principles.

Alexander's view was developed in his Gifford Lectures of 1916 to 1918 at Glasgow, published as *Space, Time, and Deity*. In Book IV of the second volume of that work, Alexander develops his famous distinction between deity and God. Deity is the fact that just beyond any level of evolution a new emergent level is to arise. "On each level a new quality looms ahead, awfully, which plays to it the part of deity."[26] God is the universe conceived as possessing deity. This view resembles humanism in regarding human consciousness as being in a sense deity. Yet it differs from humanism in holding that the human spirit is deity, not for man, but for the lower level, body; the human soul is deity for the body, but in the next stage of cosmic evolution, some unimaginable, yet inevitable, superman is deity for man. It also differs from humanism in its metaphysical objectivity; God is not identified with human aspiration, but is an objective character of nature as a whole. God is objectively real, on this view, and no mere rationalization of subjective striving.

Another naturalistic conception of God has been proposed by the distinguished American philosopher of religion, Henry Nelson Wieman. Wieman's naturalism is not in any sense an imitation of Alexander's; in fact, he has been far more influenced by John Dewey and A. N. Whitehead than by

[26] STD, II, 348.

Alexander. Nevertheless, the same general formula applies equally well to Wieman's God and to Alexander's: God is the tendency of nature to support or produce movement toward perfection. For Alexander, God is the fact that the universe is always striving for a higher level of being. For Wieman, likewise, God is the name for "the growth of meaning and value in the world." More specifically, God is "increase in those connections between activities which make the activities mutually sustaining, mutually enhancing and mutually meaningful." [27] Thus God, for Wieman, means those energies of nature which render possible the increase of rational, social experience.

Like Alexander's, Wieman's view of God is naturalistic and objective, in contrast with the much more subjective view of humanism. But Alexander's view is less empirical and less true to the facts of the history of religion than is Wieman's. There is no empirical ground for suggesting that inorganic matter ever had a "religious" attitude toward the next higher emergent, life; nor is it true to say that the present worship of the religious consciousness is directed toward "deity"—the unknown and unknowable next emergent of the evolutionary process. Wieman is much nearer the facts in holding that religion is concerned with the values of truth and beauty and love—the highest we now know—and with their ground in reality. Religion has always included an element of mystery; yet religious persons have never worshiped mere mystery as Alexander would have them do, in looking ahead to the unknown coming deity, nor has religion ever been directed exclusively toward the future. It has been concerned with adjustment to the permanent and the eternal, as well as with the improvement of the temporal. At this point, Wieman, too, is one-sided, in his definition of God in terms of growth alone. He is

[27] Wieman, NPR, 51, 137.

right that belief in God is a belief in betterment, in growth, in increase of value in the universe; but he is wrong in underestimating the factor of permanence in the idea of God. The religious worshiper would not have much confidence in God as an increaser of value unless he had a primary confidence in God as conserver of value. The thought of God as an eternally more lavish spender arouses suspicion of bankruptcy unless God is an even better saver than spender. To speak more religiously, God must be a Savior before he can be a Giver.

Suggestions like those of Alexander and Wieman are religiously useful as sincere and thoughtful endeavors to interpret God without recourse to the idea of a conscious, personal mind. They perform the useful function of tiding over religious values for those individuals who have become doubtful of historical monotheism. Yet there are many who wonder whether this naturalistic theism gives a satisfactory coherent account of the objective sources of human consciousness in nature, or of either the origins or the increase of value in nature.

§ 12. CONCEPTIONS OF GOD AS REVOLUTIONARY OR EVOLUTIONARY

There are at least three possible ways of seeking a better understanding of the facts of religious experience. One is that of rejecting its entire history and content as a congeries of error and illusion, devised either by the subconscious to satisfy its hidden cravings or by "priests" to ensure their social and economic control of society. This way is sweepingly dogmatic and naïve; nevertheless it is possible that its results may be true. The history of astrology or of magic is a history of error; perhaps the history of religion is. It is not philosophical, however, to declare that either astrology or magic is error until all experiences of all astrologers and magicians have been fully investigated. So, too, it would be unphilosophical to dismiss religion before the experiences and beliefs of religious persons have been investigated.

Leaving, then, an attitude of either acceptance or rejection of religious faith to the outcome of philosophy of religion, most thinkers regard initial skepticism as unreasonable, and devote themselves to an interpretation of religious experience: The various conceptions of God which we have been surveying are so many attempts to arrive at a rational interpretation of the facts of religion. These attempts are governed by different presuppositions, depending on different attitudes toward the monotheism which is the culminating faith of most historical religions at their maturity. Given religious experience as a fact, and monotheistic belief as a typical constituent of that experience, philosophers who respect the empirical data inquire into the direction in which rational progress in religious thought should move.

Very few thinkers, if any, believe that the essential problems have already been solved so completely that no progress is necessary. It is true that scholastics and neoscholastics speak of the Aristotelian-Thomistic synthesis as the *philosophia perennis* in such a way as to imply that the philosophical truth about God is known and is known to be unchangeable.[28] However, the constant productivity of neoscholastics implies the need of incessant rational investigation and the possibility of new discoveries. Yet, as a matter of fact, the scholastic conception of God has undergone no real change since the thirteenth century, and it is hardly to it that we should look for a principle of growth.

[28] For excellent presentations of the neoscholastic standpoint see Étienne Gilson, *The Unity of Philosophical Experience* (New York: Charles Scribner's Sons, 1937), and Jacques Maritain, *The Degrees of Knowledge* (New York: Charles Scribner's Sons, 1938), as well as the journal, *The New Scholasticism* (Catholic University of America).

If, then, we disregard for the moment those who reject religion entirely, as well as those who adhere fixedly to concepts accepted in the thirteenth century, we find the great majority of thinkers about religion agreeing on the value and the validity of religious experience, and also on the need of the scientific and philosophical criticism and interpretation of that experience. The followers of Spencer, the humanists, the supernaturalists (with reservations), the Platonists, and the religious naturalists would all agree on these points. At the same time, the group of thinkers just mentioned all represent an attitude toward historical religion which rests on the conviction that, although religious experience is valid and worthful, the ideas which religion has developed are in the main false. Most of this group, for instance, would reject the conception of God as a conscious mind as well as the idea of personal immortality; if the supernaturalists hold to these ideas, they do so in a way that constitutes a radical break with the way in which the ideas have been developed and interpreted in most of the world's religions.

The point of view of those who hold to a radical break with the history of religion is opposed by that of the large number of philosophers and theologians who think that truth is more likely to be found by a critical development of the values and beliefs discovered by historical religions than it is by a repudiation of them. If we wish to label these groups for convenience, we may call the former revolutionary and the latter evolutionary.[29] The revolutionary group wishes to do away entirely with the idea of God as a conscious spirit.[30] The evolutionary group wishes to unify,

[29] While this use of the word evolutionary refers to historical and logical rather than to biological evolution, almost all members of the evolutionary group are theists who accept biological evolution.

[30] In Bishop William Montgomery Brown there is a perfect example of the revolutionary method carried out to a *reductio ad absurdum*. Once a bishop of the

criticize, rethink, and extend the spiritual and personalistic idea of God. A revolutionary thinker tends to discredit an evolutionary one as a victim of traditionalism.[31] An evolutionary one tends to discredit a revolutionary as a victim of abstract theorizing without regard to historical realities or intellectual coherence.

The movement of religious thought, then, may be regarded as a dialectical advance. Religion starts with an affirmation of some faith: for example, God is a conscious person, whose will is revealed to us. This starting point may be called the thesis of naive dogmatism. The extreme form of protest against the thesis (within the realm of religion) is the assertion of the revolutionary antithesis. Since dogmatism is false method, so runs the antithesis, we should break entirely with its assertion that God is a conscious person, and should try to build up a new view of religion with some substitute for a personal God.[32] Wherever a thesis and an antithesis appear, there is a tendency for a synthesis to arise. The

Protestant Episcopal Church in good standing, he lost his faith in what he calls "a conscious personal God in the sky" and was found guilty of heresy. He became a Marxian Communist. The unusual aspect of his case lies in the fact that he continued, as an atheist who rejected all of the teachings of Christianity except its moral idealism, to desire still to be known as a bishop and retained belief in the Christian doctrines, interpreted as symbols of Communist ideas. See his *Communism and Christianism* (Galion, Ohio: The Bradford-Brown Educational Company, n.d.), on the title page of which is the motto, "Banish Gods from the Skies and Capitalists from the Earth." Revolutionary as is Bishop Brown, his continuation of Christian symbolism shows that a shred of evolution survives the holocaust of the most devastating revolution. In opposition to Bishop Brown's revolutionary intention is Edwyn Bevan's rejection of a new religion unconnected with the past religious experiences. See his Gifford Lectures for 1933 and 1934 (SAB, 69).

[31] Edwyn Bevan calls it "the method of anthropological intimidation" (SAB, 51) when thinkers that we have called "revolutionary" try to refute theism because of its relations to origins in primitive thought. The method of anthropological intimidation rejects all development whatever.

[32] There may be some question regarding our classification of Barthianism as revolutionary, since it still holds to a personal God. But in some respects Barthianism is substantially agnostic about God and his Word, and in all respects its method breaks with predominant methods of religious thought; it is therefore truly a revolutionary idea, whether true or false.

three do not always or usually appear in strict one-two-three order, but no matter when they arise, their relations assume the dialectical form. In the case of religious conceptions of God, the synthesis seems to be an evolutionary treatment of those conceptions, which carries religion beyond the thesis of mere dogmatism, yet takes its affirmations into account; considers the most revolutionary objections and innovations; and then builds up a revised and undogmatic form of the thesis, modified and criticized. If the danger of the thesis is its narrow dogmatism, and of the antithesis is its destructiveness, the danger of the synthesis is that of smug dogmatism. This danger can be avoided only by refusing to treat any form of synthesis as the last word of thought. Time alone will reveal all the implications of the two points of view to the thought of generations to come.

§ 13. An Evolutionary Conception: God as Conscious Mind, Immanent Both in Nature and in Values (Theism)

Modern theism is a typical evolutionary conception. Theists define God as a conscious mind (spirit or person), immanent both in physical nature and in value experiences. This evolutionary group starts its reflections from an interpretation of the facts of history, psychology, and sociology of religion, and from the monotheism which most of the higher religions have developed as their central faith. Evolutionary thinkers are mostly theists.

Theism is a special form of monotheism, as distinguished from other forms, such as pantheism and deism. Pantheists (§ 6) hold that the one divine spirit includes all that there is; man and nature are alike parts of God and there is nothing in the universe except God; God is completely immanent in everything. Deists (§ 9) hold that there is one divine spirit, but that this spirit is completely external both to nature and to man; even though God may have created the world, he now has nothing directly to do with it. He is an "absentee God," wholly "other," supernatural and transcendent. Theism may be regarded as a synthesis of pantheism and deism (as well as of the traditional and the revolutionary). Theists are evolutionary thinkers who share with many pantheists and all deists the belief in God as one supreme, personal spirit. They agree with pantheists in holding that God is immanent in nature, but they deny that spiritually imperfect human persons could without contradiction be regarded as parts of a spiritually perfect divine person. Hence they reject pantheism. They agree with deists in holding that God is other than the world of human persons, and some of them grant that perhaps God is other than na- ture; but they reject the idea that this transcendence is a complete and rigid externality. Thus they reject deism.

Theists in general agree that although God is more than all that is revealed in physical nature, he is present (im- manent) within all physical events to such a degree that those events are expressions of his power and control. Theists also hold that God's personality is expressed in the intrinsic values which are his norms and purposes and which man is gradually discovering. Theists differ about the definition of nature and the mode of God's relation to it, the importance of many of the special insights of the his- torical religions, the certainty and logical basis of our knowledge of God, and the extent to which future investiga- tions may alter or enlarge our conception of God. They agree in the repudiation of finality and dogmatism, in the critical interpretation of religious experience, and in the use of scientific and philosophical methods. In view of wide- spread popular misunderstanding, it is perhaps necessary to state explicitly that the theistic belief in God as a spiritual personality excludes entirely the idea that the divine per- sonality has a biological organism of any kind.

Some few illustrations of the theistic view will conclude this exposition. The German philosopher Lotze and the American Bowne are conspicuous for their combination of theism with an idealistic view of nature. Personalists influenced by them include men like A. C. Knudson, R. T. Flewelling, G. A. Wilson, P. A. Bertocci, and many others. But there are also many theists whose metaphysics of nature is not idealistic and who call themselves religious realists.[33]

It would be impossible within the limits of reasonable space to undertake to list the ideas of even the chief modern theists. It would be necessary to include most of the Gifford lecturers and a large number of the best-known philosophers and theologians. We select for brief mention, somewhat arbitrarily, the views of five distinguished modern theists, Bergson, Eddington, Boodin, Hocking, and Whitehead, men who have approached theism from different sides.

Henri Bergson (1859–) has devoted most of his life to psychological and biological philosophy. His view of God which had been close to that of religious naturalism, has in his most recent work, *The Two Sources of Morality and Religion* (1932, tr. 1935), arrived at a theistic position. He defines God as love, and explicitly derives this definition from the experience of the mystics, distinguishing his view from pantheism by his insistence on freedom and on God's creation of human beings as creators (see p. 243).

A. S. Eddington (1882–), best known as an astronomer and philosopher of physics, is an evolutionary theist in our special sense, in that his view of God is a scientific and philosophical interpretation of the Friends' religious experience. He starts from the empirical fact that mind or personal spirit is the only reality of which we have direct experience, and he concludes that the unseen world is the world of a spiritual, personal God.[34]

---

[33] See Macintosh (ed.), RR.　　　[34] See Eddington, SUW, 47, 81, 82.

John Elof Boodin (1869–   ), whose philosophical development has led through many phases of pragmatism and realism, develops theism cautiously. Acutely conscious as Boodin is of the complexity of experience and the limitations of our knowledge, he is nevertheless aware that mere skepticism is sterile. He approaches God through our experiences of order, life, intelligence, beauty, and goodness, and is driven to conclude that these values point to God as personality and creative love.[35]

A more idealistic theist, with a certain pantheistic trend in his thought, is William Ernest Hocking (1873–   ), whose treatment of the problem has been the characteristically evolutionary one described by the title of his great book, *The Meaning of God in Human Experience.* In the course of this analysis of the intellectual and mystical foundations of religion, Hocking defines God as "an Other Mind, an individual Subject, wholly active" and he regards any other conception of divine unity than the personal as "thinner and weaker." [36]

Finally, we mention Alfred North Whitehead (1861–   ), whose extraordinary contributions to mathematical logic, to philosophy of physics, and to social philosophy fit him to approach philosophy of religion objectively. Whitehead's doctrine of God is far from simple; but there is no doubt that Whitehead's view is theistic and evolutionary, for he holds that, in regard to God's "consequent nature," God is conscious and good, manifesting a wisdom which is "a tender care that nothing be lost." [37] Whitehead is clearly not a pantheist, nor is he a creationist; God "does not create the world, he saves it." [38]

[35] See Boodin, GOD, 46. The student will find it fruitful to consult this book carefully.
[36] Hocking, MGHE, 332, 334.
[37] Whitehead, PR, 524–525.
[38] Ibid., 526.

In bringing this chapter to a close, we cannot avoid being impressed by the variety of opinion about God. Yet what was said at the start is now seen more clearly to be true; that in all the variety of opinion there is one common insight about experience coming to expression, namely, that the object to which all religions have directed their worship and service is a divine source and conserver of values. The examination of so many different definitions of God will prepare us to evaluate the faith of religion in a larger perspective.

BIBLIOGRAPHICAL NOTE

For a good historical background, see Burtt, TRP(1939). Pringle-Pattison, IGRP(1917), treats the great ideas of God since Hume. Royce, CG(1902), and Wieman, Macintosh, and Otto, ITG(1932), are famous debates which bring out differing views of God. Various conceptions are treated critically and ably in Bowne, THE(1902), and in Lyman, MTR(1933), 229–346. A simple and clear elementary treatment is found in Harkness, CRT(1929), Chap. VIII. The variety of current views of God is brought out in popular essays by various writers in Newton, MIG(1926), and in the more critical treatments of Brightman, PG(1930), and Wieman and Meland, APR(1936). The indifference of many cultivated persons to God is well illustrated by Fadiman (ed.), IB(1939), in which some of the most famous men of letters and science show that they have not given a serious thought to God for years; the reader will decide for himself what this proves, but to some it may suggest the *New Yorker's* "Department of Utter Confusion."

SIX

WAYS OF KNOWING GOD

INTRODUCTORY

CHAPTER V has presented samples of the more important conceptions of God, both revolutionary and evolutionary. Those ideas were called revolutionary which presuppose rejection either of the predominant form which the idea of God has taken—that of a conscious, personal being (for example, humanism) —or else of the predominant conception of the relation of God to the world of human experience (for example, Barthianism); these views were called revolutionary because they rest on a break with the main historical development of religion. Other ideas were called evolutionary because they presuppose that the history of religion is a development in the gradual experimental discovery of religious truths; the evolutionary conceptions grow out of the empirical fact that all religious value is personal experience, as well as out of the historic faith that the object of worship is a cosmic experiencer and continuer of ideal values. Static or reactionary views are not profitable to examine.

It is, however, self-evident to a thoughtful mind that no classification or labeling of ideas can decide their truth. Inattentive minds may be impressed by the idea mentioned first, or by the one mentioned last; those whose emotions are suffused with a pleasant glow by the word revolution or the word evolution will suppose that the problem of God has been solved by these labels, "like a skeleton with tickets stuck all over it." [1] Philosophy of religion as well as philosophy of science or philosophy of art is based on a rational interpretation of experience, not on acceptable emotions. Religious emotion, if it is worthy, must conform to truth, not truth to emotion.

Nevertheless, to say that philosophy of religion is based on a rational interpretation of experience is far from a complete or exact statement of how God is known.[2] Experience is a word that has had so many conflicting meanings that at least one philosopher has proposed to abolish its use; and the word "known," as applied to God, or to any object whatever, opens the floodgates of epistemological theorizing. In order to clarify the problem which confronts us, preliminary definitions are essential.

The problem of this chapter is to define and evaluate proposed ways of knowing God. Knowledge is to be distinguished from experience. Experience as used in this book is a word that refers to the immediate data of consciousness; whatever is present in consciousness is said to be experienced; what at any given time is not present in consciousness is not experienced. The individual experiences his experience, lives his consciousness. But every actual experience has a double reference; it refers, as we have said, to our own consciousness as we have it; it also refers to objects not identical with our experience of them. If I say, "I experienced a change in temperature as I went from the warm house to the cold outdoors," I mean two things: first, that my consciousness changed its contents and feeling tone, and second,

---

[1] Hegel, *Phenomenology of Mind* (tr. Baillie), 110. See also J. E. Creighton, "Philosophical Platforms and Labels," in SSP, 222–242.

[2] Contrast the psychological method of James's *Varieties of Religious Experience* (1902) with the more Kantian method of the two books entitled *The Validity of Religious Experience* by A. C. Knudson (1937) and F. E. England (1938) and these in turn with W. E. Hocking's more Hegelian *The Meaning of God in Human Experience* (1912), or with D. E. Trueblood's mystical *The Trustworthiness of Religious Experience* (1939).

that I was in changing relations to objects not my consciousness (the house, outdoors, the operation of the heating system in the house and of the seasonal climate outside the house). It is most confusing to use the same word for two (or more) very different meanings. Hence we shall use "experience" to mean only the field of consciousness. It will apply to any and every item in that field, not to a set of privileged items, such as sensations or perceptions.[3]

John Dewey, it is true, stretches the term experience to include every event in nature which affects or may affect consciousness.[4] Language affords Dewey a certain basis for this usage when we say that the water experienced a change when it froze. But Dewey's treatment of experiencing and undergoing as synonyms tends to create the illusion of simplification, as if in some way direct consciousness and changes in objects become similar and well-ordered when these different meanings are reduced to one word. Perhaps consciousness and objects are of the same order of being; but it takes more than one word to prove it. While Dewey, of course, has taken far more than one word, his readers would be spared needless confusion if different words were used for different meanings. After all, there can be no doubt that immediate experience and the system of nature are not identical. Whenever we speak of nature, or of a single natural object, we always mean more than and other than anything we can possibly experience. Even if a part of a natural object can be immediately experienced, which the writer believes to be impossible,[5] the part that is so ex-

[3] Traditional empiricism (Hume's) should really be called sensationalism, on account of Hume's doctrine of impressions.

[4] See Dewey's Carus Lectures, *Experience and Nature* (1925), and his *Logic* (1938).

[5] See Brightman, ITP, 67–98, for a defense of epistemological dualism, the theory that objects known are always numerically distinct from the idea that knows them; consult Lovejoy, RAD, for a later and much fuller treatment of the same point of view. Holt (ed.), NR, is a standard attack on epistemological dualism and defense of the monistic position.

perienced is so small a part of the actual object (one's own body, for example, or a coin, or even an orange that one eats) that most of the object—the surfaces not visible or tangible and all of the interior of the object, including its atomic structure—lies beyond the range of direct experience.

The fact is, then, that our experience always refers beyond itself, sometimes to other possible experiences, sometimes to experiences which are only ideally possible (such as our perceptions of the other side of the moon), sometimes to experiences which are absolutely inaccessible (such as the past or the experience of other minds than our own), and sometimes to conceivable objects which are defined as not being experience at all (such as matter or number). The reference of our experience to something beyond its present range is far from being a proof that the object referred to (the referent) actually exists outside the realm of imagination or conceivable "essence." The critical realists are almost right in holding that existence is never given. Only our existent experience of the nature or essence present in experience is given; the object referred to lies beyond, and can be reached only by rational interpretation of or inference from what is given in experience.

When we refer to any supposed object (be it "real" or "imaginary") we are setting up what may be called a knowledge-claim. Every experience, whatever else it may be, always includes a knowledge-claim (or judgment) which refers to something beyond the experience.[6] When that reference is a spontaneous assertion of consciousness, it is called, as we have said, a knowledge-claim (Plato's opinion); when that reference is well-grounded in an examination of relevant evidence and of its logical relations, then it is called knowledge. Knowledge should not be taken to be synonymous with absolute certainty. In fact, all knowledge is

[6] See P. E. Wheelwright, "The Category of Self-Transcendence as an Essential Element in the Concept of Personality," in Brightman (ed.), P6IC, 121–128.

belief (more or less well-grounded) that the referent of the knowledge is as described. Certainty is a word that can apply, in the absolute logical sense, only to present experience while it is present. It is never so certain that we know any object correctly as it is that we are now conscious. Psychological or emotional certitude, of course, has no limits at all; one may feel emotionally certain of astrology or of theism or of atheism or of Hitlerism without either logical or empirical right to that certainty.

To summarize the postulates implied in these definitions: we experience only our present consciousness (whatever it may be); of this and this alone we are certain, as a Cartesian foundation of knowledge. Our experience always includes knowledge-claims, that is, reference to supposed objects beyond us—human persons, things, events, or gods. Knowledge-claims are never perfectly well-grounded; but when a reasonable degree of coherent empirical evidence and logical consistency supports belief in a knowledge-claim, we call it knowledge. No knowledge is absolutely certain; all knowledge is subject to revision. As Saint Paul once said, "We know in part." [7] The very essence of knowledge, whether in science or in philosophy, is to recognize its own incompleteness and to provide a method for further investigation. The so-called "pride of reason" is therefore out of harmony with the nature and spirit of knowledge.

When we are concerned, as in this chapter, with the knowledge of God, it is especially important to make clear from the start that there are special reasons for emphasizing the incompleteness and the (logical) uncertainty of any possible knowledge of God. If God is what theism takes him to be, the cosmic source of all nature and of all value experience, then complete and adequate knowledge of God would mean complete knowledge of all the evidence for

[7] 1 Cor. 13:9.

belief both in nature and in values and also complete rational understanding of their relations. Such knowledge is beyond us, although the lack of logical certainty does not prevent sincere devotion and even assurance about the religious referent.

On the other hand, this logical incompleteness and uncertainty may not properly be used as closing the door to investigation of evidence. A similar incompleteness and uncertainty attaches to all knowledge, even to the propositions of physics. The frequency with which new experiments lead to changes in theory should suffice to keep any physicist from dogmatic finality. Yet no physicist thinks of ceasing to experiment for the reason that his knowledge is incomplete. Indeed, the very incompleteness of his knowledge is the greatest possible spur to further research. So it is in philosophy of religion. Dogmatic finality is unattainable, but the very fact that we have not reached the end of religious knowledge leads the inquiring mind to further investigation. The conviction of nearly all good men through the ages, that ideal values are as truly objective as are sense perceptions, may not reasonably be rejected without examination.[8]

In the present chapter, then, it is our purpose to examine the bases of the various knowledge-claims of religious men when they have declared that they know God, and we shall call these claims "ways of knowing God." We shall first take up those ways of knowing God which arise within the religious experience itself, and then those which arise from a philosophical interpretation of that experience. Into the former group fall: (1) Immediate experience of God, (2) Revelation, and (3) Faith; into the latter: (4) A priori principles, (5) Action, and (6) Coherence. The chapter will close with further reflections on religious certainty.

[8] See Dinsmore, RCAS, 68.

§ 1. IMMEDIATE EXPERIENCE OF GOD

In the Introductory section it was said that the only certainty is our immediate experience of ourselves. Nevertheless, a great many religious individuals, especially the mystics, have asserted that they possessed an immediately certain experience of God. In Chapter II, § 9,[9] some account of mystical experience has already been given.

Of the traits of that experience, the most important for the knowledge of God is the one called by William James its noetic quality. The mystic believes that he knows God in an immediate and absolutely certain experience. The knowledge may be ineffable; in fact, all immediate experience is ineffable. No definition can tell what the quality of purple color is, or the odor of a rose; one who tries to tell of such matters can only hope that his words will be addressed to one who has had a similar experience. Otherwise the words are meaningless. So is it with experience of God. If one has experienced the presence of God, and the relation of the soul to God called the *unio mystica,* one cannot describe the mystical moment in concepts intelligible to a person who has never felt the divine presence.

Almost every human being has at some time or other felt himself lost in the presence of some overwhelming beauty or goodness or truth so immediate and convincing as to cause him to say: This is the high point of my life, yet it is more than that; it is the presence of something truly real that is higher than the highest I could have thought of if the real had not given itself to me. It is, in a word, the very presence of God. Whatever language one uses to describe the experience and whether one names the name of God or not,

[9] The devotional and psychological literature there cited may well be consulted again in this connection. In connection with the present chapter read especially Montague, WK, 54–68, and Knudson, VRE, 56–97. For a hostile treatment of mysticism see the chapter on the subject in Russell, RS.

there is no doubt that the experience itself is one that men in every civilization and every stage of religion and irreligion have enjoyed. When it is emotionally intense, prolonged, ecstatic, and dominant, the subject is a great mystic; but the most practical secularist has his mystical moments, however valiantly his hard head may resist them.

The mystical moment is an intuitive apprehension of God. It may be, and often is, preceded by a prolonged discipline of a moral, aesthetic, intellectual, or ascetic nature, but when it comes, all these preparatory exercises disappear. They are like props knocked away when the structure is completed. The mystic may prepare for the divine coming as he pleases, but when the mystical moment arrives, God is there. God and the soul are one. "Rejoice with me, for I have become God."

William James says that the theoretical outcome of mysticism is optimism and monism.[10] To these should be added epistemological immediacy. In order to understand mysticism as a way of knowing God, something must be said about each of these three points, beginning with the last named.

Mysticism, first of all, is an assertion of epistemological immediacy. Mystics declare that experience itself is knowledge and that God himself is actually present in the soul, so that what is human and what is divine in the experience are indivisibly one and indistinguishable. From the standpoint of theory of knowledge, this is a form of epistemological monism, in which idea and object are both God. It is very difficult, however, to take this claim literally. At any rate, there are apparently actual differences in the mystical experiences of Hindus, Friends, and Catholic mystics. And even if these differences are ignored, it could not be said by the most extreme mystic that his supposed union with God

[10] James, VRE, 416.

gave him an identity with all of God's knowledge, power, and character. It is more modest and more probable to say that the mystic's knowledge-claim, although exaggerated in many respects, and false in so far as it asserts identity with the divine, furnishes nevertheless important data regarding the objective source of value. No one can deny that mystic experiences occur, and it is hard to deny that they disclose aspects of the real which are not products of human will and so in some sense are objective.

What aspects of the real are discovered? William James, as we saw, thought that the discoveries are optimism and monism. Both of these words, alas, are ambiguous, and neither of them is fully consistent with all the facts of mystical experience. If optimism means that evil is only illusion and that everything real is entirely and beautifully good, then the mysticism of some forms of Hinduism and of Christian Science is optimistic. But when one contemplates the awe-inspiring and tragic factors in the mysticism of Jacob Boehme or William Blake or Rudolf Otto, one sees that the word optimism is a pale description of the mystical apprehension of the depths of reality. So, too, with monism. If monism means that everything real is one being, and that there is only one spirit, God, of whom we are but parts, then again some forms of Indian mysticism and some mystical occidental pantheism is monistic. But Ramanuja was a theistic Indian mystic, who met popular Indian theories of the dissolution of personality into the All with the very sensible problem: "When you say, 'Consciousness itself is a proof,' tell also whose consciousness, and for whom. If it is not a proof of something and for someone, it is no proof at all." [11] In other words, consciousness is always personal, and one person cannot be another. The unity of personality stands

[11] Translated from R. Otto, *Siddanta des Ramanuja* (Tübingen: J. C. B. Mohr, 1923), 55.

in the way of a cosmic monism, not only for Ramanuja, but also for the Friends, and for large numbers of theistic mystics.

Is there then no truth in James's statement that mysticism, as a way of knowing, leads to optimism and monism? It is not necessary by any means to reject them entirely merely because they are stated in exaggerated form. If optimism be taken in a less extreme sense, and be defined as the view which holds that value is objective and dominant in the universe, then mysticism is always and everywhere optimistic. And if monism be not identified with pantheism, but be taken to mean the view that a unitary spirit of good controls the universe, then mysticism is always and everywhere monistic.

To summarize this survey of mysticism as a way of knowing God, we may say: (1) that mystical experience is immediate, but cannot be called immediate experience of God; it is rather an immediate experience of the self which may be taken as a sign of the reality of God, provided philosophical thought finds this idea tenable; (2) that mysticism is not necessarily optimistic in the sense of denying all tragedy or evil, but is optimistic as a present experience of the dominance of good over evil; and (3) that it is not necessarily monistic in the sense of pantheism or absolutism, but is monistic in the sense of being "a vision of the world's unity." Thus mystic intuition furnishes data which no philosophy can ignore; even if no actual values were experienced by the mystic (a supposition impossible to defend), at least it is clear that he proposes possible hypotheses about the cosmos which are close to the pantheistic and theistic conceptions of God. Philosophers have to explore all possible hypotheses, and would be guilty of false sentimentalism if they failed to investigate any hypothesis merely because it is in some sense optimistic and monistic.

§ 2.   REVELATION

The mystics, as we have seen, lay claim to an immediate knowledge of God within the human soul.   They start from a view which postulates, and carries to an extreme, the idea of the nearness of God to man—a view often called the immanence of God.   Other religious groups have started from very different postulates.   They have usually assumed that the God that religion worships and seeks to know is entirely external to man, that is, transcendent.   They distrust the powers of human reason and the range of human experience.   They might agree with our proposition that man experiences only himself, and then infer from this that man by his own powers can never discover or experience God. God, according to these thinkers—Calvinists, Barthians, Mohammedans, Mormons, Christian Scientists, and some Catholics—would remain forever unknown, or forever only an unverified guess, an entity whose plans and nature were hidden from us, unless he revealed himself.   He is "totally other" (*totaliter aliter*) than man; man's nature and experience contain no clue to him unless and until God speaks. What he speaks is called "revelation," or "The Word."   The sacred scriptures of Hinduism, Buddhism, and Zoroastrianism, as well as of Christianity and Islam, are believed by the adherents of each of these religions to contain a revelation of God which human reason and experience could never have invented, one "free from the contamination of human hypotheses" (as Christian Scientists put it).[12]

Belief in revelation is not always held in so extreme a form as has just been stated; but it has been and is held in that

12 The Christian Scientists' view of revelation is especially interesting.   No one holds to the divine immanence more strongly than they do, and they might be expected to accept mysticism combined with some form of rationalism.   On the contrary, they hold to a rigidly authoritarian revelation.   This may perhaps be explained by their doctrine of mortal mind.   Human hypotheses fall in the realm

form so widely as to merit examination as a way of knowing God. It is open to the obvious objection as to how one may choose from among conflicting revelation-claims. The radical believer in revelation sees that if reason is allowed to creep in to discriminate one revelation-claim from another, then reason becomes the criterion of truth and revelation loses its supreme authority. Hence it is usually said that the soul is led by the Divine Spirit to accept the true revelation, by an act of supernatural faith. The extremes of this position have alienated men like John Dewey so completely from traditional religion that they have abandoned an evolutionary for a revolutionary view of religion.[13] Those who hold the view are most tenacious of it, whether Christians or non-Christians, Protestants or Catholics.

The men who at present are most prominent in dwelling on revelation as the true way of knowing God, and therefore insist on the superiority of theology to philosophy of religion, are Karl Barth (whom we have already mentioned), Emil Brunner, and Paul Tillich. These men are no superficial dogmatists. They are scholars of distinction and men for whom religious experience is a reality. They cannot be dismissed lightly, whatever our predispositions may be.

One of the favorite expressions of Barth regarding revelation is that it comes "senkrecht von oben" (perpendicularly from above). That means, it is no outgrowth of human striving and no discovery of God within man; it is a gift from God himself. Emil Brunner expresses the same idea when he declares that Christian faith differs fundamentally from all philosophy. Philosophy rests on "the complex of grounds and consequences developed by natural reason,"

of mortal mind; and divine mind is indeed totally other than it. Étienne Gilson's *Reason and Revelation in the Middle Ages* is a beautiful exposition of views held by Christian philosophers during the mediaeval period. Recent conceptions are summarized in Baillie and Martin, *Revelation.*

[13] See Dewey, CF, beginning on p. 1.

whereas Christian faith recognizes "that this complex has been broken into" by revelation.[14] Paul Tillich is decidedly more philosophical than either Barth or Brunner; yet on the first page of his treatment of philosophy of religion he says:

If philosophy of religion does not consider the revelation-claim of religion, it misses its object and doesn't deal with real religion. If it recognizes the revelation-claim, it becomes theology. . . . Revelation is the breaking-through of the unconditioned into the world of the conditioned.[15]

Such statements constitute a direct challenge to philosophical modes of thought and appear to create an absolute antithesis: *either* revelation *or* reason. It is on account of this radical opposition to reason and experience that we classed the Barthian view among the revolutionary conceptions of God in Chapter V. Yet in spite of the apparently antirational character of this view and its extreme supernaturalism, the statement of Tillich leaves at least one point of contact with philosophical thought when he asserts the obligation of philosophy to consider revelation-claims. Religious men and women have always believed that through their religious experiences they gained supernatural values and truths, that is, values and truths which are not given in the order of our sense perceptions. If sense experience be called natural and experience of ideal values be called supernatural, then religion is indeed supernatural revelation. Every experience that arises with a claim to reveal divine values ought to be impartially surveyed by reason and its claims appraised. Yet it would be fatal to rational integrity to grant that the mind should trust the Divine Spirit to guide it to accept the right revelation in the absence of reasons or evidence; for then

---

[14] Brunner. PR. 13.

[15] Tillich in Dessoir, PEG, 769, 770. Translated by the present writer. For a very different treatment, see Montague, WK, 39–53.

there would be no way whatever of telling the voice of God from the voice of the devil.

In order to clarify the problem of revelation as it is viewed by thinkers of various religions and standpoints, it is useful to distinguish between two views of the subject, which correspond only roughly to the difference between what are popularly called fundamentalism and modernism. These two views may be called the dogmatic or intellectualistic and the teleological or dynamic.[16]

The word dogmatic has here no invidious connotation. It does not mean that its proponents are irrational beings who refuse to think and who make dogmatic assertions without reasons. It means rather that they believe the essence of revelation to consist in the communication of supernatural and infallible truths or dogmas. These truths are usually thought of as propositions which the natural reason could never arrive at by reflection on ordinary experience, but which in no way contradict natural reason or experience. Christian believers in the dogmatic view of revelation point to the doctrines of the Incarnation and of the Trinity as examples of such revelation; Mohammedans, to a mass of concrete information about the future life; Hindus, to a doctrine of many incarnations as contrasted with the Christian dogma of a single and unique Incarnation of God in Jesus Christ. To any sincere believer it is perhaps painful to see the revelation-claims of the other religions placed on a level with those of his own religion, but it is a fact that equal claims are made by conflicting religions to the possession of revealed dogmas. This dogmatic view of revelation is also called intellectualistic because it treats revelation as being essentially the communication of ideas, that is, intellectual content, from the divine mind to selected and receptive human minds. It is doubtless this aspect of the

[16] See "The Way of Revelation," Chap. II of Brightman, FG.

view which once led Professor Wilhelm Herrmann to re-mark in conversation that "orthodoxy is too rationalistic." By a curious freak of thought, however, Karl Barth, reput-edly the most orthodox Protestant theologian of the present time, does not accept the intellectualistic theory of revela-tion. According to him, no human thought can ever grasp the content of the divine revelation; not dogma, but the majestic Will of God is revealed, and it is not rationally apprehended, but rather is felt as an overwhelming power.

In contrast with the dogmatic view, as was said, is the teleological or dynamic theory of revelation. According to this view, which is in some form accepted by most "liberal" or modernistic theists, the essence of revelation is not the communication of infallible truths; instead it is the guidance of human life to higher levels by divine power. To be more exact, it means the belief that, although God does not impart dogmatic eternal truths to men's minds in some supernatural way, yet the divine purpose so acts on human history that men are given impulses which lead them to move toward God. Those who hold this theory think in terms of spiritual stimulus and response, and so of divine-human coöperation, rather than in terms of divinely revealed creeds. It is clear why this view is called dynamic. It is not that there is no "dynamic power" in dogmatism; there undoubtedly is. But the dynamic view makes revelation an experience of the power and active purpose of God rather than an experience of God's knowledge. According to the teleologists (or "dynamists," as we may call them), knowledge must always be built up and tested by reason on the basis of data of ex-perience. Experience, on this view, includes many factors which are revelatory in the sense of being purposed by God in order to lead men to higher values; yet all of these factors must be interpreted by reason, and the interpretation is hu-man thinking, not divine dogma.

For the dogmatist, revelation means the communication of truth from God to man. If two men lay claim to having received revelation and the revelation of one contradicts that of the other, only one of the two "revelations" can be true. Only he who possesses the true dogma knows God; and only he possesses it to whom God has revealed it or who has learned it from some fortunate recipient of revelation. For the dynamist, however, revelation is the communicating of power and purpose, rather than truth. On this premise, if two men have contradictory ideas about God—one a revolutionary humanist and the other an evolutionary theist—both may be recipients of revelation and both may be moving in the direction of the divine purpose. If God's purpose is the development of a coöperative society of honest and good men, it is not essential to that purpose that these men agree in all points. It is essential only that they be truth-lovers and lovers of ideal value.

It is clear that the dynamic view attaches more importance to reason in revelation than does the dogmatic. Dynamists would for the most part endorse John Locke's statement in Book IV of his famous *Essay*. "He that takes away reason to make way for revelation," says Locke (xix, 4), "puts out the light of both." The dynamic view, however, does not imply that the use of reason leads to perfect intellectual insight about God. It implies only, as Kant said in his letter to Johann Caspar Lavater,[17] that "God necessarily has some supplementation of our defects hidden in the depths of his counsels, which we may humbly trust, if only we do as much as is in our power." Thus revelation for the dynamist requires man's rational response to divine impulses, but it does not require or yield infallible information.

A further distinction needs to be made if thought about revelation is to be clarified, namely, that between so-called

[17] Dated April 28, 1775.

"general" and "special" revelation. General revelation is that which is accessible under normal conditions at all times to all men. Special revelation, as the word indicates, is that which occurs only under special circumstances or at special times. There is no particular difficulty in recognizing both types of revelation, if there is any revelation at all. There are recurring and constantly accessible forms of truth about moral and spiritual values. But every person has also been aware of special moments of insight and illumination, special stirrings of his being toward God. The difficulty arises when it comes to identifying and evaluating the normative special revelations. It is at this point, fully as much as in the cleavage between dogmatic and dynamic views, that the rift between fundamentalists and modernists appears. The fundamentalist (in any religion) will tend to restrict special revelation to the holy scriptures of his own faith; while the modernist will tend to find various degrees of special revelation in all sincere forms of faith. The affiliation of Karl Barth with orthodoxy against modernism appears most sharply here; for he regards the special revelation of the first century of our era as being exclusively normative for us.

In view of the variety of opinion about revelation, may we still say that it is a way of knowing God? The reader must answer that question for himself. The dogmatist will tell him that special revelation has imparted infallible knowledge about God so important and true that all general revelation pales before it. The dynamist will tell him that no revelation, general or special, is a source of final or infallible knowledge, yet that all revelatory experience is a source of knowledge about the purpose of God for the creation and continuation of values.

§ 3. FAITH

A third way of knowing God from the point of view of religion, in addition to immediate experience and revelation,

is faith.[18] It seems evident that God is not known either
by pure reason (formal logic, mathematics) or by sense experience; or if "pure" reason and sense data enter into
knowledge of God, they certainly do not yield such knowledge apart from experience of values. God is believed to
be the supreme value, at once the source and goal of human
values. Our knowledge of values is very different from our
knowledge of logic or of sense data, so different that many
writers [19] hold that we cannot rightly speak of knowledge of
values at all. Yet religious experients in all ages have felt
assurance of a religious knowledge through faith. What,
then, is faith?

The word faith, or its equivalents in other languages, has
been used in at least three different senses. It has been taken
to mean: (1) acceptance of revelation; (2) a gift of God; and
(3) trust or obedience.

The predominant conception in the universal religions
has been that (1) *faith is acceptance of revelation,* in spite of
the almost complete absence of the idea from both the Old
Testament and the teachings of Jesus. According to W.
Morgan in ERE, this conception first appeared definitely
in Christianity in the book of Acts. "Believe on the Lord
Jesus, and thou shalt be saved" (Acts 16:31) seems to mean:
Accept the revelation of God in Christ and salvation is assured. Whether or not this was the original meaning of
the words, they soon were thus interpreted. The *regula
fidei* (rule of faith) of the early Church, resting on the dogmatic view of revelation, set forth the minimum essential
propositions of revealed dogma. This view of faith is intellectualistic; for it, faith is, as Saint Augustine said, *cum assen-
sione cogitare.*[20] (cognition with assent). In this sense, faith
is really not a distinct way of knowing God. Its difference

---

[18] See the articles in ERE on "Faith" and "Bhakti Marga."
[19] Such as logical positivists. See Ayer, LTL.
[20] *De praedestinatione sanctorum,* 5.

from other kinds of knowledge consists only of its object, the content of revelation. It is intellectual knowledge of revelation accompanied by belief.

In contrast to this first view, which prevails not only in the Roman Catholic Church, but also among many Protestants, as well as among Mohammedans and some sects of Buddhists, there is the conception of (2) *faith as a gift of God*. The first view regards man as active in accepting revelation; the second regards him as passive in receiving it. In Christianity, this conception goes back to Saint Paul, who wrote of gifts of the Spirit, and then treated faith, hope, and love as "the greater gifts" (1 Cor. 12:31, 13:13). Calvinists and modern Barthians regard faith in this light. "By grace have ye been saved through faith: and that not of yourselves, it is the gift of God" (Eph. 2:8). This point of view carried to an extreme leads to the Calvinistic doctrine of predestination, that faith is given only to those who are foreordained to be elect.

If faith is a supernatural gift, without human activity or responsibility, it is a unique and miraculous way of knowing, in a new dimension of life utterly beyond reason. If reason conflicts with it, reason must be wrong. The same conclusion follows if the first definition of faith be accepted. Human reason would not be competent to criticize a gift of God or a divine revelation. It could only appropriate and apply the one or the other. These two views of faith, then, create the famous cleft between faith and reason.

There remains the conception of (3) *faith as trust or obedience*. W. Morgan, in the article on "Faith" in ERE, writes that "the notion of trust is, indeed, vital for religion, but it has played no part in theological controversy." Perhaps this is true because trust is at once so necessary to religion and so reasonable that it cannot well be challenged. Trust presupposes something trustworthy; thus it is a value-word. Religiously, it means confident loyalty to what is believed to be of true value. Obedience likewise is a value-word; it presupposes an authority that is acknowledged as justified in demanding obedience. Religious obedience means action in accordance with what is believed to be the supreme authority. Both trust and obedience are usually thought of as directed toward God, and both are attitudes of will.

According to this conception of faith, there is no reason why the religious man should regard any experience as a valid revelation-claim or should treat any experience as a supernatural gift of God unless that experience commends itself to his reason as embodying ideal value. Then, and then only, does the attitude of faith set in; and its function is not to discover occult truths inaccessible to ordinary intelligence, but rather to act on the highest available truths about value. Faith in this sense is very close to what Kant meant by the practical reason; in spirit it is also akin to the scientific (and pragmatic) method—the method of trying loyally the best prospective experiment, and turning to a better if that fails.

Faith, therefore, is in no conflict with reason. On the contrary, without its experimental method reason has no adequate object; and without rational checks, faith has no consistency and undergoes no verification. Faith thus needs reason, and reason faith. Pascal's passionate cry that "the heart has reasons which the head does not know," taken literally, is a demand for a dual personality and for a contradictory "truth." It is the duty of reason to examine all the evidence. All religious evidence, whether of revelation or of gifts of God or of the heart, must pass under the scrutiny of reason in order to test whether it introduces chaos or order into experience. The advantage of the third, and most truly religious, conception of faith is that it directs purpose toward religious values without committing itself to any one intellectual definition of religion or of God as alone valid. In short, it dispenses with the *sacrificium intellectus*. At the same time, as a principle of action, it is to be distinguished from the Platonic "faith" (πίστις) which is an "affection occurring in the soul" below reason and understanding, yet above mere conjecture.[21] Faith is not to be defined in contrast either to reason or to certainty, but rather in contrast to unfaith, or disloyalty to the highest known values. Thus faith as trust and obedience appears also to be a form of knowledge in the famous "pragmatic" saying of the Johannine Jesus: "If any man willeth to do his will, he shall know of the teaching, whether it is of God, or whether I speak of myself" (Jn. 7:17). Similar conceptions occur in the Bhakti Marga of Hinduism and Buddhism.

By way of summary, it may be said that faith is taken to be a way of knowing God in three senses: (1) as an acknowledgment of revelation; (2) as a supernatural gift of God to man; and (3) as trust in and obedience to the highest values. In the first two senses, faith is the apprehension of a unique supernatural content. In the third sense, it is a method rather than a content; it may be called the experimental method taken whole-heartedly and applied to values.

§ 4. A Priori Principles

The three typical ways of knowing God which we have thus far discussed are immediate experience, revelation, and faith. These ways have in common the trait of being empirical in the special sense of assuming that some particular experience, a divine moment, is to be taken as bringing man into touch with God, and so as being normative for the whole life. Yet our examination of the knowledge-claims of these experiences has left us unconvinced of their authority; at least, if they have authority in their own right,

[21] Plato, *Rep.* 511DE.

it is one which reason cannot affirm without an investigation against which the extreme mystic, the dogmatic revelationist, and the authoritarian fideist, rebels. Yet we found in all these ways of knowing God something amenable to reason. All immediate experience must be acknowledged and interpreted by reason. The dynamic view of revelation stands in the light of a rational perspective, and faith as trust and obedience refers to ideals acknowledged by reason. Reason thus becomes a way of knowing God—what Royce calls a "source of religious insight."

Reason is, however, no simple entity. In fact, there are several different conceptions of what reason is, two of which are of prime importance for religion. The first (first to dominate religious thought) may be called the Aristotelian-Kantian. The second is the Platonic-Hegelian.[22] Those who hold to the Aristotelian-Kantian view define reason as a priori knowledge. "Rational knowledge and knowledge a priori are one and the same." [23] By an a priori principle is meant a principle which is necessary if a specific class of experiences in a given universe of discourse is to be possible. It is not absolutely necessary that any particular universe of discourse must be; there is no logical necessity that this world or that number must be; but if either is, or if any realm of ordered being is, there are certain principles without which it could not be at all. Deny unity, and there

[22] The reader may be somewhat surprised by this grouping. He may be inclined to say that Plato is closer to Kant than to Hegel, and Aristotle closer to Hegel than to Kant. This is true in many respects. But the terms in the text are built up with reference to logical method. Aristotle's logic was the basis of Kant's critical method; both were predominantly based on class terms, their analysis and necessary deductions from them. Kant's categories were concepts (*Begriffe*), and Kant was better able to deal with the analysis of the mind into separate faculties than with its fundamental unity. Plato and Hegel, on the other hand, were essentially synoptic philosophers, with a primary interest in wholeness and the totality of mind, experience, and reality. See above, Chap. I, § 1.

[23] Kant's *Theory of Ethics* (tr. Abbott), 261. Quoted by Knudson in Wilm (ed.), SPT, 97.

are no numbers. Deny space or time, and there is no world. Deny obligation and there is no morality. Since each a priori is thus relative to a special realm and lacks apodictic certainty, philosophers like Bowne and Knudson speak of it as an ideal. A cognitive ideal or a priori is thought of as presupposed by science; a religious (or ethical) ideal is presupposed by religion.[24] Thinkers who hold this view regard both science and religion as "autonomously valid."

In contrast to this Aristotelian-Kantian view is the Platonic-Hegelian. Representatives of this view deny that any a priori principle is to be regarded as more than relatively autonomous. They do not define reason as consisting of a priori principles, much less of autonomous ones; they regard it as the one principle of coherence, synopsis, or totality. Hegel's saying, "The true is the whole," [25] is the key to this conception of reason. For it, the only truly autonomous a priori principle is the ideal of taking all realms of experience into account in their systematic interrelations and in their totality.

Just now we are especially interested in the Aristotelian-Kantian group of thinkers, as we have called them. They hold that religious knowledge rests on a priori principles, and hence they are called religious apriorists. The leading member of this group in America is the learned and astute theologian, Albert C. Knudson. He holds that the religious a priori connotes a "native religious capacity" of the mind, which is "original and underivable" and hence autonomous.[26] This theory treats religion as being grounded in the nature of the mind in essentially the same way as are science, morality, and art.[27] Knudson's form of the view

---

[24] Knudson, DG, 81–82.
[25] *Phenomenology of Mind,* 81.
[26] See the previous discussion of apriorism in Chap. I, § 2. The phrases quoted are from Knudson, VRE, 166.
[27] Ibid., 174.

rests, as we saw in Chapter I, on a psychological rather than a rationalistic or logical interpretation of the a priori.

The chapter in which Knudson expounds his view is headed "Self-Verification." This expression appears to imply that religion is independently true, regardless of other experiences and interests. It carries its own verification with it. Knudson cites Bowne's well-known statement:

Whatever the mind demands for the satisfaction of its subjective interests and tendencies may be assumed as real in default of positive disproof.[28]

Religious apriorism has a sturdy simplicity, rational vigor, and religious confidence which make it attractive to many minds. Yet members of the Platonic-Hegelian group, while sympathizing with its clarity and force, regard it as unsatisfactory. It seems to them artificially simple and overanalytic. Hegel would call it abstract. After all, no phase of human experience is fundamentally autonomous or independent of other phases. Bowne's willingness to assume the mind's demands as real "in default of positive disproof" seems to be too lax a standard. The mere absence of contradiction is far from sufficient a basis for believing any claim that the mind sets up. Absence of disproof proves nothing. Presence of proof is required. Proof, of course, is not to be identified with what Matthew Arnold satirized as "rigor and vigor." Absolute proof is impossible. Such probable proof as we can attain and must demand for our fundamental convictions requires that no psychological claim, however native and inherent it may be in the mind, can be accepted as true until its coherence, its systematic connection with a rational view of the rest of experience, has been established. Bowne and Knudson appear to find an autonomy in religion which rightly be-

[28] Bowne, THE, 18; cited in Knudson, VRE, 176.

longs to no experience—to scientific and to moral as little as to religious experience. All autonomy is limited by the claims of the whole, just as states' rights are limited by the Federal Constitution and private rights by the principle of eminent domain.

The mind is a whole and truth is a whole. Religious faith must be justified, if at all, not by innateness nor by historical universality, but rather by such coherent and harmonious relations to all other aspects of experience as serve to establish its right to an integral place in the realm of truth.

If, then, an a priori religious principle is proposed, it must be regarded critically, as Knudson points out in his chapter. We go further. Perhaps it is no more than a rationalization—a name for the soul's intense desire that there be a God and a friendly universe. Such a principle, indeed, must be if religion is true; but it affords no sufficient insight into the fundamental question: Do we know God?

§ 5. ACTION

In opposition to the rationalists who lay claim to knowing God through a priori principles are the pragmatists who assert that the only way to know God is through action. The pragmatic movement,[29] since its somewhat abortive birth in 1878, has become one of the most influential philosophical currents in contemporary America. It has

---

[29] Pragmatism originated in America. Its first formulation was by Charles S. Peirce in his article, "How to Make our Ideas Clear," *Pop. Sci. Monthly,* 12(1878), 286-302 (see his *Collected Papers,* edited by Hartshorne and Weiss, 248-271). He coined the term pragmatism, and gave as his first definition of its maxim the formula: "Consider what effects, that might conceivably have practical bearings, we conceive the object of our conception to have. Then, our conception of these effects is the whole of our conception of the object" (258). William James, F. C. S. Schiller, and John Dewey have been the most famous thinkers to develop this point of view. For a survey of pragmatism, see Rogers, EAP, 359-410. For criticism see Brightman, ITP, 50-58; and note the bibliography, ibid., 368-369; see also Montague, WK, 131-172.

not been confined to academic philosophy, but has exerted its influence on the American system of public education, on the arts, on literature, on social theory, and on religion.

The interest of our present investigation centers not on the historical debates about pragmatism but on the use of the pragmatic method as a means of knowing God. Taking Peirce's rule of identifying an object with the effects that we conceive the object to have, then we should identify God, or a cathedral, with the effects which we conceive **God, or a cathedral,** to have. Thus a cathedral is an object which produces certain sense impressions, which arouses aesthetic reactions, and which leads the believer into a mood of worship. God is an object which arouses faith, unity of life, and loyalty to ideals. These statements are true, whether a cathedral or God is "real" or "imaginary." No one, to the writer's knowledge, ever has questioned that the experienced practical effects of an object are facts which ought to be taken into account. It is true that a pure apriorist, who relies on universal a priori principles rather than on particular empirical facts for his knowledge of God, would not attach primary importance to the effects of the idea of God on human action. Those effects, he would say, are possible only if faith or reason establishes a priori the real being of God. But he would grant that the effects are real and are to be given whatever weight should be given to empirical evidence.

If there is no difference about the duty of taking practical consequences into account, why does not everyone accept pragmatism? Is not action a way of knowing? Is not pragmatism essentially the same as the experimental method? [30] How do we ever find out anything except by acting, by seeing what we can do to objects and what objects do to us? Does not religion itself essentially rest on an ap-

[30] See the discussion of the operational method in Bridgman, LMP.

peal to action? God does not mean a theorem: he means activities which we call goodness, truth, beauty, and worship. Surely, those who are seeking to know all that can be known about God must observe the kind of action that follows from our conception of God. Much argument is empty because it ignores the plain empirical mandate to consult experience.

Nevertheless, difficulties arise when the pragmatic way of knowing God is taken, as it often is, to be the only way of knowing. These difficulties arise partly from the ambiguities in pragmatism. If action is the road to truth, does any and all action give us truth? Surely not everything that could be done in a laboratory is an experiment; much less is everything that is done in life fruitful for knowledge of God. Again, if pragmatism means that the true is the practical, we may well ask the old question, "What does pragmatism mean by practical?" If we consult Schiller, he tells us that whatever satisfies human needs is practical. But needs is a slippery word, made more slippery if stretched to cover all of human nature. If, however, we consult Dewey, we are guided away from Schiller's humanism to a more biological view; the practical means whatever tends to adjust our organism to its environment. The decisive action is thus organic. But adjust is another vague word here. What one person would regard as satisfactory adjustment, another would not.

Difficulties also arise from the vagueness of pragmatism about objectivity. Much that pragmatists say sounds as if our ways of experimenting actually make our truth and objects; and we are warned by Professor Dewey against accepting any "antecedent reality." [31] At the same time, pragmatists do assume a real, objective world of nature and a society which can make "public" verifications. The for-

[31] See Dewey, QC, passim.

mer tendency points toward a purely subjective God which we make as we go; the latter tends also to exclude an objective God from its postulates, by assuming naturalism as the theoretical framework for pragmatism. On the other hand, Schiller's humanism is in some danger of giving everyone just the kind of objective God he wants. Pragmatism thus oscillates between too subjective and too objective a view of God.

Without retracting our admission that action is a source of knowledge about God, we now repeat that action cannot be the only way of knowing because, by its very nature, it is not thought, but is only a datum for thought. The goals of action, the kinds of action, and the instruments of action must all be defined and evaluated by thought. Thought cannot survive as a set of abstract, a priori categories; neither can action survive as "blind empirical groping" (to quote Kant), and no one really supposes that it can. Actual experience is never mere action, much less mere thought. It is concrete, living union of form and content. Pragmatism is right in condemning abstract intellectualism; its critics are equally right in condemning abstract empiricism. Concrete empiricism must include not only action and experiment, but also rational interpretation of them.

§ 6. COHERENCE

The criticism of a priori principles led to a distinction between the Aristotelian-Kantian and the Platonic-Hegelian conceptions of reason. The criticism of pragmatic action led to insight into the need of supplementing the practical by the rational. We are now ready to consider reason, or coherence, as a way of knowing God.

First of all, let us make clear exactly what is meant by coherence in this connection. We are thinking of coherence as a "way of knowing" God, that is, as a way of discovering and testing truth about God. Readers of philosophy are familiar with a "coherence theory" which is a form of absolutistic metaphysics. With this we are not now concerned. Our interest is rather in coherence as a criterion of truth. Also it needs to be made clear that we are not dealing with coherence as merely theoretical consistency. It is certain that theories may be self-consistent, yet irrelevant to and incoherent with experienced facts. The coherence that we are talking about must, of course, exclude theoretical inconsistency, but consistency of theories is not enough for it. In addition to consistency among our theories, coherence requires two other attributes: first, consistency between our theories and the facts of experience, and secondly, systematic relatedness which discovers connections, laws, and purposes. Consistency is mere absence of contradiction; coherence is presence of relation.

As applied to religion, coherence is a much more rigorous way of knowing than mere consistency would be. It is fairly easy to see that there can be no logical inconsistency between observed facts and the belief that there is a God; God would be one more fact, and facts cannot be inconsistent. It is not so easy to see that there is coherent relation between the observed facts and belief in God. To say, for example, that the theory of evolution is consistent with belief in God, because evolution is God's way of working is a perfectly logical statement, free from contradiction. It is self-consistent; but is it coherent? Is it possible to show, in detail, a relation between the supposed goodness of God and the structure of the evolutionary facts?

The Schoolmen of the Middle Ages were on the whole satisfied with consistency. Formal logic was their great instrument. When modern science arose, it created a problem for traditional belief in God partly because it used methods and arrived at results inconsistent with the faith.

But it constituted an even greater challenge to theism because its results appeared to be quite irrelevant to the sacred doctrines. What has the Copernican astronomy or the law of falling bodies to do with any conception of God, especially with the God of revelation? This seeming lack of relation, this irrelevancy, this incoherence, lies at the very heart of the problem of God. For, after all, if there is a God who is to be known in any way by man, and if that God is to be of any importance to man and to human values, then it must be shown not merely that the idea of God is free from contradiction with itself and with known facts, but also that the idea of God is organically related to the facts and is needed in order to interpret them coherently. If there is not positive harmony between the facts and the conception of God, mere absence of contradiction will leave us cold, and rightly so. To assert God is to assert cosmic purpose; but it is futile to assert it with formal correctness unless the facts can be connected in detail with the asserted purpose. Thus, belief in a theistic God is an assertion of a metaphysically coherent universe, a universe organized by rational purpose for the realization of rational values.

If we are to know such a God, coherent reason is the way of knowing most suited to the problem. In fact, coherence must be the arbiter of all the other ways of knowing. Each immediate religious experience must be set in relation with our total range of experience and thought; untested experience is not trustworthy. Revelation-claims must all be judged by their coherence with our whole view of life. Faith must be seen in relation to its results, its functions, and its relations to actual experience. A priori principles cannot even be known to be a priori unless they are necessary for a coherent universe of discourse; and any such universe must be related to other possible universes and criticized with regard to its coherence. Action offers data which are mere brute facts or unsolved problems until they are interpreted by coherent rational thought and are related to the whole of our conscious resources. Accordingly, reason—concrete and inclusively empirical, not merely abstract and formal—is the supreme source of religious insight, the supreme way of knowing about God, whether he is, or whether he is not.[32]

It may appear to some readers that the present discussion is a plea for the Platonic-Hegelian against the Aristotelian-Kantian view of reason; that is, for coherence against consistency.[33] That this is not true follows from the very nature of each. Consistency does not demand coherence; hence Kant could be satisfied with his perfectly consistent, but almost perfectly incoherent, theory of phenomenal mechanism and noumenal freedom, or with his similar sharp division of the mind into sensibility, understanding, and reason, or with his conflict between speculative and practical reason. We repeat: although consistency does not demand coherence, coherence presupposes, requires, and includes consistency. To define reason as coherence is not to exclude consistency, but to demand it, and then to add to it relations, structure, and wholeness.

To other readers it may seem that the present appeal to coherence is a defection from the empirical method that was avowed in the first chapter. This would also be a misapprehension. To demand coherence is to demand full attention to all the facts of experience, to neglect none, in short, to "save the appearances," as Simplicius said in his

---

[32] See Royce, SRI, 79–116, on "The Office of the Reason." Also, Flewelling, RIF. Gilson, RRMA, should again be consulted at this point.

[33] It should be noted that both in Aristotle and in Kant there are clear traces of the coherence criterion. The contrasted pairs of names in the text are not intended as absolutely complete characterizations of the men, but as just descriptions of the main logical interest of each.

commentary on Aristotle's *De coelo*. Coherence is no repudiation of empiricism. It is simply an insistence that empiricism must be complete, well-ordered, clearly defined, and rationally interpreted.

There are at least three stages in any coherent philosophy of the knowing process. The first stage is that of gathering all the facts. The facts include the prescientific data of experience, and also their scientific formulation. Thus in knowing about God, all the facts of religious experience would be considered, plus the investigation of them by history, psychology, and sociology; further, all the facts of nature and of the natural sciences would have to be included and related to the more specifically religious facts. Thus our experiences of value and our experiences of nature and the facts about their relations would be collected in this first stage. The second stage is the construction of some working hypothesis to interpret the facts; hypotheses both regarding methods and regarding meanings would have to be tried. The third stage is the verification (or falsification) of the hypotheses, which is carried out in philosophy by relating the data to the hypotheses and considering whether the hypotheses include all of the data, and whether they organize all of the data coherently. Thus the hypothesis that God lives as an exalted human being on Mount Olympus is easily refuted by climbing Mount Olympus and finding neither God nor heaven there. The more abstruse hypothesis (of Epicurus) that the gods live in the interstellar spaces is refuted both by its failure to explain the data we have in actual experience, and also by the lack of any specific data to support it; in short, by its incoherence with experience. The simpler humanistic conception of God is consistent with all the data, but fails to offer a coherent interpretation of them.

§ 7. Knowing as Certain or as Heuristic

In the introductory portion of this chapter it was made clear that religious knowledge could not claim absolute theoretical certainty; nor is religious knowledge unique among knowledges in this respect. As long as men are men, two facts will doubtless remain true. First, alternative hypotheses for the interpretation of the facts will always be possible; and secondly, new experiences will constantly be emerging. Thus the work of thought is never done and revision and further growth are always in prospect. Yet it is the faith of religion that in all the changes that may come, certain constants of value will abide. This faith can never be asserted on philosophical grounds as a dogma, but it may be entertained as a working hypothesis used in the discovery and testing of truth about the Continuer of Value in the universe.

From a logical standpoint, then, Groos's theory of theoretical relativism is unconquerable. Final proof, complete demonstration, and logical certainty can never be reached by human skill on any matter whatever. No knowing leads to absolute certainty. But as Henri Poincaré has written, "it is a mistake to believe that the love of truth is indistinguishable from the love of certainty." [34] Groos's practical absolutism may be interpreted to mean that our most coherent hypotheses are, if not finally demonstrated truths, at least means of moving toward truth. They are not dogmatic revelation, but they fulfill the purposive function of leading man in the direction of the revealer of truth. They are therefore not certain, but they are heuristic. Such, at least, is the faith on which progress in science rests; and it is not incoherent to suppose that a similar faith is valid in the realm of religious knowledge.

[34] Poincaré, SM, 7.

Bibliographical Note

On the general problem of types of knowledge, Boodin, TR(1911), and Montague, WK(1925), are useful manuals. Macintosh, PK(1915), is a standard work; Lovejoy's RAD(1930) is more critical.

On religious knowledge, the following are general statements: Royce, SRI(1912); Flewelling, RIF(1914); Baillie, IR(1928); Hocking, MGHE(1912); Trueblood, TRE(1939); and Baillie, KG(1939). James, VRE(1902), is the psychological authority in the field. Bowne, THE(1902), 15-43, deals somewhat loosely with logical fundamentals. Numerous able scholars present their views in Bixler (ed.), NRE(1937).

Special problems are dealt with in Bennett, DRK(1931), a brilliant essay. Knudson, VRE(1937), and England, VRE(1938), are discussions of the a priori view. Bixler, Art.(1925), treats of mysticism.

On revelation: Baillie and Martin (eds.), REV(1937); Gilson, RRMA(1938); and the remarks in Münsterberg, EV(1909), 370-376.

SEVEN

THE PROBLEM OF
BELIEF IN GOD

§ 1. Why Is Belief in God a Problem?

HERE are two sorts of people, who find it unnatural to regard belief in God as a genuine problem—dogmatic believers on the one hand, and dogmatic unbelievers on the other. Dogmatic believers are so thoroughly committed to their faith that it seems to them blasphemous to treat that faith as problematic; who are we puny human beings, to doubt or even try to prove the eternal God? The refusal to make belief in God a problem has its classical religious expression in Job's "comforters." Zophar the Naamathite asks the epic hero (11:7):

> Canst thou by searching find out God?
> Canst thou find out the Almighty unto perfection?

But Job, although he does not doubt that God is, feels the necessity of an intellectual understanding of his belief, and replies (12:2, 3a; 13:3, 4a):

> No doubt but ye are the people,
> And wisdom shall die with you;
> But I have understanding as well as you.
> Surely I would speak to the Almighty,
> And I desire to reason with God.
> But ye are forgers of lies.

196

Here, then, a radical conflict among religious believers emerges; some think it is irreligious to challenge conventional belief, and others think it irreligious not to challenge it.   Unfortunately, the party of Job's comforters still outnumbers the party of Job. Similarly, among disbelievers in God, the dogmatists outnumber the critical inquirers. Not merely do Communists reject God without giving a single serious thought to the evidence, but many scientific writers [1] and philosophers do likewise. These scientists and philosophers, not unlike Job's so-called comforters, are convinced that they cannot by searching find out God. Hence they do not search. But, whereas the ancient comforters held searching to be wicked, the modern critics hold it to be useless. Such scientific and philosophical dogmatism—in the sense of atheism without investigation of the evidence for theism—is contrary to the spirit of both science and philosophy. Yet it is noteworthy that most current disbelief in God seems to have arisen from neglect of the problem and from preoccupation with interests to which belief in God is not directly relevant, such as descriptive science, mathematics, symbolic logic, historical investigations, epistemology, and other specialized investigations.[2]

The problem of God is not raised until one either undertakes to construct a coherent metaphysical view which shall include an interpretation of value experience, or at least confronts the facts of religion and tries to discover their true meaning. Almost without exception, every philosopher who has tried to do either of these things has thought

[1] See Brightman, Art.(1933). Freudianism is a conspicuous example of disbelief based on examination of limited, selected evidence.

[2] The assumption of the complete irrelevance of belief in God underlies Mr. Walter Lippmann's *A Preface to Morals*. He does not undertake to refute theism; he assumes atheistic humanism because it is the mood of his day (see PM, 133–134). It is a day well described by the Aristophanic quotation heading Part I, "Whirl is king." Yet a thinker should look considerably beyond the humanity of 1929 for an understanding of the most truly human values.

seriously about the problem of God: in recent times, such men as Samuel Alexander, Henri Bergson, William James, Josiah Royce, B. P. Bowne, W. E. Hocking, John Dewey, George Santayana, and Bertrand Russell have all found it necessary to think about God in order to arrive at clarity. But the last three differ from the first six. Dewey, Santayana, and Russell have given much less thought to weighing the evidence for and against the belief in God than they have to fitting that belief into a system that was constructed with relatively little regard to the evidence. It is just as unsound method to start in with a predetermined doubt as it is to start in with a predetermined faith. Philosophy of religion must be an investigation of experience, not a rationalization of predetermined desires. The absence from philosophical literature of any monograph which examines the evidence for and against belief in God [3] and arrives at an atheistic conclusion is evidence that modern doubt has not yet really wrestled with the problem of God.

For one trying to think philosophically, belief in God is accordingly a problem that must be faced. The scientist does not need to reflect on God; the philosopher must. To think about God is to think about a Continuer of Values—a source of the possibility and the perpetuation of value experience. Anyone who thinks persistently about value experience must inquire about its validity, its source, and its destiny. These questions cannot be fully considered without at least taking into account the possibility of a superhuman source and continuer of value. The very fact of value experience, then, raises the problem of God, altogether apart from desires or specifically religious experience.

The conflicting conceptions of God (Chapter V) force

---

[3] J. M. E. McTaggart's *Some Dogmas of Religion* comes nearest to being such a monograph, but it is not exhaustive and is the exception which proves the rule.

the mind to reject some or all of the contradictory beliefs that are or have been held. The various ways of knowing (Chapter VI) would lead to a clash of beliefs unless all of the ways of knowing are criticized and brought into harmony by the principle of coherence; and even with coherence as unifying criterion, many different hypotheses are possible (that is, conceivable) and require testing. In particular, there are mutually exclusive hypotheses about the relations between values and physical reality. The conflict among these hypotheses appears as the problem of the relation of God to nature, or of ideals to existence (in German, the problem of *Sollen* and *Sein*).

If we turn from this conflict of theories to the empirical evidence underlying all theory, we find the root of the war of ideas. There are, of course, persons who would deny this, for some say that there is no evidence for God. But such persons are using the word evidence in an esoteric sense; they may mean by it a particular kind of evidence that is absolutely conclusive to them. The patent fact, however, is that the problem of belief in God arises not from lack of evidence, but from superabundance of it. Philosophy of religion is a detective story in which there are too many clues. On the one hand, every value, every sign of order and rationality, and every experience of purpose is evidence for God. On the other hand, every disvalue, every sign of disorder and irrationality, and every purposeless experience is evidence against God. Neither body of evidence is conclusive when taken by itself.

Such theism as sweeps aside the evidence against God with a magnificent gesture and such atheism as concentrates on the negative and belittles or ignores the positive evidence are sisters under the skin—twin dogmatists, allied in rejecting the ideal of coherent reason. The one unescapable decree of reason—unescapable, that is, by all who choose to think—is that all the evidence of experience shall be faced and weighed in the scales of a logical interpretation of experience as a whole. The terms of this decree condemn with equal severity the dogmatic theist and the dogmatic atheist. For some reason, in the presence of the idea of God thought occasionally enters a state of suspended animation—not merely in an Angelus Temple, but even in a Hall of Philosophy. The idea of God is indeed overwhelming, but from its overwhelming character neither its truth nor its falsity may justly be inferred. All that may logically be inferred is the obligation to examine the evidence on both sides with impartiality. Physicists may operate as if Space-Time were ultimate; religious believers may operate as if values were ultimate. Philosophers can rely on no selected evidence, for whatever purpose it may have been selected. Philosophers must view every part in the light of the whole, and must therefore treat every belief, including belief in God, as a problem. The conflict of evidence makes it imperative for thought to wrestle with experience in order to gain truth. The question must be faced radically: Is there a God, and if so, of what kind? Is there a Continuer of Value, a "Determiner of Destiny"? Are ideals objective or subjective in nature?

§ 2.   How Could the Problem Be Solved?

If the results of Chapter VI are borne in mind, it will be clear from the start that no absolute and final philosophical solution to the problem of God will be found. The notion of absolute finality in thought is not only abhorrent to experimental science, but is also out of harmony with the spirit of religious faith and with the ideal of philosophical coherence. Scientists who apply experimental method hold all theories lightly, eager to abandon any speculation that does not accord with empirical fact and searching for truth regardless of prior commitments. Religious believers who have genuine faith in God must necessarily believe that the divine truth and reality are incomparably superior to any theory man can hold; and the history of theology confirms the poet's insight that "our little systems have their day." Philosophers who profess loyalty to the ideal of perfect coherence of all thought and experience have plainly imposed on themselves an infinite task that can never reach a neat and final completion; the dialectic of thought and the realities of experience drive the thinker inexorably on toward endless intellectual growth. Science, religion, and philosophy thus unite in the verdict that a final solution will not be reached.

If final intellectual certainty is thus known to be unattainable by anyone who respects the spirit of science or religion or philosophy, is the whole enterprise of thought vain, and must man give up in discouragement? Such a conclusion would be laughed out of court by scientist, philosopher, and religious believer alike. What the scientific investigator seeks is not a stopping place in his thought, but a stepping-stone to more truth. What the philosopher seeks is not the possession of all truth, but a unification of such truth as he has and a method of criticizing and increasing it. To give up would be essentially irreligious. What the religious man requires is not the certainty that his explanation of God is absolutely correct; he knows that "we see through a glass darkly," and he knows that his very faith in the experience and the increase of religious values requires frequent reinterpretation of his thought about God. What is the history of religion but a series of such reinterpretations?

As long as man is truly human, so long the all but infinite contrast between present insight and absolute truth in science, religion, and philosophy will never break the human spirit or cause man to cease thinking. Man knows that his life in every area is beset with uncertainty. He also knows that his life is a constant ebb and flow; the ebb is toward chaos and barbarism, the flow toward unity, civilization, and truth. Our inquiries into belief in God will never penetrate to the end of infinity, but they may serve to direct life from chaos and contradiction toward integration and coherence. One who demands more than this from philosophy of religion is doomed to disillusionment sooner or later; but one who finds this has found a method of personal growth that is superior to any unchangeable dogma.

§ 3. IS THERE NO GOD AT ALL?

The question whether there are any atheists is frequently debated. An atheist is one who denies belief in God. Yet frequently it is found that atheists deny some particular kind of belief in God (which perhaps they were taught at their mother's knee), while granting that there must be some superhuman Continuer and Source of Value. Again, many atheists direct their denial not so much against belief in God as against believers in God; against hypocritical individuals or (as in Soviet Russia) against antisocial churches, allied with wealth and corrupt politics and heedless of the injustices to which the poor are subjected. Such atheists might almost be called disguised theists, for they assert the validity of the very ideals of honesty and justice which believers in God take to be essential to a divine will. Thus the atheism most commonly met with is but a family quarrel in the religious household about the source and continuation of value; it is not fundamentally irreligious.

Truly irreligious atheism is to be found only where there is complete skepticism about any value in life. He who believes that there is nothing worth while is the thoroughgoing atheist. For him there are no value distinctions at all; in the eyes of such a person, Mr. Guest is as great a poet as Shakespeare, Mr. Berlin as talented a composer as Wagner, Mr. Hitler as just as Aristides, St. Bartholomew's Eve as benevolent as the Sermon on the Mount, ignorance as good as science, sorrow as good as joy—nothing either better or worse than anything else. With value-blindness as complete as this, if such there be, it is hardly worth while to argue. It may sometimes be found that the fierce repudiation of value which such atheists avow is an overcompensation for their failure to achieve the values they had set their hearts on, or is a veil for their own ideals, which sometimes have been put so fantastically high that peering up at them has created dizziness, and dizziness cynicism. Nevertheless, psychoanalytic diagnosis constitutes no disproof of the atheistic position. Theists and atheists should appeal to inherent reasonableness rather than to reports on mental health.

For every normal human being there are values. If God is properly defined as the Source and Continuer of Values, the question: Is there no God at all? is an unreal one. The real question is: What is God? This is the question with which theists and atheists alike are continually struggling. What is the source of values in human experience? That there is such a source is as certain as that there are values. As scholastics have said, we must distinguish between saying *that* God is and saying *what* he is. *That* a source of values is, is certain. *What* the source of values is, is uncertain. Yet for both practical and theoretical purposes it is far more important to explore concretely *what* God is than to stick in the barren, if undeniable, abstraction *that* God is.

§ 4. Is God One or Many?

The earlier stages of religion are, as we have found, polytheistic; but the tendency of religious development has clearly been toward unity—toward either monotheism or pantheism. Outcroppings of belief in nationalistic deities in modern Japan and Germany are so manifestly at odds with the main trend of religion as to constitute no important evidence for polytheism.

It is, however, not self-evident that the historical development of religion is a movement toward truth, and it is a theoretical possibility that this development may be toward error. Many errors have maintained themselves for a long time. Is the belief in monotheism such an error (regardless of how God may be defined)?

There are some considerations which lead to the view that the source of value is not one, but many. (1) While every observer must grant that there are processes in individuals, in society, and in nature which are teleological in the sense of leading up to a valued consummation, *the evidence for the unity of these value-producing processes is not decisive.* There are many axiogenetic[4] situations in experience; but it is debatable whether all axiogenesis belongs to a single unified process or plan. For a thinker like Sidney Hook, who has more confidence in the special sciences than he has in philosophy,[5] the plurality of axiogenetic processes will be much more evident than their unity. On the other hand, one who thinks that reason requires not only the variety of sciences, but also their coherence and interrelation in philosophy, will be willing to entertain the hypothesis that the many axiogenetic processes revealed by scientific observation may be signs of a common cause or ground of value.

[4] For the sake of convenience in reference, we propose as new terms axiogenesis and axiogenetic. By axiogenesis is meant the development or production of value. That which develops or produces value is called axiogenetic.

[5] The reference is to ideas expressed in discussion by Professor Hook at meetings of the American Philosophical Association, Eastern Division.

(2) A second reason for questioning the unity of God is to be found in *the variety of norms actually acknowledged in different civilizations;* what passes for recreation, or goodness, or beauty, or truth, or holiness, or worthful association in one civilization is condemned in another. This seems to point to an irreducible variety in the sources of value; that "there are gods many and lords many" is an empirical observation of the Christian scriptures (1 Cor. 8:5). But it is by no means certain that every difference of opinion among men reflects a difference in reality; a moment's thought will reveal the impossible view of reality to which such an assumption would lead. The evidence is consistent, then, either with many gods clearly known or one God obscurely known.

(3) A third consideration pointing to a plurality of gods is *the conflict of forces in nature.* The destructive forces of earthquake and tornado, the struggle between life and death, the conflict among human instincts, the existence of planets in which consciousness and value as we know them are impossible, present a picture that bears on the surface more resemblance to cosmic warfare than to the rule of one supreme axiogenetic power. This problem is so acute that we shall devote Chapters VIII, IX, and X to a consideration of it.

Over against these arguments for some sort of polytheism or pluralism of values, there are arguments for monotheism (in the broadest sense) or value monism. First of all, there is *the unity of natural law.* Value as we know it appears in a universe of law. Natural law constitutes one system; the goal of one single equation to epitomize the entire physical universe is perhaps not so fantastically unattainable as it seems. Be that as it may, natural science postulates the same laws throughout the physical universe, and adds that all laws constitute a consistent system. In such a universe value experiences arise. The unity of natural law suggests a unity in source of values.

Secondly, *the interaction of all parts of the universe* seems to be *a necessary postulate* if science is to be true or if "matter" and "mind" (whatever "matter" and "mind" may be) are to affect one another.[6] If the universe is an interacting system, one must either regard the interaction as a fortunate coincidence in the structure of independent "building bricks of the universe" or else as a product of some common cause. Value is even more intimately connected with interaction than it is with law. All social values are phenomena of interaction, and the essential nature of every intrinsic value is (as we have found) to "coalesce" (or interact) with other values in a totality of value experience. The postulate of interaction is, then, another hint that the source of value experience is a cosmic unity of some kind.

Thirdly, *the very nature of value experience itself points to one coherent system*. Every value-claim must be judged in the light of the ideal whole of value experience. Every system of value-claims which any man or his group sets up must be judged by an insight which includes, as far as possible, all value-claims and systems in their totality. This seems to leave no room for any values which are validly independent of all other values. Such autonomy as any special value possesses is that of a state in the federal republic of all values; without a federal constitution and some bar of reason corresponding to a Supreme Court, the experience of value disintegrates and becomes incoherent. Thus the choice appears to lie between a pluralism which points toward skepticism about values and a monism of ideals which welds value experience into an ideal unity. If this is the

---

[6] This argument is made fundamental by Bowne in his chapter on "The Unity of the World Ground," THE, 44–63, as well as by Lotze.

nature of value experience, it would seem probable that the source and continuer of such experience is a unity.

§ 5. Is God Human Experience Only?

In Chapter V we found that there are religious humanists who sometimes speak as though God were no more than the ideal unity of human experience of value. The acknowledgment of a supreme ideal is, of course, in a very real sense a source and a continuer of value experience, and if no other source or continuer could be found, it would be quite legitimate to speak of this ideal as God, as humanists do. However, it is doubtful whether they mean to assert dogmatically that there is no source of value experience beyond man. What they mean, probably, is that the ideal of which we have spoken is the known and effective source of human aspiration and endeavor, and that speculation about the way in which nature is able to produce the ideal in human consciousness is futile. The humanist's position is that we should take the gifts of nature gladly, that we should prize and be loyal to the ideal values of personal and social life, but that we should regard these values as purely human rather than as an expression of cosmic purpose. Their ultimate origin we cannot fathom.

The humanist is religious in practice; highly as he esteems religious values, he still finds their theoretical interpretation too difficult a metaphysical task. He stands in sharp contrast with such theists as Anselm (1033-1109) and Descartes (1596-1650). These thinkers, like the humanists, take their start with the ideal. But for them the ideal has an immediate and irrefutable metaphysical reference. Anselm held that the very highest ideal is the idea of God—a being than whom no greater can be conceived. Such a being must exist, for a God conceived as existing is greater than one conceived as not existing. Descartes added that the perfect idea of God requires a real God as its perfect cause. This movement from idea to being is called the ontological argument. Humanists and most modern theists, including the Thomists, view this argument skeptically. Its importance lies in its testimony to the presence in man of an ideal of perfection; but to move at once from this ideal to the objective reality of God is to treat the ultimate problem of existence too lightly. It may be more religious to be baffled by the problem as the humanists are than to underestimate its difficulty, as the proponents of the ontological argument do. Yet both groups are arbitrary. If it is arbitrary to declare the game of thought about God finished and won with ease, it is equally arbitrary to declare the game lost. Play must be resumed at the end of every inning; but in thought, there is no nine-inning rule. Inquiry must go on forever. Humanists and Anselmists hold complementary dogmas, in a realm where no dogmas are in order. The ideal of perfection, shared by humanists and Anselmists alike and embodying faith in the objectivity of ideals, may well be regarded, not as the end of all thought, but as a fresh beginning. It is the supreme hypothesis for all thought and experience to test.[7]

The question whether God is human experience only is not to be disposed of casually by either an affirmation or a negative gesture. It is not a solitary idea; it is the expression of one's whole philosophy of life and reality, the summation and unitary climax of all one's thinking and experiencing. It is what Hocking, in *The Meaning of God in Human Experience*, calls our "Whole Idea." Anselm is therefore right in holding, as he did, that the idea of God is different from our other ideas in its perfection; but he

[7] See Lotze, MIC, II, 470; Sorley, MVIG, 313; Bowne, THE, 47, and KS, 206–213; Galloway, PR, 387; and Hocking's chapter on "The Ontological Argument in Royce and Others" in Barrett (ed.), CIA, 45–66. The topic is treated in all important works on philosophy of religion.

and the humanists are alike wrong if they think that a mere definition of God at once solves the problem of God's metaphysical reality. Neither the faith of Anselm nor the skepticism of humanists excuses the thinker from thinking.

§ 6. Is God a Part of Nature?

In Chapter V we found that actual conceptions of God are largely formulations of beliefs about God's relation to nature. Deists and supernaturalists, we found, place God outside of nature. Their God is in external relations to the world and little, if anything, about him can be inferred from observation of the world. On the other hand, the God of the religious naturalists (of whom Henry Nelson Wieman is a leading contemporary example) stands in a diametrically opposite relation to nature. This God is a part of nature, being such processes and relations in nature as make for value, for coöperation and growth.[8]

The problem of God's relation to nature is, of course, much broader than the current views of any one philosopher or group of philosophers. First of all, the elements of the problem should be stated. God, in all the discussions of this book, means primarily the Source and Continuer of Values, and the problem of belief in God is the problem of finding a definition of the axiogenetic and axiosoteric [9] aspects of reality which is self-consistent, consistent with all known facts and valid theories, and more coherent than any other definition. Such a definition would meet the conditions of an hypothesis that would solve the philo-

---

[8] See H. N. Wieman's chapter on "Approach to God" in Wieman and Horton, GOR, 325–367.

[9] Axiosoteric is another new term introduced for convenience in discussion. As axiogenesis (adj., axiogenetic) means the production of values, axiosoteria (accent on the antepenult; adj., axiosoteric) means the "saving," that is, the preserving of values. As Source of Values, God is axiogenesis; as Continuer of Values, he is axiosoteria.

sophical problem of God. It is, however, easier to agree on a definition of God than on a definition of nature. In all religion, gods have been sources of value. But there has been far less agreement about the meaning of nature. Modern scientific investigators would probably satisfy themselves with the circular definition which declares nature to be what the natural scientists are studying. The problem of the definition of nature as a whole is really a philosophical, not a scientific problem.

The standard definition of nature among the Greeks is Aristotle's: "Nature is the distinctive form or quality of such things as have within themselves a principle of motion, such form or quality not being separable from the things themselves, save conceptually." [10] Aristotle goes on to remark that nature (*physis*) is equivalent to growth or development (*genesis*). On Aristotle's view, it is clear that he does not think of nature as a system or unified whole; it is simply the source of motion or change in things. It is, as children say, "what makes the wheels go 'round." But when a modern thinker speaks of nature, it is not of Aristotle's concept that he is thinking. He has in mind, rather, the system of nature as a whole. When it comes to defining explicitly what this "system of nature" is, there is great difference of opinion. Spinoza spoke of God or nature (*deus sive natura*) as synonymous terms descriptive of substance (*substantia*), the totality of all that is. Kant standardized a different conception which governed the use of the term in the nineteenth century and still prevails in many quarters. For him, nature means the system of all phenomena in the one "real" space and time. It thus corresponds to our idea of physical or material

[10] Aristotle's *Physics*, II, 193b, tr. by Wicksteed and Cornford in the Loeb Classical Library edition. The Loeb translation is more illuminating than that of the Oxford edition for this passage and its context.

reality, as contrasted with spirit or mind. The Germans, consequently, speak of *Naturwissenschaften* (natural sciences) as distinguished from *Geisteswissenschaften* (sciences of spirit or mind).

Kant's usage has become less and less general as its implications have become clearer. It means, for example, that the human mind is not a part of nature—a point of view offensive to psychologists and sociologists as well as to pragmatists, and one that is increasingly difficult to hold since evolution has been generally accepted by scientists and philosophers. Contemporary naturalists, like the late Samuel Alexander, E. Scribner Ames, H. N. Wieman, R. W. Sellars, and John Dewey (to mention a few typical names) have ceased to use the term in Kant's sense; for them it means more nearly what it did with Spinoza. With these men, and others, it has come to be a name for all that there is, or at least for all that is knowable by any legitimate way of knowing. This new usage, while thoroughly understandable, has introduced chaos into terminology. The word supernatural meant something when nature was the system of physical phenomena; then spirit, personality, freedom, and God, as well as revelation, could properly be spoken of as supernatural. Now the word supernatural is forced into the awkward position of meaning what isn't, since nature means all that is. It is evident that this terminological change is slippery and does not dispose of the essential realities referred to by believers in the supernatural. Nevertheless, since we are in the modern world, we must take cognizance of both the advantages and disadvantages of modern terminology. Yet we should not forget that Kant's way of putting the problem was nearer to the essential interest of religion, for he wanted to know whether there was any principle at work in experience other than the principle of physical motion. Nature is the system of all motions; but is there also a system of values, a realm of ends? Kant's question will be faced in Chapters VIII, IX, and X.

Modern naturalists restate the problem. Instead of differentiating between *Natur* and *Geist,* or nature and grace, or *Sein* and *Sollen,* or fact and value,[11] modern naturalists, holding that mind is as natural a fact as is matter, also hold that values and their sustaining grounds in the physical world are as natural as any other facts. From their postulates, naturalists readily infer the existence within nature, that is, within the realm of the scientifically observable or known, of a tendency toward axiogenesis. There certainly is experience of value and that experience must have a cause. Why not call this cause God?[12] Many perplexed minds of the present age find satisfaction in this apparently simple and secure formula, which rests on scientific presuppositions and requires no elaborate speculation as a basis for religious faith.

In order to evaluate this position, a preliminary distinction must be made, analogous to current terminology about behaviorism. When behavioristic studies and theories developed, it became necessary to differentiate methodological from metaphysical behaviorism.[13] Behaviorism as method meant the study of the behavior of organisms; and no psychologist or philosopher has objected or could rationally object to methodological behaviorism. But metaphysical behaviorism is a radically different theory; it is the thesis that, since consciousness cannot be observed in the sense in

[11] See Wolfgang Koehler's William James Lectures on "The Place of Value in a World of Facts," especially "Theories of Value" in PVWF, 35–62.

[12] For a typical exposition of such naturalistic theism (the doctrine that God is to be found as part of nature) see Wieman and Meland, APR, especially 272–306, and 332–348, where the view is often called empirical theism—a term much less restrictive than naturalistic theism.

[13] See Brightman, ITP, 183–184.

which behavior can be observed, consciousness does not exist, or if it does, had best be ignored. The extreme position, held by J. B. Watson, that consciousness does not exist at all is the typical form of metaphysical behaviorism. A similar terminology may well be applied to naturalism. Methodological naturalism may be defined as the view that nature is to be known only by observation and interpretation of the data of human experience. Sometimes (as by Bridgman) [14] methodological naturalism assumes a rigid and restricted form which would confine all knowledge to operations and their observable consequences, without interpretation. If we observe without interpreting, all our observations, operations, and actions are mere manipulations of our own experience; without interpretation we are shut up within ourselves, and solipsism is unavoidable. But if interpretation be allowed, there is no better objection to methodological naturalism than to methodological behaviorism.[15] In fact, it is very close to the method adopted at the outset of Chapter I of this book, and is the only tenable alternative to a rationalistic apriorism or a supernaturalistic revelationism; and even rationalists and supernaturalists would allow to methodological naturalism due validity within its sphere.

Methodological naturalism is one thing; metaphysical naturalism is another. The vagueness of the modern conception of nature has, however, cast a blight over the meaning of metaphysical naturalism. Yet in general we may say that, while old-fashioned Democritean and Hobbesian atomism has vanished in the presence of emergent evolution

---

[14] See Bridgman, LMP, passim, and Wieman and Horton, GOR, 345-349. The view is in many respects close to that of John Dewey, but he is less rigid in his conception of it.

[15] Professor Wieman finds it hard to classify the present writer, whether as liberal or as naturalist (Wieman and Horton, GOR, 487, n. 1.). Perhaps a reason for his difficulty is the failure to discriminate methodological from metaphysical naturalism and to define interpretation.

and the newer physics, modern metaphysical naturalism is still a kind of "physicalism." R. W. Sellars calls it "a materialism . . . of evolved unities and patterns." [16] The metaphysical essence of naturalism is the view that physical energies and forces are the only ultimately causal or determining agencies in the universe; that conscious experience is product, not producer; and that physical energy and force are totally lacking in the attributes of conscious thought or purpose. In John Dewey's identification of nature with "experience" a complex problem arises which almost baffles definition. Although Dewey is much nearer to idealism than most naturalists, it seems reasonably certain that by experience he means a realm of events which do not possess the attributes of conscious thought, reason, or purpose. Metaphysical naturalism, then, is a denial of the supremacy of conscious spirit in the universe. This goes as far beyond the innocence of methodological naturalism as metaphysical behaviorism goes beyond methodological behaviorism.

Within the limits of metaphysical naturalism as just defined there is a marked tendency on the part of modern naturalists to find a place for religious values and, in some sense, for a God. Values, as W. G. Everett used to say, are born in the womb of nature. Within nature there is something at work which actually produces value experiences in human consciousness. In his famous *Space, Time and Deity,* Samuel Alexander developed the idea that the ultimate reality is Space-Time, which, in constant evolution, is producing ever higher types of being. Deity, he held, is for any level the next higher type that follows after it, and God is the whole universe as possessing deity. There is hardly a naturalist today who does not recognize that natural processes in some degree lead to experiences of value. H. N. Wieman, whose views we have frequently men-

[16] See Sellars, PPR, 4.

tioned, finds that God is the name for all value-producing processes in nature.

It is worth while to point out explicitly the change that has taken place in the thinking of naturalists. Until the present century, most naturalists were atomistic mechanists. That is to say, they thought of nature as made up of atoms, and the only forces at work in nature were the motions of these atoms, which obeyed a rigid mechanical law, each set of motions being absolutely determined by previous motions, and so on into the infinite regress and progress of the universe. There was no place for freedom, for novelty, or for purposive control in such a naturalism. But modern naturalism has ceased to be rigidly mechanical, as nineteenth-century physics has given way to the less deterministic theories of Heisenberg. Debaters about mechanism and teleology used to set up a nature entirely free from purpose over against a God who rules entirely by purpose. Today naturalists grant a larger place to purpose and value, while personalistic theists recognize fully the reality and the importance of mechanism, insisting, indeed, that without mechanisms purposes could neither be communicated from mind to mind nor have any reliable effects in nature.[17]

The newer attitude represents to a moderate degree a triumph of the old teleological argument for God. That argument was a declaration that the adjustments and adaptations of means to ends in nature were evidence for a designer. Kant held (rightly) that the argument did not prove that there is an omnipotent designer, but at best an "architect" rather than a "creator" (*Critique of Pure Reason,* A627). In this conclusion Kant was half-unconsciously pointing to what may be true—that God is no omnipotent

---

[17] For a fuller discussion of this problem, see the Chapters, "Is the World a Machine?" and "Has the World a Purpose?" in Brightman, ITP, 249–314. See also the bibliographical references, ibid., 374–376.

creator in the traditional sense, but rather a finite controller or "architect" of eternal experience, building purpose and value as he toils. Be that as it may, Kant stated clearly the empirical fact that "this world presents to us . . . [an] immeasurable . . . stage of variety, order, purposiveness, and beauty." [18]

In reply to our question: Is God a part of nature? we are ready now to give this minimum answer. At least a part of nature contains evidence that there is an objective source and continuer of value. Man's value experiences are certainly no mere subjective creations of his fancy or his mores; beauty, order, coöperation, adaptation, have their objective grounds. There are axiogenetic processes in nature, and religion is an attitude of respect for and trust in those processes. As far as this naturalism goes, it is true. But it leaves the axiogenetic processes uninterpreted, unrelated to the rest of existence, as flowers blooming mysteriously in a hostile soil. Those who are curious as to how such soil could nourish such flowers remain unenlightened.

§ 7. Is Nature a Part of God?

Over against the view that God is a part of nature there is the antithetical belief that nature is a part of God. If God is a name for selected axiogenetic processes, then all that can be said is that God is a part of nature. But if thought does not stop with these processes, it may well move on to inquire what the source of those processes is. This question, in connection with the monotheistic arguments cited in § 4 of the present chapter, leads to the further inquiry whether there is a unitary source for all the processes in nature. Is that source the order of processes in Space-Time, or is it God? In raising the question, "Is nature a part of God?" the inquirer is asking whether nature is one of many realms

[18] CPR, A622 (tr. N. K. Smith).

within the divine, rather than being a system external to God. The question, however, does not yet postulate any view of God other than that of axiogenesis and axiosoteria. Whether God is conscious mind or is unconscious energy or matter remains undiscussed at present.

If God, the Source and Continuer of Value, is a unity, then God is in some sense related to or concerned with everything in nature. Every event in nature embodies to some degree rational law, beauty, and relation, or possible relation, to the interests of human consciousness. But if nature be defined as the order of objects and events in Space-Time, experience shows that every human consciousness apprehends values that extend far beyond nature. Natural objects and processes symbolize and generate value; but the actual experience of value is itself no object or process in the physical, Space-Time order. All experience is, indeed, in time, but not all is in space. In fact, it is truer to say (with many idealists) that all space is in conscious experience rather than that conscious experience is in space. If we look in what we call physical space we find physical processes, but not consciousness. If we look in consciousness, we find all the space-experience there is—and also much that is entirely nonspatial and irrelevant to space, such as knowledge of ideals, of love, of time, of $\sqrt{-1}$, of logical implication, and of worship. In fact all values, as conscious experiences, transcend space; it is they that give meaning to space, not space to them. In the experience of man, spatial objects occupy a large (spatially large) room; but an experience that consisted entirely of spatial objects would not admit either of a science of physics or a geometry of space, for both physics and geometry are thinking processes, and thinking is not a spatial object. Much less would purely spatial experience include moral obligation, or personal identity, or social communication, or prayer. From the standpoint of value, the whole realm of space-objects is purely instrumental. All intrinsic value is nonspatial experience.

If we build our view of God on this empirical testimony, then we may say that the spatial aspect of God is a vast, yet subordinate, area of the divine being; and that spaceless ideals and values, as well as other nonspatial types of being of which we have not the remotest inkling, make up the most important aspects of the being of God. On the supposition that God is a unity and that nature is not a created order external to God, this view is at least possible.

§ 8.   Is God All That There Is?

There have been many, as we saw in Chapter V, § 6, who have denied both of the views just discussed. For these thinkers, God is not a part of nature, nor is nature a part of God, but God and nature are synonymous terms, each designating all that there is. Spinoza is the classic representative of such pantheism in occidental thought, although he comes close to saying that nature (as the Space-Time order) is part of God, for extension is one of the infinite attributes of God.

There is much that makes some form of pantheism seem acceptable. If philosophy is "the quest for the world's unity," the formula that all is God and God is all seems to be the supreme goal of the quest. Yet philosophy is not a quest for unity regardless of facts and logic; it is a quest for such unity as the facts logically admit of. The question then arises whether it is logical to say that the source and continuer of value is all that there is, considered as a unity. But the problem arose in the first place from the fact that man knew himself not to be the source and continuer of value. The pantheist replies: Truly, man alone is not the source of axiogenesis, but man is an essential part of the whole, and it is the whole that is axiogenetic and axiosoteric.

This argument has persuaded many thinkers. (1) It furnishes *a unified system* of philosophy, (2) it satisfies *the needs of religious mystics* who long to merge their being with the divine to which they belong, and (3) it affords *a basis for optimism,* in that the whole is good, however evil the parts may be taken separately.

The objections to pantheism nevertheless outweigh the arguments for it. (1) It asserts a *unity;* but unless that unity is the oneness of an all-inclusive conscious spirit, it is really *an ineffable name.* It is the syllable "OM," it is "somehow one" (we know not how), it is transcendently beyond all experience and thought. (2) If its unity is taken to be that of a conscious spirit, then there is *a contradiction between the point of view of the infinite and the point of view of the finite.* If John Jones is a part of God, then all of the ignorance of John Jones, all of his error, must be a part of God. Now, God, if he were a conscious cosmic spirit, could well know both John Jones's errors and the correction of them, but such a God could not, while knowing the correction of John's errors also entertain those errors believing them to be truths, as John does. Spiritual or personalistic pantheism (or absolutism) requires that we believe that God at one and the same time while thinking "John Jones," genuinely and sincerely and ignorantly errs, and also corrects, supplements, and transcends those errors. To ascribe such contradictory states of mind to God is to seek unity at the cost of logic. If there is a conscious God, then, this argument proves that he cannot include as part of himself any person who errs, is ignorant, or sins. If there is a personal God, he is not all that there is. There are at least other persons, although this argument in no way disproves that nature as the realm of Space-Time objects is perhaps included within God; nature is incomplete, but it is not ignorant, erroneous, or sinful.

(3) A third argument against pantheism is related to the second. In general, it would appear that if God is absolutely all-inclusive, God would include all evil as well as all good. There might be some way in which God would include "natural" evil. But *for God to include moral evil* would make the divine an incoherent chaos and *would destroy distinctions between good and evil.* (4) Some forms of pantheism *would make freedom impossible by the determinism of the whole;* but this objection does not apply to all types, especially not to those of Josiah Royce and M. W. Calkins, who hold that when John Jones performs a free act, he is the Absolute in action and that nothing else in the Absolute determines the nature of his act.[19]

§ 9. Is God Wholly Other Than Nature?

In § 9 of Chapter V we found that many entertain the conception of God as wholly superhuman and supernatural. For this view, generally called deistic since the middle of the nineteenth century, God is not human experience in any sense; he is no part of nature; nature is no part of him; he is not all that there is, although he is the creator of nature and man.

Since religion is concerned with values, it is easy to see what considerations have led men to extreme supernaturalism. They have been aware, on the one hand, of an urge within, which beckoned them on to perfection; this urge they have regarded as a revelation of the divine. On the other hand, they, like every realistic observer of life, have been acutely aware of impediments to ideal value in human nature and in physical nature. Man's soul is weak, his

[19] See Calkins, PPP(5th ed.), 474–479.

spirituality is frail, but his evil is sly and aggressive. The doctrines of "original sin" and of "total depravity" are postulates of orthodox theologians, Machiavelli, ward politicians, totalitarian dictators, and tired radicals. Physical nature likewise seems to be, as the orthodox say, "under a curse." To achieve spiritual life, bodily desires must be tamed, physical impulses overcome, the "slings and arrows of outrageous fortune" endured—matter tamed and controlled by spirit. God, then, is neither human nature nor physical nature; he is not "in the cloud"; he is a "still small voice" other than all of nature, the creator of nature and the sole revealer of his will. Calvin began the first Book of his *Institutes of the Christian Religion* by declaring that knowledge of God "precedes and produces" knowledge of ourselves. (His method is thus completely a priori and utterly opposed to the empirical method of this book.) For Calvin, God is so wholly other than man that we learn about God not by interpreting our experience, but by turning away from it to God. It is not our values that reveal God; but we are driven to him by "our miserable ruin," "our ignorance, vanity, poverty, infirmity, depravity, and corruption." Calvin's argument evinces the desirability of there being a God, yet falls far short of proving that there is one. But for Calvin there is a God and he is utterly superhuman and supernatural. Like Christian Science, Calvinism is "uncontaminated by human hypotheses." [20]

Is this supernaturalistic deism a true account of the Source and Continuer of Values? By its rigorous realism, its moral sublimity, and its self-consistent logic, it has long maintained ascendancy over the minds of men, and is probably held by a larger number of Protestants than is any other single view.

[20] It should be noted that Saint Thomas Aquinas is far more empirical than Calvin, for he holds that God is not the first that we know; we arrive at the knowledge of God by inference from the creation to the creator. S. Th., I. q. 88, a. 3.

Its emphasis on man's inferiority to God reappears in the teaching of Schleiermacher, otherwise at the antipodes from Calvin, that religion consists essentially in a sense of dependence on God. Its logic is also roughly paralleled in the traditional cosmological argument for God, which holds that the world contains nothing necessary; all in it is contingent. But there must be a necessary being on which the contingent depends, and hence a God. Or, the world is a series of causes *ad infinitum;* but there must be a first cause, and hence a God.

Once again we ask, is the belief in this utterly supernatural God justified? The answer, from the point of view of philosophy, must be negative. (1) Calvin's argument that our very depravity evidences our need of him is equivalent to saying that the worse everything is the more we wish it were better. Such an argument expresses *a desire, not a reason* for faith, unless supported by real evidence. (2) The supernaturalist appeals to revelation; but we found in Chapter VI that *all revelation-claims must be tested* by the very evidence of coherent interpretation of experience that the supernaturalist rejects. (3) If human nature is so wretched and God so sublimely perfect, it is *difficult to see why so perfect and omnipotent a God would create creatures doomed to such imperfection.* (4) *The concept of creation is a difficult one.* It is true that any view of evolution must recognize a genuinely creative power in the universe. However, the deistic supernaturalist places so wide a gulf between creator and creation that it is all but impossible to conceive how there could ever have been any relation between them, much less so close a relation as assumed. Therefore the notion of deistic supernaturalism must be set aside as highly improbable, along with the notion of spiritual pantheism.

§ 10. Is God Unconscious Axiogenesis?

The question which is now raised is really not additional to the problems we have been considering. It summarizes a standpoint underlying the views that God is a part of nature (§ 6), or the whole of reality (§ 8), or a being of whom the physical Space-Time order is a part (§ 7), or wholly other than nature (§ 9), or an unknowable source of all being (Chapter V, § 7).

It is not logically impossible that the source of all value is itself valueless and the source of all consciousness unconscious. An effect is not bound to resemble a cause, either phenomenally or ontologically. Yet if God, the ground of all conscious value (all actual value is conscious experience) is unconscious, then we shall have to say that God is utterly unknown, if not unknowable. For we have available from our analysis of experience only three categories for the interpretation of existence. The first is the category of consciousness; the second is the category of the spatio-temporal (the physical); and the third is the category of the neutral (the purely subsistent, neither mental nor physical), contributed by the neorealists.[21] If God is unconscious axiogenesis, and he is known, then he is either spatio-temporal order or a complex of neutral entities. There are grave objections to either view. If God is purely spatio-temporal, it would appear that he can have only physicochemical properties, and never become conscious or initiate any axiogenesis. If, on the other hand, he is a complex of neutral entities, we face the problem which neorealism failed to solve, as to how existence can be derived from subsistence. It is clear how subsistence may be derived from existence, namely, by abstraction. But from nonexisting, nonmental, nonphysical, and noncausal neutral entities, how can any

21 The term neutral entity was originated, however, by Professor H. M. Sheffer.

existence whatever be concretely derived? [22] Neither matter nor mind, to say nothing of values, can be really explained in this way. Hence, if one insists on having an unconscious God, the soundest procedure is to say that his nature is wholly unknown.

The seeming intellectual humility in admitting our ignorance appeals to many minds. Furthermore, our "knowledge" of everything we say we know is so tentative, so subject to correction, so incomplete and inaccurate, that we may well profess our ignorance. Yet this well-grounded intellectual humility may be overdone. Every true scientist is humble; but his humility is expressed by his open-minded search for truth, not by ceasing to experiment or to think. Likewise, it may be a false humility in the presence of the idea of God to pronounce the word "unknown." The task of philosophy is to explore all possibilities, to try every avenue of thought, to keep searching. If thought is baffled by a physical God or a neutral God or an unknown God, then the so-called revolutionary ideas of God have led to blind alleys. May it not be possible that an evolutionary idea is worth trying, based on the idea of God as consciousness and reinterpreting the all but universal testimony of religious experience? May it not be that the conception of a personal God is the most rational road to truth about religion?

§ 11. Is God a Person?

Since belief in the personality of God is central to most living religion as it now exists in the world, and since it is indicated as the direction in which philosophy of religion must continue to explore if it is to be evolutionary rather than revolutionary, the problems attendant on this belief will

[22] For a discussion of some of the issues involved see the Chapter on "The Chief Philosophical World Views" in Brightman, ITP, 212–248, and Hoernlé, Art.(1927).

be taken up in some detail, but far more incompletely than their importance warrants. We shall first inquire what it means to ask whether God is personal,[23] and then shall present the chief evidence for and against the truth of the belief.

(1) First of all, *the popular view of God's personality must be rejected* as impossible. By "the popular view" is meant a view held so widely in nonphilosophical and nontheological circles as to amaze thinkers by its persistence, namely, that God is an old man with a beard whose chief function lies in assigning souls to heaven or to hell.[24] If there is a personal God, controlling the whole universe, it is obviously childish to think of him as localized in any sort of body, youthful or aged; and his concerns with the entire cosmos, including all human history on earth, are at least as important as those which have to do with human life after death. These latter, furthermore, must be more rational and more moral than the traditional idea of heaven and hell would allow.

(2) Furthermore, certain *quasi-scientific views* of divine personality *must be rejected* as being both philosophically and religiously scarcely above the level of the popular materialism just rejected. These quasi-scientific views center about the idea that if God is personal, then he must be *a psychophysical organism.* Does not psychology treat personality in this way?[25] The rhetorical question can be

---

[23] Professor Georgia Harkness has undertaken in discussion to distinguish between saying that God is a person and saying that he is personal, on the ground that the noun is more easily misunderstood than the adjective. Since every term may be misunderstood, even after explanation, the distinction raised does not appear to be important.

[24] Professor Alois Riehl of Berlin stated in a lecture (1910) that such was his early conception; it appears as the "modern" idea of the essence of belief in a personal God in Charles G. Norris's very twentieth-century novel, *Bricks Without Straw* (New York: Doubleday, Doran & Co., Inc., 1938), 134–135; it emerges in discussion so frequently, even among educated people, that it may be called the standard popular view.

[25] The best psychological work on the subject is Gordon Allport's *Personality.*

answered only in the affirmative. Psychology is fully justified in treating human personality as an organic phenomenon. But the belief that God is a person is, among other things, the belief that God is not a human person. It is the belief that "God is a spirit," a being whose *esse* is to be conscious, to experience, to think, to will, to love, and to control the ongoing of the universe by rational purpose. The hypothesis that there is a personal God, then, is one which denies that the earth is the only place where consciousness has emerged in the universe, and which therefore denies that consciousness is the product of any organism materialistically conceived. The assertion, therefore, that a personal God must be a psychophysical organism is mere quasi science, transferring the conditions of human existence to the whole universe. It is uncritical empiricism. It is anthropomorphism in a most objectionable sense—more objectionable than in the popular view, because it poses as science.

(3) To believe in a personal God, accordingly, is to believe that *the unbegun and unending energy of the universe is conscious rational will,* a conscious purpose that is coherent, selective, and creative. Such a will or purpose cannot exist *in abstracto;* it is the functioning of a total, unified, conscious personality, or it is nothing. Belief in a personal God (theism) does not entail of itself any particular view of matter. Some theists are dualists or agnostics about the nature of matter; others (including the writer) are idealists and regard matter as being an order of organization of the experience of God.[26] The one essential factor in personal theism is that the ultimate creative energy of the cosmos is personal will. Prior to the appearance of self-conscious beings on this earth, prior to all organic life, prior to the

---

[26] Discussion of the idealistic (personalistic) view of matter is a task of metaphysics which is with great reluctance excluded from the crowded pages of this philosophy of religion.

solar system itself and all astronomical phenomena, the eternal energy has always been and will always be personal consciousness.   James Bissett Pratt objects to the idea of a consciousness that has as much to do as, say, Berkeley's theory required, on the ground that we should thus have too busy a God.[27]   Such an objection seems almost frivolous. After all, any being that has the entire universe in its care must be very busy; to urge this busyness as an objection to the control of God over the world is really equivalent to complaining about the complexity of nature.   Let us now examine this belief in a personal God, without distress if the belief is too vast for our imagination to picture.

(4) The evidence for belief in a personal God has been stated frequently.[28]   In fact, the only "objection" which some critics have to the evidence is that it has been presented before—a singularly inept comment when unaccompanied by any refutation or counterevidence.

In connection with the previous sections of this chapter, the well-known traditional arguments have been touched on: the ontological in § 5, the teleological in § 6, and the cosmological in § 9.   The evidence for belief in a personal God will now be presented without regard to those arguments.

(i) Since *all of the actual data* empirically available *are conscious experiences,* all that is inferred from those data must be consistent with and explanatory of conscious experience.   We may call the present experience of any one of us the datum self (or the empirical situation).   If the objective source of all value experience is a personal God, the datum self is rationally explained.   It may be useful to

[27] See Pratt, PR, 215–216, etc.
[28] Bowne, THE, 150–171; Galloway, PR, 402–449; Lyman, MTR, 229–346; Wright, SPR, 376–401; Tennant, PT, II, especially 78–120, 150–179; Brightman, ITP, 315–339 and PG, 139–165; Knudson, DG, 203–241; and many other treatments.

speak of the datum self as an actual entity, [29] and of every-thing which is not now my actual experience as hypothetical entities. Other selves, the world, and God are thus always hypothetical entities. The one metaphysical qualification which a hypothetical entity must possess if it is to be regarded as real rather than unreal or imaginary, is that it be coherent with all the facts present in the actual entity, and that it be more coherent than any alternative hypothetical entity. That the hypothesis of a personal God is coherent with the facts of personal consciousness in actual entities is undeni-able. Whether it is more coherent than any alternative hypothesis is not susceptible to rigid proof. But the fact that every hypothetical entity is logically derivative from actual entities is undeniable, although the importance of this egocentric predicament has been questioned by Ralph Bar-ton Perry. After all, a fact is a fact even if dubbed a predicament, and the fact, as far as it goes, is evidence for a personal God.[30]

(ii) The previous argument was based on the data of the actual entity, as containing all the evidence for the reality other than ourselves. The second argument starts from the hypothetical entities of physics (force, energy, work) and goes on to the inference that *all physical forces are known only in so far as,* at some stage of their being, *they act on and produce conscious experience.* This fact is con-sistent with the hypothesis that physical forces are either the will of a personal God in action or are effects (or creations) of that will. Critics will rightly point out the inference to the personality of God is not conclusive, since there is no cogent reason why an effect (in consciousness) should re-semble a cause (in the physical world). Yet, although

[29] Without regard to A. N. Whitehead's technical use of this term.

[30] The standard formulation of the egocentric predicament is in Holt (ed.), NR, 11-12. See also Jared Sparks Moore's excellent criticism in "The Significance of the Egocentric Situation," *Jour. Phil.,* 35(1938), 149-156.

effects need not resemble causes, causes should not be so defined as to make their actual effects impossible. If physical causes are merely motions, there is no reason why their effects should be anything but motions (however different the effected motions may be from their causes). But if physical causes are in the realm of the conscious will of God, they are not merely motion, and both the physical phenomena and their effects on human consciousness are intelligible.

(iii) All evidence for *law and order* in a universe is also evidence for a personal mind at work in that universe. Strangely enough, the opposite has often been supposed to be the case. Anomalies, miracles, eccentricities, have been taken as evidence of a divine mind. But law which shows what Sir James Jeans has called a divine mathematician at work is plainly evidence that is consistent with regarding the physical cosmos as the energizing of a rational mind. While order does not necessitate mind, mind necessitates order, and order is coherent with mind.

(iv) All evidence for *purpose,* either *as a psychological fact* in man or other animals, *or as a biological or physico-chemical* fact of objective adaptation of means to ends in nature (see § 6 above), *or as a directive force in evolution* (such as orthogenesis, or "the arrival of the fit") is evidence for a personal God. While it is conceivable that the appearance of purpose may be caused by what has no purpose, the number of telic facts is so great that the appeal to accident or coincidence becomes less and less plausible as the evidence multiplies. That accident should produce as much purpose as actually exists would be no less than magical.

(v) The evidence of *history of religion,* with its trend toward monotheism, of *psychology of religion,* with its goal in the integration of personality, and of *sociology of religion,* with its ideal of coöperation and universal benevolence, is well explained by the hypothesis that one supreme personal God is at work in all religious experience.[31] The critic will point out that religious experience cannot be taken by itself as authentic; it may be explained by a desire for unity rather than by the actual unity of a personal God. To the critic it may be replied that while it is not philosophical to base an ontology on selected evidence, neither is it philosophical to omit any evidence. No conclusion about God, however tentative, may rightly be reached without including the area of religious experience as well as the areas of physicochemical and biological experience.

(vi) In general, the whole domain of *value experience* (see Chapter III)—of axiogenesis and axiosoteria—is even more explicitly coherent with the hypothesis of a personal God than are other facts of law and order. The latter point to an intellect which must indeed be personal, but need not be good; the former point to a personality worthy of worship. God is worshiped solely as source of value; and the hypothesis of the personality of God is, as we have seen, the rational and concrete alternative to supposing God to be wholly unknown. The supposition that "Platonic" Ideas, as abstract impersonal entities, eternally subsist might explain the validity of ideal values, but would leave unexplained the actual phenomena of axiogenesis and axiosoteria. An abstract ideal has no power to generate values or conserve them; that power inheres only in persons who adopt the ideals as their own. Value is inherently a personal experience, and if the cosmic source of value is itself a value it must be a person realizing ideals. The most serious criticism of this argument lies in the facts of evil, the sordid, tragic, overwhelming evils of mind and body and nature. This objection is so important that Chapters VIII, IX, and X will be devoted to it. No view will be true if it is based

[31] See Halliday, PRE, Chap. II.

either on the evils alone or on the values alone. Both are undeniable facts of experience in actual entities, and any rational hypothetical entity—God, or unknown power, or blind force—must give an account of both the good and the evil in experience.

(vii) *If impersonalistic naturalism be regarded as the chief alternative to personalistic theism* (or personalism), *the rational superiority of personalism may be shown by its more inclusive coherence.*[32] Impersonalism gives at least a relatively consistent account of matter; but mind and religious faith are aliens in a naturalistic world. Their emergence is an unexplained brute fact; if accepted "with natural piety," it is none the less a blessed mystery that unconscious matter should engender such offspring. On the other hand, if there is a personal God, both matter and mind are understood. Matter is an order of the divine experience (or creation), expressing divine thoughts (laws) and divine will (force, energy); mind is an order of beings other than God which are constituted as microcosms or monads, reflecting dimly, yet to some extent correctly, the nature of cosmic mind. Naturalism is an hypothesis which makes the most characteristically human facts seem most implausible; personalism, by interpreting both the human and extrahuman factors, is more rational.[33]

(viii) Finally, it may be pointed out that *the evidence for God consists of empirical facts which survive all disbelief.* Indeed, some of the most ardent denials of the existence of a personal God are themselves further evidence for such a God. Values are actually experiences, whether man believes in God or not. As has just been said, the denial of God is often, indeed usually, the assertion of some genuine value, such as sincerity, or realistic facing of facts, or (as in Soviet

---

[32] See Bowne, PER, passim.
[33] See Brightman, "An Empirical Approach to God," Art.(1937).

Russia) revolt against the antisocial attitudes of believers in God. The reality and validity of values does not depend at all on belief in a personal God; but the persistence of value experience when a personal God is denied is evidence for an axiogenetic power in the universe. As long as atheism is based on any appeal to truth or goodness or beauty, atheism itself is evidence for theism.

(5) The *evidence against belief in a personal God* is, except for the first point to be mentioned, speculative rather than empirical, whereas the evidence for such belief was largely empirical, and its speculation was justified by its empirical basis.

(i) The only empirical argument against belief in a personal God has already been mentioned (under (4), (vi) above). It is *the fact of evil*. The irrationalities of sex, of liquor, of a crazy economic system, and of the implacable cruelty of biological processes are illustrated not only in all honestly realistic literature, but also in daily experience. This problem will receive due consideration later.

(ii) *The neural basis of consciousness* is often urged as an objection to belief in a conscious God without a nervous system. The whole force of this argument depends, not on the empirical fact that man has a nervous system, but on one's metaphysical theory of what a nervous system really is. If a nervous system is what materialists take it to be, then it cannot without magic [34] produce consciousness; but if it

---

[34] A naturalist may reasonably object to having a repeatedly observed process called by the name of magic. If anything ever produces anything, then nervous systems, whatever they may be, do produce consciousness. Nevertheless, the naturalistic description of this process seems to an idealist to be magical. The reason for this radical difference of opinion lies in the fact that a naturalist appeals to a different criterion of truth from that of an idealist. Naturalists seem to be satisfied with consistency. Idealists are not satisfied without coherence, and as much coherence as the mind can achieve. Perhaps we might say that the naturalist is satisfied with a minimum of coherence, whereas the idealist seeks a maximum. The statements of naturalists are, it is true, for the most part consistent with each other and with the facts. But mere absence of contradiction,

is what idealists or personalistic theists take it to be, then the nervous system itself is no argument against a personal God, since it is an instance of the activity of that God.

(iii) The hypothesis of *a personal God,* it is urged, is *not necessary for physical science,* and consequently is superfluous. The critic of this objection admits that the idea of God is superfluous for science, but points out that science is an abstract and incomplete account of experience and that scientists do not aim at metaphysical truth. It should be pointed out that all ideals and values, and all reference to personality and personal identity, are just as superfluous and irrelevant for science as is the idea of God. This objection shows the kinship of philosophy with religion, and shows

---

as we saw in Chap. VI, is not coherence. The facts of experience as they stand, without scientific observation or explanation, are perfectly consistent; facts cannot be contradictory, only propositions can contradict each other. Now, if consistency (or minimum coherence) is all the mind needs, then thought might stop with the propositions, "Here is fact *A,* here is fact *B, . . . ,*" and so on. Science, while no more consistent than these bare-fact propositions, is much more coherent. It reveals connections not immediately observed. Scientists might well say to the exponent of bare facts: "Your view of the coming and going of experience is mere magic. You declare that the facts come and go, but you don't know how, because you do not understand their connections." So, too, the idealistic philosopher may, from his standpoint, compare naturalism to magic. He may say to the naturalist: "Sir, your view, like the view of the bare-factualist, is consistent; and I grant it is more coherent than his. But as regards the vital issues—having to do with the connections of the conscious with the material, and of value experience with neutral experience—in proportion as your view lacks coherence, it is an appeal to magic. From the standpoint of a more coherent, more connected, systematic, and purposeful explanation, a less coherent view appears like magic." The hypothesis of personal idealism, which views physical energy as the active will of the cosmic mind, consistently includes all the facts of experience and all the results of science, but illuminates with new systematic connections many facts and relations which the naturalist must take "with natural piety." Personalities require a piety that is rational as well as natural. They accept, equally with naturalists, all facts of sense observation, but they seek a rational account of these facts, free from "magic." Personalists have no need of "magic" when they view nature, including all nervous systems, as the experience of a cosmic mind that constantly interacts with all other minds. It is quite understandable that so great a mind as God's is not readily grasped as one mind on the basis of ordinary experience. But if nature is not mind at all, it is not understandable where any minds come from.

that science must omit the religious problem as long as it remains science. It does not, however, establish even a probability that the idea of God is false, any more than the "value-free" attitude of science establishes a presumption against goodness or beauty.

(iv) It is asserted that *belief in a personal God is unverifiable* and is consequently to be rejected.[35] The problem of verification is a bone of contention in modern philosophy and cannot be solved without a complete system of logic and epistemology. But it is at least possible that there is reason to believe in the real existence of objects that cannot be verified in any literal sense. It is conceivable that verification in the strict sense is confined to the individual's own conscious experience. I verify what I find in my own actual entity, my empirical situation; all else, I believe. No hypothetical entity can strictly be verified. That there was a past, even that I had a past and existed yesterday, is unverifiable, although a well-grounded hypothesis. No historical event can be strictly verified; the assertion that there are other conscious beings than myself is literally unverifiable, although these persons are objects of coherent and empirically grounded beliefs. Least of all could such an extraexperiential entity as matter ever be verified. Yet every rational mind believes that matter in some sense exists (however greatly the definitions of the particular sense may vary). The supposed unverifiability of God is logically in the same position as these other entities. We must either surrender to solipsism or believe, for good empirical reasons, in unverifiable entities.

(v) The concept of a personal God is said to be *an expression of man's arrogance*. Why should the God of all resemble man in any way? If this argument be valid, it stands in curious contradiction with the empirical fact that

[35] See Ayer, LTL.

in general religious persons have regarded all expressions of arrogance as irreligious. Believers in God have practised and taught humility and meekness. It is true that churches have often been arrogant and have allied themselves with arrogant economic secularism and wealth. But in so doing they were contradicting rather than expressing the implications of their belief in God. It is difficult to see why religious thinking is more arrogant than any thinking by scientists or philosophers, which lays claim to objectivity for observations and reasonings that go on in the minds of puny creatures such as we. What is sauce for the goose is sauce for the gander.

(vi) It is often pointed out that personality cannot be ultimate, since *logical subsistence is more ultimate than any concrete actuality.* The possible, the subsistent, the realm of essence, is what it is regardless of existence. Truth is true whether there is any exemplification of it in actuality or not. If there were no reality at all, it would still be true that there was no reality and that all logical relations are valid. As a German soldier wrote in a letter during the World War, not all the destruction of values by heavy artillery can affect the truth of the transcendental unity of apperception. These considerations, abstract and speculative as they are, have considerable weight. They prove at least that if a personal God is eternally real, the logical subsistents are not created by his will. They prove that in any possible world logic must be true. They also prove that no metaphysics is logically as necessary as is logical subsistence itself. They do not prove, however, that subsistence could produce any kind of existence nor do they render clear concretely what status bare subsistence could have in a real universe. The personalist has an answer to this last perplexing question; he suggests that subsistence defines the limits of possible thought; a subsistent is any possible object of thought—real, imaginary, hypothetical, true or false. The personalist must admit that there is a degree of logical contingency attaching to any concrete actuality, even to the actuality of God. This is another way of saying that God is actual, not merely subsistent. This does not entail the necessary or probable non-actuality of God; it is only a denial of the logical necessity of belief. It is always possible to take refuge in the unknown; but such refuge is not a place of superior enlightenment.

(vii) Finally, it is argued that there is *a contradiction in speaking of a creation of creators.* This argument against personalistic theism has been urged especially by Vatke and Bosanquet. Since it has to do with the theory of human freedom rather than with divine personality as such, its discussion will be deferred to Chapter XI, "The Problem of Human Purpose."

§ 12. Is God a Superperson?

Some philosophers, although impressed by the evidence for the personality of God, hesitate to apply the word personal to deity because it is so very human a term. They have proposed therefore the use of the term "superpersonal." [36] The famous sentence of Bradley reads: "It [the Absolute] is not personal, because it is personal and more." The "and more" is left undefined. However, Bradley explicitly admits that this superpersonal "is nothing but experience" and "contains all the highest that we can possibly know or feel," which is exactly what most theistic philosophers mean when they speak of divine personality. Yet Bradley still thinks that to call God personal makes him finite in a human sense (AR, 532).

Bradley's main objections are met when God is described

[36] Bradley, AR, 531–533, and Lighthall, Art.(1926). Some of Whitehead's references to "the primordial nature of God" slant in the same direction.

as superhuman personality. If God be a person, it is self-
evident that his experience is incomparably vaster than
man's. It is certain that he has powers unknown to man,
and goodness utterly transcending man's. It is highly
probable that he has indefinitely many types of experience
unknown to us, which are barely hinted at by such facts as
the ultraviolet and infrared rays, invisible to man. But it
is one thing to say that personality which is in part known
includes kinds of experience of which we do not yet know;
and it is quite another thing to say that there is an entity
of some sort which is lacking in all consciousness and experience and rational personal identity, and yet is higher
than personality. In the former sense we may say that God
is superpersonal, meaning superhumanly personal. In the
latter sense, since we cannot define our hypothesis except
wishfully, we cannot know whether an unconscious "superpersonality" would be better or worse than personality, and
we cannot use the concept to explain any aspect of actual
conscious entities such as ourselves. As far as we can know,
the unconscious and impersonal, if such there be in the universe, is below and not above the level of conscious personality. At best the unconscious superpersonal is but a
label for the unknown, and not a definable hypothesis.

§ 13. Religion and Theory

The discussions of belief in God in this chapter have carried us far away from the simple experiences of religious
trust and faith into many technicalities and disputes. Some
will inquire: What has all this to do with religion? Is not
religion a way of living rather than a way of theorizing?
Such questioners will sympathize with the plaint of Thomas
à Kempis, "I had rather feel compunction than know its
definition."

There is some force in this objection. Neither the present

chapter nor this text as a whole is intended as a religious experience. A philosophy of religion is an attempt to understand and criticize religion intellectually. Philosophy of religion is not religion itself any more than the science of meteorology is sunshine or tempest. To understand seismology is not to experience an earthquake, and one may readily experience an earthquake without understanding anything about seismology. So too, one may experience God without understanding any of the principles of philosophy of religion.

The issue at stake is simple: Do we or do we not believe that experience may be guided, redirected, and improved as a result of rational understanding? If we do not, we should avoid philosophy of religion. No one, even in an authoritarian state, can compel us to think. But if we believe that rational understanding is both possible and profitable, there is no reason to take it lightly. We should explore every possibility until we have reached such clarity as we can find, and then we may use that area of clarity as a center for further growth.

Religion is not theory, nor is theory religion. But it is irrational, and harmful both psychologically and morally, for a thinking man not to think about his religion. A thoughtless religion in a thinking mind leads to a divided personality and system of double entry ideals. Practical life in all its forms needs all the theoretical guidance it can secure, and theory is empty if not tested and applied in practical life. If the protester means that experience is prior to and the source of all valid theory, he is right. But if he means that religious experience can survive without theory, he has no historical basis for his thesis. All religions have had doctrines.

Specifically, religion requires the application of our best theories about God to the concrete struggle with the forces of good and evil. The facts of evil are the glaring empirical evidence against God. The struggle against evil is at once the source of human despair and the fulcrum for the Archimedean lever of religion. All argument about God remains formal until its concrete application to the goods and evils of life is made clear. Chapters VIII through XIV will be concerned with problems arising out of this concrete life situation.

BIBLIOGRAPHICAL NOTE

The entire bibliography of Chapter V bears on this chapter, and the reader is referred to the materials there cited.

In addition, the theistic position is well presented by Knudson, DG(1930), Bertocci, EAG(1938), and Hocking, MGHE(1912). The neoscholastic view is found in Joyce, PNT(1923). Critical of personalistic theism in varying degrees are McTaggart, SDR(1906), Calverton, PG(1934), Ayer, LTL(1936), Dewey, CF(1934), and Cohen, RAN(1931), esp. Bk. II.

EIGHT

THE PROBLEM OF
GOOD-AND-EVIL

P to the present chapter our thought has centered on the experience and the implications of value. Religion is allegiance to the source of value. Where there is little or no confidence in good, religion fails; but the good is not the whole story either of religion or of philosophy. A religious man is one who asserts the predominance of good in the universe, "the conservation of values." [1] Daily experience challenges his faith. While there is doubtless some value in the life of every normal human being, and a predominance of value over disvalue for a large number, it is nevertheless a patent fact that the quantity and the distribution of evils make difficult the belief in a good God who can be trusted to conserve values eternally. For many that belief is impossible. No objection to religious faith compares in seriousness with that arising from the fact of evil. If religion, as Gordon W. Allport has said, is "the search for a value underlying all things," [2] that search is rendered most perplexing by the

---

[1] It cannot be too often repeated that value experience is such that it cannot be conserved without being increased. Sorley criticizes Höffding for speaking of conservation rather than increase (or perfection) of values (MVIG, 177–181), although Höffding explicitly asserts that "value can only be retained by being increased" (PR, 11).

[2] Allport, PER, 226.

abundance of disvalue. Does value underlie disvalue? Is all evil really good? If not, what is the source of evil, the *fons et origo malorum?*

Yet this statement of the problem is not sufficient. To point out that evils are a problem for believers in God is necessary but not sufficient. Good is as much a problem as is evil, unless man is so smugly self-centered as to accept whatever he likes without even a thought. Belief in God and in the faith and practices of religion is an attempt to solve the problem of good. But the problem of good is not solved satisfactorily to the philosopher unless the solution arises from a contemplation of all the evidence. The evidence does not consist of goods alone; it also consists of evils. It is therefore equally incomplete to center (as we have been doing) on the problem of good, or to plunge (as we may be in danger of doing) into the problem of evil. We were justified in beginning with value, because it is the very heart of religion; we should not be justified in arriving at conclusions about value without examining the evidence of disvalue. Hence we confront, not the problem of good or the problem of evil, but the compound problem of good-and-evil.[3]

§ 2. Goods-and-Evils as Intrinsic and Instrumental

In Chapter III, § 2, it was pointed out that values (or goods)[4] are either intrinsic or instrumental. When we are considering goods-and-evils, this distinction becomes

---

[3] On this chapter as a whole, consult the article, "Good and Evil," in ERE, VI, by W. D. Niven.

[4] The terms value and good are used as precise equivalents. In this chapter, the compound good-and-evil is preferred to value-and-disvalue because it is both more euphonious and more familiar. The use of the term good should not mislead the reader into supposing that moral goods (character values) are intended, in contrast to aesthetic, religious, or other types. If moral or ethical good is meant, it will be so designated. Similarly, evil is any kind of disvalue, not specifically moral evil alone.

more complex. There may be intrinsic good, like truth or worship; and there may be intrinsic evil, like error [5] or blasphemy. Likewise there may be instrumental goods or instrumental evils. An instrumental good is any experience, process, or entity which contributes to producing an intrinsic good or to averting an intrinsic evil; while an instrumental evil is any experience, process, or entity which contributes to producing an intrinsic evil or to averting an intrinsic good. Intrinsic goods are inherent, and nothing can remove their goodness from them. They shine by their own light. Similarly, intrinsic evils are inherent. They are disvalues in themselves and nothing can make them into intrinsic values. But instrumental good-and-evil is relative to circumstances, and the same instrument may serve either good or evil ends. A railroad train carrying a saint like Kagawa from San Francisco to New York is an instrumental good, for Kagawa may be able to achieve worthy ends in New York which would never be achieved if he did not go there. The same railroad train may be, at the same time, an instrumental evil, for bandits may be traveling on it in order to produce both instrumental and intrinsic evil in New York or en route.

Any solution of the problem of good-and-evil must take account of instrumental as well as of intrinsic aspects of each type of experience. A perfectly optimistic solution of the problem, for example, would have to include the judgment that all apparently intrinsic evils are either essential parts of the complete intrinsic good or are necessary and perfect means to the perfect end of intrinsic good; and it would also include the judgment that all apparently instrumental evils are really instruments to good. Thus extreme optimism would in the end leave nothing but intrinsic good together with instruments perfectly adapted

[5] Involuntary error is an intellectual evil; voluntary error is a moral evil.

to achieving that good. Perfect pessimism, analogously, would explain away both intrinsic and instrumental good and would leave only intrinsic evil and instruments perfectly adapted to achieving evil. It is hardly necessary to do more than to state these views in order to create the presumption that they are both unreal, and that both rest on a torturing of the actual facts. The solution, if one is possible, cannot be reached by an easy-going general formula. It must rest on an analysis of the evidence.

§ 3. INTRINSIC GOODS-AND-EVILS

The usual method of classifying evils is to distinguish moral evils from natural evils. The former are those consequent on human volition, whereas the latter are independent of human will. Moral evil is what is known theologically as sin; natural evil would include pain, disease, death, earthquakes, and tornadoes. But this classification is oversimple, and not always clear. It has been argued that some "moral" evil is due to a pressure of natural evils which man is not strong enough to resist, or that some natural evils, like earthquakes, could be avoided by proper moral choices, such as not building cities on sites like Lisbon, Los Angeles, or Tokyo. A more careful analysis will more adequately reveal the complexity of intrinsic goods and evils.

Reference to Chapter III, § 3, enables us to gain a survey of the field. Intrinsic goods-and-evils may be classified in accordance with the table of values. Just as there are intrinsic bodily goods, so there are intrinsic bodily evils—for instance, pains, experiences of deformity, or lack of control of parts or the whole of the body in paralysis. There are recreational goods and there are recreational evils, which we call vices, that are both intrinsically and instrumentally disvaluable. There are the goods of work and the correlative evils of laziness and inaction. There are social goods and social evils; the evils may consist in the sharing of an intrinsic disvalue (such as ignorance or hate) or in an antisocial attitude such as egoism. There are goods of character and evils of character—the former the acts of a rational will and the latter the acts of an irrational will. There are aesthetic goods of the beautiful and the sublime, and aesthetic evils of the trivial, the vile, and the ridiculous. There are intellectual goods of insight into truth, and intellectual evils of ignorance and error. There are religious goods of worship and coöperation, and religious evils of irreverence and pride.

It is not always a simple matter, however, to determine just how a particular good or evil is to be classified. As we have already seen, the classification is not ultimate, and the only ultimate intrinsic value would be the rational whole of value experience. So, too, the only ultimate evil would be whatever contradicts or prevents the realization of the rational whole of good. For similar reasons, it is often difficult to judge whether an apparent good or evil (a value-claim or disvalue-claim) is a true good or true evil, either intrinsically or instrumentally.

In order to shed further light on the problem before us, let us analyze evil as we meet it in our experience. (1) Every human being experiences *a will that is more or less incoherent.* There is no one who does not at times waver in his choice of goods, at times break contracts or will mutually exclusive ends. This incoherent will is partly a "moral" and partly an inevitable "natural" evil. In opposition to it is the actual good of a partially coherent will and the ideal good of a perfectly coherent one. (2) Equally common to all is *the intellectual evil of ignorance;* this is partly a "moral" evil, in so far as we could well have known what we do not know, but preferred not to make the effort; and it is partly a "natural" evil, in so far as the ignorance was unavoidable. Any ignorance is an intrinsic evil, but ignorance of the highest intrinsic values is perhaps the worst—and most widespread—type of ignorance. Ignorance of instrumental values is both an intrinsic and also an instrumental evil. In contrast to the evils of ignorance, and possibly conquering them, are the goods of knowledge and wisdom.

(3) *Maladjustment* is an intrinsic evil, like unintended discords in music. Social maladjustment is one of the worst evils of this type. How completely it can be overcome is problematic. Religion sets up as its ideal the hope of adjustment to the will of God.

(4) *Incompetence* is another type of evil; the lack of ability in any individual to do what he undertakes to do. In the New Testament the Greek word ἁμαρτία, which means missing the mark, is the word usually translated as "sin." Yet missing the mark is no evidence of a morally evil or voluntarily incoherent will. It is evidence only of a lack of skill. It appears to be quite unjust to call a person sinful because he is unskillful; but it is not unjust to describe an unskillful person as experiencing evil. The good that overcomes incompetence is development or training which results in skill.

(5) A fifth type of evil may be called *the dysteleological surd*. The other types may sometimes be superseded by internal development: an incoherent will may become relatively more coherent; ignorance may be enlightened; maladjustments may be overcome by proper relationships; and incompetence may be supplanted by skill. But a dysteleological surd [6] is a type of evil which is inherently and

---

[6] A surd in mathematics is a quantity not expressible in rational numbers; so a surd in the realm of value experience is an evil that is not expressible in terms of good, no matter what operations are performed on it.

irreducibly evil and contains within itself no principle of development or improvement. It is debatable whether there are dysteleological surds; it is at least conceivable that such surds may exist. Take, for example, the phenomenon of imbecility. Let us grant that imbecility may encourage psychiatry and arouse pity; yet, if it be an incurable condition, there remains in it a surd evil embodied in the intrinsic worthlessness of the imbecile's existence and the suffering which his existence imposes on others. Many other possible instances of surd evil will occur to the reader. If there be any truly surd evil, then it is not in any sense an intrinsic good; good comes in opposing it, not in enjoying it. A good man or a good God, in the presence of surd evil, could only exercise control—self-control, in order not to be overwhelmed by the evil, and objective control, in order that the evil may not overwhelm all values. The problem of evil in its most acute form is the question whether there is surd evil and, if so, what its relation to value is.

§ 4. INSTRUMENTAL GOODS-AND-EVILS

Instrumental evils as well as instrumental values may be classified as natural and economic. Intrinsic goods are all to be found in the realm of personal consciousness. It is hard to conceive what the objectivity of value (or ideals) would mean other than the existence of a superhuman consciousness directed eternally toward the realization of ideal values. It is not so obvious that instrumental goods-and-evils belong entirely in the sphere of consciousness.[7] What is obvious is that, if there is a God in control of cosmic processes, such a God would be more clearly responsible for the operation of causal laws in nature than he

---

[7] Although a personal idealist defines all reality as consisting entirely of selves, so that nothing exists which is not a self, or an experience of a self, or an interrelation among selves, this metaphysical question may be left in abeyance for present purposes.

would be for the freely chosen attitudes of men toward value experiences. In other words, the experience of intrinsic evil may with some show of reason be at least partially explained by reference to man's abuse of his freedom. But if there are causal processes in nature which, apart from human intervention, lead to dysteleological results, then it is impossible to avoid the question of God's responsibility for evil.

Economic instrumental values involve human labor expended on natural objects or processes. It is plain that there are also many natural events which man can neither initiate nor prevent. Such events are taking place constantly in the heavenly bodies, in the climate, and in the interior of the earth; in particular, all events in the history of this planet prior to the existence of man belong in the class of events the responsibility for which must be traced to causes other than man. These prehuman phenomena were instrumental to many forms of life and of consciousness. Instrumental good may be found in these phenomena in so far as they were part of the cause of the development of higher types of life and mind. But by a parity of reasoning instrumental evil must be ascribed to them in so far as they produced either intrinsic or instrumental evil.

Whether one considers the means or the ends of evolution, one must admit the presence of much evil, both intrinsic and instrumental. There is no evidence for the presence of any of the higher intrinsic values in the consciousness of the saurians. Their minds, activated by small brains, appear to have entertained no ends higher than the desire to win in the struggle for survival, and even that end was frustrated. The means used in the evolutionary process were wasteful and cruel in the extreme, and for many millions of years seem to have served no intrinsic value.

The famous La Brea tar pits in Los Angeles, where masto-
dons, saber-tooth tigers, and other animals perished, illustrate the suffering and the futility which prevailed for long
ages in evolution. Yet with all this evil, there was law,
movement toward higher forms of life, and gradual striving
toward values. Nature, past and present, is a mixture of
instrumental good-and-evil.

§ 5. THE RELIGIOUS PROBLEM OF GOOD-AND-EVIL

Religion has rarely sought to evade the problems of good-
and-evil; rarely has it been a shallow optimism, facing only
the sunshine and joy of life and neglecting its shadows
and woes. In fact, Schopenhauer may not have been
entirely wrong when he declared that neither religion nor
philosophy would have arisen had it not been for the fact
of death. Religion is not merely an enjoyment of good;
it is a redemption from evil.

The problem of good-and-evil comes to expression in
religion (1) in the difficulty of believing good to be ultimate and (2) in the difficulty of achieving good.

(1) So real are the evils of life, that man's first gods
were puny, local creatures, sources of highly precarious
goods in a world of hostile powers. The gods were restricted in their power by time and place, were at war
with demons, witches, and hostile deities, and were themselves far from models of perfect goodness. The history
of religious belief shows plainly the struggles through which
man has gone before he has been able to believe in the good.
For a long time, even the highest forms of religion held
that the rule of the universe was not entirely under the control of good, but that it was a good-and-evil, an Ahura-
Mazda and Ahriman, or a God and Satan. It is true that
the intellectual difficulty of arriving at a coherent view of
God if it must be assumed that he creates or tolerates a

Satan is so great that monotheists generally have come to abandon belief in any Devil or Satan. But the negation of an incoherent, evil, Satanic personality in the cosmos leaves the problem of good-and-evil even more acute than it was; and the more coherent God of today finds many who cannot believe in him at all. It is almost as *hard for modern man to believe good to be ultimate* as it was for primitive man.

(2) *The difficulty of achieving good* in a world of good-and-evil gives religion its chief task. The intellectual interpretation of belief in God is primarily a philosophical, rather than a religious, enterprise. Religion is fundamentally practical, rather than intellectual or even emotional. The aim of religious personalities is to become good or to do good in spite of all the evil in the world. Emotion plays a part in genuine religion as a means to the practical end, rather than as an end in itself. Religious believers have undergone disciplines, offered sacrifices, abandoned pleasures, toiled, and have suffered death itself, because of their hope that thus a real and permanent good might be achieved.[8] Worship is an effort of men to concentrate on the supreme worth of existence. Most religions offer a way of salvation or redemption which rescues them from the power of evil and guarantees the supremacy of good in their lives. The essence of religion is that the highest power in the universe is on the side of value in this age-long struggle between good and evil. Most religion presupposes the reality of evil as well as of good, and finds the cosmic forces in a real struggle. Even when evil is viewed as "maya," illusion, or error, the task of religion is to banish that illusion and to aid men in the struggle against it, which in itself is actual, however evil be interpreted.

The problem of religion, then, is the twofold one of

[8] See the eleventh chapter of the Epistle to the Hebrews.

believing good and achieving good in a world in which the intermixture of good-and-evil is a constant fact of experience. Religion is a form of realistic action.

§ 6. The Philosophical Problem of Good-and-Evil

Thus far in this chapter attention has been centered on the religious interest in good-and-evil. It is sometimes said by unbelievers that the whole problem of good-and-evil is an artificial one, created by the false premise that there is a God. In this assertion there is the obvious truth that every item of evil in experience is more inharmonious with belief in God than with atheism. Those who make the assertion are nevertheless in error.

The problem of good-and-evil is a genuine problem for every philosophical thinker regardless of whether that thinker accepts or rejects religious faith or belief in God. It is true that physicists, chemists, biologists, astronomers, and geologists, for example, find within their sciences no light on intrinsic goods or evils. The causal laws of these sciences are, indeed, potential instrumental values; but so far as the sciences are concerned these laws may as well be instrumental evils as instrumental goods. From the standpoint of pure science they are neutral. From the standpoint of experience, they are Janus-faced; they may be used for education or for crime, for peace or for war. The philosopher, however, cannot abstract from all interest in values. The scientist must restrict his problem to a special field, abstracted from the rest of experience. The philosopher must take all experience for his field and seek a unified view of the whole. Therefore the philosopher is bound to include in his survey not only the results of the sciences but also the problems which the sciences were compelled to omit. Conspicuous among these is the problem of good-and-evil. There is no doubt that there are experiences of what we

regard as good and what we regard as evil. The philosopher must inquire into this whole area of value-disvalue
in order to discover what truth, if any, it contains and how
it is related to other aspects of existence.

A philosophy which did not include an investigation of
values would belie its name; it would not be so much a
love of wisdom as a barren description of facts, and it would
not be an account of the whole of experience. A philosophy
which investigated value, but not disvalue, would be so
partisan and one-sided as to lose its title to objectivity and
devotion to truth. If a philosopher will not bestir himself
into an investigation of the age-old problem of evil unless
he is prodded into it by the demands of his religious faith,
he has but feeble interest in a truly philosophical coherence
and inclusiveness. The problem is forced on the mind by
the incoherence in the claims and counter-claims of experience. The goal of philosophy is a coherent hypothesis
which will include and explain all the theses and antitheses
of experience. The philosopher's unpardonable sin is indifference toward any area of experience, especially when
that area contains such incoherences as does the battle-field
of good-and-evil. Without consideration of values and disvalues no one can hope to find more than a distorted fragment of truth.

§ 7. The Dialectic of Desire

First, then, let us examine our experience of value or good
with a view to discovering what light it sheds on our view
of experience as a whole. This problem has been adum-
brated here and there in Chapters III, IV, VI, and
VII. Now for the first time it is taken up in a systematic
way.

It seems fruitful to approach this investigation from the
standpoint of dialectic. By dialectic is meant the mind's

search for completeness and coherence. No mind can start with the attainment of wholeness. Everyone must start with his present fragmentary and changing experience. This starting point is called the thesis. If he is to understand this thesis, he must relate it to something else, contrasted with it, yet relevant to it; this is called the antithesis. Thinking, however, is more than mere contrasting of opposites. It is an understanding of their productive interrelation. This understanding leads to a new insight, known as the synthesis, which in turn gives rise to a new opposition or contrast, until the whole of experience is comprehended in philosophical insight.

Value experience is properly called the dialectic of desire, because the simplest form of good or value is always a desire striving for fulfillment. Every value-claim is such a desire. True value would be a fully coherent fulfilled desire for a fully coherent object. If such a desire is found, we may suspect ourselves of being near the truth.[9]

(1) *Desire for pleasure* (enjoying). Desire must be for something. The thesis of desire points to an antithesis which is desired. The most obvious and universal object of naïve desire is pleasure (antithesis). But reflection on pleasure shows that we make qualitative discriminations in it; J. S. Mill [10] has shown that we prefer the pleasure of a man to the pleasure of a pig because we find the former qualitatively superior. As soon as some pleasures are held to be more important than others, we experience a desire to assure ourselves of the sources of such pleasures. While pleasures are held to be all of a kind, any random experience might afford satisfaction; but when qualitative differences are recognized, the uncertainty of fulfillment of desire becomes clearer.

9 "The apparent good," says Aristotle, "is the object of appetite, and the real good is the primary object of rational wish. . . . The thinking is the starting-point." *Met.* Lambda (XII), Chap. VII, 1072 $^{a26-29}$.

10 In *Utilitarianism.*

Out of desire for pleasure (mere enjoying), thoughtfully understood, there thus arises a synthesis, which is the desire for objective grounds of the permanence of pleasure-qualities. Since the simplest ground for such permanence lies in the possession of physical things, thought about value effects a transition to the second stage.

(2) *Desire for physical things* (having). As soon as we reflect on the desire for physical things, we find ourselves haunted by their unsatisfactoriness. Mere possession of things is no guarantee of pleasure or of fulfillment of desire. Things are not desired for their own sake, anyway, but for what they will produce; we perceive that they will produce no satisfactory values of themselves. Hence they are not a coherent object or standard of value. If value is to be secured, things must be used, acted on, dealt with.

Out of desire for physical things (mere having), there arises in the reflective mind the insight that fulfillment of desire is more dependent on active transactions with things than on the things themselves. The dialectic of desire thus effects a transition to its third stage.

(3) *Desire for activity* (doing). Without activity, there is no value; no perception without apperception, no fulfillment without effort, no value without the search for value. This (pragmatic) thesis is an inevitable moment of value experience. Mere activity, however, is not necessarily valuable or desire-fulfilling. Activity must be for some end, just as desire had to be first of all for pleasure. What then is the simplest and nearest antithesis—the end for which our activity strives? Primarily, it is a relation to other persons, a social relation.

Accordingly, the desire for activity (doing) has given rise to the desire for association with others, and herewith a transition is effected to the fourth stage of the dialectic.

(4) *Desire for other persons* (sharing). When valuation is raised to the social level, it undergoes an expansion as

well as an elevation. The consciousness of respect for and association with others, the desire for experiences shared with others, the sublime experience of love, contribute to a richer and more coherent understanding of the nature of our desires. Yet, as we found earlier in our discussion of social values, the thesis of desire for other persons engenders an antithesis, in the desire for a standard by which to judge other persons and shared experiences as carriers of value. Desire is not rationally satisfied by mere association with another person or by mere sharing, unless a value worth imparting enters into the social experience. It is necessary, but not sufficient, to say that value is social sharing. The antithesis, the desire for a standard, must be considered.

A new synthesis emerges from this situation, namely the truth that shared experience is a progressive realization of ideals. Unless our relations to others and our desires for a standard were judged and fulfilled by ideals,[11] social values would be irrational. Thus arises a transition to the fifth stage of the dialectic.

(5) *Desire for ideals* (planning). In the desire for ideals, carried out on every stage of the dialectic, as enjoying, as having, as doing, and as sharing, the climax of the dialectic and the solution of the problem of good might seem to be reached. No great thinker of past or present, from Plato to Kant, from Hegel to Dewey, fails to acknowledge that ideals embody our need for truth and for insight into standards. The lower stages of the dialectic—pleasure, things, activity, and persons—are all relative to and are judged by ideals.

Yet there is something peculiarly unsatisfactory about ideals. Hegel often called attention to the weakness and emptiness of a mere ideal that was not realized. Value is

[11] See Brightman, POI, Chap. III in particular.

not achieved merely because we acknowledge an ideal, even a true one. Value arises only when the ideal is fulfilled. Thus there arises the fundamental question, whether the universe is such that our ideals can be realized in it. The dialectic of desire has not reached its consummation until the thesis of the ideal and the antithesis of the real are brought together in realized ideals, actual values. In isolated instances, this synthesis may obviously be accomplished on the level of activity. But this humanistic and practical solution leaves untouched the deeper question of the relations of ideals to existence. We confront *the antinomy of the ideal*.

Our experience of the ideal, if it means anything, means that ideals are not only superindividual, but also supersocial. Ideals, that is, are standards by which both individuals and societies are judged. The thesis of our experience of desire for the ideal is that, in order to be valid, ideals must in some sense lie beyond all human personalities as their objective goal and judge. But this thesis is opposed at once by an antithesis: ideals can be real only as the concepts and acknowledged purposes of minds. The notion of the impersonality of ideals can mean concretely only their validity for all persons. The thesis tells us that ideals must be objective; yet the antithesis tells us that they cannot be external to persons. The conflict of thesis with antithesis drives thought on to a synthesis, in which the dialectic of desire finds the solution Saint Augustine found when he declared that the soul is restless until it finds rest in God. The synthesis, therefore, is the insight that true value is an objective union of ideal and personality. The conception of a Supreme Person, guiding the universe by its ideals, is the coherent and inclusive interpretation of the whole range of value experience. Thus we move to the sixth stage of the dialectic.

(6) *Desire for the Supreme Person* (worshiping and co-operating). Logical thought about value experience thus points to the same object that religious worshipers have found—a supreme person in whom supreme good is acknowledged and actualized. Well-grounded belief in such a person affords a coherent account of the objectivity of ideals implied by value experience, and it offers reasons for the religious faith in a personal God.

Satisfactory as this outcome may be to the demands of reason and of religious faith, it must be scrutinized critically before being either accepted or rejected. Certain aspects of the conception of the dialectic which leads to belief in a personal God need to be made clearer. First, the dialectic deals only with the spiritual and logical aspects of value experience. The God of the final synthesis is a conscious, spiritual person. Nothing is yet said about physical organisms or the system of nature—except that physical things are not a rational object of value. Secondly, the dialectic shows that desire or valuation is a search for God only when it is subjected to interpretation by reflective reason. Thirdly, the previous point shows that no present insight, short of all-inclusive knowledge and wisdom, can be regarded as final truth about the mind of God. In other words, the fact that the Supreme Person is the climax of the dialectic of desire is no warrant for supposing that thought may cease, once it has found God. God is an object for inexhaustible exploration. Fourthly, the dialectic reveals the inadequacy of any view of religion or of God which makes man merely passive and dependent. In so far as a transcendent Barthian deity utters revelations which reason cannot grasp or define, such a God places himself outside the realm of intelligible value. The dialectic is compatible with the postulate that all rational value experience is a revelation of the spirit of the whole working in the humblest parts, immanent and revelatory. It is incompatible with a purely transcendent God utterly above and beyond all reason. Fifthly, the dialectic shows that we are the more surely driven to objectivity and truth when we are more loyal to our best selves. Not by divesting ourselves of reason and the highest human values do we find God, but by rigorous loyalty to them. Thus objectivity is consistent with human creativity; and the methods of humanism and naturalism, taken seriously, drive the mind beyond those positions. Sixthly, it needs to be pointed out that neither religion nor philosophy is satisfied by mere acknowledgment or assertion of a Cosmic Personality. Religion requires the development of values through worship of God and coöperation with him. Philosophy requires the critical exploration of the meaning of God and his relations to the world. Both religion and philosophy imply that what we value is not the mere existence of God as an abstract fact, but rather the concrete implication of that fact. The dialectic of desire presupposes as a religious and a philosophical foundation the actual empirical situation of each human individual. What individual human persons rationally desire is not alone the fact that a Divine Person exists, but also that the ideals of the Divine Person shall become constitutive life principles for all persons in the total cosmic society. Thus the dialectic points away from atheism and toward theism, not toward pantheism or deism. Socially, it means neither anarchism nor a totalitarian state, but organic pluralism—a society of free persons seeking a rational and valuable common purpose grounded in God, the objective principle of worthful coöperation.

(7) *Grounds of dissatisfaction.* Is the dialectic of desire, thus explained, thoroughly satisfactory? To ask this question is to answer it in the negative. It is emotionally unsatisfactory partly because of its demand for rational

thought and discipline. Exalted emotional and mystical experiences of worship are, indeed, states in which men for a time rise above all their dissatisfactions into absolute peace and joy. Human defects are transcended and forgotten. In this sense, the outcome of the dialectic may be emotionally satisfactory; but the very moment of greatest satisfaction may be a dogmatic ignoring of human defects and thus the highest emotional satisfaction may contain within it both ethical and intellectual dissatisfaction. There is ethical dissatisfaction for everyone who believes in God because of the incompleteness and inadequacy of all human cooperation with God. There is intellectual dissatisfaction because of the incompleteness of our knowledge and the insufficiency of our proofs; this dissatisfaction, however, inheres in the human situation and is the plague of honest atheists, agnostics, humanists, and pantheists, as well as of honest theists. In fact, the emotional and the ethical dissatisfactions of religion share this universality with the intellectual. Every possible point of view that the mind can assume toward its life of feeling and will, as well as toward its thinking, is haunted by its own incompleteness —what Hegel calls "the seriousness of the negative." But religious persons are in no way compelled to regard this unsatisfactoriness as a reason for rejecting belief in God; on the contrary, this perpetual unrest in man, this undying fire, this endless search for more truth, may well be viewed as "the hound of heaven" [12] pursuing man, or, to quote Hegel again, as "the guile of reason." [13]

The real challenge to the philosophical insight into a Supreme Person as well as to religious faith in that Person

---

[12] A term first applied to Diogenes by Cereidas. See Diogenes Laertius, *Lives of Eminent Philosophers*, VI, 77; also the title of a religious poem by Francis Thompson.
[13] Hegel, *Encyclopädie*, § 209.

is to be found, not in this necessary incompleteness of all human endeavor, but rather in an unnecessary and quite avoidable incompleteness of the method of the dialectic. The dialectic is precisely a dialectic of desire, that is, of the movement from value-claims to true value. It is the anatomy of good. It omits the plain and inevitable fact of evil. Its procedure in so doing is not unlike that of the natural sciences which, as we have seen, omit the entire experience of good-and-evil. Such abstractions are necessary devices if human thought is to make any headway; but they must be recognized for what they are—namely the result of deliberately incomplete thinking. C. Delisle Burns has said that "abstraction is logical forgetfulness or the art of forgetting; and it is not misleading unless you forget that you have forgotten." [14] It is not misleading to forget evil temporarily while examining good; yet it would be most misleading to give forth the results of an examination of good as truth about the whole of experience, forgetting evil and forgetting that it had been forgotten. Until evil has been examined, all conclusions about good remain insecure. The problem of evil is ineluctable.

§ 8.   Current Solutions of the Problem of Evil Examined

There is no dialectic of evil corresponding to the dialectic of good; for good is inherently rational and evil inherently nonrational. Good is a principle of totality, of coherence, of meaning. Evil is a principle of fragmentariness, of incoherence, of mockery. Hence there is no immanent logic in evil; evil is the Satan that laughs at logic. Yet there is logic in thought about evil, and many more or less logical

[14] C. Delisle Burns, *The Contact Between Minds* (London: Macmillan and Co., Ltd., 1923), 3.

solutions of the problem of evil have been proposed. Those most often discussed in the modern world will now be briefly stated and criticized.[15]

(1) *Moral evils* may be explained as *a result of human freedom*. Much weight may be granted to this argument. The objection of Kant, Vatke, and Bosanquet—that it is contradictory to suppose that God (or any reality) could create the wills of free beings without creating at the same time all the details of their willing [16]—appears to be a priori, unempirical, and to refer to a defect of human imagination rather than to a violation of reason. Surely a human being can make a machine without determining how it shall be used; it would seem extraordinary if a God could not create a free will. Such a view limits God arbitrarily. Nevertheless, human freedom leaves many aspects of evil, even of moral evil, unexplained. Why are there in the nature of things, independent of human choice, so many temptations and allurements to evil choices? And why are the consequences of some evil choices so utterly debasing and disastrous? It is very hard to reconcile some religious utterances on temptation with the facts. Saint Paul says that "God is faithful, who will not suffer you to be tempted above that ye are able." (1 Cor. 10:13.) Yet the pressure, physiological, psychological, and social, to which some men, women, and children are subjected seems to most observers to be unendurable. Is it just to ascribe all of the sins and vices of poverty-stricken refugees or unemployed families to their own freedom, or even to all human freedom

---

[15] Kant's little pamphlet, *Ueber das Misslingen aller philosophischen Versuche in der Theodicee* (1791) (*On the Failure of all Philosophical Essays in Theodicy*), raises fundamental problems. Leibniz's *Essais de Theodicée* (1710) is a classic in the field, to which Voltaire's *Candide* (1756) is a biting answer.

[16] See Kant's *Religion within the Limits of Reason Alone* (tr. Greene and Hudson), 133; Bosanquet, VDI, 136–138, and the footnote with citation from Vatke.

put together? The tendency to use human freedom too readily to explain too much is exemplified by the writer of the Epistle of James, when he denied that God tempts man, asserting "each man is tempted when he is drawn away by his own lust, and enticed" (James 1:14)—as if man's freedom actually created his own sexual nature. Freedom, we repeat, explains much of moral evil, but it does not explain either the force of temptation or the debasing consequences of moral evil.

(2) *Nonmoral evils* are sometimes viewed as *a punishment for moral evils.* This view is not logically impossible and is widely held.[17] Yet it is repugnant to the ethical sense of modern idealists. Even criminology has repudiated the motive of punishment in favor of the reformation of the criminal. Shall a good God harbor resentment? Does perfect love punish? Further, the unjust distribution of nonmoral evils, both intrinsic and instrumental, makes it impossible to suppose that any consistent desire to punish affords an explanation of more than a very few evils. This crude theory of punishment was rejected by the writer of the book of Job and by Jesus (according to Jn. 9:3). It can be maintained only by supposing (like some Theosophists and believers in Indian religions) that the incidence of evils is a perfectly just punishment [18] for sins (now unknown to us) committed in a previous incarnation (equally unknown). To say nothing of the highly speculative character of this theory, it remains exposed to all the ethical objections against the idea of punishment. The whole theory of

[17] The hurricane of September 21, 1938, in Massachusetts, was more than half-seriously held by many to be divine punishment for the nomination of an unworthy candidate in local political primaries on the previous day. Holders of this view overlooked the fact that it afforded no explanation of the worse devastation in Rhode Island and Connecticut, without similar justification.

[18] If Theosophists argue that they do not hold to punishment but only to Karma, a law of cause and effect, they have then no explanation of why that law should entail so much suffering.

punishment as a solution of the problem of evil collapses of
its own weight.

(3) *Nonmoral evils,* if not penal, *may be regarded as
disciplinary.* Their purpose is then to reform or to test, or
to elicit "rugged individualism" or social responsibility,
rather than to allot sufferings in accordance with deserts.
It cannot well be denied that many apparent evils (disvalue-
claims) turn out to be goods in disguise (true values).
Hardship often develops character. A community disaster
often elicits coöperation and a sense of human brotherhood. Many noble spirits dwell in crippled and diseased
bodies. Suffering teaches sympathy. No observer of life
has failed to perceive the growth of courage and purpose
in the experience of some victims of hard fate. Then shall
we "welcome each rebuff that turns earth's smoothness
rough"? Browning's thought seems almost to be that the
normal state of affairs is smoothness and that a little rough-
ness is welcome for variety's sake. Such a picture is too
unrealistic to need an answer. It disregards the facts. In
truth, the whole theory of evil as disciplinary falls far short
of being philosophically adequate, even when it is held in
its best form and not in Browning's unintentional caricature
of it.

Philosophy seeks for an explanation that fits all the facts
and is contradicted by none. If we test the theory before us
by this criterion, what do we find? We find that sometimes
evil facts are experienced as actually leading to nobler and
more spiritual living; also that sometimes—and perhaps
more frequently—evil facts lead to more and more re-
sentful, debased, depressed, and hopeless living. Life and
literature abound in instances which need not be cited. We
find that the good itself sometimes has the evil effect of
inflaming passion or resentment in an evil man. Defenders
of the disciplinary view, however, retort that these facts do

not show a lack of disciplinary intent on God's part, or even a lack of wisdom, justice, or power, but indicate the presence of a misuse of freedom by man in the face of disciplinary opportunities.

Criticism of the view must therefore probe deeper. If discipline is the purpose of all evil, and God is both omnipotent and just, then disciplinary evils should meet at least two conditions. First, they should appear wherever they are needed and only where they are needed. Secondly, they should be perfectly adapted to their ideal end. It is clear that neither of these conditions is met. Disciplinary evils fail to appear for the moral education of the world's worst characters; and the innocent and already overdisciplined victims of these very characters receive repeated superfluous and unjust disciplines. Even if all evils were wisely and justly disciplinary and none were wasted unjustly, the second condition would remain unsatisfied. When one contemplates the actual evils of a wild storm at sea, the experiences of freezing and starving, or the symptoms of syphilis or arteriosclerosis, it would appear most extravagant to assert not only that these experiences may be disciplinary, but also that they are the most perfect means to the ideal ends of personal and social development that an infinitely good and powerful imagination could devise. As a philosophical explanation of evil, the appeal to discipline entails incoherences so far-reaching that it cannot serve its purpose. It remains possible, and even probable, that many evils are intended to serve a disciplinary end. Perhaps all are; but a rational and good disciplinary end is very far from accounting for the empirical character of the evils and their frequent maladjustment to the ends they are supposed to serve.

The three theories thus far discussed are the ones most frequently alleged by theologians. We have found reason to reject entirely the theory of punishment, while recognizing some truth in the appeals to freedom and discipline. But neither freedom nor discipline nor the two together approach a complete or coherent account of actual evil. We turn now to other theories, which have more often been advanced by philosophers than by theologians.

(4) *Evil,* it is said, *is incomplete good.* Absolute idealists like Hegel have dwelt on the principle that the true is the whole, that a partial view of anything is inadequate and irrational, and that the whole alone is truly good. A few propositions from an argument seem almost meaningless until their relation to the whole proof is grasped. Many patches of color within a painting are ugly; but the entire painting is beautiful. Ditch-digging might seem worthless until its contribution to civilization is perceived. An operation might be judged evil before convalescence and recovery had set in. This argument from synoptic logic has real force. Yet it is cogent only if we know in advance that every whole is necessarily good, or that this is true of the universe as a whole. From incompleteness alone, the goodness of the complete cannot be derived. In fact, it is as true in some cases to say that good is incomplete evil as to say that evil is incomplete good. The joys of intoxication in a person who is forming the habit of drunkenness are intrinsic goods, but they are incomplete; the whole pattern of life, of which these goods are a part, is evil. The extreme optimism of certain tubercular patients as death nears may be merciful, but it is only one symptom of the approaching end. Satan is commonly pictured as intelligent, gentlemanly, and industrious; yet these good traits are subordinate parts of an evil whole. The question of whether the whole is good or evil must therefore be settled on other grounds than the incompleteness of our experience. Moreover, even if the whole could be proved to be good, and all evils there-

fore instrumental goods, there would still remain the question of why the perfect whole had to contain both intrinsic and instrumental evils. After all, is there any reason why our world should not be Plato's "perfect whole of perfect parts," [19] if the whole is perfect in all respects? "Perfect parts," of course, would not mean complete parts, but parts perfectly contributing to the perfection of the whole. Over against this ideal is the chaos of empirical evils we confront.

To proponents of this theory, it must be granted that complete understanding requires a view of the whole; but it cannot be granted that this principle of synoptic method sheds any light of itself on whether the whole is good or evil from the standpoint of any humanly intelligible meaning of the terms.

(5) Some adherents to the foregoing theory, as well as some who do not hold it, advance the idea that *evil is needed as a contrast to good*. A monotonous world, it is held, would be wearisome; and if all were good, no one would appreciate the goodness; perhaps no one could even define it if there were nothing by way of contrast. Consciousness, for example, we sometimes possess; we can appreciate and identify (if not define) it only because we often lose it and (if immortality is not true) shall one day lose it permanently. But if we were continuously conscious, we should never know what consciousness really means. So, too, good is in perpetual danger of being lost by its contrast and conflict with evil. This alone teaches us to appreciate its value.

The amount of truth in this view is not easy to appraise. There is surely a great variety of goods; and the diversity, the effort, and the development inherent in experiences of the good might possibly give a sufficient contrast effect. Is it necessary to visit a hospital in order to enjoy life? Does

[19] *Tim.* 32D.

such a visit enhance the value of life?   It is true that Prince Siddartha was a selfish Sybarite until he witnessed poverty and disease, old age and death; but might not a soul innocent of the evils of life still have become a Buddha? To ask a crude question, is it necessary to eat or even to see a rotten apple in order to eat a good one with satisfaction?   The theory of contrast-effect is not wholly false, for the contrasts of experience often do stimulate the good; the conflict between thesis and antithesis drives us on to a synthesis, as we saw in the dialectic of desire.   Nevertheless, as a plain empirical fact it would appear that there is far more sand in the Sahara than is needed to help farmers value their fertile soil; there is far more ignorance and misery in the world than is needed as an effective contrast to wisdom and health.   In short, there is too much evil for the purpose of contrast to good.   Contrast-effect fails to explain or justify a large number of evils.

(6) It is sometimes argued that *nonmoral evils,* as well as moral ones, *are a result of freedom.*   In a criticism of the present writer's position, Professor D. C. Macintosh [20] has given his account of the origin of evil.   He regards the universe as "the body of God," and views it as "in large part *the abiding effect of the past work of God,* and only to a limited extent his present creative work" (305).   In general, then, the universe is due to acts of divine creative freedom, no matter when they occurred.   He appears to think that some relief is found in viewing evils in the physicochemical order as due to an act of divine freedom in the remote past ("past creative activity," 305) instead of being "the immediate product of a new creative act of the conscious will of God" (306).   Why he regards the date of a free act or the instrument used by it as important in

fixing responsibility is unclear; after all "he who does a thing through another does it himself." Logically Professor Macintosh leaves the responsibility for all evils in inorganic nature on the lap of the gods—that is, in the will of God. This simply states, but does not solve, the problem. However, he does offer a partial solution in the suggestion that many evils in the natural order may be due to "an expression of the free creativity with which the divine Creator originally endowed life even in its most primordial and rudimentary forms." (306) How far down into the structure of matter this libertarian panpsychism is supposed to go, we need not speculate. We need only state that the same objections are valid against Professor Macintosh's appeal to freedom to explain nonmoral evils as were urged against that appeal as an explanation of moral evils. The misuse of freedom does not relieve God of responsibility for having placed in his creation the possibility of so many direly cruel and unjust consequences of the misuse of freedom. It may be added also that the more free beings are multiplied in the universe, the more logical need there is for some unifying, coördinating principle of totality, some Absolute or God as the responsible unifier of the order. Although J. M. E. McTaggart maintains a personal pluralism despite this argument, Macintosh holds to a God. If he does, he cannot deny God a greater share of responsibility for the structure of the universe than this theory of universal freedom entails. At any rate, evidence for it is meager and its utility, as we have seen, is limited even if it be true.

(7) Even though certain evils may be intrinsic surds so far as man is concerned, *it may be that those very evils are needed in the universe as instruments to beings other than men.* This speculation opens possible perspectives as a rebuke to anthropocentric dogmatists. It may be true that

our "evils" are necessary to the good of a race of invisible and unknown x's, angels, departed spirits, or beings utterly inconceivable to us. But this is a "may be" without the slightest ground in experience or concrete reason. Why multiply hypotheses, playing with mere possibilities, when the actual cries aloud for attention and explanation? [21] Let us, however, for the sake of clarity waive all objections and grant the supposition that all human evils are instrumental goods for superhuman or subhuman beings. In that case, we should have a perfect whole—but of very imperfect parts. For the question would still remain: Why must man suffer so much meaningless evil in order to achieve the good of alien and unknown beings? Why must humanity be fuel to the fire that warms the hands of another race? Even if man knew of the service that he was performing, could he consider such an arrangement as ideally just? Would his personality not then be regarded, in so far as the surd evils are concerned, "as a means only," and not as an end in itself? At best, such an order could be deemed ethically just only if man knew of the beings whose existence his ills were enriching and consented to that enrichment. Even then, perfect justice would hardly obtain in an order which (for some reason not stated in the explanation) required cancer, imbecility, and earthquakes in human experience in order that "angels" might enjoy goodness, truth, and beauty. As the most remote speculative refuge, this theory, although seriously advanced by some able men,[22] is only a makeshift. It offers no metaphysics and no ethics of evil, and builds its superstructure on the foundation of our ignorance. This foundation may be said to be broad, but it cannot be called firm.

[21] Nicolai Hartmann's *Möglichkeit und Wirklichkeit* (Berlin: Walter de Gruyter & Co., 1938) is a searching criticism of overemphasis on mere possibility.
[22] It has been briefly suggested by F. J. McConnell.

(8) The theory just discussed often takes a more general form in the proposition that *all evils*—intrinsic or instrumental—*serve an unknown good*. This avoids the invention of the unknown angels just discussed and leaves the solution where an agnostic would wish to have it left—in the unknown. It postulates the presence of evidence for a good God—analogous to the evidence for causality—and infers that what seemingly conflicts with that evidence will some day be explained, just as we shall some day find the cause of events which we are now totally unable to explain.[23] Here, again, we may grant the conceivability of the suggestion. Yet, like the appeal to the unknown angels, it rests on insecure foundations.

The two main objections to the proposition rest on (a) its confusion of good and evil and (b) the irrelevance of ignorance. By (a) its confusion of good and evil is meant that if we must wait for the revelation of the unknown before we decide that an apparent evil is a real evil, then we should be consistent enough to go the whole way and grant that, in the present state of our knowledge, we cannot assert that any given experience is either good or evil. The two are, in our ignorance, confusedly indistinguishable.[24] If present evil may be incomplete good, how do we know that present good is not incomplete evil? Or, if these considerations seem far-fetched (as indeed they are) and we decide that it is reasonable to act on the hypothesis that certain experiences are good, is it not equally reasonable to act on the hypothesis that some are evil? If it be argued that we know moral good and evil (with certainty),

[23] This argument has an *ad hominem* force for the present writer, since he once held to this view himself. Compare Brightman, ITP, 292–293, with Knudson's statement in DR, 208–209 and the reference to Lotze on 220. Nevertheless, the objections to it now seem decisive.

[24] This and objection (b), below, are both related to the argument above against the current solution described as (4) *Evil is incomplete good.*

but not "natural" good or evil, there arises the question: By what logic? If complete knowledge of the whole is necessary to a knowledge of the parts in the case of the one—the natural evil—why not in the case of the other, the moral? True, we must always take the whole into account; yet we must also interpret the evidence as we find it. Faith is needed for any hypothesis, but faith needs a firmer foundation than a desire for absolute perfection. If a logical method leads good and evil to become indistinguishable, then that method cannot be used for a solution of the problem of evil.

(b) "The irrelevance of ignorance" means that our ignorance cannot be used to support any particular belief. Granted our ignorance, then all assertions made in this condition are subject to the same defects. From our ignorance alone nothing whatever follows about the unknown, except the tautology that we do not know it. Our ignorance is no reason for taking apparent evils to be real or incomplete goods. If, in spite of it, we still believe in good, this belief is justified by logic and fact present and implicit in our experience, not by logic or fact of which we are totally ignorant. If we greet the unknown with a cheer, it must be for reasons, not for lack of them.

(9) In sharp contrast with the view which justifies all evil as good is the view, held by some Hindus and by Christian Scientists, that *evil is unreal*. It is "maya" or illusion; it is "error of mortal mind." Evil is neither a disguised intrinsic good nor an instrumental good. The judgment that it is real is simply a false judgment; the opinion that it is objective or permanent is an error. This view is subject to three criticisms. First: if the natural order in so far as it seems evil is nonexistent, the next step is to deny the existence of the natural order as good. If

all nature is illusory, "one grand eternal lie," [25] there is no good reason left for believing anything to be objective. Second: even if evil is error, the error exists in human consciousness and does as much harm as if it were objective. Third: how the error could arise in a supposedly perfect universe is not explained.

(10) There remains as a solution of the problem of evil the one which is most popular among nontheistic and non-idealistic thinkers, namely, the view that *good and evil are the outcome of processes or entities which are axiologically neutral*. According to this hypothesis,[26] beyond human (or animal) conscious experience there is neither good nor evil in the universe. To be exact, all intrinsic value or disvalue is found in human or subhuman conscious experience; while natural processes may be instruments either to our values or our disvalues, this instrumental good or evil is a purely accidental attribute of nature. Likewise, the intrinsic goods and evils of consciousness are purely accidental products of an order which (apart from the narrow realm of consciousness) contains no intrinsic goods nor intrinsic evils, and neither intends nor implies anything valuable or disvaluable. It is held by many that this way "around," instead of "through," the problem of evil shows that the whole problem is artificial and unreal. The problem is thus solved by being evaded, and the conclusion is that, in the cosmic causes of value experience, nothing is good and nothing is evil; as far as those causes are concerned, vile-

[25] The phrase is quoted from a now inaccessible poem by a Christian Scientist (about 1900).

[26] This view is defended by Ralph Barton Perry in *Present Philosophical Tendencies* and *The Present Conflict of Ideals;* by most naturalists, such as John Dewey and Roy Wood Sellars (Samuel Alexander is an exception, and Dewey sometimes inclines toward a certain belief in the objectivity of ideals), and by the logical positivists (see Ayer, LTL). All who deny both God and the objectivity of any ideals or values are forced to this position.

ness is just as valuable as beauty, sin as valuable as character, error as valuable as truth. Value resides only in consciousness, as a sort of miracle, created out of nothing (there is no objective value from which it can be created) and vanishing again into nothing. If experiences of value and disvalue were not actual facts and were mere speculations, this explanation might suffice as an exposure of human illusions. It has been called "a philosophy of disillusionment." [27] But it consists in offering no explanation at all for the most characteristic facts of human history and culture. It combines the marvels of Melchizedek with those of Topsy; without father or mother in the entire universe, good and evil "just growed." This explanation may be a passing phase of an age of doubt which fears to face its own ultimate problems. It is the least coherent of all interpretations of good-and-evil, although commendable for its sincerity.

§ 9. THE TRILEMMA OF RELIGION

This chapter began with the proposition that belief in God raises the problem of good-and-evil (§ 1), but went on to show that the problem must arise for any philosophy that faces the facts of experience (§ 6). An argument for the objectivity of ideals, called the dialectic of desire (§ 7) was followed by an analysis of proposed solutions of the problem of evil, which revealed difficulties in all current ideas on the subject, and showed the most popular views— the naturalistic, positivistic, or realistic views of a neutral cosmos—to be the least satisfactory of all.

By this time the reader may be willing to surrender to skepticism out of sheer weariness; yet no one who tires of thinking will find truth.

[27] By Ralph Barton Perry.

Let us therefore orient ourselves regarding the stage which our investigation has reached, in order that it may proceed in the clear light of the logic of experience. We are seeking a philosophical interpretation of religion. Such an interpretation entails an account of good-and-evil—not merely of each taken separately nor of a practical attitude toward each, but of good and evil in their relations to each other, to experience as a whole, and to the total reality in which our experience roots. The history of religion and of thought places two alternatives before thought. The first alternative is that between theism and nontheism—that is, between an ultimate personalism and an ultimate impersonalism. The dialectic of desire and most of the attempts to deal with the problem of evil point to an ultimate personalism. But the attempt—realistic or naturalistic or positivistic—to explain evil as a result of axiologically neutral processes or entities in the cosmos points to ultimate impersonalism. The inability of any such theory to cope with the problems of value and disvalue has just been shown. Yet there are those who believe that human knowledge restricts us to a universe divested of value. Holders of this view affirm that science alone gives us knowledge, but that science gives no knowledge about values.[28] What science enables us to know is a physicochemical order with no properties but physicochemical ones. It is admitted that value experiences exist; it is denied that we can have any scientific knowledge about them; and surely all would agree that values are not objects of physicochemical investigation. The point that holders of this scientific neutralism [29] overlook is that philosophy has to face the problems which science leaves unsolved. To call the problem of good-and-evil an

[28] So Russell, RS, and Ayer, LTL.
[29] Neutralism: the view that objective reality is neutral as regards value, being neither good nor evil.

artificial problem is to fly in the face of the facts of daily experience as well as of the demands of coherence.

Nevertheless, there are many who think that scientific neutralism is as far as thought can go. Of these, the great majority, in spite of their metaphysical views, are actually loyal to ethical, logical, and aesthetic ideals, and many find values in the religious experiences of the race. When the nontheistic position is chosen, with its neutralism or agnosticism, and religion is still prized, some form of agnostic humanism is usually the outcome. Religion is viewed as loyalty to human values, and the origin of those values in the objective universe is denied or left unexplained or asserted inconsistently.

On the other hand, if the theistic choice is made, there remains a further alternative from the standpoint of the problem of good-and-evil. It may be called the choice between theistic absolutism and theistic finitism. The former is the Thomistic and Calvinistic and generally accepted view: that there is a personal God who is eternal, and infinite in power and knowledge as well as in goodness.[30] The latter view also defines God as personal and eternal, and infinitely good, but denies the infinity of his power and perhaps of his knowledge. Since the solution of the problem of evil turns largely on the relations between power and goodness in God, the next chapter will be chiefly devoted to the alternative of theistic absolutism and theistic finitism. Previous discussions have shown the defects of pantheism and idealistic absolutism.[31] At all times, however, the reader should bear in mind that it is not merely a dilemma that we face, but a trilemma: agnostic humanism, theistic absolutism, and theistic finitism must all be faced; and if beyond this trilemma there is a better possibility, it too must be pursued.

[30] This view has found its best recent exposition in Knudson, DG.
[31] Note especially § 8, (4) and (5) of this chapter.

BIBLIOGRAPHICAL NOTE

The great masterpiece on the problem of good-and-evil is, of course, the book of Job.

Plato's classic treatment is well expounded in Demos's POP(1939), as is Saint Augustine's in Burton, POE(1909), and Leibniz's in the German of Lempp, PT(1910).

The recent literature has not contributed much that is new. One of the best philosophical discussions is Tsanoff, NE(1931). A mystic's view appears in Hinton, MP(1866, 1914). The characteristic thought of H. G. Wells comes to expression in his UF(1919). A popular Christian view appears in E. S. Jones, CHS(1933).

NINE

THEISTIC ABSOLUTISM
AND FINITISM

§ 1. SUMMARY OF POSSIBLE SOLUTIONS OF THE PROBLEM OF
GOOD-AND-EVIL

HE goal of Chapter VIII was an analysis of the experiences of good-and-evil. The goal of Chapter IX is a synopsis which includes and explains all of the facts revealed in the previous analysis. That analysis leaves matters undecided. Good, on the one hand, leads to a dialectic of desire that finds coherent culmination only in a personal God. Evil, on the other hand, reveals the presence of an irreducible surd (an intrinsic evil) which a good God seemingly could not approve of, much less create.

In the presence of these conflicting analyses, thought has taken one of four possible courses (or some combination of them): (1) neutralism (existence is neutral to value; all—or at least some—reality is unconcerned with either good or evil; the universe or a part of it is indifferent to value or disvalue—it is *wertfrei*); (2) optimism (existence is determined by value; good is supreme and every apparent evil is either unreal or is instrumental to good); (3) pessimism (existence is determined by disvalue; evil is supreme and every apparent good is either unreal or is instrumental to evil); and (4) meliorism (existence is partially controlled by value; in some sense both good and evil are real, but good is dominant in that the state of affairs in the universe is always susceptible of improvement).

The objection to neutralism is that it explains neither good nor evil, but leaves them as miraculous mysteries. The objection to optimism is that it is not fair to the experience of intrinsic surd evil. The objection to pessimism is that it is not fair to the experience of intrinsic good. The objection often urged against meliorism is that it states the problem and takes a practical attitude toward it, but does not solve it in principle. Yet if any solution is to be found, it must, in view of the fatal objections to other alternatives, be found in some form of meliorism.

§ 2. THE ISSUES AT STAKE

It may clarify the problem to state explicitly certain underlying issues in question form. These issues must be faced if progress toward truth is to be made. The aim of the statement of these issues is to determine, if possible, what thought is seeking when it proposes a solution to the problem of good-and-evil. What sort of answer would satisfy the terms of the problem?

(1) *Are good-and-evil to be explained away?* Would it solve the problem if it could be shown that both good and evil are "merely subjective," and that everything objective is neutral? The answer to this question must be in the negative. Even if good-and-evil be strictly subjective, a solution of the problem must show the reason why such subjective experiences occur. Nothing can be experienced subjectively which does not have some relation to and some basis in objective reality. Christian Science holds that evil is error. It would be ironical if the only further light to be shed by natural science—or by philosophy—would be an additional remark that good is also error. Neutralism affirms essentially that good and evil both are entirely erro-

neous and misleading as descriptions of the real; they are creations or figments of "mortal mind," having no objective reference or objective basis adequately relevant to them. To follow the route of explaining good-and-evil away is to assert incoherent relations between objective reality and subjective experience of value and disvalue. If this conclusion is true, then truth is a strangely incoherent chaos. Even the neatly ordered neutral systems of valueless processes could not have been discovered if men had not valued neatness and order. When men have sought to destroy value, they have had to adhere to value in some sense. Desirable subjective values are not compatible with wholly valueless objective processes. There must be a more rational view than neutralism.

(2) *Is evil really good?* When most people, whether theologians or ordinary citizens, ask for a solution of the problem of evil, what they want is some argument to convince them that all evil is really good, either intrinsically or instrumentally. They may perhaps be put off for a while with the idea that evil is unreal and illusory and so not really evil; they are then satisfied that only good is real, yet they are soon haunted by the evil of the illusion. There is doubtless a profound yearning of the human spirit for a perfectly good universe, Plato's "perfect whole of perfect parts." Furthermore, there is a certain rational motive back of this desire, for after all, the ultimate type of rational explanation is explanation in terms of purpose. Nothing is fully understood until we know its function, its end, or its final cause.[1] But the demand that all evil shall be shown to be both the expression and also the result of good purpose and of nothing else carries teleological explanation so far

[1] See Bowne, TTK, Pt. I, Chap. X, on "Explanation" (pp. 211–238) and the penetrating article by W. M. Urban, "Elements of Unintelligibility in Whitehead's Metaphysics," in. *Jour. Phil.*, 35(1938), 617–637.

that it is in danger of breaking down. It becomes so optimistic that it is irreconcilable with the facts of evil. Such an explanation overlooks the possibility that purpose may control the universe without having produced everything in it, and that purpose may order the whole in spite of the presence of genuinely evil parts. Even the writer of the J′ document in Genesis knew that nature is not perfect but is, now at least, under a curse (Gn. 3:14–18); he suffered from no optimistic hallucination. To prove that all evil is really good—a perfectly good creation of a perfectly good purpose—is to destroy every ground for a distinction between good and evil, and thus eventually undermine logic, ethics, and religion. Yet it is true that this self-defeating paradox —showing that all evil is really good—has been the aim of the predominant traditions of religious thought.[2]

(3) *Is a coherent account of the evil of evil and the good of good an adequate solution?* Let us suppose that thought cannot show all evil to be really good. Is there, then, no solution of the problem of good-and-evil? Some, among them the present writer, think that a rational definition of the evil of evil and of the good of good and of their relations to purpose in the universe would be a genuine solution of the problem, the only kind of solution we could reasonably expect. The present chapter is in the main a search for just such a solution. Critics of this kind of solution frequently say that it is no more than a restatement of the problem; but in saying that they appear to be appealing once again to the principle which admits no solution unless evil is

---

[2] Most religious thinkers distinguish between moral evil (or sin) and nonmoral (or natural) evil. The latter they ascribe to God and usually declare to be ultimately good. No one, of course, would say that moral evil is intrinsically good; yet the majority would hold that its presence in the universe is justified because without the possibility of evil will there would be no possibility of good will. Thus even sin is a factor in a good world, and it is good that sin is possible.

shown to be good. Defenders of the proposed solution reply that our desires for a spotless perfection in the universe cannot by themselves determine the truth; no desire can rightly say, "Evil, be thou good." [3] All that rational thought can do is to face the facts and then give an account of them that is all-inclusive and coherently systematic. When this is done, an explanation is reached that needs no further explanation. Explanation is needed, not when reality runs counter to our desires, but only when there is contradiction or incoherence between our theories and the facts which our theories are supposed to describe. Reason faces facts and describes them coherently; rationalization tries to see the facts as our desires dictate, uncriticized by the dialectic of reality.

If neutralism is unsatisfactory, and if pessimism builds its view on the irrational aspects of experience, then the philosopher of religion has to decide between optimism and meliorism. Concretely, this choice usually appears as the alternative: theistic absolutism or theistic finitism.

§ 3. THEISTIC ABSOLUTISM vs. THEISTIC FINITISM

Reality is always more complex than any statement about it; and religion is richer than all theory. Hasty solutions of religious problems are easy ways of avoiding hard thinking and of escaping the many-sided divine reality. Nothing that has been said hitherto should be taken as closing any question or preventing any new exploration. The arguments may have been incomplete or in some way inadequate. The reader and the author are engaged in a common adventure in thought and experience in which agreement is far less important than the love of truth and the search for a method. The worst fate of a thinker happens when he

---

[3] Although this is obviously on a higher level than the Satanic original, "Evil, be thou my good."

says, "Now I see it all; the problem is solved; no more thought is needed." At that moment, obviously, the thinker dies and rises as a dogmatist.

It is difficult to define exactly the issue that separates theistic absolutists from theistic finitists, but it can be done if we "sterilize our intellectual instruments," as Bowne said. The investigator will not be deterred by Calvin's veto: "Cold and frivolous are the speculations of those who employ themselves in disquisitions on the essence of God"; nor will he cease inquiries because that essence is called "incomprehensible." [4] If we are to speak of God at all, we must either mean something or be totally silent. If we think the divine essence to be truly and wholly incomprehensible and deem those frivolous who inquire about it, we ought not to say God, but should speak only of "The Incomprehensible which it is frivolous to try to comprehend." That any reality has ever been fully comprehended is doubtful; perhaps none ever will be. Yet the moment we cease to try to comprehend, that moment the intellect petrifies, the spark of life dies out, and the spirit is no longer open to truth. Calvin was a great man and a great thinker, not because he declared God to be incomprehensible, but because he struggled with all his intellect to comprehend what was revealed to his understanding about God.

Attempts to define God, as we saw all too clearly in Chapter V, have led to a variety of contradictory conceptions; yet critical reflection on these and their relations to experience has eliminated some and modified others, until the investigation of good-and-evil has confronted us with the choice between theistic absolutism and theistic finitism. The two forms of theism agree in the proposition that God is an eternal, conscious spirit, whose will is unfailingly good. The difference between the two may best be brought out by

[4] Calvin, *Institutes*, Bk. I, Chap. II, ii; and Bk. I, Chap. XI, iii.

saying that theistic absolutism is the view that the will of God faces no conditions within the divine experience which that will did not create (or at least approve), whereas theistic finitism is the opposing view, namely, that the will of God does face conditions within divine experience which that will neither created nor approves.

These two views reflect a paradoxical antithesis in religious experience. On the one hand, religion is an assertion of an ideal of perfection.[5] It is in the interests of this ideal to explain evil away, and to ascribe the supposition that there is surd evil to our ignorance. The faith of religion from this point of view is that God "saw that it was good" and still sees all things working together for good in a perfect harmony regulated by his will. Matter, as divine activity, and freedom, as divine creation, are perfect products of the perfect will of God.

On the other hand, religion is an assertion of the need of salvation from real evil. From this point of view, the world as it is is not good. Obviously sin is a real evil. But the maladjustments in physical nature are real evils, too; most great religious leaders have either been (like Jesus) healers of disease or (like Buddha) teachers of some way of escape from the evil effects of disease. In this mood, the religious teaching is that matter is inferior to spirit—an acute illustration of the paradox of religion. For if matter is the unadulterated expression of the perfect will of an all-powerful God, it is strange that it should be regarded as inferior to free and sinful man who never expresses perfectly his divine vocation. Religious spirits, then, far from minimizing evil, paint it all the blacker. Spirit must be saved from matter, "this body of death"; the whole order of time is somehow corrupt and inferior to the perfection of eternity.

The first-mentioned view, then, overemphasizes the per-

[5] Compare the traditional ontological argument; see Chap. VII, § 5.

fection of God and declares his whole creation to share in that perfection. The second view expresses so strongly the imperfections of the creation as to raise questions about the perfection of the creator. Theistic absolutism expresses the former mood, theistic finitism the latter. Both are rooted in the realities of religious experience.

The contrast between the two is akin to the contrast between philosophy and religion. Philosophy starts with the whole field of existing experience; religion starts with its eye on value. The philosopher asks: Is the existent valuable? The religionist asks: Is the valuable (V) existent (E)? For philosophy, the problem reads: Given E, is there V? For religion it reads Given V, is there E? E for philosophy is the existence of experience; for religion it is the existence of God. Both problems are legitimate and no philosophy is complete until it has given full weight to the religious problem. It is evident, however, that philosophy, thus conceived, would be more likely to incline toward a finite God, while religion would incline toward an absolute one. Yet the paradox of religion and the differences of approach among philosophers (empirical vs. rationalistic) make this distinction only a rough and provocative analogy rather than a precise distinction.

§ 4. HISTORICAL SKETCH OF THEISTIC ABSOLUTISM

In order to understand man's struggles for truth about the fate of value in his universe, it will be fruitful to examine a few of the most decisive historical expressions of the two competing views. Since absolutism is more widely known than finitism, it may be treated more briefly.

The historical root of theistic absolutism is to be found in Aristotle, whom Saint Thomas called "The Philosopher," and whose thought has dominated the history of scholasticism since the thirteenth century. The classic statement of

Aristotle's personalistic absolutism [6] is found in the magnificent passage in Book Lambda (XII) of the *Metaphysics,* Chapter VII, from which Hegel quotes at the climax of his *Encyclopädie.* Let Aristotle speak for himself: [7]

> It is a life such as the best which we enjoy, and enjoy but for a short time . . ., since its actuality is also pleasure. . . . The act of contemplation is what is most pleasant and best. If, then, God is always in that good state in which we sometimes are, this compels our wonder; and if in a better, this compels it yet more. And God *is* in a better state. And life also belongs to God; for the actuality of thought is life and God is that actuality; and God's self-dependent actuality is life most good and eternal.
>
> We say therefore that God is a living being, eternal, most good, so that life and duration continuous and eternal belong to God; for this *is* God.
>
> Those who suppose, as the Pythagoreans and Speusippus do, that supreme beauty and goodness are not present in the beginning . . . are wrong in their opinion . . . for the first thing is not seed, but the complete being.
>
> There is a substance which is eternal and unmovable and separate from sensible things. . . . This substance cannot have any magnitude, but is without parts and indivisible. . . . It is impassive and unalterable.

This sublime prose poem defines an absolute, self-sufficient, and complete deity—an *actus purus* [8] of eternal goodness. Aristotle may be said to have written the history of theistic absolutism, for the idea has experienced no important modification from that day to this.[9] In the nature of the case,

---

[6] The statement of Fuller in HP, I, 151, that Aristotle's God cannot be viewed as personal, rests on some esoteric definition of personality not current in philosophy.

[7] In Ross's translation, excerpts from *Met.* 1072^{b14}–1073^{a12}.

[8] "Pure actuality"—a being in which all potentialities have become actual. In God all possibilities of thought are perfected as complete pleasure and complete value.

[9] There have, of course, been numerous changes in defining the relation of God to the world (and to Christ); but there has been no important alteration within this tradition regarding the concept of divine absoluteness.

further development of so climactic an idea is impossible. The concept of such a being could no more change than could God himself. "In deo," wrote Saint Thomas Aquinas, "nulla est potentialitas."[10] God is infinite intelligence. For Aristotle and Thomas it is inconceivable tha⸲ the will of God should confront any conditions in which that will was not already perfectly and eternally fulfilled. References to Thomas in the work of an eminent theologian like Knudson make clear the essential harmony of a modern Protestant liberal with Aristotle and Thomas, concerning the divine absoluteness.[11]

But—and this "but" is momentous—Saint Thomas and most modern theistic absolutists agree that there is one necessary limitation on the power of the absolutely perfect God. To quote the Angelic Doctor again: "Voluntas Dei non potest esse eorum quae secundum se sunt impossibilia."[12] Bowne Americanizes the thirteenth century when he says that "God can do only the doable." Knudson specifies that this restriction of God's power is traceable to "limitations within the structure of reality."[13] Thus, even the absolute God is, in a sense, limited; but not in any such way as to thwart or divert or hamper his will.

[10] "In God there is no potentiality." That is, he is his essence, and his essence is eternal goodness, with no admixture of anything else. See *Summa contra Gentiles*, Lib. I, Chaps. XXI, XXXVIII, and XXXIX, and also XLIII. Consult Robert Leet Patterson, *The Conception of God in the Philosophy of Aquinas* (London: George Allen & Unwin, 1933). For a modern specialized study, see J. K. Mozley, *The Impassibility of God* (Cambridge: University Press, 1926).

[11] It is fitting and respectful to refer to this distinguished, ancient view as traditional theism. That it has enjoyed a long tradition proves nothing for or against its truth.

[12] "There can be no will of God regarding those things which are inherently impossible." *Summa contra Gentiles*, Lib. I, Cap. LXXXIV. "There are," he adds, "impossibles which cannot be." Note Leibniz's concept of the best of *possible* worlds.

§ 5. HISTORICAL SKETCH OF THEISTIC FINITISM

If theistic absolutism began with Aristotle, theistic finitism began with his teacher, Plato. But there is a marked difference in the history of the two concepts. Theistic absolutism, like logic and mathematics, has remained virtually unchanged in its fundamental principles; whereas the idea of a finite God has experienced almost as many changes as has empirical science itself.

Before beginning an account of the history of finitism, two conceptions should be excluded from consideration as not belonging strictly under theistic finitism. The first is limitations of logical possibility and the second is divine self-limitation. As to the first, we have already seen that Saint Thomas grants that God cannot do the inherently impossible. Although logical possibility is thus recognized as a limit on divine will and thus becomes a barrier to literal absoluteness, it is so universally recognized by adherents of theistic absolutism as to constitute no special contribution of finitism.[14] As to the second, it is clear that if God be in any sense a good will, he is a self-limited will. The will to be good, the will to create other free persons, and the will to entertain an eternal purpose of any specific kind are all instances of self-limitation. But such self-limitation is perfectly consistent with the principle of absolutism, for it is an expression of God's all-powerful will. A limitation

---

[14] Its purely formal character comes to expression in the work by William King, Archbishop of Dublin, *Concerning the Origin of Evil* (Cambridge: William Thurlbourn, (1731) 1739. He undertakes to show that evil necessarily follows if an omnipotent God is to be rational. It is impossible, he holds, for a created being to be made perfect. The "universal war" among animals is perfectly rational, for the weaker were made "on purpose to afford aliment to the others" (184–185). Evil could not be avoided without a contradiction (220), partly because the perfect God had to create out of nothing, which is imperfect (217)! The inadequacy of such abstractions to explain the concrete evils of existence is patent. The Archbishop is a poor exhibit for the absolutist tradition.

would constitute God as finite only if it were not a product of his will. Leaving, then, these two conceptions to one side as belonging properly to traditional theism, let us proceed to trace the history of finitism.

There is a fundamental reason why Plato should regard God as finite.[15] In the *Philebus* he discusses at length the finite and the infinite. He holds that these two elements (23C) are to be found everywhere in the universe. But, contrary to our modern mood, he feels no awe before the infinite; it inspires in him only confusion. Goodness and beauty are not to be found in the in-finite, the un-limited; on the contrary, they exist only where the indefinite is made definite, the limitless is limited. Socrates says that a divinity,

beholding the violence and universal wickedness which prevailed, since there was no limit of pleasures or of indulgence in them, established law and order, which contain a limit. You say she did harm; I say, on the contrary, she brought salvation.[16]

As Socrates puts it a little later, it is "the infinite bound by the finite" (27D) that creates "the victorious life." Thus, all meaning, goodness, and order are limitations on infinity by the finite. Plato's doctrine is akin to Saint Thomas's admission that the infinite God cannot do the impossible, yet differs from it by the fundamental principle that infinity as such is not admirable or sublime. It is not even good unless there are limits to it.

The rejection of mere infinity as divine prepares us for Plato's dualism. If God were infinite, he would have to be regarded as all-inclusive, or at least as the ground of

---

[15] No student of Plato's philosophy of religion should fail to read the *Timaeus*. The commentaries by Taylor and Cornford are illuminating. Robert L. Calhoun's essay on "Plato as Religious Realist," in Macintosh, RR, 195–251, is an invaluable survey of the field. Since this section was written, Raphael Demos's book, *The Philosophy of Plato*, has appeared, which supports the view taken in the text.

[16] *Phil.* 26BC, translated by H. N. Fowler in the Loeb Classical Library edition (published by the Harvard University Press).

everything that is. Plato, profoundly concerned about the problem of good-and-evil, puts into the mouth of Socrates the principle that "God is not the cause of all things, but only of the good things." [17] This is explained more fully in the *Timaeus,* where divinity is represented, not as omnipotent creator of all, but simply as a good God who desires "that, so far as possible, all things should be good and nothing evil" (30A). So far as possible! His will, then, did not create the conditions under which it worked, but "took over all that was visible, seeing that it was not in a state of rest, but in a state of discordant and disorderly motion," and "he brought it into order out of disorder." [18]

Plato's picture of God is now before us. God is a will for good, not infinite but finite, limited on the one hand by rational principles of order and control (*Philebus*) and on the other by "discordant and disorderly motion" (*Timaeus*) which he finds in existence. All human life is an "undying battle," requiring "wondrous watchfulness," in which gods and daemons give us aid. (*Laws,* 906A) God's will, in this battle, confronts limits of reason and limits set by the uncreated discordant and disorderly (infinite) aspects of being. But Plato's ultimate metaphysics remains unsatisfactory and disunified, because both the principles of reason and the disorderly infinite seem to be external to God. Thus Plato preserves the goodness of God at the cost of metaphysical coherence. Plato seems to have believed that axiological coherence was more important than cosmological coherence; if he could not say, with Lotze, many centuries later, "I seek in that which *should* be the ground of that which *is,*" [19] he could at least say that what should be *is* ruler over what *is,*

---

[17] *Rep.* II, 380C.

[18] The similarity to Gen. 1:2 is obvious; Plato's God did not create what was "without form and void."

[19] Lotze, *Metaphysics* (Eng. tr.), II, 319.

yet *should not* be. Thus Plato had a well-reasoned view of a finite God which Aristotle rejected in favor of an absolutism of Pure Form, as we have seen.

Plato's profound yet incompletely unified insight seems to have been ignored by most of his readers. The *Timaeus* was almost the only work of Plato that survived continuously throughout the "Dark" and Middle Ages; but it was doubtless read through the blue glasses of the absolutistic interpretations of the Neo-Platonists, which prevented any insight into Plato's real meaning. However, Epicurus (341–270 B.C.) had no such excuse for ignoring Plato's solution. Yet Epicurus presented thought with a pointed alternative:

God either wishes to take away evils, and is unable; or he is able, and is unwilling; or he is neither willing nor able, or he is both willing and able. If he is willing and is unable, he is feeble, which is not in accordance with the character of God. . . .[20]

Thus Epicurus considers and rejects the idea of a finite God as being too "feeble"; he concludes that God is indifferent to evils. But since the only reason for believing in God at all lies in the evidence of our experience of good-and-evil, there is far more reason for believing in a finite God than in an indifferent one. Good Father Lactantius, however, stands by his absolutist guns and asserts that God is able to take away evils, "but he does not wish to do so." His point is that evils discipline our wisdom, and without them "we should not be a rational animal." On the other hand, Epicurus solved the problem of the conflict between omnipotence and benevolence by rejecting both; at least, if his indifferent and nonbenevolent gods are omnipotent, there is no reason to assign that attribute to them and no occasion for them to exercise it. In a roundabout way, then, he re-

[20] Cited by Lactantius (fl. A.D. 313) in *A Treatise on the Anger of God*, Chap. XIII.

jected one kind of finite God (a good one) in the interest of another kind of finite God (a morally neutral one).

The rise of Christianity made the problem of the relation between goodness and power in God far more acute than it could have been for the dignified Epicurus and his gods, who asked no more than to be left alone with their pleasures. Jesus taught that goodness and sacrificial love were at the very center of divine character, but he proposed no metaphysical theory. Saint Paul is more interested in explaining matter ("this body of death") than is Jesus, but he, in turn, offers no systematic theory. During its second century, Christianity developed some bold and sincere, but untrained and sadly muddled, thinkers called Gnostics, of whom Marcion (A.D. 85–159) was the most striking.[21] Marcion was impressed by the glaring contrast between the Old Testament's God of Battles and the New Testament's loving Heavenly Father. Another contrast fascinated him—that between matter and spirit. Faced with the good teachings of Jesus, which he accepted in the form they assumed in the Gospel of Luke, and with the good-and-evil facts of history and the physical world, Marcion concluded that the power for good in the world must be finite. He proposed a most extraordinary solution, a *tour de force* if ever there was one. There are, he taught, three fundamental powers in the universe: (1) the loving Heavenly Father, revealed by Christ but unknown previously—perfect in goodness, yet limited in power by the other two environing forces; (2) a realm of evil matter (an echo of the *Timaeus?*),[22] ruled by the devil; from this Marcion deduced ascetic practices, including prohibition of marriage; and (3) the God of the Hebrew Old

---

[21] The classic treatment of this thinker is in the fascinating volume by Adolf Harnack, *Marcion: das Evangelium vom fremden Gott* (Leipzig: J. C. Hinrichs'sche Buchhandlung, 1924). It is worth while to learn German, if only for the sake of reading this book—provided one has human or historical or religious interest.

[22] Clement of Alexandria compares Marcion with Plato in *Stromata*, III, 4, 25.

Testament, who (like a Platonic Demiurge) [23] forms a world out of the devil's matter, and is finite not only in power but also in goodness, as is evidenced by the cruelty of his commands.

Marcion's view need not detain us long. It is obviously mythical and incoherent; but it is a serious attempt to give an account of the place of both good and evil in the Cosmos. He wished "to justify the ways of God to man," and made his foundation stone the principle that what is unjustifiable cannot be one of the ways of God. He was far from the flat optimism of Alexander Pope's "Whatever is, is right." He took sides against the neutralists, the optimists, and the pessimists, and allied himself with the meliorists. For this he merits praise despite his aberrations.

Another more erratic genius contributed to the history of thought about the finite God. He was named Mani (A.D. 215–276) or Manes, and his followers were called Manichaeans. His doctrines were a mingling of Babylonian, Persian, Buddhist, Greek, and Christian ideas, but were closer to those of Zoroaster than of anyone else, although they are sometimes classified as Gnostic. Mani was treated as a heretic both by Zoroastrians and by Christians. For a time (A.D. 373–382) the great Augustine was a Manichaean. Our information about Mani has until recently been chiefly derived from Mohammedan writers. Now some genuine documents of the faith are available.[24]

Mani's solution of the problem of good-and-evil was less complex than Marcion's. It was dualistic, as Zoroaster's had been. The universe is an eternal struggle between the force

---

[23] "Demiurge" is a word meaning artisan; one who shapes the world out of pre-existing matter, rather than creating it out of nothing.

[24] See A. V. Williams Jackson, *Researches in Manichaeism* (New York: Columbia University Press, 1932), from which source the main facts in the text are derived. Henry Neumann's article, "Manichaean Tendencies in Philosophy" in *Phil. Rev.*, 28(1919), 491–510, is instructive.

of light and the force of darkness, that is, between spirit and matter. The realm of light and spirit was presided over by the good Father God, and the realm of darkness and matter was presided over by a diabolical Ahriman. The eternal history of the universe is that of a struggle between these two powers, which Mani elaborated in fantastic detail. For us, the main point is that God is not the creator of matter, but rather its enemy; the good God is limited by conditions external and abhorrent to him. The human body is a prison for soul and light and is created by the devil. It is the task of God to free the soul from this prison. The Manichaean metaphysics is chaotic, but it represents an effort to face the realities of good-and-evil with a mind untrammeled by fetters of tradition—or logic.

When Boethius (A.D. 475–524) brought the classic tradition to a close in his *De Consolatione Philosophiae,* the problem of good-and-evil was still recalcitrant. "Si quidem deus . . . est, unde mala? Bona vero unde, si non est?" [25] The solution that God is good but not omnipotent seemed not to occur to him.

Passing over profound insights into a struggle within God, expressed by mystics like Jakob Boehme (1575–1624), we note that the learned, half-skeptical, secular mind of Pierre Bayle (1647–1706) was frequently occupied with the problem of evil. He was greatly influenced by Mani and to some extent by Marcion. His thoughts were expressed in his amazing *Dictionaire historique et critique,* one of the first encyclopaedias and amply provided with footnotes, documentation, and appendices. The first edition appeared in 1697, the second in 1702, followed by numerous others. Articles in the first edition on Manichaeans, Paulicians (Armenian Christian Manichaeans), Zoroaster, Xenophanes,

---

[25] "If there is a God, whence come evils? But whence come goods, if there is none?" *De Cons. Phil.,* I, 105–106.

and Marcionites manifested so much sympathy with the heretics (heightened in the second edition) as to draw a rebuke from the ecclesiastical authorities.[26] Bayle argued that the doctrine of predestination held both by the Catholic Augustine and the Protestant Calvin logically made God the seat of the evil principle as well as of the good. To this he preferred Manichaean dualism; he therefore viewed history as a conflict between the good God and the bad one (the devil). He looked on the devil as "superior in the battle," since a great many more are damned than are saved. The power of the good God is, for Bayle, so finite as to avail for the salvation of barely one soul in a million. Bayle concluded, tongue in cheek, that the only way to cope with the Manichees was to exalt faith and abase reason.

The idea of a finite God appears also in the thought of David Hume (1711-1776). In Part V of the *Dialogues Concerning Natural Religion* (1779), Philo [27] analyzes the arguments of Cleanthes, who has deduced God from the facts of nature, and declares that Cleanthes must "renounce all claim to infinity in any of the attributes of the Deity," adding that

the cause ought only to be proportioned to the effect, and the effect, so far as it falls under our cognisance, is not infinite; what pretensions have we, upon your suppositions, to ascribe that attribute to the divine Being?

Philo finds the whole view of Cleanthes too anthropomorphic, yet does not examine the evidence closely. Like Bayle

[26] See the section on "Original Sin" in Howard Robinson, *Bayle the Skeptic* (New York: Columbia University Press, 1931), 206–215, to which the discussion in the text is indebted.

[27] Norman Kemp Smith in his edition of the *Dialogues* identifies Philo with Hume himself, although most previous interpreters, following a hint by Hume (at the end of Part XII) had taken Cleanthes for the true Hume. Philo is certainly closer to the skeptical spirit of Hume than is Cleanthes.

who, tongue in cheek, appealed to faith, so Philo, tongue in cheek, appeals from the finite God to the absolute one.

There are many inexplicable difficulties in the works of nature, which, if we allow a perfect Author to be proved *a priori,* are easily solved.

Again, in Part X, where the problem of suffering is considered, Philo defends the incomprehensibility of God against "the anthropomorphites," and appeals twice to the old argument of Epicurus.   In Part XI, Cleanthes takes up the idea that God is "finitely perfect."   Philo, however, answers that there can be no grounds for an inference to divine goodness "while there are so many ills in the universe." He plays for a moment with the Manichaean belief, then concludes that "the original source of all things is entirely indifferent to all these principles," and thus takes his stand with Epicurus and neutralism.   It is noteworthy that Hume in these Dialogues considers good and evil separately, but never treats the joint problem of good-and-evil.   His exclusively analytic method blinded him to a synoptic view.

Immanuel Kant (1724–1804), with Plato, Aristotle, and Hegel, one of the world's greatest thinkers, contributes to the idea of a finite God only in an indirect way.   In the course of his famous refutation of the traditional proofs of God in the *Critique of Pure Reason,* he (like Hume and others) expressed highest respect for the teleological (or "physico-theological") argument.[28]   He complains, however, that it does not prove a "world-creator, to whose idea everything is subjected," but at most a "world-architect, who would always be greatly limited by the suitability of the stuff with which he works."   It is odd to have a great mind

[28] See Chap. VII, § 6, above.   The passage from Kant is in the *Critique,* A627(B655).

admit that the evidence points to a finite God, yet decline to consider the conception. This evasion can be explained only by the a priori grip which the idea of theistic absolutism had on his mind because of the ontological argument.[29]

From the time of John Stuart Mill (1806–1873) on, the idea of theistic finitism has had an increasing number of adherents. In Mill's posthumous *Three Essays on Religion* (1874), he comes to the conclusion (not publicly stated during his lifetime) that "there is a large balance of probability in favor of creation by intelligence" (174). But he maintains that all evidence for design, for the use of means to attain ends, is "evidence against the Omnipotence of the Designer" (176). Therefore "the author of the Kosmos worked under limitations" and "was obliged to adapt himself to conditions independent of his will" (177). Those conditions Mill takes to be provided by the eternal and uncreated factors, "Matter and Force" (178). The whole section on "Attributes" (176–195) is a strong argument for the finiteness of God, and against any Manichaean dualism (185). Mill is able to render probable the goodness of God (191) because he is not "incumbered with the necessity of admitting the omnipotence of the Creator" (186). The arguments of Mill are sometimes discounted by believers on the ground that he stood outside of religious traditions and lacked a Christian experience; yet this very fact makes his arguments seem to others to be the more objective and convincing. At any rate, Mill would not have to be asked, as Voltaire was by Rousseau: "Why do you wish to justify his power at the expense of his goodness?" [30] Mill did not, however, develop clear ideas about the relation of God to

[29] See Chap. VII, § 5.
[30] Rousseau's letter to Voltaire, August 18, 1756. See also Brightman, Art.(1919).

matter and force. His metaphysics was undeveloped and therefore his concept of a finite God lacked philosophical vigor.

In 1891, F. C. S. Schiller (1864-1937) took the position that a finite God "may be proved." [31] William James (1842-1910), in his famous little book of Lowell Lectures, *Pragmatism* (1907), rejecting all "tender-minded" absolutisms, went the "tough-minded" road of the finite (273). He turned from neutralism, optimism, and pessimism, and accepted meliorism. God, for him, is the chief, *primus inter pares,* of "the shapers of the great world's fate" (298). At the same time, James's eloquence of style and realistic facing of facts are not supplemented by a clear definition of the relation of God to the limits of the "great world." James's view, like so many others, is an intuition rather than an explanation.

In 1906 two important treatments of the finiteness of God appeared. J. M. E. McTaggart (1866-1925), the acutely logical British metaphysician, published in that year his work, *Some Dogmas of Religion,*[32] in which he argued that if any conception of God is to be adopted, that of a finite God is preferable to that of an infinite one. Although McTaggart is a metaphysical personalist, holding that nothing but eternal persons exist, he is an atheist, since he does not see why a unifying cosmic person is needed in addition to the society of finite known persons. McTaggart's definitive treatment of the problem appears in *The Nature of Existence* (Vol. II, 1927), especially in the chapter on "God and Immortality" (176-187). God means for him "a being who is personal, supreme, and good" (Sec. 488), supreme not

[31] *Riddles of the Sphinx* (rev. ed., New York: The Macmillan Company, 1910), 302-316.

[32] This work is notable as being one of the very few serious examinations of theistic thought in recent times by a competent thinker who rejects theism. It is available in a second edition (London: Arnold, 1930).

meaning omnipotent. Guided by this definition he rejects the supposition that God is the universe as a whole, since he holds that no self could be part of another self, and we could therefore not be parts of God. He then rejects the supposition that God creates other selves on the ground that this presupposes the reality of time, which he rejects; he admits that if time were real, it might be hard to disprove a creative God.[33] Finally, he disposes of a God who controls and governs without creating, by appeal to the same consideration—the supposed unreality of time. Nevertheless, he admits that the statement that there is a God, while not true, may be as true as that there are mountains in Switzerland (Sec. 496). No one should suppose that McTaggart's thought is absurd if this summary sounds absurd. His arguments are worthy of close attention; yet a theory that hangs by a single thread—the unreality of time—seems to partake of the quality of gossamer. It lacks the "tough-mindedness" of William James.

The other work appearing in 1906 is S. S. Laurie's *Synthetica,* important because of its frank treatment of the problem of evil, its recognition of "superfluous evil" (what we have called "surd evil"), and its description of God as a "spirit in difficulty," who is genuinely limited in his struggle against evil. Laurie faces both good and evil, yet fails to propose a well-knit theistic philosophy on the finitistic basis.

F. H. Bradley (1846–1924) subjected the idea of a finite God to searching analysis in his essay on "God and the Absolute" (1914).[34] Bradley holds with McTaggart that God cannot be the all-inclusive Absolute. God must be

---

[33] Bergson, Alexander, Whitehead, and many others hold that time is real, against McTaggart and Kant. See arguments for the reality of time in Leighton, Art.(1918), Brightman, Art.(1932), and Gunn, PT.

[34] In Bradley, ETR, 428–451.

finite. A finite God, he admits, is compatible with heroic religion, but imperils the peace and satisfaction that religion needs. The essential point about Bradley's "finite God" is that its finiteness consists primarily in the fact that it is not the whole; God is limited by that in the Absolute which is external to God. The notion that God may have created that which is not himself, or that there may be a limitation within God, does not enter into his calculations. He is concerned only with an antinomy of religion: that religion needs the peace that only an Absolute can give, whereas the only God religion can have must be finite-heroic but unsatisfying.

Herbert George Wells (1866–   ) is the first modern writer to devote an entire book to the concept of God's finiteness. *God the Invisible King* (1917) is a curious compound of diluted Gnosticism and Manichaeism, with Wellsian imagination. In it Wells proposes the distinction between the creator of the universe, a Veiled Being of whom nothing is known, and God, the Invisible King, a finite, youthful, developing deity, who is known, is good, and is the object of all noble aspiration. The trouble with this Neo-Manichaeism is that the good God, having been born, will doubtless some day die, that the Veiled One can't be relied on not to interfere even before the King dies his natural death, and that the King is hardly to be distinguished from the social mind as it was among aspiring British souls in 1917. Intellectually, Wells's idea of a very finite God added nothing to religious thought; but it performed the historical function of keeping the problem before men's minds.

There is an obvious resemblance between the philosophy of Henri Bergson (1859–   ) and the idea of a finite God. Concepts such as those of the reality of time, the waste in the onward movement of the *élan vital,* the importance of freedom, novelty and struggle, all connect him with the thought of a limited, but ever-creative, cosmic force. One of the first to see this aspect of Bergson was Frank H. Foster (in 1918).[35] Bergson himself did not clearly avow the religious implications of his philosophy until 1932, when *The Two Sources of Morality and Religion* (TSMR) appeared (Eng. tr. 1935). In this book, Bergson develops his ideas about religion and God. He plainly rejects the absolute deity of Aristotle for a dynamic personal God of love—one too good to have willed suffering. He asks why anyone should suppose that, even if God is not so omnipotent as to be the creator of suffering, he should therefore not properly be regarded as God.[36] His answer is that the trouble arises from a priori thinking; we suppose ourselves to know in advance that God must be both omnipotent and good, and then we become atheists when we are able to prove that good is not omnipotent in experience. Bergson pleads for a rejection of this a priori method in favor of the empirical approach. If we question experience, we find reason for belief in a real God, but we find no reason for calling him omnipotent.

This historical sketch began with Plato's conception of a finite God. The greatest Anglo-American philosopher of the present time, Alfred North Whitehead (1861–) is in a sense a modern Plato, who builds on the *Timaeus*, and develops a modern version of the Platonic Demiurge.[37] At about the time of the appearance of Whitehead's *Process and Reality*, there was a spontaneous outburst of thought favorable to a finite God. It appeared in H. B. Alexander's *Truth*

[35] See his article, "Some Theistic Implications of Bergson's Philosophy," *Am. Jour. Theol.*, 22(1918), 274–299, and H. R. Mackintosh's criticism in *Expositor*, 16(1918), 346–361. Compare Brightman, PG, 9–12.

[36] TSMR, 249–251 presents the kernel of his thought.

[37] See *Process and Reality* (1930), esp. 67–68, 519–533. One might compare J. E. Boodin's definition of God as "the concrete, finite and individual embodiment of form" in *A Realistic Universe* (1916), 336.

and the Faith (1929). William Pepperell Montague in *Belief Unbound* (1930) described God as a self struggling with recalcitrant factors within himself (84). The present writer began in *The Problem of God* (1930) the development of the idea of a personal finite God whose finiteness consists in his own internal structure: an eternal unitary personal consciousness whose creative will is limited both by eternal necessities of reason and by eternal experiences of brute fact.[38] These limits he called The Given—an aspect of God's consciousness which eternally enters into every moment of the divine experience and into everything that is, either as obstacle or as instrument to the will of God. In 1931 Radoslav A. Tsanoff published *The Nature of Evil,* in which, although he did not use the terminology of the finite God, he expressed substantially the same idea by contrasting the drag (The Given) with the urge (the will) in the cosmic process (27, see also 364–401).

Limits of space prohibit the listing of the names of more than a few of the recent writers who have shown interest in the idea of a finite God. Some of the more prominent (most of whom find The Given external to God) are W. K. Wright, John Bennett, Robert L. Calhoun (who speaks of "rigidities" within God), W. T. Marvin, Henry Nelson Wieman, Vergilius Ferm, Georgia Harkness, and Peter A. Bertocci. Religious poets like Studdert-Kennedy and Edwin Markham, and the very different Rainer Maria Rilke, have expressed the conception in deeply moving verse.[39] It may be said that philosophically-grounded belief in a finite God

---

[38] See also *The Finding of God* (1931) and *Personality and Religion* (1934). The view will be treated more fully in the next chapter.

[39] Consult R. H. Dotterer, "The Doctrine of a Finite God in War-Time Thought" in *Hibb. Jour.,* 16(1918), 415–428; "The Doctrine of a Finite God" in Webb, GP, 134–155; "Pluralism and the Finite God" in Perry, PPT, 316–330; also Reeman, NIG, and Lupton, RSC (the last two being popular treatments). See also writers like Howison and Rashdall.

is more widespread in the present century than at any time since Plato. It must be added that antifinitism has also come to its most intense expression in the theology of Karl Barth. We live in days of intellectual, as well as of social, conflict.

§ 6. What Theistic Absolutists and Theistic Finitists Have in Common

The foregoing historical survey may well have left the reader with the impression of an almost unmitigated opposition between Platonic finitism and Aristotelian absolutism. The latter seems suffused with the serenity of Olympian calm; the former appears to be erratic and inconsistent. Yet this first impression is false to the resemblances, as well as to the differences, of the two views. In the face of the facts of evil, how can the absolutist be quite so serene? And in the face of the facts of good, how can the finitist be quite so erratic? As a matter of fact, the two views, in their best form, have considerable common ground.

(1) *Absolutists and finitists agree that God is a person.* Of course, there are certain types of absolutistic and also of finitistic philosophy which deny personality to God, but we are not now concerned with such views.[40] We are examining differences among theists, and all theists agree that God is personal. That is, they hold that the eternal reality which is the ultimate source of everything good in the universe is a conscious spirit—a mind that is eternally rational and good. The only "theistic" finitists to deny this are H. G. Wells, whose finite God is neither eternal nor, probably, a self-conscious person, and H. N. Wieman, whose finite God, although probably eternal, is not a person. These thinkers are exceptions.

[40] See Chap. VII, esp. § 11.

(2) *Both groups agree that ideals are objective.* "Eternal values," as they have often been called, are essential to the character of God, whether he be absolute or finite. Whatever limits may or may not restrict the power of God, his will is eternally directed toward the realization of ideal ends. Belief in a God is belief that egoism and ethical materialism are not only false in their human utility, but also false to the eternal purpose of the universe.

(3) *Both agree that God is worthy of worship.* This follows from the previous point. Man worships the good, the true, the beautiful, and the holy in their highest expression. He worships God not because God commands it and has power to enforce his commands, but because the eternal will of God is eternally loyal to those ideals which impart value to existence. God is worshipped not because he is omnipotent, but because he is good.

(4) *They also agree that God is responsive to man.* According to both, God is not only conscious of himself, but he is also conscious of every event in the universe. God, whether absolute or finite, is conscious of man's appeal to him, and is conscious of the ideally best response to those appeals. How, then, could he fail to respond? Both absolutists and finitists hold that the life of religion is actual experience of divine response to human need.

(5) *Both hold that God is in some sense in control of the universe.* The nature of the control in the two theories is very different, it must be granted, and those differences will reappear in later discussion. Meanwhile, we point out that the finitist, as well as the absolutist, holds that the will for law, for rational order, and for good, is the eternally dominant force in the universe. In this sense, at least, the finitist believes in eternal divine control as truly as does the absolutist.

(6) *Both also agree that in at least two senses God is limited: namely, by the principles of reason and by his own self-limitation in his creation of free beings able to sin.* Neither absolutist nor finitist supposes that the laws of reason were created by an arbitrary fiat of will; reason is an eternal and uncreated attribute of God, not dependent on his will. Neither absolutist nor finitist would doubt that God limited himself when he created beings with a power of choice. But the absolutist insists that both of these limitations are "ratified" [41] by the divine will. He regards the reason as an integral part of the will and the created beings as products of the will. On the other hand, the finitist insists that these two limitations taken together fall far short of explaining the surd evils of experience.

Such are some of the chief agreements among theistic absolutists and theistic finitists. These agreements show that, in the main, both types of theism are "evolutionary" rather than "revolutionary." Both represent great change from the earliest stages of religious belief; but both conserve and develop the values which historical religion has discovered, without any radical or revolutionary break, such as is involved in the denial of the personality of God by certain thinkers. Yet the rate of evolutionary change is more rapid in finitism than in absolutism. Hence, with all their agreements, it is not to be forgotten that finitism and absolutism propose fundamentally different solutions of the problem of good-and-evil, and imply fundamentally different practical attitudes in many concrete situations. Absolutists hold that, ultimately, God wills what we call evil, and sees that it is good; whereas finitists hold that there is ultimate evil in the universe which God has in no sense willed and against which he always exerts his full energy.

[41] A term often used in this connection by A. C. Knudson.

Bibliographical Note

In recent literature, one of the best statements of the absolutist view, and the best criticism of the finitist view, is to be found in Knudson, DG(1930), and DR(1933). In DG, see especially Chapter VII, on "The Absoluteness of God." In DR, the relevant material is in Chapter IV, on "Suffering." Ferm, FCRP(1937), 145-183, is an objective and concise survey.

It is not necessary to list further references here, in view of the abundance of material cited in the footnotes to § 3 and § 4 of this chapter.

TEN

IS GOD FINITE?

§ 1. Argument for Theistic Absolutism

OR general considerations bearing on belief in God, the reader is referred back to Chapter VII. At this point, we shall now consider only the specific arguments that may be urged in favor of theistic absolutism.

When man faces his experience thoughtfully, the first impression life makes on him is certainly not that of the omnipotence and absoluteness of good. Man's world looks much more like a battlefield than a triumphal entry, more like a problem than a solution. The religious man sees the evil facts. Indeed, they look more evil to him than they do to an irreligious or nonreligious man, because he is judging them by a divine standard. The lofty demands of his faith make evil all the blacker. He sees clearly that there is a state from which he needs to be saved. He sees that matter (however it may be explained metaphysically) is inferior to spirit. He sees that time is less glorious than eternity; "now we see in a mirror, darkly; but then face to face." Seeing all the evil, he nevertheless affirms the supreme reality of good.

The argument for theistic absolutism is based essentially on the religious experience just described. In a world of apparent evil, man finds within himself an ideal of perfect good; in a world apparently accidental he finds within himself an ideal of rational purpose. Using this ideal to interpret his

305

experience, he discovers that much that was apparently meaningless acquires meaning in the light of the ideal. He finds, it is true, that there is much that he cannot explain, but he retains his trust in the ideal and believes that somehow all apparent evil will be shown to be real good. Logically, he may compare this trust to the trust of a man of science in the ideal of causal explanation. There is much that scientists can explain; much is left that is not explained by any investigator. But the fact that the causes of some phenomena are unknown does not lead anyone to suppose that they have no cause. Confidence in the ideal is undisturbed by our ignorance; we keep seeking for causes, assured that we shall find them. So, too, the theistic absolutist is assured of a perfect good even though his knowledge and understanding of it are very imperfect.

Just what is this ideal? Kant, in his *Critique of Pure Reason,* calls it "a mere ideal, yet one free from flaw."[1] It is essentially Aristotle's Pure Form,[2] as well as the God of the ontological argument.[3] It is the ideal of the best and greatest that man can think, and includes perfection of power and knowledge, as well as perfection of goodness.

This ideal is not merely an outgrowth of man's religious nature. It is also an expression of his logical nature. The search for truth is a search for completely coherent thought about experience. Complete coherence is an unattained ideal—perhaps forever unattainable by man. Yet no one could deny the validity of coherence merely because he could not be coherent. Now, if the true and the real are coherent, there arises before the mind an ideal of completely coherent value, power, and eternity. Thus logic leads to the absolutist's God, as did religious experience.

[1] A641 (B669).
[2] This chapter, §§ 3 and 4.
[3] See Chap. VII, § 5.

Such, in the main, is the sort of argument that leads men—and has led them through the ages—to accept the absolutistic God. Many, in fact, will say that God must be as this argument describes him, or else there is no God at all. Perhaps they are too sure.

§ 2. ARGUMENT AGAINST THEISTIC ABSOLUTISM

The logic of the case for the infinite, omnipotent God marches with a magnificent sweep which thrills the mind. Yet the sweep of logic is one thing and its cogency is another. Rationalistic method cannot define a priori the content of experience, human or divine. That the existence of an absolute God (or of any God) is not demonstrated with logical necessity is generally admitted since Kant's searching analysis of the traditional proofs and his doctrine of the primacy of the practical reason.[4] As B. P. Bowne has said: "The arguments, carefully considered, turn out to fall short of demonstration."[5] N. K. Smith remarks that "it is no longer regarded as possible to demonstrate by dialectical argument the existence of God."[6] Many other philosophers and theologians could be cited to the same effect. The pragmatic movement is an extreme counter-revolution against the equally extreme claims of rationalism.

Theistic absolutism, then, cannot be regarded as syllogistically certain. In order to make this point clearer, let us subject the two arguments presented for the position to a critical examination. They were the religious and the logical. The religious argument is defective for four reasons. (1) It is *not historically true that all religions* or even that all Christian believers, *have found an absolute and omnipotent God to be the natural implication and fulfill-*

[4] See the "Transcendental Dialectic" of the *Critique of Pure Reason,* and Abbott's, *Kant's Ethical Theory,* 218.

[5] Bowne, KS, 207.

[6] In *Phil. Rev.,* 29(1920), 24.

ment of their faith. In fact, many ordinary Christians practically identify God with Christ or even with the Virgin Mary. Practical religion tends toward picture-thinking and a far too finite view of God. (2) Historically, much may be said for the position that *the supposed religious demand for an absolutely infinite God is largely a result of the influence of Aristotle* on Christian thought. (3) The vitality of Gnosticism, Manichaeism, and other finitist sects proves that *religion can flourish when absolutism is denied.* The decay of these sects may be due to their ascetic practices and irrational dogmas rather than to their finitism. (4) Most serious of all is the fact that *metaphysical conclusions cannot be grounded on the inspection of any limited area of experience,* even so important an area as the religious. Let the religious values be as autonomous and unique as they possibly can be, it nevertheless remains true that no metaphysically objective inferences can be drawn from religion until the religious values have been considered in relation to all other values, and until the whole range of value experience has been related to the empirical facts of existence.[7]   The religious argument for an absolute God leaves us just exactly where we were at the close of the argument from the dialectic of desire and before the empirical facts of surd evil had been considered.[8] Religious faith may, indeed, triumph over the evil facts; but a philosophy of religion must be not merely a triumph, but also an explanation.

If the religious argument is defective, the logical one is even more so. The logical argument rested in part on an analogy between the ideal of teleology and the ideal of cause. It was held that each ideal is wholly valid, and that this validity is in no way impugned by the absence of com-

[7] See Chap. III, §§ 4–7.
[8] Chap. VIII, § 7.

plete empirical verification. The analogy, however, leads in surprising directions when the concept of cause is carefully examined. Anyone who recognizes any factor of chance or of freedom [9] in the world, or who has considered Heisenberg's principle of indeterminacy, is aware that the rigid ideal of cause as held by Newton, Kant, and nineteenth-century physics no longer remains unimpaired. Its absoluteness is marred by the facts of experience. So, too, with the ideal of an absolutely infinite teleology. The remainder of the logical argument was an appeal to coherence. But this appeal carries with it no a priori information about the object which is coherently thought about. Coherence as such implies no claim that reality shall be perfect. It implies only a demand that true thinking shall include a systematic account of all the facts of experience; and it is precisely in this respect—the inclusion of all the facts of good-and-evil—that the belief in theistic absolutism is weakest.

There are five objections to theistic absolutism which, taken together, render it a highly improbable view. These are (1) *its appeal to ignorance,* (2) *its ascription of surd evils to divine will,* (3) *its tendency to make good and evil indistinguishable,* (4) *its cutting of the nerve of moral endeavor,* and (5) *its unempirical character.* Let us consider these in order.

(1) *Its appeal to ignorance.* The argument for theistic absolutism entails the admission that we cannot explain the surd evils—the waste, the cruelty, the injustice of nature— and that we must admit our ignorance, while retaining the faith that the fuller light of immortality will make clear what we do not now know.[10] That we are ignorant requires no elaborate argument. None of our ultimate insights

9 See E. G. Spaulding, *A World of Chance,* passim.
10 See Knudson, DG, 208–209.

achieve certainty. But if the absolutist believes that we truly are ignorant, what right has he to assert at the same time that we have knowledge? If we do not know, how dare we infer that the surd evils are real goods? "Verily thou art a God that hidest thyself," says the Second Isaiah (45:15). In so far, then, as we are dealing with a *deus absconditus,*[11] it is the part of wisdom to admit that we do not know, rather than to infer God's absoluteness from our ignorance (as Royce in *The Religious Aspect of Philosophy*). Spinoza wrote bitterly of "voluntas dei, asylum ignorantiae"—"the will of God, the refuge of ignorance." Hume spoke more moderately in Part XI of the *Dialogues Concerning Natural Religion:*

There may, for aught we know, be good reasons, why providence interposes not in this manner [i.e., to turn evils into goods]: And though the mere supposition, that such reasons exist, may be sufficient to *save* the conclusion concerning the divine attributes, yet surely it can never be sufficient to *establish* that conclusion.[12]

In a word, our ignorance must lead either to silence or to further investigation; and further investigation will always have to be based on the evidence that is available, not on data of which we are totally ignorant.

(2) *Its ascription of surd evils to divine will.* Since theistic absolutism includes the belief that the divine will is omnipotent and faces no conditions which it did not create, an upholder of that view must find the ultimate source of all surd evils in the will of God. Martin Luther was frank enough on this score. He declared that all men find the omnipotence of God "written in their hearts," and that the Omnipotent One wills the existence of sin and suffering as the just and best way to reveal his power, mercy, and

---

[11] "A hidden God"; compare Wells's "Veiled Being."
[12] P. 254 of N. K. Smith's edition of the *Dialogues.*

honor.[13]   He goes on to add that if this could be comprehended by reason, then faith wouldn't be necessary.[14]   Francis Bacon was doubtless less religious than Luther, but he
may have thought more worthily of God when he wrote
the following sharp words:

> It were better to have no opinion of God at all, than such an
> opinion as is unworthy of him.   For the one is unbelief, the other
> is contumely: and certainly superstition is the reproach of the
> Deity.   Plutarch saith well to that purpose: *Surely* (saith he) *I had
> rather a great deal men should say there was no such man at all
> as Plutarch than that they should say that there was one Plutarch
> that would eat his children as soon as they were born;* as the poets
> speak of Saturn.[15]

Belief in an absolute God is, of course, no mere superstition;
yet in so far as it ascribes surd evils to his will it is in principle not utterly different from belief in Saturn.   Appeal to
an omnipotent will about which we profess ignorance may
enable us to say that even Saturn's act is good; but such an
explanation, as D. W. Gottschalk has pointed out, would
serve to account for any kind of world whatever.[16]   Since it
would apply to any possible world, a priori, it has no special
use in accounting for the particular features of our world,
whether good or evil.

(3) *Its tendency to make good and evil indistinguishable.*
Since absolute theism entails the proposition that all apparent
evil is real good, it is in danger of producing complete skepticism about values.   It commands us to declare that an experience which, from every rational and empirical standpoint, seems an irreducible surd evil shall nevertheless be
judged to be good.   If what seems evil is really good, an
inquiring mind would naturally go on to inquire whether

[13] Dittrich, LE, 9, 10.
[14] Ibid., 12.
[15] Quoted by Perry, PCI, 250, but without indication of primary source.   It is
from Bacon's *Essays*, XVII.   "Of Superstition."
[16] See Gottschalk, SR, 228.

what seems good is not really evil. Again, if devastating earthquakes in Japan and Chile are justified by their purifying effects, is not the absolute God unfair in withholding those purifying effects from New Englanders or Germans? Saint Augustine concludes his survey of the universe in Chapter XXXII, Book XIII, of his *Confessions,* with the words: "videmus haec et singula bona et omnia bona valde" ("we see these things—they are good taken separately, and exceedingly good as a whole"). So anyone must judge who holds to theistic absolutism; he must hold that all things are good, whether they seem evil or not.

(4) *Its cutting of the nerve of moral endeavor.* From a theoretical standpoint, theistic absolutism, like other types of absolutism, removes all incentive for moral reform of the individual or of society, and that for two reasons. First, because the absolutistic view denies the reality of time; what happens in time is reduced to the level of phenomenon or even an illusion. Striving to make changes in the time order thus becomes unimportant and loses its militant cast.[17] Secondly, absolutism holds to an optimism which implies that the world is already timelessly perfect. If it is perfect, why try to improve it? If every evil is really a good, why try to eliminate evils? Fortunately, however, theistic absolutists have not been theoretically consistent; the moral imperatives of theism have overcome its metaphysical quietism, and even Calvinists have labored for their God just as though all were not predestined and as though they were free. Yet a conflict between theory and behavior affords no justification for the theory, even when the behavior is better than the theory.[18]

---

[17] See Perry, PCI, 249.

[18] Even Christian Scientists, who deny that error or evil is real at all, are active in seeking to eliminate this nonexistent illusion from the world. See the editorial, "Theodicy," by Clifford P. Smith in *The Christian Science Journal,* 47(1930), 691.

(5) *Its unempirical character*. The root of all objections to theistic absolutism is that it is a theory founded in an a priori faith, which in turn grows out of desires found in certain types of religious experience. Many thinkers regard it as improper to consider our desires at all; but after all, desires are facts and they constitute part of the evidence about the kind of universe this is. Theistic absolutism is, therefore, not to be condemned for taking desires into consideration. In so far as it does so, it is properly empirical. Its defect lies in treating a favored set of religious desires as ultimate intuitions—which are taken as absolute and a priori. Because of his predilection for a few experiences, the theistic absolutist sweeps to one side great masses of empirical fact with the a priori faith that some day they will be explained. In this he is unempirical. Our interpretation of experience should grow up out of contact with the whole of experience, not with some provincial corner of it that pleases us most. It is true that a survey of the whole may lead us to regard religious experience as crucial; it is also true that only a survey of the whole justifies us in any of our assertions about the meaning and the object of religious experience.

The essential basis for the difference of opinion between theistic absolutists and theistic finitists lies precisely herein. The absolutists neglect or explain away the harsh details of experience in the interests of their rationalistic faith, while the finitists find their faith growing up out of the concrete rough-and-tumble of experience.

§ 3. ARGUMENT FOR THEISTIC FINITISM

A theistic finitist is one who holds that the eternal will of God faces given conditions which that will did not create, whether those conditions are ultimately within the personality of God or external to it. If those conditions are external to the divine personality, the position is a kind of dualism (or dualistic personalism); if they are all within divine personality, then the position is a variety of idealistic personalism.[19] All theistic finitists agree that there is something in the universe not created by God and not a result of voluntary divine self-limitation, which God finds as either obstacle or instrument to his will.

Having considered the main arguments for and against theistic absolutism, we should recall that the arguments against theistic absolutism may all be regarded as pointing toward finitism. If we compare with § 2, we find the following contrasted results. (1) The hypothesis of a finite God *does not need to derive any of its basic evidence from our ignorance.* All that it asserts is based on an interpretation of actual experience. (2) *The surd evils are not ascribed to the will of God,* although idealistic personalists assert that the surds are to be found within God's experience of himself as an eternal person. (3) Finitism maintains *the eternal distinction between what is good and what is evil.* (4) Finitism is *an inspiring challenge to eternal cooperative moral endeavor*—a coöperation between God and man.[20] (5) Finally, *finitism is empirical.* It is based on the truly empirical motive of giving a complete and a rational account of all of the experiences of man.[21] It resists

---

[19] It would be a terminological blunder to identify personalism with finitism (since great personalists, like Bowne and Knudson, are absolutists) or with idealism (since most scholastics and many religious realists are dualists, yet are also personalists in the sense of holding that personality is either the only ultimately creative reality, or else is the controlling reality, in the universe).

[20] See Brightman, "The Gospel as Co-operation" in Nall, VR, 45–50, which is relevant here although the concept of a finite God is not mentioned.

[21] Donald C. Williams has in correspondence suggestively defined empiricism as "saving the appearances." See Hoernlé's chapter under that title in SCM, 99–140. The much-quoted phrase seems to come, not from Plato, but from Simplicius (fl. A.D. 530), the Neo-Platonic commentator on Aristotle. See his Commentary on *De coelo.*

attempts to explain the known by the unknown; starting from the known, it explores the unknown.[22]

It is not, however, sufficient to show that finitism is strong where absolutism is weak. If there is no independent positive evidence for a view, it should not be accepted merely because an alternative view is defective. Such positive evidence will now be presented.[23]

(1) *Evolution.* An investigation of the data of prehuman evolution is a desirable starting point for metaphysical thought about God, since it shows something of what God does and is when man with his desires, his values, and his faiths, is absent from the picture. A survey of the facts of evolutionary process such as one gains from reading Darwin's *Origin of Species,* or any more recent manual, furnishes a mass of apparently contradictory data. Most conspicuous, perhaps, is the struggle for survival. There is a vast and almost unthinkable waste in the production of life. Hegner, in his amusing and informing book, *Big Fleas Have Little Fleas,* mentions a protozoon one individual of which is able to have 268,000,000 offspring in a single month—a rate of propagation such that, if unchecked, it would fill the physical universe with this species.[24] The struggle for survival entails a death rate among protozoa which causes the figures of the national debt to pale into insignificance. Sutherland, in *The Origin and Growth of the Moral Instinct,* has calculated that the number of fish that are eating other

[22] Technically it is preferable to distinguish the terms experience and knowledge. In this sense, the most certain experience is not knowledge merely because it is experience. Experience becomes knowledge only when (a) it is rationally organized and (b) it refers beyond the moment's experience to something else. The statement in the text is to be interpreted in the light of this definition.

[23] The reader may perhaps allow the author to present the arguments roughly in the order in which they impressed themselves on his own mind. A more strictly logical order would begin with the fifth of the positive arguments.

[24] See Hegner, BFLF, 8.

fish in any given minute is about equal to the number of drops of water going over Niagara Falls in that minute. Not only is there colossal waste in the life process; there is also what appears to be a great deal of unsuccessful experimentation. Whole species are developed which are unfit to survive in the struggle for existence; museums are full of dinosaurs and saber-tooth tigers and countless other beings that were failures. Their line is extinguished. Even the innocent and relatively well-adapted heath hen has died out within the past decade; the last known specimen in the world died on Martha's Vineyard Island. One is inclined to quote the sardonic tombstone lyric: "If she was so soon done for, I wonder what she was begun for"; or else the solemn lines of *In Memoriam:*

> Nature, red in tooth and claw
> With ravine, shriek'd against his creed.

An honest mind can hardly face the facts of the life process without grave perplexity from the standpoint of religious faith. It is superficial to say that evolution affords no problem to religion. The problem, however, does not lie in the descent of man from the lower animals in accordance with law. This descent is simply proof of one universal and unifying power at work in the universe; it is evidence for, rather than against, God. The real difficulty for religion arises from the cruel and irrational waste and the seemingly aimless futility which evolutionary studies have revealed. The evidence of such facts points toward the purposeless, the dysteleological, in short, surd evil. Chance rather than reason seems revealed in these facts.

Evolution is not completely described when it is called a wasteful and aimless struggle. Much of the life process is wasteful and much is aimless. Yet not all is wasted and not all is aimless. In fact, if the entire history of life were wasteful and aimless chance, it is difficult to conceive how a single organism would ever arise that was fitted to cope with the environment and pass on its powers to later generations. If that aspect of evolution which is called the survival of the fit points to a mechanical and accidental aspect of reality, the fact that there are any organisms at all that are fit to survive points to a purposive and creative power at work in evolution. The survival of the fit presupposes the arrival of the fit.[25] Not only do fit organisms arise occasionally, but they are produced in vast quantity. He who views the past in perspective sees the movement of life as a creative or emergent evolution,[26] in which the earliest stages show organisms fit to survive for a relatively short time in a relatively restricted environment, and the later stages show organisms, such as the human, equipped to survive for a much longer time in a world-wide environment. Evolution shows a marked increase in the power of life to alter the environment to suit its needs, in the ability of consciousness to foresee and plan for the future, and in the range of values enjoyed.

Thus the evidence of evolution is seemingly contradictory. It points toward purposeless waste and futility; and it points toward purposeful creation and value. Center on one half of the evidence, and you become an atheist. Center on the other half, and you become a theistic absolutist. Take both together without any explanatory hypothesis, and you become a skeptic. Yet the facts themselves point to an hypothesis. It is an undeniable fact that law, creative evolution, and purposive advance are revealed in evolution. It is equally undeniable that this purposive advance marches on in the presence of the difficulties of waste and purposeless

[25] This cogent stating of the case was a favorite argument of B. P. Bowne's.
[26] "Creative evolution" is, of course, Bergson's term, and "emergent evolution" is Lloyd Morgan's. Both expressions are titles of important books.

facts. As far back as our knowledge goes, and as far into the future as science and philosophy can penetrate, we see purpose at work under difficulties; but we also see purpose as the growing edge of the universe, the dominant, never ultimately-thwarted factor. After all, death is really only an episode in the life process; disease is itself a form of life; and in the long run health and hope, for the race as a whole, triumph over disease and despair. The hypothesis which these facts force on us is that of a finite God. Let us suppose a creative and rational will at work within limitations not of its own making. Then the world of life as we see it is what would be expected if the hypothesis is true; it appears to be the work of a spirit in difficulty, but a spirit never conquered by the difficulties. Particular purposes may be thwarted; the dinosaur and the heath hen may perish. Nevertheless, the general purpose of life and mind and value always finds new channels, new avenues of expression. It is never entirely dammed up. The *élan vital* rushes on. Such is the argument from evolution for belief in a finite God. It is the hypothesis which best "saves the appearances" of the good-and-evil of evolution.

(2) *Coherent account of surd evil.* What has been said about the futilities and waste of evolution may be extended to apply to all the "surd evil" which figures so prominently in the entire problem of good-and-evil. There seems to be evil in the universe so cruel, so irrational, so unjust that it could not be the work of a good God. The attempts that have been made to show surd evil to be good serve rather to break down distinctions of good and evil or to build faith on our ignorance of what is good. This outcome has led to the utter abandonment of religious faith on the part of many, or to a religious dualism that is almost a "double truth" on the part of many others. The hypothesis that God is finite brushes aside these cobwebs, and shows that the

whole difficulty arises from supposing that, if there is a God, he must be omnipotent and infinite in all respects. There is no evidence that power is infinite. All power is under limits; indeed, the mountain sometimes "labors and brings forth a mouse." If we suppose the power of God to be finite, but his will for good infinite, we have a reasonable explanation of the place of surd evils in the scheme of things.

(3) *Goodness more fundamental than power.* As we have seen, the coherent account of surd evil rests on the experience that rational purpose controls the brute facts. In the choice that Epicurus posed between benevolence and omnipotence, the choice lies with benevolence. Ends are determinant; means derive their meaning from the ends which they serve or defeat. There is nothing worthy of worship in power as such; only the power of the good is adorable, and it is adorable because it is good rather than because it is power. God is the goodness in the universe. If there is power for evil, it cannot be the will of God.

(4) *The structure of all experience as activity, rational form, and brute fact.* Any statement about "all" experience is manifestly a sweeping one, and subject to correction. The statement that "all experience" is a structure that includes, in every phase of it, some activity, some rational form, and some brute fact is intended as an empirical hypothesis, not as an absolute, a priori necessity. Yet as an empirical hypothesis it has the support of all the experience we now have, all we can remember, and all that we can imagine or conceive. There is a theoretical possibility that there may some day emerge a kind of experience that is now inconceivable and unimaginable; but the philosophical task is to interpret actual experience, and if different experience arises, different interpretation will be in order. Meanwhile we take our stand on the actual.

Every moment of actual experience, and every concrete

real object [27] to which our experience can refer, is a complex which can be analyzed into factors of three kinds—activity, form, and content. In every empirical reality there is some sort of activity or agency. Leibniz and Bowne go too far when they assert that to be is to act; but they are partially right. All real being is active, although its being may not be completely described by the word "activity." In addition to being active, every real object embodies "form"; that is, it conforms to the laws of reason and embodies rational principles. Certain aspects of what we commonly call form may be no more than a name for the kind of activity that is going on; but the formal principles of logic and the laws of rational coherence (including the Platonic Ideas) are not the result of any activity whatever. They are present no matter what the activity is; no activity can begin them, change them, or end them. They are the principles to which any possible (conceivable) being must conform. Besides the activity and the form, there is a content of brute fact—the ultimate qualities (or *qualia*) of experience, the sense qualities, the pleasures and pains, the desires and impulses of experience. This brute fact is a stimulus and a challenge to activity, but is not itself activity. It is the content on which the activity operates, the matter which it has to form. In fact, all experience is a constant activity, which seeks to impose the forms of reason on the content of brute fact.

This statement should not be taken to mean the false and unempirical proposition that activity, form, and content are separate states or entities or processes. Rather, they are discovered by "analysis in situ" to be inseparable constituents of every pulse beat of actual consciousness and of every object to which we refer.

If this be true, we have important evidence for theistic

---

[27] Certain abstractions, such as mere subsistents, are not "concrete and real," and the statement does not apply to them.

finitism. Our experience of activity would be evidence for the cosmic will of God; our experience of "form" would be evidence for his uncreated eternal reason; [28] and our experience of brute fact would be evidence for his uncreated non-rational content. To assert that divine activity created reason would be to assert that the activity was intrinsically irrational and that reason needed to be created; on the contrary, reason must be coeternal with the will of God. To assert that the brute fact content was created is to assert that God wills the surd evils, which in turn is to assert that his will is evil and his power greater than his goodness. The hypothesis of a finite God thus affords a coherent account of the structure of all experience; to deny it contradicts the implications of experience and makes God evil (or unknowable).

(5) *Empirical adequacy.* The case for belief in a finite God may be summed up by saying that it is empirically adequate. If God is an eternal person, whose will is limited by the eternal laws of reason and the eternal brute facts of his experience, then the observed empirical nature of the world we experience can be understood. All of its features are explained by reference to the eternal ground of all human experience—namely the divine experience.

There are empiricists, however, who are not willing to acknowledge that this procedure is empirical. Their objections, voiced in discussion, in correspondence, and in print, are twofold. They argue, first, that truly empirical method appeals to social verification, and, secondly, that true empiricism restricts itself to experience without seeking any explanation or ground of experience. They maintain that any belief in God, even in a finite God, falls short of meeting these conditions.

Let us examine these objections. Scientific experiments are types of verification which may be socially tested. Any-

28 The "pattern" of Plato's *Timaeus* 31A.

one who understands the terms of the experiment may repeat the experiment and his results objectively tested are socially recognized. But the belief in God cannot be similarly tested; no experiment verifies it, and different persons facing the same facts may interpret them differently. There is, however, a logical flaw in this argument.[29] If it is right to believe only such propositions as can be socially verified in experiments on observable data, by what right can we assert that society itself exists? No mind can observe another's mind as a sense object; no experiment can prove conclusively that any mind exists other than our own. Yet, in order to carry on experiments, we must first grant the existence of other minds which do not appear in the subject matter of the experiments. Our belief in other minds, and so in society, is a reasonable hypothesis for the explanation of our experience, but it is not one that can itself be experimentally verified. It is a presupposition of experiment.[30] Assuming that belief in society as other than my experience is well-grounded in my experience, even though not experimentally verifiable, the same logic would lead me to postulate a God among the other minds, if my entire experience is to be explained. The essence of the reply to those who insist on social verification is that social verification itself rests on appeal to uses of reason which are more fundamental and broader than experimental verification. Experimental verification, without such use of reason, cannot give us society or nature or God; it leaves us shut up in solipsism.

A further answer to this objection lies in the fact that the argument against the empirical verifiability of God is also an argument against the empirical verifiability of values. The logical positivists in general hold that propositions about

[29] The argument has much in common with logical positivism, although the criticism offered does not deal with that movement as a whole.

[30] See Brightman, "The Presuppositions of Experiment." *Personalist,* 19(1938), 136–143.

value are "nonsense." They declare that such propositions
have no meaning and cannot be verified; they are neither
true nor false.[31] Thus the logical positivists have unduly nar-
rowed the range of verification; but they have performed a
service by forcing the dilemma that values (and disvalues)
either have or have not a meaningful empirical status. If
they have, then, like sense data, they must be taken rationally
into account in our characterization of objective reality. If
they have not, then they are not available even for a subjective ethics. In the former case, empirical thinking would
justify both ethics and theistic faith. In the latter case,
neither would be justified.

The second objection, ably voiced in a review by Sterling
P. Lamprecht,[32] holds that empiricism is "a method which
takes experience itself as needing no explanation" (75) and
argues from this that we have no empirical right to "want
more than experience furnishes" (74). Hence God is superfluous and unempirical. There are two answers to this
argument. (1) If its proponents mean only to assert that
nothing is more real or ultimate than experience, they are
asserting what all theists assert. Theists, however, hold that
all experience is self-experience and that there is therefore
no substance or subsistence or conceivable entity in the universe more real than self. (2) If they mean literally what
Professor Lamprecht says, that "experience itself" needs "no
explanation," and by experience they mean the actual concrete experience of any human being, they are simply asserting solipsism. Surely my experience of the moment is in
dire need of explanation by reference to some sort of larger
context. The theist, appealing to the law of parsimony,
avoids the supposal of nonexperiential entities; on the other
hand, he cannot suppose that the order of nature is purely

[31] See, for example, Ayer, LTL, Chap. VI, "Critique of Ethics and Theology."
[32] See Lamprecht's review of Bertocci, EAG, in *Jour. Phil.*, 36(1939), 73–76.

human experience. He but follows the most rigorous empirical logic when he postulates a cosmic experient and cosmic experience as the explanation of the disordered flashes of experience which we live through. Yet, since these disordered flashes are all we actually possess in our immediate experience, we must construct our view of the larger cosmic experience on the basis of the structure revealed in our own. This structure points, as we have seen, to a finite God.

§ 4. ARGUMENT AGAINST THEISTIC FINITISM

The argument for theistic absolutism (§ 1) is manifestly at the same time an argument against finitism. But the rapid growth of belief in a finite God during the past few decades has been accompanied by numerous criticisms of the idea, some of which have been superficial and others acute and penetrating. No attempt will be made here to present all of them. Criticisms directed against crude Manichaeism, or against the imaginings of H. G. Wells, or the incompletely defined idea of William James will be ignored, as will arguments based on sheer misunderstanding. The most weighty objections to finitistic theism are five in number: (1) *its supposed religious inadequacy;* (2) *its anthropomorphism;* (3) *its failure to absolve God of responsibility for creation;* (4) *the supposed implication that God has developed from zero;* and (5) *the supposed unworthiness of man as an object of divine love.*[33]

(1) *Its supposed religious inadequacy.* Religion, it is said, desires and demands a God perfect in power as well

---

[33] The literature criticizing the idea of a finite God is abundant. By far the best statement of objections is to be found in Knudson, DR, 204–212. An acute treatment by Andrew Banning, "Professor Brightman's Theory of a Limited God. A Criticism," appeared in *The Harvard Theological Review,* 27(1934), 145–168. The fullest account is in Baker, CLG, 139–178, but reviewers generally have pointed out its lack of objectivity. Many criticisms are summarized and answered in Brightman, Art.(1932)[2]. Lyman, MTR, 426–437, discusses the view critically, yet without setting it in its proper context of the problem of good-and-

as in goodness. Believers in a finite God, however, ascribe eternal limits to the power of God; although they hold to the perfect goodness of the divine will, they admit that that goodness is not in perfect control of the universe, on account of the presence of natural evils either as uncreated factors within God's eternal experience or as some eternal being (matter or devil) external to God. It may readily be admitted that Jewish, Mohammedan, and Christian orthodoxy (Catholic and Protestant) hold dear the position of theistic absolutism; also that, to one accustomed to asserting the absolute infinity of God's power and goodness, the thought of a finite God comes with a shock similar to the impact of democracy on a mind that is used to belief in the divine right of kings. But to be shocked is not necessarily to be a possessor and defender of truth. There are reasons for regarding the identification of religion with belief in an absolutely infinite God as more than dubious.

(1) First of all, *most religious believers have regarded God as finite*—far too finite. This is true of all the early stages of religion, of all polytheism, and of most vital religion that has not come under the influence of Aristotle's Pure Form. The living religion of the Catholic Christian does not center on the theological concept of Saint Thomas's God; but it feeds on finite objects—the crucified Jesus of Nazareth, the Virgin Mary, and the saints. Most ordinary people cannot grasp the sublime ideas of theistic absolutism; whatever the theories of theologians may be—Christian or Hindu—the common man seeks finite pictures, images, icons—idols of

evil, and Pratt, PR, 372, treats it courteously, but wishfully. Ferm, FCRP, 170–174, is a sympathetic treatment, as is Harkness, RI, 161–182 and 223–225. Wieman. in Wieman and Horton, GOR, 356. disposes of theistic finitism hastily by calling it a mere reformulation of the problem; what he objects to especially is the idea that surd evil is in God. It is noteworthy that the few casual pages which Walter Lippmann devoted to the problem of evil speed so rapidly to the conclusion that God is impersonal as to avoid all consideration of the possibility of a finite God; see Lippmann, PM, 213–217.

one sort or another. These facts are mentioned, not as a defense of idolatry or of picture-thinking, but as a refutation of the supposed universal demand of religion for an omnipotent absolute.

(ii) Furthermore, even if all religious persons desired a God who was omnipotent and entertained a sincere and exalted faith in such a God, it would not follow that he is omnipotent. *Every desire,* whether of religious believers or of unbelievers, *must be subjected to the dialectic of reason and fact.* Wishful thinking is not valid merely because it is widespread and has inspirational qualities. The foregoing arguments against theistic absolutism have revealed reasons for doubting the validity of this particular desire.

(iii) After all, *the object of religious worship is a perfect ideal rather than a perfect power.* It is true that belief in the reality of God is belief in the reality of the ideal; but the eternal reality of the ideal does not entail the unreality of the unideal. That way lies Christian Science; yet even Christian Science ascribes some sort of status to "error of mortal mind," which is unideal. It might well be judged more irreligious to hold the world as we experience it to be the best possible expression (to date) of an unlimited power for good than to regard it as the best possible expression of a limited power, for if this world is intended to convey the omnipotent's idea of perfection, then perfection must be much worse than we supposed. In short, the limiting of the ideal by theistic absolutism is more irreligious than the limiting of power by theistic finitism.

(iv) Finally, *there are certain positive religious values that attach to the idea of the finite God.* It is true that some able thinkers are most emphatic in their denial of such value. Knudson holds that it is "inconsistent with the spirit . . . of true religion." [34]   Hocking expresses agreement with Mc-

---

[34] Knudson, DR, 208.

Taggart's contention that the finite God "is of no worth." [35]
Over against the judgment of these distinguished men is the
fact of the persistence of belief in a finite God on the part of
those who are more concerned about value than they are
about power. In particular, there is no doubt that Plato
held to the conception of a finite God.[36] Would Hocking
hold that Plato's God was "of no worth" or that Raphael
Demos and Paul Elmer More err in finding that God to be
finite? Far from regarding finiteness as of no religious
value, F. H. Bradley insists that it is essential to any idea of
God that shall have any religious value at all. He says: [37]

> Once give up your finite and mutable person, and you have parted
> with everything which, for you, makes personality important.

Bradley is quite right in this statement (provided by "mut-
able" he does not mean "capricious"); his error lies in rejecting personalistic finitism as "absurd" and even "intellectually dishonest" without subjecting it to examination.

From the conflict of authorities we turn to the specific
religious values in the idea of a finite God who is potent, but
not omnipotent. At least five such values may be mentioned. First, there is the greater assurance of divine sympathy and love; if God is finite, he is not voluntarily impos-
ing any unjust suffering or "surd" evils on other persons,
but is exerting all his power against such evils. A God who
is doing that is seen to be on man's side in a sense in which
the Omnipotent One is not; the omnipotent God may be a

---

[35] Hocking, MGHE, 225-226. McTaggart differs from Hocking in holding that
the arguments for theistic finitism are better than those for absolutism. The
judgment of both regarding the religious worthlessness of finitism is so contrary
to experience and so casually grounded as to arouse some surprise. Hocking's
great work shows that theistic absolutism is religious; it does not show that
theistic finitism is irreligious.

[36] See More, POD, passim, and Demos, POP, 43, 120, 125, 337. Demos explicitly defends the religious value of a finite God (120), on the ground of its
"absolute distinction of good and bad."

[37] Bradley, AR, 533.

God of love, yet it requires far more faith to believe it of him than it does if God is finite in power. Secondly, there is something awe-inspiring and favorable to mystical and "numinous" experiences in the magnificent cosmic struggle of God against the "fire of anger," "bitter torment," "the abyss," and the "demonic," to use expressions of Jakob Boehme and Paul Tillich.[38] The divine control of that in the universe which the divine will did not create is a spectacle of suffering and victory—an eternal Calvary with an eternal Easter—which is fitted to elicit the profoundest religious emotions of reverence, gratitude, and faith. Thirdly, belief in a finite God furnishes those incentives to coöperative endeavor toward ever higher moral and social values which we found lacking from theistic absolutism. Fourthly, the concept of a finite God with an eternal task affords ground for belief in creative cosmic advance; thus the inexhaustible perfectibility of the universe gives meaning to immortality and warrants a religious attitude toward the future. Fifthly, it is more natural to pray to a finite God, who may be moved by our infirmities, than to an Absolute, whose decrees are eternally fixed.[39]

(2) *Its anthropomorphism.* The argument against belief in a finite God which most impresses some minds is that it humanizes God too much. A naïve student once remarked that it seems to make God "a glorified college pro-

[38] See Georgia Harkness, "The Abyss and The Given" in *Christendom,* 3(1938), 508-520.

[39] A thinker as acute as Hugh R. Mackintosh in his TMT, 299, expresses the belief that Karl Barth has blown "all Manichaean notions sky-high" in the following quotation from his *Romans,* 321. Let the reader judge for himself, using his semantics:

In our apprehension which is not-knowing, and in our not-knowing which is apprehension, there is shown forth the final and primal unity of visibility and invisibility, of earth and heaven, man and God. In that duality, which now and to the end of our days is alone accessible to our perception, is announced the ultimate unity which is the glory of the children of God and our hope.

fessor." An eternal professor who includes within himself and controls the entire cosmos and is able to create other
persons, including many nonprofessorial ones, is a being
to whom the name of professor is definitely inappropriate.
Yet it must be admitted that all theism and all idealism
alike assert that the ultimate reality of the universe is to
some extent akin to human consciousness and human
values. Having said this, we must say more. Not only is
religious idealism anthropomorphic, but so, too, is science.
Natural science rests on the foundation of human sensations
and human logic; it makes no statements about objects
which are not logical interpretations of our human sensory
experiences. In fact, all thinking, whether good or bad,
must be anthropomorphic. All of our experience is human.
Philosophy cannot reject human factors from our thinking;
it must retain them and view them coherently. One condition, and one only, must be imposed on religious beliefs: that
they shall give a coherent account of human experience—coherent within itself and coherent with all the experienced
facts and also with our interpretation of nonreligious realms
of experience. In so far as this ideal is attained, we have
religious truth. A belief, then, may be cogently criticized
not for anthropomorphism but only for incoherence.

If we apply this test to belief in a finite God we find it
to be coherent with the facts of good-and-evil, with the
scientific theory of evolution, with modern physical science, and with religious experience. The only sense in
which it is anthropomorphic is the desirable one of including a coherent account of all the facts of human experience.
Antitheistic and anti-idealistic philosophies, such as naturalism, give an account of the physical aspect of man's
experience. In the etymological sense they are therefore
more literally anthropomorphic than is theism, for they take
man as a form or shape, a spatial object, and offer exclusively

spatial hypotheses to explain man's spatial being. A physical universe explains only physical man. Naturalism leaves consciousness and values in the realm of unexplained miracle, as far as coherent explanation is concerned.[40] However, if we think of the universe in such a way as to account for man's memory, his reason, his imagination, and his ideal values, as well as for his sensory experiences, we find it difficult to avoid theism; theistic idealism is indicated as the most adequate hypothesis.

The absolutist may admit all this and still insist that his criticism is sound. Finitism, he holds, is so close to the facts as to be a mere recapitulation of them; whereas theistic absolutism, he thinks, is an explanation. The finitist's reply is that he would rather have the facts unadorned than have an explanation that confuses good with evil. Both contentions, however, are extreme. Finitism is much more than a restatement of human experience; it is an hypothesis about the eternal experience which is the source of all being. On the other hand, the absolutist's theory may be consistent with the facts, but it is so remote from them as to lack the coherence essential to truth. Truth must not only abstain from contradiction; it must also "save the appearances." Here, absolutism fails.

Professor W. Macneile Dixon reports that a traveler found an African tribe which believed God to be good and to wish good for men; but they held that, unhappily, God has "a half-witted brother, who is always interfering with what he does."[41] This is an uncritical anthropomorphism, indeed; but is it not more coherent with the facts of experience than a theism which declares that all the deeds of the half-witted brother are parts of the perfect expression of perfect good will by omnipotence?

[40] The reader is referred to the note in Chap. VII, § 11, (5), (ii) for fuller explanation of the miraculous character of naturalism.
[41] Dixon, HS, 83.

(3) *Its failure to absolve God of responsibility for creation.* The strongest objection to the theory of theistic finitism is that if God is regarded as a creator, however finite his power, he must still be held responsible for having created man, knowing that man would necessarily suffer from surd evils.[42]

Comment on this argument necessitates some remarks about creation. Obviously, the theory of a finite God entails a view of creation different from that of traditional theism. According to the traditional view, God created the world "out of nothing" (*ex nihilo*) by a fiat of will. A creationist theory has the problem of evil on its hands, and theistic absolutism is also creationism. The problem of evil may be avoided by a complete denial of creation, as in the thought of H. N. Wieman. He regards nature as uncreated and defines God as the principle of growth within nature.[43] Such a view holds to the finiteness of God, yet without being subject to the criticism which may be directed against belief in a creator-God. Its impersonalism is philosophically unsatisfactory; it gives no satisfactory account of the source of consciousness and value or of the unity of nature. It gains exemption from the problem of evil by failing to cope thoroughly with the problem of good. Furthermore, we cannot brush aside the problem of creation. After all, there is creative evolution, and the population of conscious persons in the universe is constantly being added to; the bodies of these persons might conceivably be regarded as made out of pre-existing stuff, but their conscious personalities must be viewed as creations.

How then is creation to be viewed? Let us sketch a working hypothesis from the standpoint of finitistic personal idealism. According to this hypothesis, the reality

[42] This argument is best stated by Knudson, DR, 207–208.
[43] See Wieman and Horton, GOR, 325–367.

of the physical universe is located wholly within the conscious experience of God. Physical space-time is God's standard space-time experience; energy and force are God's will controlling and directing this experience; the sense qualities of physical things are the "content" aspect of The Given in God's experience, while the mathematical formulae of physics result from God's will that his given "content" shall be controlled by "form." Biological evolution is God's progressive, creative [44] control of The Given, partly successful, partly unsuccessful, as we have seen (§ 3).

This hypothesis is objected to by numerous modern theists (or deists) who think they can save divine dignity and responsibility by a dualism which sets nature apart from God both quantitatively and qualitatively. But dualism is a superfluous hypothesis for one who believes in God; it needs Occam's razor. If nature is created, then God and God alone is the ultimate explanation (although his will is not the cause) of the surd evils in nature. If it is not created, it nevertheless limits God as effectively as if it were within him, and God's experience of nature is then a "Given" within God just as truly as though the additional external nature were not there. Such dualism is an hypothesis with no religious or philosophical function; it serves only to delay the day of reckoning with God about good-and-evil. It is but a cushion for reverent feelings, with no further use. On the other hand, personalistic finitism solves the problem in so far as it gives a coherent account of all the elements of good and evil.

The personalistic theory of creation needs further definition. All events in physical nature are events within God. But physical nature is not all there is, either for God or for man. Man's personality is no part of his body nor of any of

---

[44] The word creative here means only productive of novelties within divine experience, not productive of beings in any way external to God.

the physical objects that surround him. He is a personal self. As such, he cannot be thought of as a part of God nor as a rearrangement of matter (however matter be viewed). He is a creation, but not an arbitrary or "special" creation. He is brought into being by the will of God under the given conditions. When God creates, he has to create as a will limited both by reason and by nonrational content. Thus when man is created there enter into his being the same constituents that obtain eternally in God and in all his deeds.

This brings us back to the main problem we are now considering. If God creates man under these conditions, is he just as responsible as though he had created him *ex nihilo* and had willed all of the evils man is heir to? After all, if The Given is in man, God gave it to him. If this argument is sound, then a finite creator God no more solves the problem of evil than does an infinite creator. In fact, it is a better argument for atheism than it is for an infinite God; it makes evil an insoluble problem and an insuperable difficulty for rational faith.

Before yielding to skepticism (an easy way to avoid hard thinking), let us examine the situation more carefully. On the hypothesis of absolutism, God regards all so-called evils as instrumental goods and therefore approves of them. He created voluntarily and wisely; "and God saw that it was good." On the hypothesis of finitism, God sees that there are real evils which are ideally unjustifiable, yet he creates other persons. The motive of creation is rational love.

One may suppose that there lay before God only two alternatives: that of creating other persons whose existence must contain many irrational evils and that of not creating at all. The latter would forfeit all the values in a social universe, and all the possibilities of human existence. The former would lead to the world of society as we experience

it. One may well think that a good God would be willing
to endure all the added suffering that would be entailed,
and to help humanity to endure and control it, rather than
to have a universe without human values. Who would
deem this choice wrong? Yet it is one thing to say that
creation is justified in spite of surd evils entailed by The
Given and quite another thing to say, with Knudson, that
the finite God "regarded the unavoidable evils as justified
by the total outcome." [45] Neither man nor God can
rightly call evil good. A wise finite God could not possibly
judge the evils to be justifiable. He judges them to be
unjustifiable as well as unavoidable, yet in spite of the dross
of creation, he creates because gold may be obtained. To
create evils unnecessarily would be monstrous. The creation of persons whose lives must contain unjustifiable evils
is nevertheless justified if redemption is possible. Unless
the creator is also a redeemer, as Irenaeus held, our doom
is sealed. But the fact that evil must enter into any possible creation does not mean that the act of creation is evil.
Creation means only that God is responsible for exercising
redemptive love; it does not mean that he is either responsible for or acquiescent in the evils which his will does
not create, but finds. If we hold to creation and regard it
as the act of an unlimited will, there is no escape from
Bowne's *obiter dictum* that the "world-ground, by its independent position, is the source of the finite and of all its
determinations." [46] On this basis, no rational solution of
the problem of evil in creation is possible; one must take
refuge in an almost blind faith. The hypothesis of a
finite God makes a rational, open-eyed faith possible.

[45] Knudson, DR, 208.
[46] Bowne, THE, 64. But see his MET, 295-296, where he finds "the purposes
of the system mostly inscrutable."

(4) *Its supposed implication that God has developed from zero.* One aspect of belief in a finite God is its temporalism [47] and evolutionism. In some sense, God is moving on, creating novelties, progressively. There is, as we have said, following Whitehead, creative advance. Now, the idea of future expansion to more and more in God suggests the idea of a past that is regressively less and less, until one reaches the limit of zero. Thus the idea of a finite God leads to the absurdity that everything developed from nothing. This argument is a perplexity (an *aporia*) arising from the nature of infinity. However finite God may be in some respects, he must be infinite in some ways (as we shall see in § 5). For example, he must be infinite in time, of unbegun and unending duration. The thought staggers imagination and leads to many difficulties. If time is really unbegun, then infinite time has already elapsed. Why, then, has not everything happened already? To this there is only the double answer: it is necessary that time be unbegun (for there would be a time before any possible beginning); and experience shows that everything has not yet happened. On similar principles the difficulty about a zero beginning must be dealt with. However much a finite God may progress, he has infinite stages and varieties of progress behind him; and at all stages of progress, he is the fullness of all actual objective being, the creator of all created being, the unity of all energy. His inexhaustible perfectibility for the future presupposes a past series of inexhaustible perfectibilities. The conception of a beginning with zero is due to picture-thinking resting on the analogy of diverging (and so converging) lines, and ignoring the necessities of infinite duration.

[47] Brightman, Art.(1932)1.

(5) *The supposed unworthiness of man as an object of divine love.* In his little book, *Religion and Science,* Bertrand Russell offers as his ultimate argument against all theism, finitist or absolutist, and against all religion of every type, the assertion that the values of human life are not worthy of a God. Man's existence, he thinks, has all the marks of being an accident rather than a work of rational purpose. One may make an *ad hominem* reply and point out Lord Russell's own devotion to human social values and his protests against social wrongs as an indication that he takes man more seriously than his words imply. Without recourse to personalities, however, we may appeal to the ideal experience of the race. Everywhere spiritual values have been recognized in some form or other; everywhere man has dreamed of something better than he now is. Lord Russell's objection, taken with these facts, reduces to an argument against divine omnipotence (which he rejects) and an argument for an eternal finite God (whose existence he does not even entertain as a possibility).

None of the arguments against theistic finitism is conclusive, not even the strongest one; and all of them when closely examined show that a finite God is a much more probable and coherent object of belief than an infinite and absolute one.

§ 5. RESTATEMENT OF THE HYPOTHESIS OF A FINITE-INFINITE CONTROLLER OF THE GIVEN

At the cost of some repetition, it may be well for the sake of clarity to state in a more precise and connected form the definition of God which has emerged from our investigation.

God is personal consciousness of eternal duration; his consciousness is an eternally active will, which eternally finds and controls The Given within every moment of his

eternal experience. The Given consists of the eternal, uncreated laws of reason [48] and also of equally eternal and
uncreated processes of nonrational consciousness which exhibit all the ultimate qualities of sense objects (*qualia*),
disorderly impulses and desires, such experiences as pain
and suffering, the forms of space and time, and whatever
in God is the source of surd evil. The common characteristic of all that is "given" (in the technical sense) is, first,
that it is eternal within the experience of God and hence
had no other origin than God's eternal being; and, secondly,
that it is not a product of will or created activity. For The
Given to be in consciousness at all means that it must be
process; [49] but unwilled, nonvoluntary consciousness is distinguishable from voluntary consciousness, both in God and
in man. God's finiteness thus does not mean that he began
or will end; nor does it mean he is limited by anything
external to himself. Strictly we should speak of a God
whose will is finite rather than a finite God; for even the
finite God is absolute in the sense of being the ultimate
source of all creation.

God's will, then, is in a definite sense finite. But we
have called him "finite-infinite." [50] Although the power
of his will is limited by The Given, arguments for the objectivity of ideals give ground for the postulate that his will
for goodness and love is unlimited; likewise he is infinite
in time and space, by his unbegun and unending duration
and by his inclusion of all nature within his experience;
such a God must also be unlimited in his knowledge of all
that is, although human freedom and the nature of The
Given probably limit his knowledge of the precise details
of the future.

[48] Including logic, mathematical relations, and Platonic Ideas.
[49] Note Whitehead's category of process in *Process and Reality*.
[50] See "A Finite-Infinite God" in Brightman, PR, 71–100.

The further predicate of "Controller of The Given" needs explanation. God's will is eternally seeking new forms of embodiment of the good. God may be compared to a creative artist eternally painting new pictures, composing new dramas and new symphonies.[51]   In this process, God, finding The Given as an inevitable ingredient, seeks to impose ever new combinations of given rational form on the given nonrational content.   Thus The Given is, on the one hand, God's instrument for the expression of his aesthetic and moral purposes, and, on the other, an obstacle to their complete and perfect expression.   God's control of The Given means that he never allows The Given to run wild, that he always subjects it to law and uses it, as far as possible, as an instrument for realizing the ideal good Yet the divine control does not mean complete determination; for in some situations The Given, with its purposeless processes, constitutes so great an obstacle to divine willing that the utmost endeavors of God lead to a blind alley and temporary defeat.   At this point, God's control means that no defeat or frustration is final; that the will of God, partially thwarted by obstacles in the chaotic Given, finds new avenues of advance, and forever moves on in the cosmic creation of new values.[52]

The view may be clarified by comparing and contrasting it with Plato's conception of a finite God.[53]   According to Demos's sound analysis, which rests on the *Philebus* and the *Timaeus* as the definitive formulation of the Platonic phi-

[51] But God cannot be called "an unhampered artist," as Pratt does in PR, 376. His will is genuinely hampered by The Given.

[52] Bowne once wrote that "the finite as we experience it is not worthy of God" ST, 442.   Proper inference from that is that the finite is not an expression of God's will.   Instead, Bowne postponed (and never solved) the problem by inferring immortality from this unworthiness of the finite.   Treating the available evidence as incomplete, he relied on what is unavailable as evidence.

[53] Raphael Demos's *The Philosophy of Plato*, which appeared while this chapter was being written, presents an interpretation of Plato which coincides with that of the present writer at nearly every point.

losophy, the creative factors in the universe for Plato are: God (the Demiurge or cosmic Artisan), the Pattern (the eternal ideal, corresponding to the Ideas in the earlier dialogues), and the Receptacle (the primordial chaos of space, discordant and disorderly motion). The actual world is caused by union of the forms (or Pattern) with the Receptacle. The motive of creation is the Good, the principle of value.[54]

It is easy to see that the Pattern corresponds to what we have called the formal aspect of The Given, while the Receptacle is the content aspect of The Given. But there is an essential difference between Plato's view and that which has been developed in this chapter. Plato is a dualist or pluralist. The Receptacle (certainly) and the Pattern (probably) are external to God. The relations among them, and their ontological status, are therefore obscure. Much of this obscurity and unrelatedness is removed by our hypothesis which enlarges the idea of God so that Pattern and Receptacle are both included in God.

The Pattern becomes the system of conscious rational and necessary laws to which divine thinking conforms; the Receptacle becomes the spatial aspect of the stream of divine consciousness. The relatedness of these factors is established by their presence within one personality which controls and directs them all by its will to the Good. When we transform Plato's inspired and illuminating, but obscure, dualism into a personalism, his dualism is transcended through a monism of purpose and personal identity; and yet the pluralistic phase is retained by the analysis into will and Given as well as by the concept of a society of interacting selves and persons.

This personalized Platonism, which may also be called organic pluralism, owes much to Hegelian influences. The

[54] Demos, POP, 3–7, is the source of these ideas.

dialectic of thesis and antithesis, the principle of negativity, and the union of finite and infinite have been fructifying contributions. A rather remarkable parallel is found in the Yoga analysis into rajas, sattva, and tamas, which mean energy, intelligence, and materiality, and correspond closely to will, reason, and content.[55]

§ 6. PERFECTION OR PERFECTIBILITY?

Along with the notion of a finite God goes a revised notion of perfection. Etymologically the word perfection means completion; divine perfection would thus mean ideal completion. For a theistic absolutist who denies the reality of time and who acknowledges nothing given in God which his will did not determine (save the laws of reason, which his will approves or "ratifies"), it is quite possible to conceive of God as timelessly completed ideality, perfection in the literal sense. Yet such "perfection" is as far above human comprehension as it is above concrete imagination; and it is so remote from the facts of experience as to be incoherent (although doubtless consistent) with them.

If the universal human longing for perfection is to be coherently fulfilled it cannot be by the traditional conception of a timelessly perfected, completed God. When, however, we substitute for perfection the ideal of inexhaustible perfectibility, we have a concept applicable to both God and man and adequate to man's religious need. Not optimism but meliorism; not completeness, but ever new tasks in accordance with the eternal principles of the Good; not timeless perfection, but inexhaustible perfectibility in everlasting time—these are the perspectives which open for the cosmos and for every enduring person in it if the empirical evidence for a finite God has guided us toward

---

[55] Kovoor T. Behanan, *Yoga: A Scientific Evaluation* (New York: The Macmillan Company, 1937), 31–36.

truth. The wearisomeness sometimes ascribed to this perspective does not exist for anyone to whom the variety of the values of life and the joys of creation and communication, even amidst pain and struggle, are profoundly real. For the Buddhist, perfection may be the cessation of all desire; but for him who values personality, coöperation with the unshakable purposes of the Eternal Person and joint responsibility for the creation of new forms of control of The Given elevate life to its loftiest ideal plane.

That the proposed solution of the problem of evil and the idea of a finite God are an advance toward the truth seems highly probable to the writer. Whether these views are true or not, it is certain that philosophers will not fulfill their true function by following the popular mood of indifference to God. Until they wrestle more earnestly with the problem of God, the meaning of the whole, what they say of the parts is in danger of making a crazy patchwork— far from the rational Pattern of Plato.

Bibliographical Note

All of the bibliography of the previous chapter is relevant to the present one. The reader is also referred to the numerous references in the footnotes, especially in §§ 4 and 5 of Chapter X.

ELEVEN

THE PROBLEM OF
HUMAN PERSONALITY

§ 1. The Importance of Man for Religion

ELIGION is a characteristically human experience. As far as we know, the lower animals have no religion. If there were no men, and if there existed only pure intelligences with no ideal save that of scientific knowledge, physics and mathematics would be as true for them as for men, but they would have no religion. They would experience no worship, no coöperative realization of values, no prayer, and no faith. Religion is man's aspiration toward the source of his highest values, and his sense of coöperation with and dependence on that source. Religion is man's concern about his own value and destiny. Hence every religion has required a conception of man (the religious subject) as well as of God (the religious object). No philosophy of religion can omit an investigation of human personality.

§ 2. Why Not Then Begin with Man?

If religion is essentially human, the student may well inquire why we did not begin our philosophy of religion with a study of man. After all, we know more about man than we do about God and it might have been simpler to start with human personality. Yet these considerations are plausible without being conclusive. The most successful sciences seem to have been the objective ones that have ignored man—physics and chemistry, for example; and re ligious experience is as objective in its original intent as is the sense experience which physics and chemistry interpret. Furthermore, it is impossible to arrive at a philosophical understanding of man unless we consider him in relation to his world and to his God. In any event, one's starting point is not decisive in a philosophical investigation. The main thing is to include the whole range of relevant experience before we are through.

But there are special reasons which made it seem wiser to follow the procedure of the text rather than to begin with human personality. In a philosophy of religion, the center of interest is in man as a religious being. If there is no evidence of religion in human life, there is no philosophy of religion at all. Therefore we did not begin with a theory of personality, but rather with man's religious experience. From that experience we learned that the idea of God in some form is the highest religious affirmation of man's value and destiny. Hence we proceeded directly to the central problems of value and God, as the main topics of philosophy of religion.

If we had begun with human personality, our results would have had to remain very incomplete and tentative until our view of the relations of man to God could be investigated. In a sense, of course, all human thinking is incomplete and tentative, and we may gain further light on God as we study man's personality. Yet the advantage of beginning with God is that in order to think about God at all, especially about the problem of good-and-evil and the finiteness of God, we have been forced to take into account wide ranges of man's personal experience. Our method has, therefore, forced us from the start to be inclusive, objective, and hence philosophical. To have started with a view of personality that omitted religious values and God would have been merely to survey the general psychology and philosophy of personality without advancing philosophy of religion one whit. We have plenty of psychology without God as it is. We need an understanding of what human personality means when it declares that it is experiencing God.

§ 3. WHAT IS THE PROBLEM OF PERSONALITY?

As soon as we raise the question: What is human personality? we are confronted by a whole jungle of answers. Psychology and philosophy offer an embarrassment of riches. Fortunately, matters are somewhat simplified when we remember that many psychological details about personality are unrelated to a philosophy of religion. Experiments on the knee jerk or Weber's Law or conditioned reflexes are irrelevant to our understanding of man as a religious being and an experiencer of ideal values. In fact, C. C. Pratt has stated that psychology has shed practically no light on "the determinants of man's higher activities." He would send us to Shakespeare and Goethe rather than to "literary psychology" for light on our problem.[1] If we were to trust this psychologist, we might ignore most of the work of psychology without loss to philosophy of religion. Exception would have to be made of psychology of religion, which we have already considered in Chapter II.

The reasons for the relative unimportance of much technical psychological research in our field are almost self-evident. The religious interest in personality is not an interest in the sense organs as such, the brain and nervous system, or any isolable conscious process or response to stimulus. It is rather an interest in the personality as a

[1] C. C. Pratt, *The Logic of Modern Psychology* (New York: The Macmillan Company, 1939), 166–167.

whole, and in an evaluation of the ideals for which it is striving.[2] Accordingly, the religious problem of personality is much closer to philosophy than it is to psychology. It concerns the philosophy of psychology or of personality. In this chapter we shall deal chiefly with philosophical presuppositions and implications of psychology, although making free use of psychological data whenever they shed light on the problem.

In order to illustrate the philosophical approach to personality, as distinguished from the psychological, let us consider very briefly the presuppositions of experiment, for the psychologist relies chiefly on experiment, while the philosopher is chiefly concerned with interpreting the presuppositions and the results of experiment. Experiments do not occur in a vacuum; they are initiated, observed, and reported by a mind. Every experiment presupposes, therefore, at least the following items: (1) a self or person, (2) the unity of the self during the entire experiment, (3) data of consciousness which are the observable aspect of the experiment, (4) a purpose, (5) the validity of reason, (6) memory, (7) the experience of time, (8) the acknowledgment of an objective world, and (9) society.[3] In short, if any experiment is to produce valid results, it is necessary that there be a unitary, purposive, rational, self-remembering personality, interacting with its environment. Just such a personality is also presupposed by religion. Any experiment which seems to question this personality is a "self-refuting system," for it denies the very condition on which it depends for its validity. But this insight is far from solving either the psychological or the philosophical problem of the nature of personality.

---

[2] Let the reader recall William James's definition of the self as "a fighter for ends."

[3] See Brightman, "The Presuppositions of Experiment," Art.(1938).

§ 4. DEFINITION OF PERSONALITY

One who is inclined to approach problems empirically may well define personality in terms of consciousness.[4] Each one of us experiences his own consciousness; that experience is private and can be literally shared by no one else. We cannot inspect the consciousness of anyone else as we can inspect our own. This may be proved by the simple experiment of trying to tell another person exactly what is in his mind. Each person reads off his own consciousness directly; he approaches that of others indirectly. Even if he is as sure of the other's thought as he is of his own, it is in a different way. To be precise, he must infer the consciousness of others from certain appearances in his own consciousness, either his sensory consciousness of the other's body or his more complex consciousness of the other's language.[5] To infer from our reference to the other's body, as Watsonian behaviorists do, that the other person is a mere body and not a consciousness is as unreasonable as it would be to infer from the reference to language that the other person is a disembodied language. Actually, our experiences of body and of language lead to the conclusion that the other is a person. My mind is not alone. I am an experient; there are other experients.

[4] This statement will strike some readers as untenable, for physiological psychology is commonly regarded as more empirical than introspection. However, the process of experiencing is always a conscious process and the actual empirical situation (see Chap. VII, § 11, (4), (i)) is what a real empiricist must build on. For such an empiricist, all objects other than present consciousness are hypothetical entities, deduced from it. The facts of physiological psychology are such hypothetical entities—objects of a rational belief that is well-grounded in experiences of the actual entity. This belief, of course, presupposes causal action of nervous system on consciousness, as well as causal action of consciousness on nervous system.

[5] See the penetrating article by H. H. Price, "Our Evidence for the Existence of Other Minds," in *Philosophy*, 13(1938), 425–456, where the evidence of language is emphasized. There is, however, no reason for supposing that language alone solves the problem of communication and interaction. How do we communicate language? Consult Urban, LAR(1939).

To regard personality as consciousness [6] is not to deny the body or to minimize physiological psychology or behavioristic method. It is only to insist on the most fundamental fact of experience, namely, its consciousness.

It is necessary to distinguish between Situations Experienced and Situations Believed-in. A "situation" means any state of affairs. No situation is a Situation Experienced unless it is actually present in consciousness. Experience is given only as a conscious state of affairs. To experience is to be aware. A man cannot properly say that he is experiencing a fire in his house merely because the fire is going on; he experiences the fire only when it makes a perceptible difference to his conscious experience. More exactly, the man can never say that he is experiencing the fire, even when perceptions of its odor or heat occur; yes, even when the fire burns his body, the Situation Experienced is excruciating pain, not actual fire. The fire is always a Situation Believed-in, no matter how painfully well-grounded the belief may be.

The only Situation Experienced by anyone is his own consciousness. From this, if he is able to observe and reason even in an elementary way, he is able to infer with varying degrees of accuracy, the presence in his environment [7] of fire, or, if he be religious, of the God who is called a consuming fire. The only basis we have for any knowledge, belief, faith, truth, or error, is to be found in Situations

[6] In agreement with Whitehead's correct interpretation of Descartes's *cogito ergo sum*, in MT, 228.

[7] Environment is here used to mean whatever is not my conscious experience, but affects it so as to produce observable changes in it, or, more generally, so as to make its very existence possible. Hegel's *Phänomenologie des Geistes*, for example, is not my conscious experience, no matter how often I read it. My experience of the book is not the book itself. But the book affects my experience, and my experience could not be as it is without the book. For a further discussion (in other terms) of the problem of Situations Experienced and Situations Believed-in, let the reader consult the treatment of knowledge claims in Chap. VI, Introductory, and of actual and hypothetical entities in Chap. VII, § 11, (5), (iv).

Experienced. Whatever is not in the Situation Experienced is a Situation Believed-in or Disbelieved-in—for example, a person's brain, or the bottom of the ocean, or God. A Situation Experienced is a self, a person, or an experient, because it is a self-experiencing whole which includes thinking, choosing, remembering, anticipating, and purposing, as well as feeling and sensing. A whole self includes all those Situations Experienced which are related by self-identifying memories and anticipations. It is true that, for any present experient, its own past is no longer a Situation Experienced. Now, that past has become a Situation Believed-in; but the belief that it was once a Situation Experienced by the experient may be well-grounded in coherent interpretation of experience.

However, no portion of an experient's nervous system nor any part of his body has ever been or can be a Situation Experienced by that experient. When I see my hand, for example, the hand is not itself actually in my consciousness. The Situation Experienced consists of a whole within which there is observed a certain pattern of sense data. That pattern is part of a personal Situation Experienced; the hand itself is a Situation Believed-in. Many Situations Believed-in we must postulate to be actually there. All such situations belong in a universal interacting system which itself interacts to a greater or lesser degree with all Situations Experienced.

This distinction, once clearly made, helps to remove much of the confusion pervading contemporary philosophy.[8]

[8] The Situation Experienced is what the author has elsewhere called the datum self. The concept is close to many now in use. It corresponds to the field of attention, to James's stream of consciousness (although treated as a unified Gestalt), to the specious present, and to Royce's span of consciousness. It is related to Whitehead's actual occasion and to Dewey's situation; but the former seems to be more narrow in its scope than the total Situation Experienced, while Dewey's situation includes, if it does not entirely consist of, Situations Believed-in, found in the biological and social matrix of which he writes in LOG(1938). Dewey thus leaves

Truly radical empiricists should be the first to welcome the sharp distinction between actual experience and the beliefs to which it gives rise. They should see that personal consciousness alone is experience, and that all bodies, brains, and gods are objects of belief. Many of the Situations Believed-in, and also many unknown situations, exert their energies on us; but only chaos ensues when we identify ourselves with the energies that affect us. My brain, the stimuli which affect my nervous system, the sun in the sky, and God are all essential to my continued existence in this world. But I—the experient, the person, the Situation Experienced—am not to be identified with what sustains my being. I am not my nervous system, the sun, or God. I am what I experience myself as being—a conscious self.

This radically empirical point of view, which takes my personality to be my consciousness, is also a religious point of view, for religion is concerned with man's conscious experience of values, with man's spirit, and with religious experience. The goal of religion is the development of worthy consciousness.

On this foundation we can build our definition of personality—the quality of being a person. What, then, is a person? [9] Is any consciousness whatever to be regarded as a person? Supposing a paramecium to be conscious, is it a person? Is the consciousness of an ant, a pig, a horse, a dog, or an ape personal? These questions necessitate a

---

the mental, the actual experience, in an orphanage for sterilized children of unknown parents. The Situation Experienced includes all of Santayana's essences, and the concept of the Situation Believed-in agrees with Santayana's teaching that existence is not given, as well as with his doctrine of animal faith, with the qualification that animal faith is too narrow a basis for a well-grounded belief in existence. Santayana enjoys values, but excludes them as grounds of belief. The relation of our terminology to Lloyd Morgan's experienc*ing* and experienc*ed* remains to be clarified.

[9] See Brightman, "What is Personality?" Art.(1939), for a brief treatment. Gordon W. Allport's *Personality* is the best book on the subject from a psychological point of view; see the footnote on p. 159.

distinction in terminology. The word *self* is used for any and every consciousness, however simple or complex it may be. A self is any conscious situation experienced as a whole. Each "empirical situation" is a self. All consciousness is self-experience; but self-experience is not properly called self-consciousness (reflective consciousness) unless the self in question has the special attribute of being able to think about the fact that it is a self in addition to the fact that it experiences sensations and desires. A *person* is a self that is potentially self-conscious, rational, and ideal. That is to say, when a self is able at times to reflect on itself as a self, to reason, and to acknowledge ideal goals by which it can judge its actual achievements, then we call it a person. There is no reason on the basis of known evidence to draw the line sharply and say that only human beings are persons; pigs, dogs, apes, and horses seem to be at least elementary persons. But this consideration is of no vital importance to a philosophy of religion, for the very good reason that, as far as we know, human persons are the only ones who have religious experience.[10]

The brief definitions of self and person need fuller explanation. Individual psychology reveals to us a great variety of persons; and comparative psychology makes it probable that self-experience, if not reflective self-consciousness, extends to the lowest forms of animal life. We can barely surmise how the consciousness of a dog or a cat feels to the animal that has it; to conceive the consciousness of a protozoon passes all our imagination; yet there is good reason to believe that every living being experiences itself as a self. The various levels of selfhood and personality merge into each other and defy classification. It is possible, however, to indicate the range of these levels by not-

---

[10] The question whether "subhuman" persons are immortal is one which cannot be answered, since sufficient evidence is not available.

ing the chief characteristics of the most elementary type of
self that can be and contrasting the marks of this minimum
self with the chief characteristics of a person.

The *characteristics of a minimum self,* the simplest possible consciousness, may be listed tentatively under eight
headings, as follows: (1) *Self-experience*—a unified complexity of consciousness (Stern's *unitas multiplex*). Every
item of consciousness is owned, and belongs to a whole.
There are no floating experiences, but only selves. (2)
Qualia—distinguishable qualities, at least sense qualities and
perhaps other qualities of feeling. (3) *Time and space.*
All selves must necessarily experience time because this is
a world of process; it is highly probable that some kind of
space-consciousness is also universal. (4) *Transcendence of
time and space.* The complexity of the specious present and
memory (however dim) elevate every self above time to
some extent; and probably the humblest self transcends
space both by its ability to aim at distant spaces and by its
nonspatial experiences (such as its unity). (5) *Process
and conation.* All selves are in constant process of change,
which includes striving for ends (conation); to be a self
is to experience a desire for future experience, if only the
eating of food and the continuance of life. (6) *Awareness
of meaning.* The simplest self treats its experiences as signs
of further experience; thus it is in an elementary way aware
of meaning. To feel conation is also to refer to an object.
Sophisticated as it may sound, the humblest paramecium
experiences objective reference in every one of its pursuits
and avoidances. If only by "animal faith," it reaches beyond
itself to something "meant" whenever it darts toward food.
(7) *Response to environment.* Every self lives in an environment which is constantly stimulating it. A minimum
self doubtless has no awareness of the causal relation or of
reasoning processes, and so is not conscious of a difference

between itself and its environment. Yet its "animal faith" leads it to respond to the effects of the world in its experience. (8) *Privacy.* Every self is directly experienced only by itself. "The monads have no windows" in this sense. However, a minimum self is not aware of this property of its experience, since any understanding of the concept of privacy presupposes reasoning processes.[11]

If we contrast a minimum self with a person, we find that each of the eight characteristics just mentioned has been developed to a higher level. (1) *Self-experience* is far more complex and highly organized; reference to past and future plays a much larger part in the present experience of the self. (2) New *qualia* emerge, such as feelings of moral obligation, of aesthetic taste, and religious obligation, which come to be recognized as *imperative norms.* (3) The range of *time* and *space* experience is vastly *extended.* (4) *Time-transcendence* is extended by the development of a more complex field of attention and of a richer and more accurate memory accompanied by recognition. The self of the present is thus identified with the self of past and future. *Space-transcendence* is increased by a multiplication of non-spatial interests in spiritual values and abstract ideas. (5) *Conation* rises to the level of *free* purposive *self-control* and control of environment. The self desires; the person is, within limits, freely selective and critical of its desires. (6) *Awareness of meaning* becomes conceptual thought and *reasoning.* This has often been given as the unique attribute of man, but we now know that it is present in some degree among the apes and other forms of life. Reflective self-consciousness, as distinguished from mere self-experience, arises on this personal level. (7) The *response to environment* is

[11] Mary W. Calkins, in her article, "The Self in Scientific Psychology," *Am. Jour. Psych.,* 26(1915), 519, listed the following traits of the self: identity (our (1)), change (our (5)), uniqueness (our (8)), totality (again our (1)), and relatedness to environment (our (7)). See also her *First Book in Psychology,* p. 14.

increasingly a response to a social and ideal environment, and the responses are more freely selective rather than mechanical. (8) Although *privacy* is transcended by language and by understanding, it remains a fact that all communication is sent by and received in private experience; and developed persons respect the fact and the rights of privacy.

Among these emergent traits of personality, the most important are the consciousness of imperative norms, freedom, and reason. By reason is meant the power of testing truth-claims by logical and empirical standards; the principles of deduction and induction; and, above all, the perception of the relations between parts and wholes (analysis, synthesis, synopsis). Coherence, the principle of reason, is identical whether its subject matter be the physical world (Kant's theoretical or speculative reason), the realm of values (cf. Kant's practical reason, which is the rational will), or social relations ("social reason"). The consciousness of imperative norms is man's experience of his destiny as obligation to pursue the ideal values; personality grows as these ideals are transformed into concrete value experiences. Freedom, as Driesch has well said, is the power of saying yes or saying no (*Jasagen, Neinsagen*) to given experiences. In a word, freedom is the power of choice. Reason, imperative norms, and choice enter into every higher personal experience, especially into religion. "I will pray with the understanding," "love your enemies," and "choose you this day whom ye will serve" are typical religious expressions of these three principles of personality.[12]

§ 5. THE UNITY AND IDENTITY OF PERSONALITY

For various reasons, the unity and identity of personality are of special importance to religion.[13] If a person is not a

[12] 1 Cor. 14:15; Mt. 5:44; Josh. 24:15.
[13] For a psychological treatment of this topic, see Allport, PER, Chap. XIII.

true identical unity through all the changes in his experience, then spiritual development is impossible. Moral growth, for example, rests on the postulate that I am responsible to myself for my past purposes and contracts; yet if I am not the one who entertained those purposes and made those contracts, I experience neither responsibility nor continuous growth. Unless I am one person, identical through change, all hope for immortality becomes irrational, especially if the apparent unity which we experience be traced wholly to physiological causes, materialistically interpreted.[14] Finally, if personality is not a true identical unity, it is absurd to regard God as a person, whether infinite or finite.

The problem of the unity and identity of personality may be approached from the standpoint of four different theories, namely, the epiphenomenal, the analytic, the substantialist, and the organic.

According to the theory of *epiphenomenalism* (which is held by some psychologists and philosophers), consciousness is to be regarded solely as effect, never as cause. It is the end term of physiological processes and is to be understood exclusively as a physiological product. Hence any unity or identity it may appear to have is illusory. The real unity is that of brain and nervous system, not of consciousness. At least two weaknesses may be pointed out in this view. The first is that our physiological knowledge is not sufficient to warrant so sweeping an assertion. The second and more fundamental one is, as we have previously pointed out, that

[14] The unity of human personality must be due to a cause beyond man. The nervous system is the area where that cause operates. If the nervous system is known to be material substance, independent of any mind, then personality is an "epiphenomenon" and its unity is only that of a shadow. But if the nervous system is what idealism and theism take it to be, namely, an expression (or creation) of mind, then the dependence of human personality on its nervous system is an instance of the dependence of human mind on cosmic mind. The choice between these two explanations will ultimately be determined by the relative coherence of each with all the empirical facts of personal experience.

all experimentation presupposes a unified and identical self as observer and interpreter of the experiment. Physiological psychology, therefore, in so far as it is experimental, presupposes the unitary self which epiphenomenalism denies. The theory is, therefore, self-contradictory.

The *analytic* theory, which might also be called relational, rests on the method of analysis as the ultimate procedure of both science and philosophy. The most famous example of analytic theory of the self is the associationist psychology developed by David Hume and many others. According to this view, the complex structure of mind is revealed by analysis to consist of simple elements, either sensations (impressions, as Hume called them) or neutral entities (as modern analytic realism views them).[15] It is obvious that the unity and identity underlying mind, if this view is true, must be found, not in personality as a whole, but in its simple elements. Two chief objections are urged against this theory. First, it is highly improbable, both psychologically and logically, that the "elements" of mind enjoy any separate and continuous existence apart from the self to which they belong, and even more improbable that (purely subsistent) neutral entities can account for any actual existence whatever. Secondly, important and necessary as is analysis, it is not a method suited to the discovery and interpretation of the properties of wholes as such. The unity and identity of personality may well be not elements or relations of elements, but pervasive properties of each personality as a whole.

The *substantialist* point of view, following the thought of Aristotle and the scholastics, rests on the postulate that every real object is a substance, either material or spiritual, and that substance is a necessary category, although not an object of sense perception nor discoverable in consciousness. Since

---

[15] See Brightman, ITP, Chap. VI and Lexicon.

substance is other than experience, the spiritual substance is called a transcendent soul. Epiphenomenalists deny spiritual substance, and usually declare that all real substance is material. Analysts deny the category of substance entirely, holding that analysis reveals no such element as "substance" in addition to observed properties. Substantialists point to the inadequacy of both epiphenomenalism and analysis, and declare that their view is the necessary and only valid alternative. For it, the unity and identity of personality are found neither in the brain nor in the elements of consciousness but in the soul as a spiritual substance, which underlies and produces the phenomena of consciousness.

Although the theoretical argument for this position appears strong, there are cogent objections to it. In the first place, if one asks *exactly what is meant by this transcendent soul substance* as distinguished from consciousness, one receives no more than a pronoun or two for answer. The soul, we are told, is "that which" supports or causes consciousness. As distinguished from matter, it is a spiritual "that which," and it is equipped with the faculty or power of doing whatever appears in consciousness as its deed. Many thinkers regard this as an empty concept and, in fact, reject substance as a mere abstraction lacking any concrete definition. In the second place, even if there is such a substance as is alleged, *it is of no philosophical or religious importance in interpreting personality.* All that we need for the philosophical understanding of personality is the experienced reality and unity of consciousness and its interaction with its environment. To add to consciously experienced unity and identity the further unity of a substance is philosophically to create a needless hypothesis. Religiously, it is only our conscious experience of ourselves as realizers of value that is of any importance; what happens in a supposed soul substance is not of religious moment until conscious experience of God occurs. And if a soul were to be immortal, the only possible value in its immortality would lie in its conscious experiences, not in the persistence of a substance. The traditional theory of substance seems unempirical and otiose.

There remains what is called the *organic* theory. The term "organic" is not used here as referring to the bodily organism, but rather as pointing out the wholeness of personality. The organic theory is usually called *self psychology,* and posits an immanent self as distinguished from a transcendent soul. That is to say, the self of the organic view is a living whole of conscious experience, whose parts have no existence in isolation from the whole and whose nature is to be conscious as a whole. This view of the self is closely related to Gestalt psychology, purposive psychology, and so-called "personalistics." According to it, the unity of the self or person is the wholeness and indivisibility of its consciousness, its identity is the experience of self-identification in immediate experience and in processes of memory and anticipation. This view recognizes the interaction of the unitary personality with the bodily organism and thus finds a partial truth in epiphenomenalism; it insists on the need of analysis for understanding but supplements analysis by synopsis; it grants that substantialism is right in seeking for a unity, but holds it to be wrong in the unempirical unity asserted. The chief arguments against the organic theory are, first, those in favor of the opposing views and, secondly, the assertion that the self cannot be found by experimental psychologists. With reference to this second point, two remarks may be made. First, if the methods of experimentalists are directed toward objective phenomena of behavior, as they usually are, it is obvious that they are not looking for the self and hence naturally will not find it. Secondly, we may repeat that the unity and identity of the self are empirical presuppositions of every experiment. If I do not experience myself as one identical mind, I cannot conduct any experiment. Therefore the organic view of self psychology is the most tenable theory of personality, precisely from the experimental standpoint.

In Chapter VII attention was called to the datum self (or the empirical situation) as the source of all evidence for belief in society, the world, or God. It is evident, however, that the actual experience of ourself which we enjoy at any moment is far from being our whole self. The empirical situation is always a self; it is an experience of wholeness and identity, of complex unity, of purpose, and of awareness of an environment. But every datum self contains signs of a larger self to which it belongs; memory and anticipation assert the identity of the present person with a person that has been and a person that will be. Thus the whole self, or person, is a total conscious process which is never present to itself in one single experience, but which is aware of its identity and wholeness by means of its backward-looking memories and its forward-looking purposes. The whole self, or person, then, consists of all the conscious experience that is or has been or will be present in all the empirical situations that constitute the history of the person. The unity of personality, therefore, is the unity of consciousness; personality includes consciousness only, and does not include any of its environment—physiological, subconscious, or social —as part of it.

§ 6. Personality and its Environment

The distinction between a personality and its environment is not always made so sharply as in the preceding paragraph, but the distinction is a useful one; in fact, it is necessary if we are to have any clear concept of personality. The conscious person is not the brain; the Situation Experienced is not to be confused with its cause in any Situation Believed-in. Nevertheless, the person is in a constant process of dependence on and interaction with its environment. The action of the environment is not dependent on the person's being conscious of it. A person is usually not conscious of his brain, unless he is reflecting on physiology; nor is he usually conscious of the sun. But brain and sun are environing causes which incessantly affect his consciousness, and without which (in this world) it could not exist.

Taking the conscious person as our point of reference, we may describe its environment as (1) *biological,* (2) *physical,* (3) *social,* (4) *subconscious,* (5) *logical and ideal,* and (6) *metaphysical.*[16] (1) The *biological environment* is the brain and nervous system, which stand in immediate causal and interactive relations with the person; also the whole system of living beings in organic nature. (2) The *physical environment* is inorganic nature—the earth, the air, the sun; in short, the physical universe. (3) The *social environment* consists of all the other interrelated persons whose individual or group activities are mediated to us by the physical and biological environment, and perhaps also by telepathy. (4) The *subconscious* consists of those conscious processes which are connected with our organism and from time to time affect the normal datum self without being actually present in that self. We call them conscious because the evidence indicates that they are in themselves processes of conscious sensation, desire, or even reasoning; we also call them subconscious because they are not experienced as an integral part of the conscious datum self and so they are environment of the total person, rather than part of it.[17] In quite another sense we

[16] See the fuller discussion in Brightman, POI, 25–28.

[17] The subconscious is in one sense nearer to being part of the person than any other environmental factor, because it is a series of conscious processes which almost always (perhaps always) accompany the person as satellites accompany a planet, yet act on the person more intimately than the tidal action

may speak of the logical and ideal environment. (5) *Logical and ideal entities,* although not causes in the sense in which physical objects are, certainly enjoy a subsistence of some sort beyond our experience of them, and so may be called environmental factors. (6) The *metaphysical environment* is the total reality on which we are dependent. Reasons have been given in the previous chapter for defining the eternal, controlling metaphysical power as a finite God. The five previously mentioned aspects of environment may all be viewed as instances of God's control of The Given. The sixth is God and his creation as a whole.

Although from the points of view of experience and knowledge all of these environing factors are hypothetical entities, not actually present in the datum self but only believed-in and referred-to, our reasons for believing that there is an environment on which our very existence depends, and with which we stand in constant interaction, are so cogent that hardly anyone seriously denies it.[18] Two extreme views have been advanced: the Leibnizian and the epiphenomenalist. Leibniz held that the monad (the person) "has no windows." It is active from within, but nothing from without can affect it. The seeming interaction is due to a pre-established harmony among monads. On this view, persons are causes, but not effects. Epiphenomenalists hold that personal consciousness is entirely an effect of the nervous system, and lacking in all causal power. The fact seems to be that persons are both causes and effects, both

---

of any moon; but in another sense the subconscious is more definitely excluded from the person than is biological and physical nature, for our knowledge of it is more clearly inferential. Yet even the so-called direct observation of physical nature is no more than a personal experience which leads to the belief that an environment is present. For any experient, his subconscious consists of Situations Believed-in, which are no part of Situations Experienced by him.

[18] For a concise statement of the inadequacy of the point of view of the datum self, see Hegel, *Encyclopädie*, sec. 71. Pratt's arguments in PR are a good recent statement of the case for interaction.

active and passive; able to choose and initiate certain systems of bodily behavior, yet dependent on the environment for their existence.

Like science and philosophy, religion accepts this dependence of man on his environment. In fact, Schleiermacher regarded the consciousness of dependence as the most characteristic trait of religion. The difference between a religious and a nonreligious interpretation of this relation does not consist in any fantastic denial of physiological facts; it consists, rather, in the metaphysical view of the environment that is adopted. If the environment on which persons and their values depend and out of which they grow be regarded as in itself unconscious and valueless, then no religion is possible except such humanism as can survive the wreck of any objective basis for faith. If, on the other hand, the world of nature and its metaphysical ground be regarded as at least under the control of conscious, value-seeking personality, then man's dependence on and interaction with his environment may be viewed as coöperation with God.

§ 7. The Reality of the Spiritual Life

It is not the bare existence of conscious selves in the universe that is the source of religion and the evidence for a God; it is rather the fact that there are persons—selves who are able to develop ideal values. One who confronts the facts of social, economic, and political injustice in the world, to say nothing of the private miseries and futilities of countless individuals, is impressed with the honesty of the title of Henry Churchill King's book,[19] *The Seeming Unreality of the Spiritual Life*. Yet over against all that makes man's higher values seem unreal is the fact that they have survived despite the injustices of nature and man's inhumanity to man. Wherever humanity exists, there moral, scientific,

[19] Published by The Macmillan Company, New York, 1908.

philosophical, artistic, and religious ends are sought. Far from being unreal, spiritual ideals are what make men human, as well as akin to the divine. Man's desperate wickedness is often due to the inaccessibility of precisely these ideal values, or to the unjust distribution of the means of access to them. Without these spiritual values man would be depersonalized and dehumanized; he would be a mere brute. For all their seeming fragility, the spiritual values are the only clue to any real meaning in history or in individual life. To use the language of German philosophy, it is spirit (*Geist*) that gives meaning to nature or finds meaning in spite of nature; [20] to quote an authority: "Howbeit that is not first which is spiritual, but that which is natural; then that which is spiritual." [21] These words summarize the development of personality. A self is given; a personality is achieved. Personality is, of course, achieved on many different levels, through sharp and prolonged conflicts, through dialectical struggles, through sin, forgiveness, and redemption. But it is the reality of the spiritual values that measures the evils as well as the goods of personality. Pessimism could not even be thought of if it were not seen that the true destiny of man was the achievement of values worthy of him.

§ 8. Personality Human and Divine: Likenesses

The term personality has been applied in the course of our discussions both to man and to God. In view of the differences of opinion that prevail with reference to divine personality, it is of the utmost importance that the term be used precisely. In previous chapters arguments for and against supposing God to be a person have been considered. We are now ready to explain more fully exactly what is meant by saying that God is a person. Let us consider first

[20] See Paul Tillich in Dessoir, PEG, 779.
[21] Saint Paul in 1 Cor. 15:46.

the respects in which human and divine personality are similar, then the respects in which they differ.

(1) *All persons, human or divine,* in order to be persons must *share in the essential marks of personality* listed in § 4 of this chapter. To summarize: God and man both enjoy complex self-experience, *qualia* (including ideal norms) which low grade selves are not conscious of, a wide range of temporal and spatial consciousness, time-transcendence and space-transcendence, free purposive self-control, rational awareness of meaning, free response to environment, and privacy of consciousness. All these traits belong to the essence of personality. None of them is inconsistent with the idea of God (as empirically derived) except perhaps privacy; but, since privacy means only that no one else can experience a person's consciousness directly, as he can himself, the inconsistency is only apparent. Only the most fanatical mystic would lay claim to experiencing God from within as God experiences himself. And human privacy is compatible with interaction, communication, and knowledge of and by other selves. Privacy, therefore, is consistent with what the idea of God requires.

(2) *No other person, human or divine, can be perceived by the senses, but must be inferred from the data* of our own personal consciousness. It is debatable what we do perceive by sense—whether we perceive only our own sensuous consciousness or external material objects; it is not debatable that consciousness is imperceptible to sense. No one ever had a sense perception of thinking, or feeling, or choosing, or even of sensing itself. No sense quality which we experience can possibly be regarded as a direct awareness of another's consciousness. From sense data of our own personal datum self we infer the presence of other persons, human or divine. We have no direct sensuous evidence of either human society or divine personality; both can be affirmed only as

rational objects of belief based on interpretation of our experience. We do not see other persons; we think them as inferences from our perceptions. For us they are hypothetical entities. This fact is related to the space-transcending attribute of all persons. We think a space world. Ultimately, for the theist and the idealist, minds are not in a space independent of them, but all space is in minds as their experience.

(3) *All persons, human or divine, possess an active will* (a power of choice and hence of the organization of experience). Without this selective power a person could not pursue ideal norms, nor could he direct his life by reason. Without it he would be a thing rather than a person.

(4) But *every person, human or divine, has experiences which his will does not produce, but finds.* It is patently true that man's will confronts given factors in his heredity, his sense experience, and his rational nature. If our view of the finiteness of God is correct, the divine will also finds given content which it did not create but which it has to direct and control. The experiences with which will thus deals may be called The Given.

§ 9. Personality Human and Divine: Differences

In spite of the numerous resemblances which we have found between human and divine personality, their differences are equally important. In one sense, their differences may be said to be infinite, since man's life has a beginning in time, while God's has neither beginning nor end. The differences which we shall discuss include those entailed by the idea of a finite God which we developed empirically.

(1) The *divine personality* (as was just said) *is eternal and uncreated.* That something must be unbegun follows from the principle *ex nihilo nihil fit.*[22] If there had ever

[22] "Nothing is made out of nothing."

been a state in which there was nothing, then that state would have continued forever. It is impossible for our imagination to grasp unbegun duration, but the failure of our imagination is overcome by the necessity of rational thought. As surely as there is anything now, so surely there must always have been something. The postulate of our philosophy of religion is that the ever-enduring reality, unbegun and unending,[23] is the divine personality. This earth, and the life on it, had a beginning; the divine personality is the unbegun source of all beginnings. Those who deny an eternal divine personality have to show that the postulation of an eternal unconscious force, entity, or complex of forces or entities could explain the properties and the development of the conscious empirical situation, which is the being of each one of us, better than could our postulate of an eternal personality. The postulate of personality has its great advantage over alternative hypotheses in its ability to interpret concretely the combination of form, content, and activity found in every experience and in every object which we experience or acknowledge to be real. The propositions of logical positivism may account for form; the neutral entities of neorealism may describe content; concepts like energy or life may refer to activity; but only concrete personal consciousness unites form, content, and activity in an actually experienced whole. Hence we are justified in postulating divine personality as the eternal and uncreated reality, in contrast with every human personality, which has a beginning in time.

(2) *The Given* (see § 8, (4)) *in the divine personality is coeternal with the divine will as an integral aspect of the divine personality.* In man, The Given has to be explained

---

[23] Unending, because a cause without any effect (which would be an absolute end) is as unreasonable as an effect without a cause (which would be an absolute beginning).

as prior to his birth and therefore coming from some source beyond him. In God, The Given cannot be regarded as coming from some external source without supposing an incoherent ultimate dualism in the universe; nor can it be regarded as willed by God without compromising the eternal subsistence of logic as well as the coherence of the divine will. We, therefore, have a choice between consistent agnosticism (which if thoroughly consistent will not postulate any God at all) and consistent finitism. Acceptance of this finitism makes it as unreasonable to ask, "Whence The Given?" as to ask, "When did eternity begin?" or "Who made God?" Divine personality is not dependent for any of its content on any power external to itself, except for such changes in its content as arise from the choices of other personalities. But no other personality is eternal, hence all others depend for their existence on the divine will.

(3) *The divine person has,* in contrast with man, *no body and especially no nervous system.* The postulate that there is a God means all real energy in the universe is the will of conscious personality, and that the human nervous system can be a cause of human consciousness only if it is itself, in its inner being, a conscious reality. The view that nervous systems are systems within the divine personality, rather than separate consciousnesses or complexes of conscious "monads," is supported by the unity of the system of physical nature as well as by the evidence that a nervous system is a divisible complex and not a true unity. Only personality, with its experiences of self-identification, is a true, indivisible unity. The divine personality is the locus and the divine will the energy of the whole physical universe, including the human nervous system. Metaphysically, personality is not caused by nervous system, but nervous system is caused by personality—that is, by the personality of God. The evolution

of nervous systems is part of the cosmic process of the divine personality in its control of The Given.

(4) *The divine person creates other persons.* This has been presupposed under point (2). The concept of creation is difficult but unavoidable. Whether one is a theist or an atheist or an agnostic or a skeptic, one must acknowledge the fact that novelties emerge in the evolutionary process. Evolution is creative. At one time there was no Goethe; then Goethe came into being. Whatever may be said of his biological origin, it cannot reasonably be maintained that Goethe's personality, his actual conscious experience, had any sort of actual being in the world before Goethe began to be. When he was born, a new person was created. At one time in the evolutionary process on this earth, there were doubtless no persons, but only elementary selves. Before that, there were no individual selves at all, but perhaps only the ongoing of inorganic matter (which we view metaphysically as a phase of God's own conscious personality). But it cannot be said that selves were made out of matter and persons out of selves. It must rather be acknowledged that evolution creates new beings and new kinds of being. On our view, evolution is God's will in action, imaginatively controlling The Given and creating such qualities and beings as can be created under the given limitations. Among the creations of God are human personalities with their experienced traits. That they are creations is shown by their novelty; that they are other than God is shown by the incoherences which ensue when human consciousness, with all its ignorance and limitation, is thought of as literally part of a divine consciousness which transcends human limits.

(5) *The divine person undoubtedly has types of experience unknown to us.* Possibilities of such experience are

hinted at by our knowledge of infrared and ultraviolet rays. There are energies unperceived by us; there are countless gaps in our knowledge of the physical world, of the realm of values, of the social realm, and of ourselves. In these gaps there is no reason to suppose that there are no surprises or novelties now utterly unknown and unimagined. Yet, however great the varieties of divine experience may be, there is no adequate empirical or rational ground for asserting that there is anything in God which is not experience. Although this statement is regarded by some as anthropomorphic, the burden of proof lies on those who assume existences which by their very nature are excluded from being in experience at all. Why such entities should be supposed or what it means to suppose them remains a mystery. There is enough mystery implied in real experience; mysteries should not be multiplied beyond necessity.

(6) *The divine person alone is completely and perfectly personal.* Man is only fragmentarily conscious. No human being is conscious of his own whole self, to say nothing of the whole world. Man's consciousness is dimmed by weariness and illness, and is interrupted by sleep and by death—although, as it is resumed after sleep, so it may be resumed after death. In contrast with man's consciousness, God's is uninterrupted, inclusive of his whole personality, fully and immediately conscious of the whole physical universe, aware of and consciously coöperating with all persons other than himself, foreseeing all of the future that can be foreseen, and planning for all contingencies. So vast a consciousness almost paralyzes our imagination, and leads even a wise thinker like J. B. Pratt to infer that the sustaining of such an overwhelming range of consciousness is too great a task to be assigned even to a God. Yet a God must be superhuman and must be sufficient to account for the entire universe. The inability of our imagination to picture God—an eternal

spiritual personality—does not deter our mind from thinking him. The sublimity of God [24] is one of the perpetual sources of worship.

We have asserted in § 8 that there are likenesses between human and divine personality; in § 9 we have found differences. Some critics of theism hold that the likenesses debase God to the human level, whereas the differences are so great that we cannot even call God a person. The reply of the theist is that the concept of personality is rich and meaningful enough to include within its realm all beings from the humblest and most elementary personal creature to the supreme and eternal cosmic person. The reader will decide for himself which interpretation is the truer. The least that can be said is that personalistic theism is an hypothesis which interprets experience and its implications without contradiction.

BIBLIOGRAPHICAL NOTE

The literature of personality, both psychological and philosophical, is so extensive that even the 3341 items in Roback's bibliography, BCP(1927), were far from exhausting the material available in 1927; and almost as many items again have appeared since that date. A very few representative selections will be made for our purposes.

The most useful current text in general psychology is Vaughan's GP(1939), which is concrete and accurate. Boring's HEP(1929) affords needed orientation on the history of experimental psychology. The logic of psychology is suggestively, although inadequately, examined in Pratt, LMP(1939).

A survey of the elements of the problem is found in Brightman, ITP(1925), 166–211, with a selected bibliography, 372–373. Fundamental issues are ably analyzed in Moore and Gurnee, FP (1933). The best and most comprehensive psychology of personality is Allport, PER(1937).

A valuable little book on the philosophy of personality is Pratt,

---

[24] See Kant's discussion of the sublime in his *Critique of Judgment*.

MS(1922). Pratt develops his views, including a brief discussion of Brightman's standpoint, in his later PR(1937), 220-334, where he treats the self, the mind-body problem, and the finiteness of God. The problem is discussed from the standpoint of philosophy of religion in Brightman, PR(1934), more fully in Laird, *Problems of the Self*(1917), and most thoroughly in Tennant, PT(1928, 1930), especially Vol. I.

Of special interest is the article on "Mind and Near-Mind," Hocking, Art.(1927). Brightman, Art.(1931), Art.(1932)[3], and Art.(1939) may also be consulted.

TWELVE

THE PROBLEM OF HUMAN PURPOSE

IN the previous chapter persons have been defined as conscious selves capable of reasoning and valuing. Selves that can seek food without a thought of anything other or better than food are not persons. Thus we have established a level of purpose as the criterion for distinguishing selves from persons. Persons are essentially purposers, and purposers of rationality and value.

There are, of course, experiences which are not purposes. Mere awareness of sense qualities, of space and time relations, or of logical necessity, is not in itself purpose. But, as substantially all psychologists agree, some sort of purpose almost always accompanies our nonpurposive consciousness, so that in almost every conscious complex unpurposed elements such as have been mentioned are always attended by some striving or conation or desire or plan. A wish to give or to divert attention, a longing to maintain or to alter the present state of consciousness— something of the nature of purpose is present in all consciousness which is not mere neutral indifference. Whether this state ever occurs is debatable. If a conscious being continued permanently in that state, it would not be a person.[1] In his

[1] It is questionable whether Nirvana is such a state. Nirvana certainly is a conquest of all desire for selfhood. But whether it is to be regarded as the

371

oft-quoted phrase, William James calls selves "fighters for ends." Persons are selves who may become fighters for ideal ends, pursuers of good, avoiders of evil. Some end is sought by all normal human consciousness. Whatever else it may be, all personal living is purposing.

§ 2. RELIGION AS CONCERN ABOUT PURPOSE

Pervasive as purpose is, not all human interests are interests in purpose. Science "abstracts" from purpose; the pure physicist does not investigate the bearing of physical laws on human purpose. His purpose is to ignore all purposes except that of knowing the laws of matter and motion. The technologist or engineer applies the results of physics to the achieving of practical purposes; but his chief interest is not in the inherent value of the purpose so much as in the means of realizing it.

Religion, on the other hand, is primarily concerned about purpose. Religion asks, with the Westminster Shorter Catechism, "What is the chief end of man?" [2] To raise this question is to emphasize the connection between value and personality as the two fundamental concepts of religion. Purpose is that concrete personal experience which aims at the production and conservation of values—at axiogenesis and axiosoteria as we have called them. Religion is faith in a divine axiogenetic and axiosoteric power—a superhuman purposer of value. A God that is merely a cosmic power or a cosmic mathematician [3] is of no religious interest or value. Only when this power or this mathematician becomes a setter of goals and a coöperator with man in the

---

conquest of all purpose or the fulfillment of the highest purpose of existence is a point that will have to be left to Orientalists. At worst, then, the religion of the Buddhist is the purpose to overcome purpose.

[2] This is illustrated even by Feuerbach's assertion that "the divinity of man is the end of religion."

[3] As Sir James Jeans has called God.

achieving of those goals is he a God in the religious sense. Similarly, belief in life after death is not a religious belief merely because it asserts endless survival. It is religious only in so far as it is purposeful.[4] The religious man is not concerned about bare facts or pure existence; his concern is always with the control of facts by purpose. Religion finds its problem in the scientific data; but its solution is always in the realm of purpose.[5]

§ 3. Teleology and Mechanism: Problem and Definition

Purpose is an undeniable fact of personal experience. Even subpersonal selves, including all of the so-called "lower" animals, are purposers. The adaptation of means to ends in nature, the "fitness of the environment" [6] for the survival of life, the origination of organisms that are fit to survive, the beauty that is immanent in nature, the harmony between mind and body—these and like facts incline the mind naturally to suppose that purpose is manifested in external nature as well as in human experience. Substantially all religion and most philosophy until recent times have supported the view that man and his world are alike the work of a cosmic purpose. Sir Thomas Browne said in the *Religio Medici*,[7] that the principle "natura nihil agit frustra" (nature does nothing in vain) is "the only

[4] The distinction between science and religion set forth in the text is related to the views of Koehler in PVWF and of Whitehead (in his discussions of "importance") in MT. The logical positivist, Schlick, holds that science is "the pursuit of truth," while philosophy is "the pursuit of meaning" (see GA, 126). This view, frequently held today, restricts the word "truth" to statements about empirical fact, and thus implies that there can be no truth about ideals. The language is unfortunate; but it is at least an attempt to rephrase the distinction between description and evaluation.

[5] This is to be related to Kant's doctrine of the primacy of the pure practical reason.

[6] The phrase is the title of a book by L. J. Henderson of Harvard.

[7] Pt. i, Sec. 19.

undisputed axiom in philosophy." Not to recognize this purpose is to ascribe to blind chance or coincidence a series of purposive adaptations that stretch back as far as human knowledge goes and point ahead as far as mind can think.

Over against this view of nature as purposive there is an opposed view which explains events in nature as necessarily conditioned by previous events without regard to any supposed design or purpose. As long as the view of nature was dominated by a search for purpose (or "final cause," as Aristotle had called it) no laws were discovered which rendered reliable prediction possible. Nature could not be successfully controlled by speculation about her purposes. But as soon as experimental method was applied and laws of cause and effect discovered, nature began to be mastered. "Natura vincitur pariendo" (nature is conquered by obedience), said Sir Francis Bacon; and obedience meant for him what it means for all inductive scientists—observation, experiment, and generalization.

As a result of the scientific progress that has ensued from ignoring final causes and centering on principles of what Aristotle called efficient cause, Sir Thomas Browne's Aristotelian axiom has been challenged by many. If man's power over nature increases as purpose is disregarded and if scientific laws are most exact when no account is taken of purpose, what is the importance, the relevance, or the truth of the supposition that purpose rules nature?

Thus there has arisen the conflict between teleology and mechanism. A view which regards the cosmos, or at least some cosmic power beyond man, as expressing purpose through the realization of ends is called teleology. A view which explains all events according to laws which are not guided or controlled by purpose is called mechanism.

No thinker denies the facts on which teleology rests, nor does any thinker deny that there are mechanical laws. But thinkers differ widely about the interpretation of the teleological and the mechanical aspects of experience.

§ 4. Stages of Thought About Teleology and Mechanism

Primitive thought was in the main a confused pluralistic teleology. It was not supposed that one purpose unified the meaning of all existence, but many conflicting purposes were at work in spirits and demons, forces of nature and magic, gods of many natures and functions. As religion moved toward monotheism, the idea of one controlling purpose developed. Meanwhile man had observed some of the regularities of nature. The laws of the heavenly bodies and of the human organism began to be roughly understood long before Sir Francis Bacon and modern inductive science. The first clear statement of the radical difference between explanation by purpose and explanation by mechanical laws is put into the mouth of Socrates by Plato in the *Phaedo* (97B–99D). Socrates here rejects the idea that the cause of his being in prison was his bones and sinews or any material thing, in favor of finding "the real cause" in what the Athenians decided and what Socrates decided. For Socrates and Plato teleology was true. Yet at the same time the Democritus whose name Plato does not mention in the dialogues was developing a philosophy of atomism which explained every event in the whole universe, including every mental event, as an instance of the motions of material atoms and as a necessary result of previous motions. While Plato was asserting teleology, Democritus was asserting mechanism. Aristotle, by his theory of the four causes—formal, material, efficient, and final—thought that he could reconcile the strife; but by making final cause supreme he definitely sided with teleology, and his solution remained dominant until the rise of modern science to which reference has already been made. Then at the end of the eighteenth century, Kant undertook to solve the problem by turning over the realm of phenomena (the space-time world of sense objects) entirely to mechanism and assigning purpose, especially free moral purpose, to a realm of noumena (a spaceless and timeless order of "things in themselves"). The Kantian solution left mechanism and purpose universally valid in their respective realms, but "never the twain shall meet."

"Nineteenth century physics," which was rigidly mechanistic, seemed so thoroughly to confirm Kant's view of phenomena as to leave no room at all for purpose. Meanwhile (1859 on), the theory of evolution was exhibiting the combination of purpose and mechanism in the development of life; psychology was moving from the mechanical views of associationism to the more purposive conceptions of functional and hormic psychologies, self psychologies, and *Gestalt;* physics itself was modifying the mechanical rigidities of the nineteenth century by such conceptions as the quantum theory, the theory of relativity, and Heisenberg's principle of indeterminacy. A new appraisal is in order.

§ 5. The Validity of Mechanism

Experimental physics, chemistry, physiology, and psychology, as well as astronomical observations and predictions, have so well established the presence of mechanistic processes in the universe that it would be the height of absurdity to deny them or even to raise a serious question about their existence. Repeated experiments in the form "If X, then Y" have been performed. Every time X has been observed, Y has followed. When an apparent X has not been followed by Y it has been found that we did not have a pure case of X; we had $X + n$, in which case it is clear why Y did not ensue. So frequent and uniform has been the verification of this principle that we have occasion only to point to it as true, not to challenge it in any way. There are mechanisms in this sense in all fields of scientific observation. For example, in the physical there is the correlation between lines in the spectrum and the elements; in the chemical, the green flame of copper; in the physiological, the knee jerk; in the psychological, memory; and in the astronomical, an eclipse. Mechanisms vary widely in their nature and complexity but the principle is the same in all instances.

§ 6. The Limits of Mechanism

The philosophical problem of mechanism is, accordingly, not the problem of whether or not there is mechanism in the universe. It is rather the problem of the adequacy (that is to say, the coherence) of mechanism as the sole and complete explanation of all events. To admit the reality of mechanistic processes is to imply no sort of contradiction with our experiences of purpose. Contradiction between mechanism and teleology arises only when two assertions are made: (1) that mechanism is the sole and complete explanation of all events (as we have just said), and (2) that reference to purpose as a nonmechanical principle precludes the validity of mechanism.

When these two sources of contradiction are analyzed, they are seen to be far from certain. If we declare that mechanism is the sole and complete explanation of everything we are going far beyond scientific verification into the realm of philosophical speculation. There is no objection to philosophical speculation; every human being who seeks for unity must speculate about the total meaning of his experience. But such speculation must conform to the fundamental maxim of philosophy: Give a coherent account of all aspects of your experience. It is arbitrary and unphilosophical to take one aspect of our scientific experience, such as the principle of mechanism, and extend it so as to cancel the meaning of our most meaningful experiences; moral, aesthetic, and religious values, as ends of purposive striving, are as well verified empirically as is the principle of mechanism, although by different types of experience. Even more arbitrary is it to declare that the conscious pursuit of these ends cannot be made an explanatory principle without abandoning mechanism. It is not "saving the appearances" to clamp the mechanistic formula down on value experience in such a way as to deny importance to the truly important. Thus arises the question of the limits of mechanism.

We must distinguish scientific mechanism from philosophical mechanism. Scientific mechanism is valid in so far as it is verified in experiment or observation. But in the nature of the case, scientific mechanism is abstract. It applies to an isolated state of affairs: that is, it presupposes a closed system. The X must be conceived as a perfect instance of its type and as affected by no forces of any sort external to itself. But such an X is clearly an ideal abstraction, never perfectly realized in fact; there is no perfect vacuum, no frictionless oscillation, no observation free from the personal equation.

The fundamental limit of mechanism, then, is that it is explanation in terms of an imperfectly realized ideal, which ideal itself is a purpose of the scientific mind. There is no experiment without purpose. Furthermore, the chief empirical reason for man's search for mechanistic knowledge is his purpose to apply mechanisms for the control of experience and the realization of values.

It is not necessary to examine here the many arguments which have led an increasing number of philosophers to reject mechanism as a universal and sufficient explanation of everything. Such an examination belongs to metaphysics.[8] Suffice it to say that the formula "if X, then Y" gives no account of how any X arose in the first place and no account of why there should be the striving for value which is experienced as a factor in all stages of X. Mechanism rightly describes the survival of the fit; but it leaves the arrival of the fit—the source of the valuable and purposive—in the dark. Even if only one organism in a billion survives, how did that one come to be adapted to survival? Mechanism lacks any principle which accounts coherently for the slightest gleam of adaptive purpose in the universe—to say nothing of the light which has illuminated the growth of religion in the world.

§ 7. The Evidence for Teleology

In § 3 the evidence for teleology has been summarized. It consists of all personal experience of purpose, end, or plan; the signs of purpose or conation in subpersonal selves; the adaptation of means to ends (of inorganic to organic, of organic to conscious) in nature and hence "the fitness of the environment"; the arrival of the fit, the beauty in nature; the harmony and interaction of mind and body; and, we may add, the spiritual life—the striving for ideal values—that arises wherever man develops the possibilities of his consciousness, whether in China or Japan, India or Babylonia, Greece or Israel, Egypt or Rome, among Teutons or among Incas.

An essential difference between mechanism and teleology is that the evidence for teleology is so plainly factual that it is undeniable, whereas philosophical mechanism is a speculative theory. Long before man was sophisticated enough to think of scientific mechanisms he had observed

[8] See the treatment of "the limitations of mechanistic explanation" in Brightman, ITP, 259–279.

the facts of purpose and built a world view, letting his imagination play freely by conjuring up magical and demonic purposive forces. The crude teleology of primitive thought and of modern wishful thinking has led many honest thinkers to revolt against all teleology. But to do this is to fly in the face of the empirical evidence for purpose. The fact that men have distorted the facts does not prove that the facts are not there or justify the thinker in seeking, by a panmechanistic theory, to explain the facts away. Such a reaction is both logically and psychologically on a parity with the view of those who would reject evolution because some evolutionists have interpreted it as precluding any truth or value in religion.

Let us repeat then: there are teleological facts which are there before any philosophizing begins. Any reasoning which aims to be philosophical must give an account of these facts, if philosophy is a coherent description of experience. In this respect, then, teleology has a logical advantage over mechanism. Mechanism, even in its scientific form, is an explanation, not a given fact. It is a well-verified explanation, yet we have seen so many changes in theory that mechanism may be forced to change with the advance of science, as to some extent it is. But the facts on which all science and philosophy rest cannot be altered by progress in human interpretation of them. Facts are stubborn things. And the facts of purpose, of organization, of pursuit of value, are just as real and undeniable as the facts of our sense observation on which mechanistic theory rests. If the mechanist appeals to experience, to experience he shall go. In experience he will find purpose, whatever else he may also find.

§ 8. The Problem of Freedom

Experience is not wholly purposive (as we shall see in § 9). My purpose never determines the whole of my consciousness; much less does it determine all of the consequences which flow from it. Indeed, human purpose may be said not so much to determine as to discover what consequences follow from this or that purpose. Purpose, then, is a use of mechanism. But conscious purpose is more than that; it is also a choice of mechanism. To this choice we give the name of freedom. There may perhaps be purposive organization of some sort which is not consciously chosen. Such organization might arise by chance or coincidence, or as a result of a single drive with no alternative. On the other hand, purpose as we actually experience it in its highest forms is usually a complex series of choices.

Let us illustrate the nature of freedom. A sculptor, for example, is asked to produce a statue. First of all, his purpose releases the mechanisms of his imagination—fires his imagination, as we say. Among the many conceptions of a possible statue that crowd his mind, he chooses one. Then, after preliminary sketches, he finally begins chiseling the marble. Every blow of the mallet is directed by purpose and is guided with reference to the ideal conception in the sculptor's mind. Finally, after a series of indefinitely many free acts, each chosen with regard to its fitness for shaping the marble, the finished statue stands in view. It is impossible to describe this process adequately without describing the dominant purpose, the free choices, and also their mechanical conditions and effects.

From this illustration we see why Hans Driesch defines freedom as saying "yes" or "no" to a given content. We also see why it is absurd to regard freedom either as nonexistent or as all-determining. The free person acts in every choice; but he acts on the material given by previous experience (the sculptor's imagination) and by the environment (the block of marble). To put it otherwise, in harmony with our previous theory, freedom is control of The Given; it contradicts the concept of the free creation of The Given by the self as well as that of the completely mechanistic determination of the self by The Given.

§ 9. Relations Between Mechanism and Teleology

The purposes revealed in personal experience, in values, and especially in religion, suggest once more that faith in God is a rational hypothesis for unifying and interpreting our world. But if that faith is soundly based in the facts of experience, one who holds it must bear in mind our earlier discussion of good-and-evil, and must remember that experience contains both teleological and dysteleological factors.

It is, of course, possible to exaggerate the dysteleological and even to suppose that everything mechanistic is on the dysteleological side of the ledger. This is far from correct. There is a close relation between the purposive and the mechanistic aspects of experience. On the one hand, without purpose, mechanisms would achieve no order (except by chance), no beauty, no goodness, no worship, no rational personality. On the other hand, without mechanisms, purposes would have no effective means of expression or communication. Mechanistic laws are principles of co-operative procedure in a personal world. Mechanism and purpose are both essential to the ongoing of the world, as well as for the development of human culture. Both of the two principles, that of order in objective nature and that of values in human consciousness, show that purpose is dominant and controlling. Unless free purpose were actually in control, guiding and using the mechanistic aspect of things, the aspects of relevance (to which Whitehead calls attention), of order, and of value would be seeming miracles in the cosmic process.

§ 10. PURPOSE AND COMMUNITY

The importance of purpose for philosophy of religion may be shown in various ways. Religious experience is social in its ultimate aim, however private and individualistic some of its manifestations may be, for the reason that religious values point every individual beyond himself toward God. The same forces that bind men to God bind men to each other by a common devotion and aspiration.

Religion has, therefore, almost always expressed itself through a religious community—the community of those who share a common purpose. There is difference among religious believers about the source of this purpose. Some regard it as a supernatural gift of God (Calvinists, Barthians, and Mohammedans). Others regard it as a natural aspiration of man (humanists). Still others regard it as a cooperation between God and man (most theists). Yet in every case, a religious community is constituted, as every community is, by a shared purpose. Some communities purpose to tolerate a wider variety in the purposes of their members than do others, but all communities rest on purpose. When the purpose is clearly and intensely shared by all members of the community, the community is strong. When awareness of purpose weakens and falters, the community weakens and falters. No other principle suffices to build a community. Homogeneity of race or geographical propinquity may result in chaos if the members of the group cannot agree on ends to be sought. Hence no totalitarian state can be built on race alone; if religious faith or political ideals divide the group, the state, in order to preserve itself, will demand a common purpose and will suppress dissident members. The harshest repression of free purpose is thus a dialectical proof of the necessity of free purpose in any community.

§ 11. Purpose and Time

A further illustration of the religious importance of purpose is to be found in its relation to time. All experience is temporal, always moving ahead into a future as if it were reaching for purposes yet to be attained. The very movement of time is teleological. The life of value consists in the creative guidance of the time process by ideals which can never be fully and finally realized, and so are inexhaustible. The ideal of beauty implies the never-ending creation of new forms of beauty. The ideal of goodness implies the endless discovery of new expressions of rational will, individual and social. The ideal of rationality implies inexhaustible exploration, discovery, and interpretation; for the ongoing of the time process means that the purpose to be reasonable will always have fresh materials and problems. All the more does the religious ideal imply a task which never can be exhausted in the time process—unbegun and unending as it is. The creative purpose of God is the controlling force in the entire process, the source of its meaningful novelties, the principle of its movement. Hence man's relations to the purpose of God are the source of impulses toward higher ends, and they stimulate man to the remaking of his purposes on a higher level.

Human history, as well as the eternal history which religion envisages, is an enduring time process. In that process, some goals are fixed and unchanging—the divine purpose to be rational and to seek the realization of the best possible values. Other goals are new creations, by the very nature of the creative imagination and purpose of personality, human and divine. The fixed goals we may call the eternal purpose of God and the teleological constants of history. In addition to these, there are not only the creative novelties, but also the empirical factors of The Given (both formal and material) and the deviations of human purpose from the good. To view the time process and history as such a combination of eternal purpose, creativity, mechanism, brute fact, and human good-and-evil is far more realistic than to suppose it a pure expression of absolute purpose or of absolute mechanism. A God who can guide toward ideal goals such a chaos as we find and make in experience is (so it would seem) more to be honored, worshiped, and loved than a God who, having omnipotent power and goodness, creates this seeming chaos in order to manifest that power and goodness. Thus the consideration of purpose and time leads to a further confirmation of the hypothesis of a God, limited in power but unlimited in goodness, whose power nevertheless suffices to control The Given; and it makes both the wildness and the purposive striving of human history more intelligible.

§ 12. PURPOSE AND ETERNITY

It was impossible to treat time without touching on the eternal. We may define the eternal as what is true at all times. As regards purpose, the eternal is what is purposed at all times.

Many religious believers have thought of the eternal as utterly different from time in every respect—absolutely different in its quality. There is something overwhelming in such a conception of the eternal, before which, as before an utter mystery, man abases himself. Yet such a view of the eternal is far from satisfying to one who approaches religion empirically. If the evidence for religious faith is to be found in experience, then no religious believer has grounds for supposing that his God is utterly unrelated to what is revealed in experience, and no property can justly be ascribed to God for which there is not some basis in experience. It is a meaningful extension of experience to conceive a purpose that unfailingly directs the universe at all times; to think of the eternal as utterly timeless in all respects and as wholly other than temporal process is to think of it in a way that may be edifying, but it is useless for the understanding of religious or of any other experience.[9] All our conceptions, including that of the eternal, derive their meaning from their reference to purpose.[10]

BIBLIOGRAPHICAL NOTE

The specific problem of the present chapter was anticipated in Chapter VII, § 6. The discussion of values in Chapter III and the treatment of good-and-evil in Chapters VIII, IX, and X also bear on the problem. The reader is therefore referred to the Bibliographical Notes on those chapters for suggestions.

The first treatment of the topic is in the *Phaedo* 97B–99D. Kant's analysis of the antinomies, in the Transcendental Dialectic of the *Critique of Pure Reason,* is another *locus classicus.* Almost every textbook on introduction to philosophy and on philosophy of religion has sections on the problem of mechanism and teleology, to which special reference would be superfluous. Bibliographies in Brightman, ITP(1925), 374–376; Wright, SPR(1935), 338; Ferm, FCRP(1937), 303–304, and Drake, PR(1916), 293–294, refer to the chief literature.

For the development of the science of physics, Einstein and Infeld, EOP(1938), is excellent. Barnes, STR(1930), presents able arguments for a teleological interpretation. Whitehead, SMW(1925) and AI(1933), deals with the issues of this chapter, as does Bergson, CE(1913) and TSMR(1935).

[9] See Leighton, Art.(1918), and Brightman, Art.(1932)[1].
[10] It is interesting to note that this view is shared both by Whitehead, in MT, 184, and by his critic, Urban, Art.(1938), 628. Urban says that "the only thing that is ultimately intelligible to us (intrinsically intelligible) is a will directed toward the good or value."

THIRTEEN

THE PROBLEM OF HUMAN IMMORTALITY

§ 1. Religious Belief in Immortality

ELIEF in the survival of bodily death is so widespread that some have called it universal. Traces of it may be found in almost every primitive tribe,[1] as well as in almost every developed religion. There are, it is true, some religions (such as Old Testament Judaism) in which belief in conscious, personal immortality is inconspicuous, and others from which it is entirely absent (such as Hinayana Buddhism). But, like belief in the personality of God, it tends to develop in the later stages of a religion, even if it was lacking from the earlier. Judaism gives rise to Christianity, a religion which "brings life and immortality to light." Hinayana Buddhism develops into Mahayana, in which belief in the future life is a prominent feature. This historical tendency of religion has been opposed by a relatively small number of questioning spirits within the ranks of religion. Spinoza is one to whom personal immortality was meaningless. Today the proportion of doubters is probably greater than ever before; but the power of belief in immortality is evidenced by the fact that among all of the men of science whose beliefs he investigated (except psychologists), J. H. Leuba found that a greater proportion believed in immor-

[1] See Frazer, BI, 25, 33, and Leuba, BGI, 1, where Frazer is quoted.

387

tality than in God (as Leuba defined the two terms).[2]

Man is so tenacious of faith in his own immortality that for him to give up that faith is sometimes equivalent to his giving up not only religion but even a healthy-minded attitude toward life. Yet the existence of many religious believers who do not accept immortality, and nevertheless are thoroughly healthy-minded, is evidence that man can adjust himself to life without this belief.

The question that confronts the student of philosophy of religion when he investigates this belief does not concern primarily the number of its adherents nor the psychological helps or hindrances attendant on the belief. The question which he seeks to answer concerns primarily the truth of the belief. Does the personal consciousness survive the death of the body? If so, does it continue to exist forever?

§ 2.   Belief in Immortality as Extension of Experience of Purpose

In order to evaluate the belief in immortality intelligently, we should first have some conception of its roots in human nature. The belief does not arise from observation by the senses. Sense perception tells us that the body dies and that the personal consciousness no longer communicates with us through its accustomed organism. The belief seems in the first place to have been suggested by dreams in which spirits of the departed seemed to appear. But the developed forms of the idea of immortality no longer rest on dreams as their ground. When civilized man accepts faith in immortal life, he does so because of his experiences of purpose. Purposes are strivings for value experience. The seat of purpose and value is personality. A chief trait of the values which we actually realize is their incompleteness, their im-

---

[2] See Leuba, BGI, 278. Leuba defined God as one that answered prayer.

perfection and their evanescence. Many, perhaps most, of our ideals remain unrealized dreams; those that are partially realized often do not come to completion; those that are, in a way, completed do not satisfy our ideal demands; and many of our highest value experiences pass away so quickly that after a while they can barely be remembered.

Our life, then, is essentially a life of purpose, but of uncompleted purpose. Our potentialities are to a great extent unrealized when death comes. Browning's poem *Cleon,* infers faith in immortality from the unrealized purposes of the poet's soul. In general, faith in immortality is an extension of the experience of purpose beyond this life. Man observes that purpose is the most constant and characteristic feature of his existence; he observes that his ideal purposes are capable of indefinite variety and growth in their realization; and he observes the fact of death, which seems to bring purposing to an end. The belief in immortality is the belief that purpose is a better clue to man's real nature and destiny than is death. Both purpose and death are facts. Which gives truer insight into man's future? If death is final, that fact must be faced realistically, and the values of life enjoyed while we possess them. But if purpose is the clue to cosmic reality, there is reason to suppose that the cosmic purpose may cause personal consciousness to continue after the death of the body. No careful thinker would say that the solution of the problem of immortality can be regarded as self-evident.

§ 3. Weak Arguments

Discussion of immortality has been confused by the exceptionally large number of weak and even trivial arguments that have been urged for it and against it. The inferior force of these arguments has had the unfortunate effect of confirming each side in its beliefs without shedding any light; proponents of each side believe their own arguments and find it quite possible to refute the arguments of the other side. Such superficial thinking is on the level of a poor debate, and must be avoided if we are to have any hope of approaching truth.

Against the truth of the belief in immortality weak arguments such as the following have been adduced.[3]   Immortality must be a mere fancy because *belief in it originated in dreams.* (There is nothing to show that a true idea might not be suggested in a dream or be inferred from a dream.)   Or, it must be false because *we have no evidence in sense perception of life after death.*   (Sensation is not the criterion of all truth, nor is sense experience our only source of knowledge of reality; experiences of value and purpose are the evidence for immortality and absence of sense data is to be expected if the belief is true.)   Or, it must be false because *the desire for immortality is selfish.* (The selfishness of a belief is irrelevant to its truth, since a miser's selfish desire for accumulation is consistent with the truth that there is money and that he can accumulate it; further, the desire for immortality is no more selfish than the desire to live tomorrow; and the desire of an unselfish person for immortality is a social desire that all humanity may survive death and may engage in social development of value.) Or, it must be false because it is a law of nature that *what begins must end,* so that if souls begin at a point in time they must perish at a point in time; this argument is admittedly not valid if souls are eternally pre-existent and so birthless as well as deathless. (There is no proof of a universal law that what begins must end; the principle may perhaps be true of physical motion, but it is not true of a mathematical line beginning at point *a* and infinitely pro-

[3] Each argument will be stated as concisely as possible, followed by a remark in parentheses showing its weakness.

duced in the direction of *x;* appeal to pre-existence is thus not necessary to "save" immortality, nor is there good evidence for pre-existence in view of the failure of most persons to remember it.)

Or, it is alleged that immortality must be rejected because *"easy belief" is a "crime."* (Obviously this is an argument against gullibility rather than against immortality, and it may equally well be urged against "easy belief" in mortality and in atheism.) The *disbelief of many scientists* is regarded by some as a reason for doubting immortality; J. H. Leuba has laid particular stress on this argument. (But the opinions of scientists on problems outside their field have no more weight than the opinion of a geographer about biology; scientists are not experts in philosophy of religion.) It has even been suggested that immortality would be undesirable because *the universe would eventually be overcrowded with souls.* (It is hardly possible that William James proposed this seriously; aside from the point that a spirit occupies no space at all, all arguments for immortality presuppose that God can and will provide room for all.) Finally, it is held that *the permanent social influence of the individual is an adequate substitute for immortality.* (Although social influence is a real and important fact, yet, if immortality is true, why seek a substitute for it? This view makes each person a means to the welfare of others, leaving the intrinsic value of each person to perish, and it must look forward to the ultimate extinction of all society, thus impugning the goodness of God.)

None of these arguments, as the parenthetical comments show, has any real cogency against the belief in immortality. They may be paralleled by numerous equally weak arguments in favor of the belief.

It is said, for example, that belief in immortality must be true because *the desire for immortality is universal.* (The desire is not universal; some do not wish for it; and if it be universal, it is no more universal than the desire for bodily health, which is not permanently fulfilled. Mere desire is not a test of truth.) The same weakness inheres in the related contention that there is *a consensus of belief in it.* (There may be agreement in error, and when there is agreement in truth there must be some reason for the agreement; furthermore, there is not complete agreement, for some who desire immortality do not believe in it, not to mention those who neither desire nor believe.) It is argued that *the belief is true because it is inspiring,* giving man faith and confidence, reconciling him to the tragedies of life, and creating in him hope for the future. (That the belief may thus inspire those who hold it is undoubtedly true; but the history of religious, social, and political beliefs affords many instances of inspiring ideas which are partly or wholly false. This argument shows that, if belief in immortality be true, it is a very useful truth, but it does not show it to be true.) It is further declared, as by Bishop Butler, that *the analogy of certain natural processes,* such as that which leads from the caterpillar to the butterfly, *points to a new life for the soul after the death of the body.* (The facts on which this analogy rests show that experience may reveal what pure reason could not infer, but they are all confined to changes from one type of biological life to another, and hence lack cogency in proving a transition from the biological to the spiritual realm.)

Some declare that immortality is true because *the mind is the guide and controller of the work of the brain.* (The experiences of choice and purposive direction are important items in any philosophy, but even the most remarkable therapeutic influence of the mind on the body would fall far short of proving immortality; the influence of the body on the mind is at least as certain as the reverse process. Just as the one does not prove the immortality of the body, so does the other not prove the immortality of the soul.) Others rest the case for immortality on *evidence from so-called psychic phenomena;* communications from departed spirits are said to have been obtained through mediums, and they are regarded as irrefutable empirical proof of life after death. (It may be granted that "psychic phenomena" show that the human mind has powers and sources of information which do not appear on the surface and are not ordinarily accessible; but the more or less trivial content of most supposed communications from the departed, the error in many of them, the failure of many serious attempts to establish communication, and the possibility of explaining many of the most remarkable cases by means of subconscious or telepathic processes in the living—all these leave the spiritistic evidence inconclusive. Even if they were established, no more would be proved than that some souls survive bodily death for a while; immortality—endless life—would still be problematic.)

Many who admit that the arguments for and against the future life are inconclusive rest their faith in it not on experience or reason, but on *revelation.* Belief in divine revelation is common to most forms of developed religion; and among the truths believed to be revealed, the immortality of the soul is prominent. It is not equally prominent in all religions; Confucianism says little about personal immortality, and Hinayana Buddhism, with its doctrine of Nirvana, seems flatly to deny it. Egyptian religion, the Greek Mystery Religions, Christianity, and Islam are examples of religions for which the truth of immortality is an article of faith revealed by God to man. (The presence of belief in the revealed truth of immortality is an important religious phenomenon. However, the validity of a revelation-claim requires for its support more than the bare claim. While it is true that all experience may in some sense be viewed as a "revelation" of reality, and that certain striking experiences of beauty, goodness, truth, and holiness may by the same logic be regarded as "special revelation," it is not true that any experience should be taken as authoritative or revelatory until it has been tested by all the means at our disposal. If there is divine revelation, as believers in God maintain, such revelation cannot rightly be the object of a blind and unquestioning faith, for then there would be no way of distinguishing the wildest and falsest revelation-claim from a true revelation. It is therefore not decisive to say that immortality is a revealed truth; the belief in immortality must be subjected to all the tests to which any other revelation-claim is subjected, and the real evidence for or against the belief will be found in those tests.)

We have now surveyed several of the arguments for and against immortality and have shown their weakness. It is perhaps natural that arguments which lack logical cogency should meet with wide popular favor in a field where the emotions are as deeply involved as they are in man's attempt to peer beyond the grave. But emotional acceptability (whether it favor skepticism or belief) is not proof. Let us therefore turn from the weaker arguments to those which are really crucial.

---

[4] It is the function of theology rather than of philosophy of religion to consider the beliefs of any special religion, such as Christianity, which are peculiar to that religion. It should, however, be noted that the remarks in the text apply to the resurrection of Jesus, as well as to all other religious beliefs. However much true revelation there may be in the records of the resurrection, philosophical belief in immortality cannot rest on those records alone.

§ 4. Crucial Argument Against Immortality: Physiological Psychology

The only really strong argument against immortality is that based on a materialistic interpretation of physiological psychology. It runs somewhat as follows: consciousness is proved to depend on brain; if brain is injured, consciousness is injured, and the contents of consciousness are determined by bodily states or external stimuli which in turn are communicated to the brain. When the brain ceases to function, consciousness ceases; the death of the body destroys the cause of the "soul," and it is absurd to suppose an effect to continue after its cause has been destroyed. This argument is strong because it follows logically from its premises and because its premises seem to have the full support of empirical science. Corliss Lamont, in his searching investigation, *The Illusion of Immortality,* rests the case against belief chiefly on this argument, which he calls "monism in psychology," because it implies the indissoluble union of personality with body.[5] If personality is simply a function of body, lasting as long as body lasts and disintegrating as soon as body ceases to be body—that is, ceases to be living organism—then obviously there is no shred of truth in the belief in immortality.

We have here a crucial argument. No educated person can fail to be aware of it. Yet many educated persons are not convinced by it. Why? Is it merely because their emotions blind them to the evidence? Or is the argument after all not strictly crucial?

As the scholastics say, we must make a distinction here. There are points of view from which the physiological argument is crucial, and there are points of view from which it is not crucial, depending on one's metaphysical postulates.

[5] Lamont, IOI, 109-110; cf. 99, 105-106, 112.

Let us consider some possible postulates and their consequences.

First, we might take positivism, a very popular view at the present time, as our postulate. It must be admitted that positivists at present are changing their views so often that positivism is a veritable Heraclitean river. Out of the stream we may rescue, perhaps arbitrarily, a definition of positivism, based on A. J. Ayer's discussions in *Language, Truth, and Logic*. From Ayer's book we gather that logical positivism is the view that there are two kinds of meaningful propositions, the logical and the empirical. Logical propositions are necessary because tautological, but give no information about the world. Empirical propositions are probable and refer only to sense experience.[6] From such premises it is both simple and necessary to infer, as Ayer does (177) that there is no meaning, no "factual content," in the proposition that there is a "transcendent" God or a future life. Physiological psychology rests on observations of sense data and is meaningful and verifiable; belief in immortality rests on no such observation and so is meaningless, or, as the positivists like to say, it is "nonsense."

Since the postulate of positivism is a fundamental rejection of all aspects of experience except sensation, it is plain why it does not convince most minds as a disproof of immortality. There are two reasons for rejecting the positivistic definition of meaning, as applied to immortality. The first is that immortality "is an hypothesis about our own future experience, and our understanding of what would verify it has no lack of clarity."[7] If any hypothesis about future ex-

---

[6] See Ayer, LTL, Chap. I, esp. pp. 16, 19, 24, 31, Chap. II, p. 42, and Chap. IV entire.

[7] The quoted words are from the brilliant presidential address of Clarence I. Lewis, "Experience and Meaning," *Phil. Rev.*, 43(1934), 143, which is a critique of one aspect of logical positivism. Moritz Schlick, in an article on "Meaning and Verification," *Phil. Rev.*, 45(1936), 357 (reprinted in *Gesammelte Aufsätze,*

perience is meaningful, statements about immortality have meaning. But the second reason for rejecting positivism is even more important. If all meaningful statements (except logical tautologies) must refer to sense experience, then all such statements as the following are meaningless: "I remember, I anticipate, I share a meaning with you, I experience values, I criticize my values, I seek for truth about values, we love truth, we worship." A postulate which requires us to consider meaningless experiences as universal as these reveals itself as arbitrary in the extreme. The empiricist who appeals to experience has no right to restrict his attention to specially favored parts of experience. If experiences of sense give us access to probable knowledge about certain aspects of the universe, it is at least possible that experiences of value and of personal unity and purpose may shed light on other aspects.

Positivism, however, is not the only postulate which, if true, would be fatal to belief in immortality. More important, more deeply rooted in the human spirit, is the postulate of materialism, which is the most ancient, the most instinctive, and the most perplexing "animal faith" of the race. Like positivism, materialism rests on the postulate that sensation is the gateway to knowledge. However, while the positivist limits his statements to what he can verify, the materialist goes far beyond the verifiable, for he declares that the universe consists, not of verifiable sensations, but of (essentially unexperienceable) material things and processes. Then he adds to his postulate the thesis that the

---

356), grants to Professor Lewis that "the hypothesis of immortality is an empirical statement which owes its meaning to its verifiability," but adds that "it has no meaning beyond the possibility of verification." If Schlick meant by "possibility" actual possibility, then he denied meaning not only to immortality but also to statements about the past or the interior of the earth. If he meant ideal possibility, the positivistic case against immortality as meaningful has collapsed.

only true *substance* or *cause* in the universe is material substance and its activities. By introducing such categories as substance and cause,[8] the materialist has on the one hand departed far from positivism; on the other, he has made a greater appeal to ordinary common sense.

The bearing of materialism on belief in immortality is very clear. If materialism be true, then the material objects and processes investigated in physiological psychology are the real causal substances which produce consciousness. Once accept the materialistic postulate, and immortality is impossible. Our body causes our personal consciousness and when the body ceases to function, its effect will necessarily cease to be. We should notice, however, that the force of this reasoning derives not from the scientific observations of the physiological psychologist, but rather from the philosophical postulate which underlies the interpretation of those observations.

If materialism is true, there is no basis for immortality. But is the materialistic postulate really true? We have said that many educated persons were not convinced by the physiological-psychological argument against immortality; the chief logical reason for this is the unconvincingness of materialism. In several previous discussions in this book arguments against materialism have been presented. At the cost of some repetition, let us briefly review some of the chief difficulties of materialism. Materialism means that the universe is supposed to consist of nothing but physical substances and their causal activities. If we had no experiences other than sensations, this supposition might appear acceptable,

---

[8] Reference to these categories makes it evident, if it was not already evident for other reasons, that philosophy of religion is a branch of metaphysics and that its problems are intertwined with metaphysical ones. No philosophy of religion can be complete in itself. A study of metaphysics should both precede and follow a study of philosophy of religion. Bowne's *Metaphysics* remains one of the most useful introductions to the field.

were it not for the annoying empirical fact that sensations are not physical but mental in character. Yet, even in dealing with purely physical objects, materialism fails to account for the rational order of things, even for mechanistic regularities; the uniformity of law is an inexplicable coincidence, a sheer miracle, if each physical object is endowed with its law-abiding properties without any common cause. Thus theism (or personalism), which defines matter as the will of God in action (or at least as an effect of that will), accounts more consistently for the material facts than does materialism itself.

Further, the immediate empirical situation which contains all the facts that are to be explained is the field of consciousness. Materialism postulates that what is always experienced as conscious and immaterial must be explained by what is never conscious or immaterial. We can understand how motions can be explained by other motions, as in physics; but we cannot understand how motions of matter can produce consciousness. If we say that they do, and that's an end of it, we should ask ourselves how we are so sure that there is any unconscious, substantial, causal matter in the first place. If the postulate of materialism is a false dogma, then the mystery of the interaction of mind and body, although still inscrutable, becomes the more manageable mystery of the interaction of mind and mind. If materialism is false, the body may be itself part of the activity of the Cosmic Mind. If materialism is true, consciousness is a stranger in the universe and its intrusion must be accepted as a miracle; if theism or personalism be true, the facts of consciousness are clues to the nature of all reality.

The more closely we inspect conscious experience, the more difficulties emerge for materialism. We experience personal identity, unity, memory; materialism offers no account of these facts that explains their characteristic features. We experience purpose; materialism has to try to explain purpose away. We experience values and ideals; materialists also experience them and often are loyal to them, but their philosophy renders the very experience of ideal value unintelligible and offers no theory of obligation. In short, materialism, based as it is on an exclusive preference for sensations, cannot in the nature of the case give a coherent description of experience as a whole, and cannot even include sensations themselves in the domain of matter.

If the postulates of both positivism and materialism are questionable, it is clear why the argument against immortality based on physiological psychology is not truly crucial, even though it seems to be so. It is the strongest objection there is, but it is not decisive. While asserting the dependence of the mind on the body, and fully accepting all the facts of physiology, the philosopher may still inquire into the nature and the cosmic relations of the reality that appears as his body. If the body is viewed as materialistic postulates require, death is final. But if the body is interpreted on theistic postulates, the destiny of personal consciousness in the world will not be determined by the laws of matter but rather by the purpose and will of the God whose activity is very incompletely revealed in the object we call the human body.

No science can settle the question of immortality, not even physiological psychology. Neither can it be settled by intensity of hope or desire or faith. The ultimate question at stake includes but transcends science and religion; it is metaphysical.

§ 5. Crucial Argument for Immortality: the Goodness of God

Just as there is really only one vigorous argument against immortality (which reduces to the argument for a materialistic philosophy), so there is only one vigorous argument for immortality ₍which reduces to the argument for a theistic philosophy). If there is a God—a supreme, creative, cosmic person—then there is an infinitely good being committed to the eternal conservation of values.[9] That being is the controlling and directing power in all natural processes and is engaged in a process of immanent coöperation with all other persons. Since all true values are experiences of the fulfillment of ideal purposes by persons, the existence of values. depends on the existence of persons. Value is personality at its best. God, the conserver of values, must be God, the conserver of persons.

We have found reason to regard God's power as finite; but there is no sufficient reason for supposing it to be so finite that he cannot conserve values. In a word, every argument for God, whether as absolute or as finite, is an argument for God's power to control his universe so as to achieve value; and every argument for God's goodness is an argument for his obligation to maintain persons in existence as intrinsic values that could not be lost without a total failure of God's good purpose. For if all persons were to perish with their bodily death, God would be in an unenviable position. He would either continue forever to create new persons, or he would give up the enterprise of creation. If he continued to create new persons, then he would be conducting a cosmic bonfire, with each new generation warmed by the burning of the previous one; God and man alike could look back on centuries of effort with no permanent results, no persons treated as ends in themselves, no life coming to full development. Or if he abandoned the enterprise of creation, then there would finally be no result at all from the entire race of personal beings except in God's memory; the eternal ideals would be as ab-

[9] This argument is stated simply and effectively by Charles R. Brown in *Living Again* (Cambridge: Harvard University Press, 1922).

stractly valid as they were before creation, a disappointed and frustrated God would remain—and all the intrinsic value of each person (except God) would be irretrievably lost. That the arguments for God are at the same time arguments for immortality is indicated by the fact that there has been only one well-known philosophical believer in immortality who denied theism, namely, J. M. E. McTaggart, and the correlative fact that substantially every theist has accepted immortality.

The arguments for God [10] are either directly based on the spiritual value and meaning of personality or else point to traits in objective nature which reveal personality at work there. On the other hand, no argument for immortality which leaves out the reference to God has any cogency; hence no argument that rests the case on any one intuition or fact carries weight.

The ordinary Christian believer doubtless bases his faith largely on the accounts of the resurrection of Jesus in the New Testament. Those accounts, however, cannot be regarded as conclusive, taken by themselves. Historical criticism shows that it is very difficult, if not impossible, to determine exactly what happened on the first Easter. The only historical certainty is that somehow the early disciples became convinced that Jesus was living. This conviction, however caused, does not constitute evidence for immortality unless taken in connection with the total personality of Jesus, his faith, its grounds, and its influences. Only when interpreted in the light of a theistic world view does the resurrection story become validly symbolic of immortality.

Just as the argument from physiological psychology rested on materialistic postulates, so the argument from the goodness of God rests on theistic postulates. The initial data of materialistic (and positivistic) postulates are found in sense

[10] See Chapter VII.

experience. The postulate of theism is that the real universe, to which our experience refers and in which it arises, must be conceived in such a way as to include and account for all the initial data, that is, the entire range of conscious experience: for sense data, and also for personal consciousness, reason, memory, purpose, freedom, and value—in short for all that materialism included and for all that it omitted in its postulation.

Does this mean that the theistic argument for immortality is truly crucial, whereas the materialistic argument against it was not? Let us be fully clear. It cannot be asserted on any empirical or rational basis that theism is the only possible view. Rigorous necessity cannot be ascribed to the proof. But it may justly be said that as between materialism and theism, the former accounts for a narrower range of the evidence and advances a postulate more remote from experience than does theism. Whereas materialism leaves the existence of consciousness and of spiritual life a mystery, theism shows it to be a rational expression of the nature of the universe. Thus materialism is an improbable inference from the total initial datum of experience, while theism is more probable, because more inclusive. "Matter" cannot be ultimate, because it is an hypothesis incoherent with experienced facts. God can be ultimate, because the concept of God is coherent with all the facts.

Rationally, then, faith in immortality is better grounded than is materialistic denial of that faith. Yet neither the argument from physiological psychology nor that from the goodness of God is crucial in the sense of being absolutely decisive. For the ultimately decisive information we must await the experience of death and of what lies beyond it. Meanwhile, it would appear that doubts of immortality are to some extent emotional. "Animal faith," deriving from our bodily sensations is often emotionally more powerful than "moral faith," [11] deriving from our ideal natures. But the thinker dare not allow emotional intensity, animal or moral, to weight any argument. In philosophy and in religious faith, as well as in practical life, there is a perpetual struggle of spirit to control the brute facts of The Given and to wrest meaning from them. Rational purpose has to test and guide emotion—a task of supreme difficulty. Spinoza rightly says, "All things excellent are as difficult as they are rare."

§ 6. IMMORTALITY AND THE PROBLEM OF GOOD-AND-EVIL

Supposing now that belief in immortality is a more probable interpretation of the evidence than is the denial of it on positivistic or materialistic grounds, we may well ask what bearing the belief has on the central problem of life— the problem of good-and-evil.

Some have regarded immortality as the solution of all problems. If the evils of the present are transitory, they may be endured bravely. There is an "eternal weight of glory" which outweighs all the tribulations of this life. "All tears shall be wiped away." The perfections of that life will wholly compensate for the imperfections of this. When the familiar picture of heaven is realized in experience, the memories of earth will fade. Eternity will solve all of time's riddles by its healing touch.

This picture of immortality as a state of painless absolute perfection presents an ideal that has comforted many religious souls and may possibly correspond to truth. Yet it offers difficulties to the thinker whose view of immortality rests on an interpretation of the empirical evidence. In this life there is constant struggle; there may be progress or there may be retrogression. If immortality is a fulfillment

---

[11] Santayana refers to a moral faith once in an often-overlooked passage in SAF(1923), 221.

of the highest promise of this life, it will not be an experience of effortless and complete perfection, it will rather be an experience of unending creativity, new discoveries, and growth. To suppose that there are no obstacles to be overcome, no difficulties to be conquered in the future life is to suppose that The Given, which seems a necessary part of all of God's work in this world, is entirely eliminated in the future life. For such a supposition there is neither empirical nor rational basis. Only desire, weary with effort, or else supernatural revelation could point thither, and such considerations lie outside of philosophy.

The law of spiritual continuity [12] points rather toward the future life as continuous with this life, preserving memories of it, devoted to its ideal values, yet solving the problems of existence on ever higher and more creative levels. If The Given is always in the universe, creative development may enable the spirit to mold its clay (as we may call it figuratively) into lovelier forms. We may suppose that many problems of The Given may be permanently solved, as many diseases in this world have been almost banished by the advances of science. Yet there will always be more to do. The immortal universe of persons is not striving toward a completed state of finished perfection. Its perfection is rather its eternal perfectibility. Browning's final insight is, from this standpoint, essentially correct:

> "Strive and thrive!" cry "Speed,—fight on, fare ever
> There as here."

Now we return to the question whether immortality is a solution of the problem of evil. To this question, a negative answer must be given. If the future is a life of pure and

[12] To adapt Leibniz's *lex continui.*

unadulterated perfection, the problem of why the earthly life is so bad becomes all the more acute, by way of contrast. If the future is a development of personality, on principles like those we find in this life but on a higher level, it offers no account of the mixture of good and evil at all stages of eternity. Unless here and now we find reason to believe in God, it is futile to appeal to immortality for our theodicy. Faith in immortality is reasonable and well-grounded; but it is reasonable only in proportion as belief in God is reasonable. In our view of God we must find our solution of the problem of evil. If we hold to an absolute God, the solution will be that all seeming evil (except sin) is a real good. If we hold to a finite God, the solution will consist of a rational account of the relation of the eternal purposes and choices of God to eternal given factors in his experience (or perhaps, as some think, external to his experience). Certainly the traditional view of heaven and hell was no solution of the problem of good-and-evil, but was a radical perpetuation of it. In our view of God, and in that alone, can we find any insight into this baffling problem.

§ 7. CONDITIONAL IMMORTALITY

A special problem must be faced by anyone who entertains the faith in immortality. He must ask whether all souls are immortal, or only some.

The usual view is that all souls (all persons, according to our terminology) are immortal. Yet one who takes seriously the arguments presented in this chapter will be cautious in such a generalization. If belief in immortality is an inference from belief in a good God, then as many persons will be immortal as God wills shall be immortal. This suggests two possible limits to the immortality of all persons, namely, the power of God and his goodness.

For the absolutist, there is no limit to the power of God

other than his own free, rational purpose. For the finitist, God's power is indeed limited. But since experience shows that the limits within which the Creator works are compatible with his own control of The Given at every stage of which we have knowledge, it seems a reasonable faith that he who creates and sustains personalities in this world has resources sufficient to continue their existence in another order. If personality be compared (in a very imperfect metaphor) to a tune played on a guitar by the master musician, we may well conceive that the destruction of the guitar (the body) would not mean the destruction of the music. In some sense, it would always live in the soul of the musician, who would surely find some other instrument on which to express the music; it might be a cornet, or a harp, or a violin, or a piano. There seems to be no reason for supposing that a finite God is restricted to the present physical order as his only field of operation. That is to assume materialism was right in holding sensation to be our only access to objective reality. If, as theists believe, sensation reveals only one aspect of reality, the other aspects of reality revealed by the experience of value and personality suggest the presence in God of resources sufficient to provide for immortality. There is no definite reason for regarding the finiteness of God as a barrier to universal immortality.

The question accordingly depends solely on the goodness of God. Religious believers have entertained widely varying conceptions of the future life, many of which ascribe to God an attitude toward "lost souls" which seems to the modern mind entirely inconsistent with goodness. Traditional belief in hell makes God a being as cruel, vengeful, and unrelenting as the most hateful and arbitrary human sinner. To make the soul's eternal destiny rest entirely on choices made in the short span of three-score years and ten is to act out of all proportion to a human sense of justice. But it is not the purpose here to discuss the variety of traditional views. Our interest is rather in the bearing of divine goodness on immortality.

Let us now attempt to clarify the discussion by setting up an hypothesis based on the goodness of God. It runs: Those persons are immortal whom God judges to be capable of developing worthily at any time in their future existence. By developing worthily is meant choosing and realizing ideal values, individually and socially. It may be that some conscious beings born of human parents—some imbeciles, for example—may be hopelessly unable to appreciate ideal values. It would be more just to let them enjoy what they can while they live and then to let them die when their time comes, rather than to preserve them as aimless immortals. On the other hand, perhaps some "subhuman" animals may be gifted with conscious powers so great that, given immortality, they might undergo a lofty spiritual evolution in the course of eons. Again, it is conceivable that some human individuals, once responsive to the divine impulse, may become so vicious that even God may despair of arousing them to any higher aspirations.

The hypothesis thus defined may be called that of conditional immortality. The term means that immortality is not inherent in every person or every human being as such, but is conditional on the presence in the person of genuine potentialities for spiritual development. The hypothesis, as presented, refrains from any further attempt to define the exact conditions which make immortality possible; it leaves them to the goodness of God.[18]

[18] The belief in conditional immortality has been rather widely held. Many think that it is found in Saint Paul, who is notable for the lack of any doctrine of hell, and who associates sin and death. A typical Christian presentation of the view is found in J. Y. Simpson, *Man and the Attainment of Immortality* (New York: George H. Doran Company, 1933).

§ 8. The Religious Value of Belief in Immortality

There are many who question the value of giving special attention to the belief in immortality, even if it is true. They point to the asceticism and otherworldliness that have developed where the glories of the other life have led to a scorn of this life—a *contemptus mundi*. They think that hope for an assured beautiful future beyond the grave tends to paralyze social action and to foster acquiescence in social evils, which may be endured for the sake of the coming "pie in the sky."

That belief in immortality sometimes has unfortunate, and even debasing, results must be granted. Yet we cannot judge the value of a truth by the misuse to which men have subjected it. After all, the truths of physics, chemistry, biology, logic, and mathematics are daily put to flagrantly evil uses by evil men. If weak and foolish persons have been so dazzled that they cannot see immortality in a proper light, that fact should not lead us to repudiate immortality any more than we repudiate mathematics for the uses made of it by cheats and gamblers.

The religious values of immortality may be briefly summarized. The good life is a life of goal-seeking; it is a life of forward-looking purpose. Immortality symbolizes the faith that good purpose never fails to all eternity. The taproot of all human endeavor is in the hope that purpose can achieve values. Those who deny immortality continue to strive largely because they believe that they are laying foundations for the next generation. If courage and meaning are imparted to life by a short look into the future, how much more dignity, hope, and perspective arise from the faith that every life capable of purposive development is eternal. Immortality symbolizes the intrinsic value of the individual person, the intrinsic value of shared, coöperative living, and the goodness of God.

BIBLIOGRAPHICAL NOTE

The careful reader will have noted the omission from the chapter of certain historically important arguments in which modern thought has lost interest. Such are Plato's argument from the simplicity of the soul in the *Phaedo,* and Kant's argument from the categorical imperative in *The Critique of Practical Reason.*

A predominantly historical approach is found in Baillie, LE (1933), Frazer, BI(1913), Pringle-Pattison, II(1922), Tsanoff PI(1924), and Brightman, IPKI(1925).

Suggestive arguments are found in Brown, LA(1922), Bevan, HWC(1930), Hicks, HPFL(1934), and Galloway, II(1919). The treatment in McTaggart, SDR(1906), is noteworthy as a defense of immortality by an atheist. Unfavorable to the belief are Leuba, BGI(1921), and Dewey, CF(1934). The most objective treatment by a disbeliever in immortality is Lamont, II (1932). Lamont's later work, IOI(1935), is a strong argument against the belief.

FOURTEEN

THE PROBLEM OF
RELIGIOUS EXPERIENCE

§ 1. Religion as Experience

ELIGION is one of the many forms of human experience. The purpose of our whole investigation has been to interpret religious experience; and since this book is a philosophy of religion, it may appear that more stress has been laid on the interpretation than on the experience itself, despite the empirical method used.

A sound instinct continually calls the philosopher back from his speculations to the facts about which he is speculating. Now that we have examined the main beliefs of religion, it is fitting to turn back to religious life and view its experiences in the light of our philosophical reflection. On doing so, we are struck by the apparent contrast between religious theory and religious practice. Those who are most expert in the interpretation of creeds, doctrines, and ideas are often barren in practical religious experience; and those whose religious practice is the most vital and simple, the most prayerful and devout, are often indifferent to creeds, doctrines, and ideas. "Give us religion without theology," is the demand of many such folk. They do not want philosophy, they say; they want life.

In the commonplace that the facts of experience are more fundamental than any theory about them, there is surely a partial truth. But sometimes a partial truth functions as error in concealing the whole truth. It may be that the ancient distinction between practice and theory is not a distinction between experience and some realm remote from experience. It may be that it is simply a distinction within experience, and that, if all theory were removed from practice, the practice itself would utterly collapse, or would become something quite different. It might reduce to a series of mechanical reflexes, without any guidance from intelligence or ideals. In the field of religion, it may be that the plea for experience as opposed to speculation may sometimes be a disguised way of saying that the religious person is so well satisfied with his present speculations that he does not wish to be disturbed in them. Modernists have used the appeal to experience as a way of asserting modernism against fundamentalism; and fundamentalists have taken their experience as a complete and final proof of their theology.

These facts suggest that it is of the utmost importance to make clear exactly what is meant by experience, and in particular, by religious experience.

§ 2. The Meaning of Experience

The word experience has been used with so many different meanings that it has almost become a philosophical scandal. Scientists are not unjustifiably impatient with the variety of definitions which philosophers connect with a term. One philosopher [1] proposed a few years ago to drive out the word experience entirely from philosophical discourse because of the confusion it has created. Yet this would add nothing but confusion, if only because the word would still appear in the history of thought and a veto on its present use would cause an awkward break in philosophical development.

[1] The late Professor Theodore de Laguna.

The Latin verb *experior,* from which *experientia* and experience are derived, means "to try, to prove, to test," and comes from the root PAR-, PER-, which means "through" (*per*), "fare, reach, try." *Periculum* (experiment, hence peril), *porta* (gate), the German *fahren* (compare *Erfahrung,* experience), *Gefahr* (danger), and the English fare, far, fear, and expert, all come from this root.[2] Experience thus brings with it suggestions of movement, testing, danger, skill, and completeness (*per*). In current popular usage experience means frequent observation and testing, particularly, personal observation and testing. Philosophers, however, have frequently used the word much more narrowly, restricting it to the data of sense. Others have extended it to cover the whole of conscious awareness.[3] Still others, like John Dewey, mean by it the whole world of natural events and persons,[4] thus including within experience not only the fact of experienc*ing,* but also everything that may be said to be experienc*ed.*

Underlying these (and other) uses of the word are far-reaching differences of opinion. For present purposes, we shall have to leave to epistemology and metaphysics the detailed investigation of these differences, and shall propose as a working hypothesis that we use the word experience to mean all the data and processes of consciousness. Thus experience for us includes all that is in consciousness and nothing else; and it is only the conscious or mental.[5] The reader, for example, is now conscious of himself as experiencing patterned sensations, some of which he ascribes to his body,

---

[2] These data are derived from Charlton T. Lewis, *A Latin Dictionary for Schools* (New York: American Book Company, 1916) and Webster's *New International Dictionary,* Second Edition.

[3] The present writer prefers this usage.

[4] See *Experience and Nature,* 28.

[5] The view is in especially sharp contrast to that of Dewey in EN, Chap. I.

some to the book, some to the rest of the environment, some to his memory and imagination. In ordinary language, we say that we experience the book; but the book is certainly not literally in my conscious experience in the same sense as my perceptions of it are. My perceptions (the "essences" of critical realism) are directly given; the book, however, is inferred or at least referred to and believed in, rather than immediately experienced. As Santayana says, it is an object of "animal faith." [6] If this distinction between experience and the objects referred to in experience is not made, we are reduced to a choice between solipsism (which denies that there are any objects other than my experience of them) and epistemological monism (which asserts that the independent objects and my experience of them are somehow identical without disparagement to the independence of the objects). Both of these possibilities have been explored by philosophers. No one has found the solipsistic position tenable. Epistemological monism has been accepted by a considerable number; neorealists and religious mystics, though differing in most respects, agree in being epistemological monists.[7]

If our hypothesis is correct (as opposed to solipsism and epistemological monism) we may infer from it that we experience only the datum self (or experient). In the literal sense, I experience nothing but my present self; I know (refer to, believe in) my past self by inference from present memories, and know my future self by inference from present anticipations; I infer a society of other selves and a world of nature from my own experience of myself. Epistemologically every referent other than my present self is a

[6] This description of experience is consistent with epistemological dualism, critical realism, and personal idealism. It is presented (but in too extreme a form) by P. W. Bridgman in *The Intelligent Individual and Society*.

[7] For a searching criticism of monism see Lovejoy, RAD. This criticism seems to the present writer conclusive.

hypothetical entity, an object of more or less well-grounded belief.[8]

Since my experience includes all of my present consciousness, with all of my choosing and feeling, as well as my knowing, inferring, and erring, it is now clear why the distinction between theory and practice is not absolute. There is no practice—no conscious, active experience—which is not attended by some degree of inference and theory as a constituent of the experience.

From this it further follows that the presence of an item in experience is of itself no guarantee of the reality of the object (the hypothetical entity) which the experient believes to be the object of this item. There are illusions of sense and errors of thought. Experience always points beyond itself, but its testimony is always subject to tests by further and more critical experience. The tests for all hypothetical entities are to be found only in someone's first-person experience.

§ 3. THE MEANING OF RELIGIOUS EXPERIENCE

Religious experience is *any experience of any person taken in its relation to his God*. Religious experience is not a unique kind or quality of experience;[9] it is rather a unique way of apprehending experience. There are therefore many degrees of religious experience. The experience of believing nature to be a deed (or creation) of God is a religious experience; so is the experience of prayer. But the latter, being less apparently impersonal than the system of nature and being more directly concerned with spiritual values and hence

---

[8] Even epistemological monists must, if they are logical, admit that their knowledge of the past, the future, and the spatially absent or inaccessible—that is, their knowledge of everything not directly observed at the moment—requires hypotheses about what-is-not-now-observed. A doctrine of hypothetical entities must therefore be accepted by all who reject solipsism.

[9] In spite of Rudolf Otto's theory of "the numinous" as such a quality.

with the essential nature of God, is more intensely religious.

In the proposed definition, perhaps the most elusive important word is "taken." What makes an experience religious is the way it is taken. The words of a prayer might be repeated by an elocutionist without the slightest religious experience, because the words are taken histrionically. Unless the words are taken as relating the soul to God, there is no religion in saying them. In that word "taken" there is implicit the hypothetical reference of all meanings in our experience. The meaning of any experience lies in the way it is taken; that is, in the hypothesis which explains it, giving it coherence and value.

Faith is a name characteristically given by religious believers to their hypothesis. Religious experience is any experience viewed with the eye of faith. Whether faith is regarded as a gift of God (as by the Barthians) or as an a priori principle (as by the religious apriorists), its practical working is that of an hypothesis accepted as unifying and interpreting our experience by referring it to an object and an objective.[10] It is a way of "taking" life.

The proposed definition of religious experience uses the words "any experience," which are intended to convey the idea of the wide variety in religious experience. That variety has already been sketched in Chapters II and III of this book. We shall now undertake a brief interpretation of it, considering first the foundations of religious experience and then its development.

[10] Among discussions of religious experiences, James, VRE, is the best known, with Hocking's MGHE a close second. Otto's IH has aroused much discussion. Knudson, VRE, is the most penetrating recent treatment, although somewhat abstract. England, VRE, is less vigorous, MacMurray, SRE, less critical. Bertocci, EAG, and Moore, TRE, are valuable critical treatments of recent thought. Baillie, KG, is able, although not fully consistent.

§ 4. FOUNDATIONS OF RELIGIOUS EXPERIENCE

(1) *Faith.* Faith we have already found to be essential to religious experience. It is the belief of man in his God, and the conduct of life in the light of that belief. Empirically, faith arises partly out of man's experience of prereligious values [11] and partly out of his sense of insufficiency, his perception that his values are neither created nor guaranteed by his own will alone. Thus faith is a combined product of the experienced reality and the insecurity of values. It is man's response to the complex situation of good-and-evil in which he finds himself. But no religious believer, certainly no theist, would be satisfied with this merely subjective and empirical account of faith. The religious believer finds that experience justifies his faith. Thus he has a standing ground for a metaphysical interpretation of faith. Faith so interpreted is still a human experience, but an experience divinely caused, expressing the divine purpose to lead man toward God. It is man reaching beyond himself for higher meanings; it is also God reaching into man's life so that the spirit of the whole is at work in the individual. To deny or minimize either aspect of faith is to maim religion. Religion is not merely a human effort; nor is it merely a divine operation. Each partial view makes a strange miracle of religion; the former makes man impossibly self-sufficient and the latter removes faith in God from all organic and intelligible relation to experience.

(2) *Revelation.* As soon as experience becomes religious by the presence of faith, so soon there arises the experience of revelation—that is, the faith that God himself is imparting insight and guidance to man.

[11] By a "prereligious value" is meant any experience of an empirical value (whether or not it be a true value) which is not yet "taken" as related to a cosmic source of value.

Religious thinkers distinguish between two types of revelation, general and special. General revelation is that which is in principle accessible to all men, and we shall consider this first. Faith in God as creator and sustainer of man's existence implies that the creation contains signs of its creator. We find that all human experience includes factors which man's will can neither produce nor alter. Unless these factors are at least clues to a revelation of the real, no knowledge at all is possible. The postulate that experience is revelatory of the real is essential to rational thinking; the alternative to it is solipsism which is the abandoning of rational interpretation of experience. Sense experience, taken religiously, is a revelation of the power and rationality of God; value experience adds a revelation of his loyalty to goodness, beauty, truth, and holiness as the principles of his being and of all personal development. It is just as unreasonable to suppose that man's will has created value experience out of nothing as to assume that it has thus created sense experience; and, since value experience calls more clearly on man to transcend himself (and to change himself) than does sense experience, it is a higher revelation. Yet faith sees God at work in all experience at all its levels.

Over against general revelation, there is the principle of special revelation, which F. J. McConnell in one of his earlier books called "the diviner immanence." [12] All experience may be a general revelation of God; but it is certain that this revelation is not equally clear and evident at all times. There are moments when faith gropes in the dark, and even a Jesus cries out, "My God, my God, why hast thou forsaken me?" There are other moments when the meaning and value of life are concentrated in a single overwhelming experience of insight or beauty or worship. Such moments are well called special revelations. As it is with the individual, so it is with

[12] That is, the greater spiritual significance of certain special events in experience.

the race in its historical development No one would be likely to call the twentieth century an era of special revelation. It is rather a time of struggle with spiritual obscurantism. But the period of the prophetic movement described in Chapter II may well be described as one of special revelation, in which the great moral and religious ideals of humanity were imparted to the minds of spiritually receptive leaders. It is no Christian provincialism which sees in the life and teachings of Jesus a high point of that special revelation.

There is radical difference of opinion as to the relative importance of general and special revelation. Some reject the idea of special historical revelation as unjust and as leading to excessive emphasis on tradition. In his famous *Reden über die Religion,* Schleiermacher declared: "He does not have religion who believes in a Holy Scripture, but rather he who needs no Scripture and who could make one himself." [13] In a similar vein, Ralph Waldo Emerson once wrote these words:

> Men make their religion a historical religion. They see God in Judea and in Egypt, in Moses and in Jesus, but not around them. We want a living religion. As the faith was alive in the hearts of Abraham and of Paul, so I would have it in mine. I want a religion not recorded in a book, but flowing from all things. [14]

It is to be noted, however, that both Schleiermacher and Emerson were relatively immature when they expressed these views, and that they were perhaps carried away by a youthful enthusiasm. It is right to revolt against bondage to tradition and to base religion in present experience. [15]

---

[13] Translated from the first German edition, p. 122.

[14] From Emerson's Sermon No. 158, cited in McGiffert, *Young Emerson Speaks,* xxxv.

[15] The most striking ancient statement of this truth is in Jer. 31:31–34, where Jeremiah proclaims "the new covenant." In prophetic ecstasy he sees a day when

But to "need no Scripture" and to insist on a religion "not recorded in a book" is to cut off the present from the past, to refuse to learn from the experience of the race, and to begin afresh at the level of naïve ignorance and untutored instinct. It is like Rousseau's revolt against civilization.

On the other hand, there are those who distrust and repudiate general revelation and base their faith entirely on special historical revelation. This tendency, represented in one aspect of Saint Paul's thought, appears in Tertullian, in some of Augustine's utterances, in John Calvin, and most emphatically today in Karl Barth and Emil Brunner. The breakdown of the spiritual life in the World War of 1914 and in postwar phenomena has furnished a background for the astonishing growth in Christian thought of what is called neosupernaturalism, which is essentially an insistence on the sole validity of the special revelation in the New Testament as interpreted by the Reformers. According to the neosupernaturalists, man is a fallen creature, so sinful and corrupt that all of his undertakings are poisoned and doomed from the very start. There is no hope of man's finding God by his own efforts. Either God must reveal himself or man is utterly lost. But God has revealed himself in Christ. Therefore salvation is possible only through faith in this special revelation.[16]

Here we have exclusive belief in special revelation over against exclusive belief in general revelation. To one who consults experience for the grounds of his beliefs it would

---

the historic religion will be superseded by inner religion; "and they shall teach no more every man his neighbor, and every man his brother, saying, Know Jehovah; for they shall all know me." It is evident that a religion thus independent of history, of education, and of society lies far in the future; and even as an ideal, it is a one-sided value-judgment rather than a literal statement, for our knowledge of what God is can never rightly be severed from our knowledge of what God has done in history.

[16] For an elementary treatment of this point of view, see Wieman and Meland, APR, 61–95.

appear that both extremes are inadequate to represent the facts. It is not empirically true that spiritual values are equally accessible at all times to all persons. There are special moments, special persons, special ages, unusually favorable to the reception of religious truth. On the other hand, it is not empirically true that spiritual values are accessible only to those who have found their salvation through faith in Christ. To reject all evidence for God except that of special revelation is to make agnosticism the soil for faith and to ignore both the roots of value experience in nature and the spiritual life that has developed in every civilization.

Another approach to the problem of revelation is through reflection on the relations of reason and revelation. Ever since Saint Paul struggled with those relations in 1 Corinthians 14, the bearing of reason on faith has been a bone of contention. Much of the difficulty has arisen from confused definitions. Some have taken reason to mean the rules of formal logic; others, the inherent structure of mind including its "innate ideas"; and others (more soundly), the principle of coherence. Again, some have taken revelation to mean the Bible alone, while others have extended it to cover the whole range of general and special revelation. Revelation is independent of ("above") reason, or perhaps even in conflict with it, if reason is merely formal logic and revelation is merely the Bible. But if reason is the principle of coherence (the systematic interpretation of all experience), and if revelation is experience, both general and special, taken as related to God, then there is no ground for any conflict in principle between reason and revelation. Saint Augustine said that "we could not even believe if we had not rational minds"; [17] and to this may be added Locke's word: "He that takes away reason to make way for revela-

[17] *Epist.* 120, 3.

tion puts out the light of both." [18] When, in contrast with this synthetic view, Emil Brunner declares that "the complex of grounds and consequences developed by natural reason" has been "broken into by revelation," [19] it is evident that he does not interpret reason as coherence or revelation as experience.[20]

A further distinction should be made in order to clarify thought about revelation. There have been two different ways of regarding revelation in the Christian Church, and they have been paralleled more or less in other religions. They may be called the doctrinal and the functional theories of revelation. The doctrinal theory is the view that revelation is a communication of absolutely valid divine truths, acceptance of which is a condition of salvation. This is an authoritarian conception. The functional theory is the view that revelation is a series of purposive divine acts which so stimulate human experience as to lead man nearer to God. It is a teleological conception, rational rather than authoritarian. Fundamentalists and neosupernaturalists in general accept the doctrinal theory; liberals and modernists, the functional.[21] The two views have in common the metaphysical faith that the ultimate initiative in the rise of revelation is with God, rather than man; their differences have been stated. Humanists obviously have no view of revelation, since for them all religion is human endeavor, not in any sense divine revelation.

(3) *Conversion.* The psychology of conversion was discussed in Chapter II, § 8. Conversion is an experience of many persons, regardless of how it is interpreted. Faith

---

[18] *Essay,* IV, xix, 4.

[19] See Brunner, PR, 13. By "natural reason" he seems to mean reason directed to the interpretation of nature as revealed in sense experience only.

[20] For historical light on the problem, see Gilson, RRMA.

[21] For a discussion of this and other topics about revelation, see Brightman, FG, 33–51.

interprets it as an experience in which an act of human will is in immediate interaction with a coöperating act of divine will. One who is persuaded that the evidence for a theistic world view is cogent, will regard conversion as an expression of divine purpose. The half conversions, the relapses, and the abnormal phenomena which sometimes accompany conversion will then be ascribed either to incomplete human coöperation with God or to the presence of The Given in the universe, as retarding the full expression of divine purpose. There is no empirical or theoretical reason why a theist should either look with disfavor on a so-called crisis conversion, or should regard it as typical. The aim of religion is the movement of life toward divine values; the mode of initiation of that movement is irrelevant.

Faith, revelation, and actual initiation of religious living (whether by "conversion" or by natural growth) are the foundations of religious experience. We turn now to consideration of its more developed forms.

§ 5. Development of Religious Experience

(1) *Meditation.* In the language of world religions one of the most frequent terms to appear is "contemplation" or its equivalents.[22] Thought about God and divine things, reflection on the relation of the soul to God—in short, religious meditation—constitutes a large part of the inner life of vital religion. This is evidenced by the large body of devotional literature. In the Bible, meditation abounds in the Psalms and the Gospel of John. The Bhagavad Gita, the *Imitation of Christ,* the *Theologia Germanica,* the *Journal* of John Woolman, and the writings of Rabindranath Tagore are specimens of the meditative aspect of religion. Religious poetry and philosophy offer a wealth of matter for religious contemplation. Religion is more than ideas about

[22] See the article "Adoration" in Hastings, ERE, I.

God, and more than ritualistic or moral behavior. It is an organization of the whole of life. Hence meditation on religious values and beliefs is of great importance in the integration of a religious personality; repeated concentration of the mind on religion fills the memory with religious ideas, and causes religious feeling to suffuse the entire being, conscious and subconscious.

The religious worth of such meditation is obvious. Without it, religion tends to become external and mechanical, or purely moralistic; in either case, religion loses its power. But the perils of religious meditation must not be ignored. The mood of acquiescence and adoration is not favorable to intellectual analysis and criticism. The very meditation which is essential to the life of the mind as religious may lead to the death of the mind as intellectual. Yet it would be unreasonable to infer from this defect of meditation that it would be better to avoid it altogether. Many of life's most precious experiences—the enjoyment of music, of humor, or of human love—are, like religious meditation, perilous enterprises. Any partial value becomes an evil when it crowds out other values and arrogates to itself the place of the whole. So it is with meditation. Its worth depends on its being held within bounds. A life that is all meditation is not preferable to one in which there is no meditation. To think of God all the time is to preclude doing the will of God. The cultivation of meditative habits is doubtless more needed in our age than is the caution against too meditative a life; yet both are essential.[23]

(2) *Prayer.* The chief difference between meditation and prayer [24] is that he who meditates thinks of the divine in the third person; he who prays thinks of the divine in the

---

[23] The discussion of the principle of alternation by Hocking, MGHE, 405–427, is illuminating in this connection.
[24] See Chapter II, § 10, for a reference to the psychology of prayer.

second person. Prayer is therefore more personal and more expressive than meditation. Feuerbach has called it "the innermost essence of religion" and this view is shared by saints, mystics, and psychologists.[25]

The philosophy of prayer, like the philosophy of immortality, depends on the idea of God. If God is not a conscious person, then prayer is only a dramatization of meditation, and its second-personal form is illusory. To say "thou" to an unconscious power is a misuse of terms. The religious impersonalist should confine his devotional expressions to statements of his desires and aspirations; he should not only suppress the second-person "thou," but also the personal "he" in his worship of God. The resultant forms will be awkward; the theist believes that this awkwardness suggests the religious unnaturalness and the philosophical inadequacy of impersonal conceptions of God.

For the impersonalist, the philosophy of prayer stops at the point of aspiration. For the theistic personalist, however, aspiration is only the beginning of the philosophy of prayer. Heiler well states the theistic view of prayer when he calls it "a living communion of the religious man with God." [26] The word communion, however, is somewhat ambiguous, for on the 'one hand, it covers all spiritual intercourse among persons, and on the other it is used more narrowly for a special type of relatively passive and mystical experience. We shall use the term only in its broader sense.

The main types of prayer may be classified under six heads: petition for physical things, petition for personal spiritual values, petition for forgiveness, prayer of adoration, intercessory prayer, and prayer of thanksgiving and praise.

[25] See Heiler, PRA, xiii–xvi. Heiler's book is the only really scholarly treatment of prayer.
[26] Heiler, PRA, 358.

It might appear that the first type, that of *petition for physical things,* is so materialistic and mercenary as to be essentially irreligious. But a realistic awareness of the dependence of the spiritual on the physical banishes this objection. Prayer for physical things (or for physical states, such as health) is religious in so far as the physical is desired as an instrument for the development of spiritual values. If physiological psychology reveals dependence of the spiritual on the physical, psychotherapy equally reveals dependence of the physical on the spiritual. Add to these facts the theistic philosophy of the immanence of God in all of nature, and it will appear that no limit in principle can be set to petition for physical things as means to spiritual ends save the empirical one of actual experiment. Some experiments, such as walking through fire, would be unspiritual bravado, tainted by insincerity; but no one can predict in advance of experiment the extent to which prayer may contribute to physical health and perhaps to other modifications of natural processes.

The prayer of *petition for personal spiritual values* is perhaps the commonest type. Men are conscious of their weakness and feel their need of divine aid. Conscious striving in prayer for specific ends, such as increase in patience or in honesty, is beneficial. Two objections may be raised against this type of prayer: first, that it is selfish, and second, that it is weak. Neither objection seems well-grounded. An act is selfish only if it seeks to take a benefit from another or to exclude another from a benefit; but answer to prayer for personal spiritual values, far from excluding others, would benefit all with whom the pray-er associates. The loose use of the word selfish to cover every desire of a self is to be deplored. The other objection is more subtle; in a sense, it does appear weak to ask God to do what our own will ought to do for itself. No one else, not even God, can be honest for me; I must will my own honesty or it does not exist. This objection, however, overlooks the fact that prayer is itself an expression of my will to achieve spiritual value, and that it can be honest only when I have exerted that will to its utmost. It also rests on an artificially individualistic psychology; there is no act of our will which does not to some extent involve the coöperation (or the results of the coöperation) of other wills, human and divine. For prayer to ignore this fact would be unempirical.

The *prayer for forgiveness* is not common to all religions. It is especially Christian, yet is not confined to Christianity. It is the prayer of one who is conscious of having sinned, that is, of having been voluntarily disloyal to what he believed to be the will of God. Its classical instance is the prayer of the publican: "God, be merciful to me a sinner" (Lk. 18:13b). This may be regarded as a special instance of prayer for personal spiritual value, but it is so marked a type as to be worthy of special mention. While it may be abused when attended by a morbid sense of guilt, its religious value in contributing to the restoration of an impaired religious relation is proved in countless experiences.

The *prayer of adoration,* in contrast to the three types just mentioned, is objective. The previous types are subjective in the sense that they are primarily directed toward the enhancement of value in the actual experience of the person praying, the religious subject. The prayer of adoration is objective in that it is conscious contemplative appreciation—reverent admiration—of the person prayed to, God, the religious object. While such prayer is remarkably purifying and exalting and is sometimes regarded as the highest type of prayer because of its disinterestedness, it is subject to certain limitations. It is relatively passive in its relation to God, rather than active; relatively general, rather than specific and concrete in application; and (like all the types thus far mentioned) relatively individual, rather than social. It is, however, the type of prayer to which least theoretical objection of any sort has been raised.

Intercessory prayer is the name given to prayer with a definitely social purpose. Like adoration, it is objective. It is prayer for others, petition for physical or spiritual benefits to other individuals or to groups. It takes the form of requesting God to influence others who themselves are not praying.

On the one hand, intercession seems to be the loftiest type of prayer. It is even more disinterested than adoration. In adoration, the pray-er may himself be rewarded by a glimpse of the divine glory. In intercession, the mood is wholly altruistic and selfless. It is the keynote to the prayer life of Jeremiah and of Jesus ("Thy will be done on earth as it is in heaven" is universal intercession). If there is a divine goal of cosmic process, that goal must surely include a coöperative society. Furthermore, intercession is active, concrete, and social, as distinguished from the passive, general, and individual character of adoration.

On the other hand, over against these admirable traits of intercession, there are two objections that have been raised against it on ethical grounds. The first is that it may serve as a deterrent to or a substitute for social action; and the second is that it is unjust for persons who happen to be objects of prayer to receive spiritual benefits without any effort of their own. The first of these objections is the less serious. It is true that prayer may be a substitute for action; but it may also be an effective supplement to action, which may secure divine coöperation in my social endeavors, and divine action in cases where I am helpless to act. The truly religious man will never utter an intercessory prayer unless he is doing and will continue to do his best; otherwise the prayer is magical and irreligious, abandoning the whole principle of religious coöperation. The second objection is more weighty, yet not conclusive. The social structure of life is such that every individual receives daily from God and from society countless benefits without any effort on his own part; and there is no abstract justice in the distribution of these benefits. Intercessory prayer, in so far as it bestows benefits without effort, is therefore quite in harmony with the general nature of social process. Further, it should be added that no truly spiritual benefit can come to one who has been prayed for until he voluntarily avails himself of the new opportunity for spiritual growth which God has given to him in view of the interceder's prayer. To minimize intercessory prayer, as many moderns have done, is to betray at that point a lack of confidence in a cosmic social purpose.

The *prayer of thanksgiving and praise,* essentially joyous in nature, is the sixth type of prayer. Subjective in origin, resting on a specific consciousness of benefits received from God, it is objective in purpose. It asks for nothing, not even for a vision of God; it is the unselfish overflow of a grateful heart. No objection has been raised to this type of prayer except by those who deem it unworthy of God to be pleased by praise and thanksgiving. It would indeed be unworthy for God to demand adulation; but for him to prize the personal gratitude of human beings is for him to manifest his insight into the intrinsic value of personal relations. This objection is trivial and applies only to the lower levels of authoritarian religions, not to religions of the spirit.

We have considered the six main types of prayer and have shown the religious value of each. But religious value is one thing; objective metaphysical validity may be another. There are certain fundamental objections to prayer which must be weighed before the claim of prayer to metaphysical truth can be properly estimated.

First of all, it is urged that *prayer is inconsistent with the goodness of God.* If there is a good God, it is absurd to ask him to be better. He will do the best possible without being petitioned. This argument would not affect prayers of adoration and thanksgiving, but it would veto all prayers of petition, whether for physical or for spiritual or for social goods. Petition is a request for God to improve, presupposing that he is unwilling to do good unless entreated to do so. Such is the moral argument against petitionary prayer. It is undoubtedly true that some petitions actually do imply the crude idea of God which this argument attacks, but such prayer at its best is immune to this criticism. The critic, concerned about abstract logic, fails to consider the concrete facts of personal relations. If the purpose of God is to elicit free spiritual effort in man, and to encourage coöperative personal relations between man and man and between God and man, it is reasonable to assume, with the critic, that God will always do the best possible. It is not, however, reasonable to assume that the best possible is a fixed a priori quantity, independent of all facts of experience. In a coöperative society, the best possible when men pray would be better than the best possible when they do not pray. The human attitude of prayer creates a situation in which a good (finite) God would be able to do what he could not do in the absence of that attitude. Thus the logic of God's goodness creates no obstacle to petitionary prayer.

A second argument seems to be more serious, for it rests on the appeal to *natural law.* According to this argument, all events in nature conform to natural law but answers to prayer would be natural events which occurred in response to human purposes and hence not in accordance with the formula of a law. This argument has considerable force, since the concept of law is equally necessary to science and to religion. A lawless universe would be a godless one, although religion includes among God's principles not only all natural laws, but also all principles of true value. The force of the argument reduces to the question whether natural law is inconsistent with purpose.[27] Now, all laws are abstractions stating what will occur under the ideal conditions of a closed system. Most of the so-called laws of nature are statements of what takes place when purpose, for example, does not interfere. But every scientific experiment is a purposive undertaking, so that the proof of law depends on the validity of purpose. Further, it is an empirical fact that human persons can express their purposes in a universe of law. It would be extraordinary if the divine person were unable to do what man does every day. If man makes purposive responses to purposive requests without detriment to law, a fortiori God can do so. In fact, man's every conscious act calls on nature (or God) to make responses which would not otherwise occur. Only if I will to rise will my body leave this chair. The law of will is also a law. We may properly speak of the law of prayer, which calls on God to act purposively in a prayer situation as he would not act in the absence of the prayer. Thus there is no theoretical objection to prayer in the fact of law.

A third argument is practical. *Prayer, we are told, is not answered as we desire.* It is pragmatically unsuccessful. It must be freely granted that it would be impossible for all prayers to be granted; and if God is wiser than man, it would be strange if many prayers were answered exactly as desired. It may also be granted that some "remarkable answers to prayer" are mere coincidences or results of other causes than prayer. The crucial question is not whether men get what they pray for; the question is whether prayer makes life better. To decide this question, no theory suffices. Experience alone is the final court. If prayer is

[27] Compare Chap. XII, esp. § 6 and § 9.

found empirically to elicit powers which no other experience can reach, then it is validated. It is a unique response of the cosmos to man's striving. But no theorizing about prayer is of any importance except as an interpretation of the actual experience of prayer.

(3) *Mysticism.* The topic of mysticism has already been touched on in this book.[28] There is abundant literature on the subject, in contrast to the poverty of the treatment of prayer. We may therefore deal with it briefly in this connection.

Mysticism is a term used to cover a wide variety of experiences—from the quiet and peaceful to the blissful and ecstatic. The mystical is not a clear-cut, separate type of experience; it is a quality that pervades most religious life to a greater or lesser degree, although there may be predominantly moral or intellectual religious experiences from which the mystical is almost entirely absent. By mysticism we mean an immediate consciousness of God,[29] not believed to be mediated by the intellect or the will of the individual or of society, but attributed directly to God himself.

Mystical experience is an empirical fact which no one can doubt, but there is great difference of opinion regarding the interpretation and evaluation of the fact. Most extreme mystics emphasize the "noetic quality" of the experience, to which James referred. They regard the testimony of the experience itself as absolute knowledge. Yet the most superficial comparison of the deliverances of the mystical consciousness of a Taoist, a Hindu, a Mohammedan, a Jew, a Catholic Christian, and a Protestant Christian reveals at

---

[28] See Chap. II, § 9. In addition to the references there given, the writings of Baron von Hügel, Evelyn Underhill, and Rufus M. Jones are valuable treatments of the subject.

[29] Let it be noted that the word God is used here, and frequently in the text, to designate the object of worship, whether that object be defined as a conscious person or not.

once the fact that equal immediate certainty may attach to very different conceptions of the divine. One mystic "experiences" God as impersonal, another as personal; one views God in terms of pantheism, another of theism; one approaches the divine through the Blessed Virgin Mary, another regards this approach as spurious. In short, the experiences of the mystics may be interpreted as were the claims to revelation. On the one hand, they may be viewed doctrinally, as immediate apprehension of certain divine truth; then they are chaotic and contradictory. On the other hand, they may be viewed functionally, as means whereby the divine person draws humanity nearer to itself; then they are seen to serve a cosmic purpose. Mysticism thus becomes one more witness to the fact that actual contact with the real is more fundamental than our rational interpretation of it.

In the light of what has been said thus far, the mystical experience appears to be of cosmic importance and integral to normal religion. Mysticism, however, has been subject to attack on at least four grounds. It is said to be antisocial, otherworldly, psychologically abnormal, and morally defective. Each of these points is a sound criticism of excesses of which some mystics have been guilty. There have been mystical hermits who have withdrawn from society; there have been mystics whose interest in the divine world has caused them to lose interest in the affairs of this life; there have been fanatical and hysterical mystics; and there have been mystic "antinomians," [30] who have violated the commonest moralities.

Over against these extreme types, there are many mystics who are open to none of the criticisms mentioned. Such mystics are not antisocial; although they prize their individ-

[30] This term refers to those who believe themselves justified in disregarding all law.

ual relation to God, they find in God the universal source of love and brotherhood. It is to mystics like the Friends that we owe some of the most practical of social movements, such as prison reform, the abolition of slavery, and protest against war. Nor are these mystics otherworldly, in the sense of lacking interest in the affairs of this life. It is true that all religion sees more meaning in personal existence than is visible to the senses, and most religion includes faith in immortality; but those who have been otherworldly in the fanatical sense have been disloyal to the values which they ascribe to the other world by betraying them in this world. The "trust God and keep your powder dry" of Cromwell is more typical of the best mysticism. Again, the mystics whom we are now considering are not psychologically abnormal. Who could be more healthy-minded than our contemporary American mystic, Rufus M. Jones? Even William Blake, for all his visions, lived a sane and normal life in ordinary relations.

Mysticism is an area in which error and fanaticism lie near; but it is also an area in which discipline, objectivity, and new insights are often found. If the mystic shares the perils of the pioneer, he also shares his achievements.[31]

(4) *Coöperation.* Meditation, prayer, and mysticism are the relatively more passive aspects of religion; in them, man thinks of himself as dependent, receiving rather than acting. Essential as these factors are to the development of religious experience, it would be untrue to the facts to picture religion as consisting entirely or chiefly of these more passive and objective attitudes. There is a sense, indeed, in which religion is passive and requires, as Schleiermacher held, a sense of man's absolute dependence. There is another sense

---

[31] The term worship has not appeared in Chap. XIV. Worship is a name given to the total movement of religious experience toward God. For a discussion of it see Brightman, RV, 173–237.

in which religion is perhaps man's most powerful impulse to activity. When one's experience takes the form, "Thus saith the Lord, Go!" action is in order. Religion, as devotion to the loftiest ideal values, presupposes that the will of God is not now done in the world and that it should be done. Hence come such utterances of Jesus as "By their fruits ye shall know them," and "If any man willeth to do his will, he shall know of the doctrine." There are some religious persons, it is true, who seek the passive experiences for their own sake; but those who have entered most deeply into the spirit of religion have used the insights gained in the passive experiences as norms and incentives for religious action. The moral idealism, the missionary and reform activities, and the social interests of the great religions all point in this direction.

The essence of religious activity is that it is coöperative, not merely individual or merely subjective. In the first place, it must be *coöperation with God*. It is an elevation of the soul toward God, which involves both a receiving and a response. Without experienced commerce with the divine, involving activity on both sides for a common value, there is no religion. In the second place, it must with equal necessity be *coöperation with man*. Religion is a devotion to personal values as expressing the purpose of God; not to coöperate with men for the social realization of those values is at the same time not to coöperate with God's purpose. Religion, when conscious of its own destiny, is best defined as *coöperation with God and man for the realization of individual and of shared values*.[32]

The practical, active, coöperative nature of religion may be illustrated by comparing "pure" science, "pure" art, and

---

[32] This definition is, of course, intended to be normative; it represents the author's view of what religion ought to be; it manifestly does not describe what religion always is. On the other hand, it is not restricted to Christianity; it repre-

"pure" religion. Pure science is knowledge for its own sake, without regard to applications; that devotion to pure science has often led to discoveries of practical importance is of no moment to the pure scientist. "Pure" art, likewise, is often thought of as art for art's sake; beauty, or form, or expression are regarded as ends in themselves by the pure artist, regardless of their effect on life. But pure religion is in its very essence practical; its aim is to change the whole of life and to realize the ideal in human experience. The writer of the epistle ascribed to James embodies this thought in classic language: "Pure religion and undefiled before our God and Father is this, to visit the fatherless and widows in their affliction, and to keep oneself unspotted from the world." [33] For this writer, religion is coöperation with God in social action and individual character. Otherworldly quietism is so sharp a contrast to this as to contradict the main function of religion—the realization of values.

§ 6. THE VALIDITY OF RELIGIOUS EXPERIENCE

Let us view the results of this chapter in the light of principles discussed in earlier chapters. Religious experience is a complex body of empirical facts, which include many conflicting beliefs about the facts. The same may be said of our biological, and, all the more truly, of our aesthetic experience. In view of our philosophical method, we must reiterate that no single experience, religious or nonreligious, carries its truth with it. Every experience or intuition must be tested by its relation to the claims of other experiences and our synoptic insight into experience as a whole. Yet all ex-

---

sents the ideal striving of all religion. The great documents of religion for the most part emphasize right social action as the will of God. Compare the Code of Hammurabi, the Code of the Covenant (Exodus 20:22–23:33), the Decalogue, Deuteronomy, the Sermon on the Mount (Mt. 5–7), and the Koran. The duty of action is the central problem of the Bhagavad Gita.

[33] James 1:27.

perience is in a sense revelation; for all experience, however illusory it may be in some respects, involves the impact of the universe upon our personality. The fact that no single religious experience can stand by itself as authoritative is not to be taken as a discrediting of religious experience. The function of religion is not to ascribe absoluteness to a single moment; that is more nearly the work of the Faustian Mephistopheles. The function of religion is rather to relate each moment to the meaning and purpose of the whole universe. Thus the validity of religious experience, like the validity of reason, is to be found in its appeal to the largest and most inclusive view of experience.[34]

BIBLIOGRAPHICAL NOTE

The references at the end of Chapters I, II, III, and VI, all contain material bearing on the subject of this chapter. The footnotes in this chapter, especially those on § 3, refer to the essential literature.

Works of special interest for the interpretation of the chapter are Bowne, SC(1909), Brightman, RV(1925), Knudson, VRE (1937), and Baillie, KG(1939). On the underlying epistemology, see Brightman, ITP(1925), and Lovejoy, RAD(1930).

[34] The point of view expressed above is related to Kant's statement that "being is evidently no real predicate" (*Critique of Pure Reason,* A598, B626). No single experience can reveal the difference between a real hundred dollars and an imaginary hundred dollars; between a real God and an imaginary God. Reality is a system, and the meaning of any experience must be found by its place in that system.

FIFTEEN

INTERNAL CRITICISMS
OF RELIGION

§ 1. PHILOSOPHY OF RELIGION AS CRITICAL INTERPRETATION
OF RELIGION

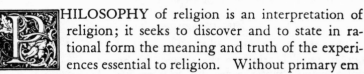HILOSOPHY of religion is an interpretation of religion; it seeks to discover and to state in rational form the meaning and truth of the experiences essential to religion. Without primary emphasis on this constructive task of interpretation, philosophy of religion is in danger of becoming either a mere dogmatic restatement of tradition, or else a polemic against tradition without clear understanding of what the content of the tradition is. It must, however, at once be added that this very emphasis on constructive interpretation is also in peril of becoming dogmatic, unless the interpretation is critical. Criticism means re-examination of fundamentals: consideration of objections, of alternative possibilities, of starting points different from the ones hitherto favored.

The treatment of religion in the text thus far has been predominantly interpretative, although accompanied by no little criticism of the ideas considered. Now that we have completed the main task of interpretation, so that we know what religion means and have seen what some of its chief beliefs imply, we might be inclined to say that a philosophy of religion has been presented and that *finis* should be written. Apart from the fact that thinking is an infinite task that can never reach a final conclusion,[1] no philosophy of religion can reach its proper goal without making the need of criticism more explicit than we have yet done.

§ 2. INTERNAL AND EXTERNAL CRITICISM

In general, criticism may be classified as internal or external. Internal criticism is one that starts from the point of view under discussion and then reveals within that point of view the presence of incompatible elements. For example, our discussion of the finiteness of God was an internal criticism of the idea of God, revealing contradictions between the omnipotence and the benevolence which that idea had included. Internal criticism makes use of no argument and no principle that does not grow out of the area under criticism. It is the most fundamental, the most persuasive, and the most intelligent type of criticism, for it meets a position on its own ground and proceeds from premises granted by all concerned.

Internal criticism, however, is in some danger of smugness and dogmatism. It may strive only for more effective statement of a position that is essentially false. Hence any point of view needs also to be confronted by external criticism, that is, by criticism which rests on different assumptions and which therefore challenges the validity of the whole position criticized. In its cruder forms, external criticism means that I, the critic, judge all other views by their consistency with my opinions, which I have arrived at without considering the evidence or the arguments on which the other view is based. In its more mature forms, external criticism leads me to examine that evidence and those arguments in detail, yet to judge them by my own criteria—the criteria of my point of view, not of the one under criticism.

---

[1] This lack of finality in philosophical thought, which leads some to skepticism, may well be viewed as an opportunity for faith and also as a ground for belief in immortality, since the work of thought might well occupy a soul forever.

The distinction between external and internal criticism is not to be confused with that between favorable and unfavorable criticism. As we shall see, much internal criticism of religion is very unfavorable to tradition; and some external criticism is in a sense favorable, as when an atheist says that the church is commendable as a means of keeping the masses under control. The distinction between, and the proper use of, internal and external criticism are among the most difficult and important lessons for the mind to learn. Most criticism is external: it was the greatness of philosophers like Socrates and Hegel, and of a religious personality like Jesus, that they relied chiefly on internal criticism.

§ 3. History of Religion as a Process of Internal Criticism

Internal criticism is a method which may be applied by anyone, whether or not he personally shares the views of the position criticized. From the coolly objective point of view, a criticism derives its force from its logical cogency, not from the personality of the critic. Humanity, however, has not usually been coolly objective in arriving at its decisions. Hence criticism made by a member of a group is often more successful than exactly the same criticism made from outside the group. Citizens of Alabama resent advice from New Yorkers. Protests of foreign nations against a policy of our country are less welcome than the same protests when raised by our own nationalists. So it is in the field of religion. A criticism of religion by an unbeliever, however honestly propounded and however just it may be, is regarded as sinister and almost blasphemous by many adherents of the religion criticized, whereas the same criticism coming from a believer may be seriously heeded and may lead to revolutionary changes in the religion. "Boring from within" is as effective in religion as it is in politics or economics.

If religion is a form of life, it is natural that internal criticism coming from religious believers should be the most effective form of criticism; for the living organism maintains itself over against its environment, and its growth is from within. What comes from without must be transformed by processes characteristic of the organism before it can enter into the life of the organism.

The history of religion is an illustration of this principle. In fact, it would not be far wrong to describe that history as a process of internal criticism. Religion is often said to be conservative and static; and there is some truth in this description. The Jewish, the Christian, and the Mohammedan churches are by far the oldest international organizations in the world today; they perpetuate many ancient traditions and usages. Nevertheless, it would be incorrect to describe these churches as being nothing but conservative forces. Neither Judaism nor Christianity nor Mohammedanism is today what it was at the beginning. As in every other human institution, there have been changes, some for the better and some for the worse. The history of religions may be compared to the history of universities; in both we find a combination of conservatism and liberalism, of loyalty to the past and of new hope for the future. It is perhaps true that changes in religion have occurred more slowly than in most other fields, but this may be accounted for by the importance of religion to the sincere believer, its pervasive influence on his entire life—individual and social, emotional, intellectual, and volitional. It is no light matter to change one's religion. Fashions in clothing come and go with breath-taking speed; the growth of religion is a more gradual process. Slow movement is not necessarily less important than fast movement; some of the most rapid motions of the stars seem to the eye to be no motion at all, because of our point of view. Fundamental economic changes are as slow as religious changes, because they, too, involve important issues of life.

Illustrations of this process of religious self-criticism abound. Take, for example, the development from polytheism to monotheism, or from naïvely materialistic views of God to a spiritual conception, or from merely ritualistic and often grossly immoral religious practices to the highest moral idealism. The prophetic movement, referred to in Chapter II, was a striking example of the internal self-criticism of religion in these respects by forward-looking leaders of many different faiths and lands, all of whom felt themselves divinely moved to criticize beliefs and aspirations popular in their own religion. Plato's criticism of Homeric ideas about the gods, the attitude of Jesus (Mt. 5–7) and of Paul (in the epistle to the Galatians) toward the religious traditions of the Jewish people, the protests of Mohammed against the Arabic religion of his day, the theses of Martin Luther nailed on the door of the church in Wittenberg in 1517, the growth in tolerance and appreciation of other religions as a result of Christian missions, the rise of modernism with its attack on authoritarian aspects of religion—these characteristic episodes and movements are all evidence of the tendency of religion to internal criticism.

The very nature of religion is such that self-criticism is inherent in it. If the religious man is one who is devoted to the objective source of the highest values, which he calls God, such a man will be moved by a consciousness that the best that he and all humanity have ever done falls far short of the purposes of God. Nothing could be more irreligious than a sanctification of the *status quo*.

§ 4. Religious Criticism of the Present as Disloyal to the Past

The self-criticism of religion assumes many different forms. One of the commonest consists in an attack on those tendencies within the religious group which deviate from the idealized traditions of the group. The conservative is often the sharpest critic. His criticism may take the form of excommunication or even of the torture or the burning at the stake of heretics.

It might appear erroneous to call conservatism or authoritarianism a critical force; but it would be erroneous only if criticism had the sole function of changing generally accepted ideas. Conservatism is criticism, and it is internal criticism, directed against certain deviations from a religious norm. To deny that it is criticism would be to take too narrow a view of the scope of criticism. Criticism is rational examination, even when its primary aim is to support what is taken to be established truth.

The modern temper has been unfavorable to conservatism, and the excesses of conservatism are glaring. The Inquisition, Blue Laws, heresy trials, and acts of intolerance are abhorrent to the liberal mind; and well they may be. These evils do not, however, reveal the true nature of conservatism. The religious conservative starts from the not unreasonable assumption that the experience and thought of past centuries is worthy of respect and has a greater probability of being true than the speculations of any individuals working independently. There is a certain analogy to scientific method in this assumption; for it rests, as does science, on the appeal to experience and on the repeated testing of hypotheses through the ages. The faith of science and the faith of religion have both been tested by many experiments in human living. Therefore the conservative has a useful function to perform when he challenges the radical who deviates from the beaten path. In view of this recurring process of internal criticism, any religious innovator has to run the gantlet before his idea is treated seriously. Thus religion is protected against disintegration by the activities of fanatics or fanciful speculators.

Despite unlovely extremes to which the authoritarian mood has led, it has the useful function of warning that human history does not begin afresh every morning, but is rooted in the past. It may be that the only lesson that we learn from history is that we learn nothing from history; the religious conservative is one whose work it is to point out the folly of history-blindness and the superficial modernity of the present moment.

§ 5. RELIGIOUS CRITICISM OF THE PRESENT AND PAST AS DISLOYAL TO THE IDEAL

However justified conservatism may be, religion could not consist entirely of loyalty to tradition. What is handed down as living religion must originate at some time, and when it originates it is an experience of, or faith in, some ideal value. Loyalty to this value involves critical rejection of lower values and an attack on disvalues, especially when they are parts of existing religion. The adjective prophetic evokes the noun denunciation. A harsh negative note, quite foreign to the soft modern demand for "constructive criticism," sounds in the messages of Amos and Isaiah, Xenophanes and Socrates, Buddha and Jesus; and this negation is directed not merely or chiefly against the irreligious and profane, but against adherents of the established, traditional religion.

Internal criticism of religion on the grounds of its disloyalty to the ideal has taken at least three main directions. It has been a criticism lodged against (1) *mere traditionalism,*

(2) *immoral practices,* and (3) *materialistic conceptions.*

(1) The *criticism of mere traditionalism* is a major interest of prophets like Isaiah and Jeremiah. During the years 705–701 B.C., Isaiah was saying: ". . . all vision is become unto you as the words of a book that is sealed" (29:11); that is, living insight into divine truth is being crushed by loyalty to the letter of an unintelligible tradition. The prophet went on (as God's spokesman) to remark bitterly of the "religious" men of his day that "their fear of me is a commandment of men which hath been taught them" (29:13), or, as Moffatt translates it, "a mere tradition, learned by rote." Jeremiah a century later continued the prophetic plea for living religion and the criticism of traditionalism. After a poetic picture of the naturalness of religion (8:7), where he compares religion to the seasonal flight of birds, Jeremiah asks: "How do ye say, We are wise, and the law of Jehovah is with us? But, behold, the false pen of the scribes hath wrought falsely" (8:8). Life points to God, says Jeremiah; but tradition hides and distorts God. In the Sermon on the Mount, Jesus quotes several passages from the Old Testament (in Mt. 5:21, 27, 38, 43), introducing them with the words "Ye have heard that it was said," and in each case he shows the inadequacy of the traditional view with a "but I say unto you." Buddha's life work was largely an attack on Hindu traditions, and Martin Luther's an attack on Catholic traditions.

These great religious personalities did not, it is true, "come to destroy the law or the prophets"; they came "not to destroy, but to fulfill" (Mt. 5:17). In short, their attacks on tradition were evolutionary, not revolutionary. They aimed to build on the best in the past, but they did not hesitate to assail ancient traditions when they stood in the way of religious growth.

(2) The *criticism of immoral practices* that are indulged in by religious believers, often as an integral part of religion,

is another important phenomenon. Immoral here means whatever man's enlightened conscience rejects as contrary to ethical principles. Devotion to moral progress is so marked a characteristic of religion that many people, both religious and irreligious, tend to a somewhat superficial identification of religion and morality. The growing edge of man's moral idealism has been found largely in the self-criticism of religion. It was the Hebrew religion that repudiated the religious rites of child sacrifice and of temple prostitutes. It was the prophet Amos who turned the traditional doctrine of Israel as an elect nation into a doctrine of Israel's moral responsibility. "You only have I known of all the families of the earth: therefore I will visit upon you all your iniquities" (Amos 3.2). This has been called the most significant "therefore" in all literature. Its force may be imagined by reflecting on the fate of men in modern totalitarian states today who make similar utterances.

The Sermon on the Mount (Mt. 5-7) is largely a criticism of the Mosaic religion and its interpreters from the standpoint of morality; Jesus substituted a spiritual view of morality for the external behavior-codes of the old law. The first and second chapters of Romans are a scathing criticism of the association between the religion of Paul's day and the vilest immorality. Wherever we discover traces of "the prophetic movement" or its influence there we see religious leaders holding up moral ideals and mercilessly criticizing moral delinquency among the religious. The Old Testament prophets were as bitter against the sins of the church as against those of the state. Buddha found the caste system of Hinduism degrading and the Hindu treatment of woman unworthy; he protested vehemently against both abuses. Where the Christian church has tolerated slavery, war, and unjust economic conditions, Christians have themselves pointed out the inconsistency of the church long before skeptics or Communists have leveled their external criticisms. There have been "reformations," so-called, in the churches of many religions; in almost every instance, the reformation included a self-criticism of religion on moral grounds. The teachings of Confucius and of Buddha consisted almost wholly of moral ideals; Martin Luther was as much concerned by the immoral consequences of the system of indulgences as by their theological "unsoundness." New religious movements are often occasioned by the moral laxity of existing religious practices. Mohammedanism was a long step forward in moral development because of its bold break with the older Arabic religion. The development of religion is a development of the moral self-criticism of religion and also a development of higher ideals.

(3) A third type of internal criticism of religion is religion's own *protest against religious materialism.*

There can be little doubt that man is naturally materialistic. If Saint Augustine is right in declaring the soul naturally Christian, then the soul has a dual nature. In each human being there is "the man with the muck rake" as well as Bunyan's Pilgrim. Man's first thought is for his material well-being—for food and clothing and shelter; and for many men material comfort and material pleasures are not only their first thought but also their last. It is easier for the successful man today to be a materialist than to be an idealist. So it is in religion. Man first conceives the divine as a power (mana) residing in physical objects; spirit itself is thought of as attenuated matter. The gods have physical forms, physiological organisms, and feel hunger, wage war, live a sex life, and in short are crudely material beings. Even in the Hebrew religion, according to the early records (the document J)[2], Jehovah walks in the garden in the cool of the day; there are "sons of God" who take "daughters of men" as

²See Brightman, SH, 19-111.

their wives. God has to come down to see the tower of Babel
and the wickedness of Sodom. Jacob wrestled with God;
"I have seen God face to face, and my life is preserved."
Like man, Jehovah repents and changes his mind. He even
waylays Moses and tries without success to kill him (Ex.
4:24). He becomes visible in a theophany described in Ex.
24:1-2, 9-11. Moses, according to Ex. 33:23, sees his back
but not his face. It would be idle to pile up further evidence
of religious materialism. The religious conceptions of aver-
age modern Christians and Jews are not only materialistic in
their views of God, but also, in many cases, materialistic in
their religious aims—with primary emphasis on physical
health, economic prosperity, and vocational success. Christian Science, despite its spiritual philosophy, is best known
for its emphasis on the body. The Church of the Latter Day
Saints, an organization of far more moral force and genuine
devotion than most of its critics suppose, looks on God as a
literally material being and lays great stress on the material
goods of life.

It cannot be said that all emphasis on the material is
materialistic. Religion is an organization of the whole of
life under the principle of supreme value. The material cannot be ignored. There is a proper religious evaluation of
matter, both as an expression of the immanent creativity of
God and also as a means to spiritual ends. Nevertheless,
religious practice, begun on the level of regarding material
values as intrinsic, is in danger of remaining permanently
on that level. Materialistic paradises and, even more, materialistic rewards in this life are readily taken by man's unspiritual nature as a surrogate for true ideal values.

Therefore it is noteworthy that the history of religion has
been a series of protests by its most deeply religious leaders
against man's natural materialism. Religion was for a long

time universally idolatrous. Nonreligious materialists, as far as is recorded, made no protest against idolatry—the worship of material substitutes for spiritual reality—until long after religious believers had declared idolatry irreligious. The thoughtful priests of Egyptian and Indian religions, like the Greek philosophers, taught that the divine reality is spiritual and the images only symbolic of the spiritual (as the Catholic regards the images of the saints). But the greatest prophets were iconoclastic, and protested with all their vigor against any material images of the imageless, spiritual God. In the sixth century before Christ, the Greek Xenophanes in Elea and the Hebrew Second Isaiah in Babylonia independently saw the absurdity of trying to express the spiritual personality of God by any physical medium. The Second Isaiah carried to its logical extreme the ideal of the Decalogue: "Thou shalt not make unto thee any graven image." An image, he says, "is profitable for nothing" (Is. 44:10).

From the sixth century on, religious thinkers have opposed the tendencies to anthropomorphic views of God and to the ethical materialism which makes man's life consist "in the abundance of the things that he possesseth." The sayings of Jesus in the Sermon on the Mount are a rebuke to the materialistic standards of Deuteronomy 28. The teachings of the Buddha attack the materialistic practices of Hinduism. The mystics and saints of the Catholic church repeatedly rebuke the materialism of its priests and ecclesiastics. The Quakers and other spiritual leaders of our own day—men like Gandhi, Kagawa, Stanley Jones, or Rufus Jones—whatever one may think of their practical merits, are men who put moral and spiritual values above all material considerations. Such men are even more concerned with attacking the indifference, the unspirituality, and the materialism of organized religion than they are with assailing these vices among the irreligious. These men appear to regard the presence of such evils in religion as treasonable; whereas their dominance in secular life, while evil, is after all to be expected.

These three internal criticisms—attacks on traditionalism and immorality and materialism—are only specimens of the vitality of the critical spirit in religion. Detailed researches would reveal far more than has been hinted at in this cursory treatment. Indeed, if religion is devotion to what are believed to be eternal values, no truly religious mind could be content to endorse as fully adequate any present embodiment of the religious spirit. True religion cannot be acquiescence in the *status quo* of the church, any more than it can bless the *status quo* of the state or of the economic order. The essence of religion is a continual remaking of the temporal in the light of the eternal.

§ 6. Religious Criticism of the Present as Disloyal to Spiritual Growth

The eye of the religious man is primarily on the eternal ideal. But the eye of faith cannot see the eternal except in its relation to the temporal. If the eternal values are not revealed in actual temporal experience, they are not revealed at all; for actual temporal experience is all that we have. If eternal values are revealed in experience, they are revealed not merely as eternal divine validities, but also as goals for human action. In the light of this tension between the eternal and the temporal, there is a sense in which religion is more truly a practical demand than it is either a body of doctrine, a revelation of truth, or an emotional satisfaction. Most of the great scriptures of all religions are exhortations or commands to act. A religion that in no way changes the conduct of a man or a society is regarded as defective or hypocritical.

It is generally recognized that to be religious means to act in accordance with ideals which faith regards as pointing toward the eternal will of God.   It has been less generally perceived that true religion requires growth, not only in the practice and in the apprehension of eternal ideals, but also in man's very conception of what those eternal ideals are.   If the ordinary religious person is asked to designate whether loyalty to received truth or openmindedness toward new and higher truth is more religious, he will usually reply that loyalty is more fundamental than openmindedness. There is a certain canny secular instinct of self-preservation in this judgment; for many individuals and groups are so settled in their habits and so lacking in plasticity that any change may mean death for them.

But the greatest religious personalities have almost without exception been on the side of openness to new truth. The Sermon on the Mount is obviously an openminded document, with its repeated criticisms of what has been "said to them of old time."   The message of Socrates and Plato was that of subjecting all religious traditions to the test of reason. It is true that a fervent and cautious spirit like Tertullian rejected the principle of openmindedness in favor of orthodoxy; but he paid the price by cracking under the strain and losing the orthodoxy he was so bound to defend for the fanatical Montanism which led him toward spiritual disintegration instead of toward growth.   On the other hand, Justin Martyr, Clement of Alexandria, and Origen were loyal to the rational spirit of Greek philosophy and they contributed to the continued growth of Christian thought.

When the rediscovery of Aristotle in the Middle Ages challenged the thought of men, a great Arab like Avicenna and a great Christian like Thomas Aquinas welcomed the new light and sought rational truth openmindedly.   With the rise of modern physical science in the sixteenth and seventeenth centuries, religious thinkers like Descartes and Berkeley, Spinoza and Leibniz, reinterpreted the fundamental concepts of religion. Again in the nineteenth century, the theory of evolution led James Ward and C. Lloyd Morgan, John Fiske and Borden Parker Bowne—to mention only a few religious leaders—to new insights into the nature of divine activity and the developing character of religion. The evolutionary view in the broader sense has led many to reject the traditional view of the Bible and to accept a developmental view. The same principles have led to analogous reinterpretations in Judaism, Mohammedanism, and Buddhism.

It is true that the religious critics of religion have often been assailed as heretics and cast out of the synagogue (as was Spinoza). But it is usually they, rather than their orthodox opponents, who have represented the essential nature of religion as spiritual growth.

§ 7. RELIGIOUS CRITICISM OF THE TENDENCY OF RELIGION
TO EXTREMES

No frank observer of religion (or of any other human phenomenon) could fail to note the tendency of beliefs and practices to go to extremes. Life is a structure of dialectical tensions, in which "claims and counter-claims," [3] theses and antitheses, war against each other. But spiritual warfare is rarely one of extermination, and almost never a *Blitzkrieg*. Extremes develop in religious or social life because there is some reason for them. One extreme is a partially justified protest against another, or is a reaching of the human spirit for needs left unsatisfied by the existing order. There is always some thesis against which the antithesis justifiably rebels, even if the form of the rebellion is not justifiable.

The very existence of extremes within religion is itself an instance of the immanent self-criticism of religion. Isa-

[3] The phrase is Bosanquet's.

iah's "Come now, let us reason together" (better translated as, "Come now, let us accuse one another") illustrates the fact that the very life of religion is self-criticism.

But self-criticism in the form of a mere setting up of one extreme against another results only in dogmatic recriminations. In fact, such intellectual cat-and-dog fights are not worthy of the name of criticism, for criticism means judgment. When real criticism sets to work, sooner or later each extreme is analyzed, discriminated, appreciated—and altered; a new insight arises, sometimes quickly, sometimes after long centuries, which embodies the fruits of critical examination in a new synthesis. This is the true spirit of dialectic, which, it must be said, is sharply in conflict with Karl Barth's conception of dialectical theology. In Barth's dialectic there is no critical advance, no new synthesis, no growth of insight; there are only God and the world as thesis and antithesis, each over against the other, each saying "No" when the other says "Yes," and "Yes" when the other says "No." But if the world is so utterly evil that God can say "Yes" to nothing in it, how then can it be believed that God created such a world, and how can such a world ever receive or accept God's contradicting Word?

The actual history of religion contains many illustrations of the dialectical criticism of extremes by religious thought. This is not to say that where criticism has been needed it has always been forthcoming, or that the movement of religious development has been a straight line of progress. The facts render such judgments absurd. Nevertheless, we perceive reason at work among religious believers, continually criticizing aberrations and irrationalities and calling religious thought and practice to a more balanced and more inclusive view of truth.

A few illustrations will suffice. The tendency of religion toward curbing human excesses is exemplified in the Greek

view of *hybris,* that proud human insolence which leads the
individual to lord it over his fellows and even compete with
the gods; *hybris* is one of the worst sins in Greek religion.
The story of the Tower of Babel (Gn. 11) is the Hebrew
equivalent of the Greek condemnation of *hybris.* Yet here
we have perhaps not so much a criticism of religion as of
irreligion; although there may be doubt whether the Promethean theft of fire from heaven (a nobler deed than building the Tower) was an act of irreligious *hybris* or of religious
aspiration, so that the Zeus who tortured Prometheus was
really himself guilty of *hybris.*

One of the areas in which religion is most prone to extremes is that of action or inaction. On the one hand, religion is intensely practical. It experiences the obligation
to achieve the highest values as a divine command.[4] It gen-
erates action which the nonreligious man views as either
futile or fanatical. On the other hand, religion is faith in
divine sovereignty and submission to divine will. Salvation
depends on divine mercy and divine initiative; it is a gift
which no man can earn by his own efforts. In the fullest
development of religious life, a dialectical tension exists between these two aspects; religion is both faith and work, both
submission (Islam) and obedience (Judaism), both the
Word of God (Barth) and the deed of man (humanists).
Yet if either one of the two poles dominates the other, the
current of religion runs awry. It is here that the self-criticism of religion has repeatedly set in.

The great book of devotion in Hindu religion, corresponding in many ways to the Gospel of John in Christianity, is
the Bhagavad Gita. The theme of this work is the supreme
value of mystical union with God. At the end of Chapter
VI, the deity says to Arjuna:

[4] Note Kant's idea that religion consists of regarding our duties as divine
commands.

The devotee is esteemed higher than the performer of penances, higher even than the men of knowledge, and the devotee is higher than the men of action; therefore, O Arjuna! become a devotee.[5]

Here the writer commits himself to faith as opposed to knowledge or works. Yet the central purpose of the Bhagavad Gita is to show the religious duty of action. Arjuna is represented in Chapter I as entertaining humanitarian (Promethean!) and religious doubts about the value of military action. "I do not perceive any good," he sagely says, "likely to accrue after killing my kinsman in the battle." But the deity in Chapter II regards Arjuna's compunctions as "base weakness"—a pale inaction unworthy of the religious man, on the metaphysical ground that "weapons do not divide the self into pieces; fire does not burn it; waters do not moisten it; it does not dry up." The climax is reached in the words: "Having regard to your own duty also, you ought not to falter, for there is nothing better for a Kshatriya than a righteous battle."

Thus we see that the religious consciousness which developed the most mystical and metaphysical heights of faith in India at the same time developed a self-criticism which pointed out the religious duty of action in the world. Needless to say, the kind of action recommended—relentless, pitiless military warfare—is itself another extreme which religion had already begun to criticize in the Hebrew prophets' dreams of a warless world.

They shall beat their swords into plowshares and their spears into pruning-hooks; nation shall not lift up sword against nation, neither shall they learn war any more. (Is. 2:4)

Jesus makes the prophetic ideal a maxim of conduct, with explicit rejection of the militaristic maxims of the older religion and its *lex talionis:*

[5] The translation of K. F. Telang in the SBE is followed, except for the spelling of Arjuna.

Ye have heard that it was said, An eye for an eye, and a tooth
for a tooth: but I say unto you, Resist not him that is evil: but
whosoever smiteth thee on thy right cheek, turn to him the
other also. (Mt. 5:38, 39)

It would be a mistake to interpret Jesus as advocating a return to the quietistic mysticism which the Bhagavad Gita
had repudiated. Jesus commissioned his disciples to a life
of action. He said: "I send you forth as sheep in the midst
of wolves: be ye therefore wise as serpents, and harmless as
doves." (Mt. 10:16)   In criticizing the action of wolves and
serpents, Jesus was not criticizing action; he was criticizing
wolfish and snakish action only.   His point was that religion
commands action guided by social intelligence rather than
rapacity and violence.

Thus we see how religion develops extremes—extremes of
mystical devotion and extremes of fanatical action; and how,
at the same time, the spirit of religion tends to correct and
criticize the extremes which it has developed.   If the correction of quietism goes too far, as in the Hindu classic, and
even praises unworthy military action, it is religion again
that criticizes the appeal to the violent retaliation against
wrong.

Another illustration of the law that religion tends to correct its own tendency to extremes is found in the Christian
thought of the second century.   After the great contributions
of Jesus and Paul in the first century, there was a descent
from their lofty heights; Christianity began to be institu-
tionalized and conventionalized, as every great social movement tends to be.   But within the church there were radical
extremists ready to protest against the tendencies of the
times.   These extremists were in two main groups—one
representing the interests of the intellect and moral idealism,
and the other the interests of emotional loyalty.   The party

of the intellect and moral idealism rejected the unworthy and cruel deeds and motives ascribed to Jehovah in the Old Testament and hence refused to identify Jehovah with the loving God taught by Jesus as Father. This party also carried its moral criticism of sins of the flesh to the extreme of ascetic refusal to regard the marriage relation as Christian. Its teachings were so widespread at one time that they threatened to conquer the entire Christian movement. But this Gnosticism, as it was called, was opposed by another movement known as Montanism. The Montanists regarded the Gnostics as laying altogether too much stress on human speculation and human endeavor. The Montanists felt themselves called to chasten the *hybris* of the Gnostics. Montanism was a highly emotional experience of what was believed to be the power of the Holy Spirit in the life of the individual. Its adherents turned from rational speculations and moral disciplines to the joy of feeling God's Spirit present in the human spirit. A mystic ecstasy above all reason carried the Montanists away until they believed that somehow they and the Holy Spirit were one. Then the rational judgment of the church reasserted itself. From the Gnostics, the church learned a new lesson in the importance of philosophical thought and moral idealism; from the Montanists, she learned the need of vital emotional life if religion is not to become arid. Gnostics and Montanists thus showed religion in the process of self-criticism; and there developed as a result of this critical process in later thinkers, such as Irenaeus, Clement, and Origen, ideas on a much truer and more adequate level.

It is not necessary to accumulate further evidence. The student of the history of past and present religious life and thought will find countless other instances of the rise of extreme tendencies in religion, each of which has some justification as a criticism of unsatisfactory conditions, but each of which in turn has to be criticized by the religious consciousness.

One aim of this chapter has been to show that religion is not, as is sometimes supposed, a static tradition. Rather, religion is a developing process of self-criticism, what Hegel calls a dialectical movement. The purpose of religion—that of coöperation with the source of the highest values in the universe—is one which, by its very nature, can never be attained in finite time, and which requires every religious believer to criticize all of the actual achievements of religion in himself and in others.

BIBLIOGRAPHICAL NOTE

Since the subject of this chapter has received no extended discussion in the literature of philosophy of religion as far as the author knows, the student's reading will have to be confined to the primary sources—which is no misfortune.

Illustrations of the internal criticism of religion are abundant in the Bible, especially in Amos (760–750 B.C.), Isaiah (740–701 B.C.), Jeremiah (626–586ff., B.C.), Mt. 5–7 (spoken about A.D. 28, written about A.D. 80), and Galatians (A.D. 52). *The Gospel of Buddha,* edited by Paul Carus, gives Buddhistic writings from many periods; it has been used as a textbook by Buddhists in the Orient, and contains evidence of the criticism of Hinduism by Buddha (624–543 B.C.?). Various translations of the Koran are available; one should be consulted for the religious criticism of Mohammed (A.D. 578–632). Among the Greeks, Xenophanes was the first internal critic of religion. His extant writings may be found in Burnet's *Early Greek Philosophy* (1926) or in Bakewell's source book.

Some light on the problem may be found in Brightman's "Dialectical Tensions in the Christian Idea and Experience of God," in the *Seminar Quarterly,* 6(1937), 7–18, 18–21.

SIXTEEN

EXTERNAL CRITICISMS OF RELIGION

§ 1. The Meaning and Value of External Criticism

IN the previous chapter the internal criticism of religion was discussed and the difference between internal and external criticism was to some extent explained. Internal criticism is that which may discover inconsistencies or inadequacies within a given system; it shows that if the postulates on which the system rests be accepted, certain aspects of the system must be modified in order to agree with those postulates. External criticism, on the other hand, takes its stand without the system and challenges the very postulates on which the system rests. It would be a serious internal defect in plane geometry if a proposition were introduced involving three dimensions. To note this defect would be internal criticism. On the other hand, a person who needed to know about the properties of three-dimensional space might well offer an external criticism of a consistent plane geometry, to the effect that his interest was not in planes but in solids and that plane geometry as a whole was therefore insufficient for his needs.

Internal criticism is more fundamental than external criticism. If a system cannot be made coherent within itself, then it must be false. It must be internally coherent before external criticism is needed or is profitable. Without grasping the internal coherence of a system, no critic can know clearly what he is criticizing. Many critics of religion suffer from this defect and attack religion for beliefs which are rejected by most religious thinkers today and which in no case are essential to religion. The external critic must first be an internal critic unless he is to be a mere partisan propagandist for an opposing view.

From this it should not be inferred that internal criticism is all good and external criticism all bad. The principles of coherence and synopsis, which logic and sound method require for exploring the truth about experience, prevent us from separating any area of experience from the rest and treating it independently. We have a perfect right to stake out the domain of religion, to investigate it, and to develop its internal meaning and coherence. But we have no right to stop at that point and proclaim that we have now found the truth about religion merely because we have been able to tell a straight story about what religion appears to its adherents to be. External criticism is necessary. The claims of religion must be subjected to the scrutiny of the claims of other types of experience, such as the aesthetic, the moral, and the scientific. Furthermore, the beliefs of religion, as faith, are (intellectually considered) hypotheses. An hypothesis proposes a possible explanation of experienced facts. No hypothesis can be called proven until it is shown to be the best possible one. Obviously ideal proof therefore requires the examination of all possible hypotheses, preliminary to the determination of the best.

To summarize: the great tasks of external criticism are, first, to point out areas of experience which have not been included in the realm under investigation (in our case, religion) and, secondly, to suggest alternative hypotheses for the explanation of the facts. The first of these tasks has in the main already been performed in the course of our previous discussions. We have at least touched on the great problems involved in the relations of religious values to other values, and of values to evils; but we have not laid sufficient stress on alternative explanations. In finite time it would not be possible to exhaust all possibilities of thought, and a book like the present one cannot aim at completeness. The present chapter will not be so much concerned with the alternatives furnished by competing types of philosophy (which have already been considered incidentally) as with the attempts of external criticism to discredit religion by nonreligious explanations of religious experiences.

The external critic of religion, if he believes religion to be essentially erroneous, thinks of the religious man much as a psychiatrist thinks of the victim of delirium tremens, who sees snakes. The snakes seem real and altogether too coherent to the victim from the standpoint of such internal criticism as he can offer; but the external critic, the healthy-minded psychiatrist, perceives that the snakes are all hallucinations caused by a diseased physiological condition of the patient. The patient's problem is: The snakes are real, and how can I escape them? The psychiatrist's problem is: How can I cure the patient of the delusion that there are any snakes at all? This somewhat unpleasant illustration shows the imperative need of external criticism as the sole treatment in certain abnormal cases. There are some who regard religious beliefs as being in this same category. We shall proceed to examine their main contentions.

§ 2. RELIGION AS OUTGROWTH OF FEAR

An ancient external criticism of religion is that religion originated in fear and is therefore an attitude unworthy of man. Epicurus (341–270 B.C.) and after him Lucretius (99–55 B.C.) were perfectly willing (for reasons unrelated to their materialistic metaphysics) to admit that gods exist and live a life of ease in the interstellar spaces. But the existence of gods is one thing, and religion is another. The Epicurean School tolerated gods, but viewed religion as something evil. As Lucretius put it:

When man's life lay for all to see foully grovelling upon the ground, crushed beneath the weight of religion, . . . a man of Greece was the first that dared to uplift mortal eyes against her.[1]

Lucretius continued with a description of the courage of Epicurus against religious intimidations:

Neither fables of the gods could quell him, nor thunderbolts, nor heaven with menacing roar, nay all the more they goaded the eager courage of his soul. (I, 68–70)

The aim of the religious is "fortunasque tuas omnis turbare timori" (I, 106), "to confound all your fortunes with fear." Prometheus, Lucretius, and Nietzsche are all figures that embody man's refusal to cringe, and his heroic assertion of human right against any conceivable superhuman might.

Religious believers assert that man's experiences of value are signs of the presence in the universe of an axiogenetic power, friendly to man, with which man can coöperate. Epicureans start from the same facts, but offer an alternative hypothesis, namely, that the pursuit of religious values is due to man's fear of a malevolent divine power which really does not exist. The world is not the work of gods, but of unconscious atoms; and such gods as there are live in a state of indifference to man.

No one can doubt that the hypothesis of Epicurus (with or without his happy gods) is a conceivable one and that

[1] This and other citations from Lucretius, *De rerum natura*, are from the translation by W. H. D. Rouse in the Loeb Classical Library. The above is from I, 62–66.

there is some ground for it. Some religion is based on fear. The hells of most religions are proof enough of this thesis. But it is far from certain that the presence of fear as an element in religion constitutes evidence against religion in favor of the antireligious alternative. Anyone who could live in this world of storms, disease germs, hereditary ills, insanity, earthquakes, lightning, wild beasts, insects, and human crime without any feelings of fear would surely be abnormal. Military experts testify that there is no normal soldier who does not feel fear; the hero is he who, being afraid, still goes ahead. Fear is both normal and intelligent, and any true philosophy or religion must take account of the fearful aspects of man's world.

Natural as fear is, fear alone is not religious and can never be religious. In so far as religious believers come to be entirely dominated by fear in their attitude toward God, they have ceased to be religious; they are merely terrorized victims of power. Fear is not religious unless it is fear of goodness and justice. A cosmic power is not God merely because it inspires fear; it is God only if it embodies true values—goodness, beauty, truth, and holiness. It may well be that weak and sinful man may tremble with fear in the presence of perfect goodness; such fear is a religious fear. But it is religious not because it is fear but because it is in the presence of perfect and eternal goodness. The highest levels of religion, moreover, remove all empirical basis whatever from the external criticism of Lucretius. The keynote of such religion is "Fear not." Whether one reads the Bhagavad Gita or the New Testament, the same idea is found: "Perfect love casteth out fear." [2]

It may be added that even if the Epicureans were right about the origin of religion in fear, they would have proved nothing about religion as a mature experience. Every hu-

<hr />

[2] 1 Jn. 4:18.

man being was once an infant—Alexander the Great and Buddha, Jesus and Hitler the Aggrandizer. By contemplating their infancy we can learn little or nothing about these characters. We must observe their growth and development if we are to understand them at all. So is it with religion. If fear was the infancy of religion, contemplation of this fact is unenlightening to the philosopher until he perceives what the infant became as it matured. Perhaps Epicurus and Lucretius were right in seeing that much of the religion of their own times was based on superstitious terror; but they were wrong in failing to consider the nobler and more courageous religion of Socrates, Plato, and the Stoics, of Zoroaster, the Hindus, and the Hebrew prophets. At any rate, we of later times should be most narrow-minded if we were to base our judgment on so limited an area of facts about religion as Epicurus and Lucretius took into account.

§ 3.   Religion as a Rationalization of Desire

The religious believer looks on his beliefs as true, at least as approximations to truth or movements of the spirit in the direction of truth. The modern psychologist who criticizes religion from an external point of view holds that religious beliefs are essentially false because their true nature is concealed from the believer. According to this critic, religion is simply a means of assuring man that his deepest wishes will be satisfied, an assurance which the critic takes to be obviously groundless.

As compared with the Epicurean view, the modern explanation of religion as a rationalization of desire is on a far higher level. To trace religion to fear alone is to distort the facts of experience. To find it the fulfillment of man's deepest wishes is far truer to the facts. Not fear or even submission, but fulfillment of value is the essence of religion. Sigmund Freud sees this when he says:

Critics persist in calling 'deeply religious' a person who confesses to a sense of man's insignificance and impotence in face of the universe, although it is not this feeling that constitutes the essence of religious emotion, but rather the next step, the reaction to it, which seeks a remedy against this feeling.[3]

The three men who have perhaps contributed most to the conception of religion as wish-thinking are Feuerbach, Freud, and Pareto. Ludwig Feuerbach (1804–1872) expressed his views in a series of thirty lectures on "The Essence of Religion" (*Das Wesen der Religion,* 1849). At once more broadly psychological than Lucretius and more consistent in his opposition to religion, Feuerbach taught that God was an imaginary creature of human desire.

Gods [he declares] are the wishes of men, either actualized or represented as real beings. God is nothing but man's drive for happiness, satisfied in imagination. . . . The heathen have different gods from the Christians because they have different wishes.[4]

"The gods," he asserts, "are objects of our striving simply because man wishes to preserve the pleasant and the good, and to avert the unpleasant and the evil." Accordingly, he lays down as his fundamental principle that "theology is anthropology" and "God is nothing but the deified nature of man." [5] The Freudian view is essentially the same as Feuerbach's. Religion, Freud holds, is an illusion "derived from men's wishes." "It would be very nice if there were a God . . . and a future life," he adds, "but at the same time it is very odd that this is all just as we should wish it ourselves." [6] Freud thinks we treat God as personal since it is "natural to man to personify everything that he wishes to

[3] Freud, FI, 57.
[4] Translated by the author from the Kröner Taschenausgabe of Feuerbach's WR, 274 (the 25th lecture).
[5] Feuerbach, WR, 19 (3d lecture).
[6] Freud, FI, 56, 58.

comprehend, in order that later he may control it." [7]   In *Totem and Tabu,* Freud explained the origin of the God-idea as due to the father-complex in the subconscious of every child.   In *The Future of an Illusion,* he traces it to man's helplessness, his need for protection, of which dependence on one's father is but one instance.[8]   Man wishes to develop in a hostile world; hence he assumes that things are as he wishes them to be.

Vilfredo Pareto (1848–1923) is another external critic of religion.   His position is more external to religion than that of Feuerbach and Freud, both of whom remained all their lives intensely interested in a reinterpretation of religion.   Pareto was entirely destitute of sympathy for or interest in religion, except in so far as he discovered religious phenomena to be social facts.   His view, as presented in *The Mind and Society,* may be summarized briefly.[9]   All true knowledge comes through the logico-experimental method of science.   Most so-called knowledge consists of "derivations"—variable elements in nonlogical actions—"derived" from residues, which are constant elements that correspond to sentiments (instincts, sensations, preconceptions, inclinations).   Religion falls in the class of derivations, a subject treated at great length in Vol. III of Pareto's work.   Chapter IX is a biting attack on all religion and all metaphysics, on the ground that they are derived from sentiments rather than from experimentally observed facts.

Thus we find Feuerbach, Freud, and Pareto agreeing that religion is no more than an elaboration of man's desires.   In their view there is some truth, for religion certainly is concerned with man's experiences of value, and valuing is desir-

---

[7] Freud, FI, 38–39.

[8] See Freud, FI, 39–42, and Martin, MR.   Martin says, for example, that "the subject has learned to forgive his own sins, by conceiving of them as having been forgiven by the Father." (192)

[9] See Brightman, "Vilfredo Pareto," in *Religion in Life,* 5(1935–36), 295–303.

ing. If we desired nothing, there would be no religion, and, we may add, no science either. These thinkers have also emphasized the familiar truth that a belief (religious or otherwise) cannot be taken uncritically at its face value. There is more to almost any belief than appears on the surface. It reflects man's total nature (Feuerbach), the influence of subconscious complexes (Freud), and of group interests (Pareto). All of these aspects should be carefully weighed before one arrives at a decision about the truth of a belief. All beliefs, including the scientific ones as well as religious, are in some sense an expression of man's aspirations, his desires, his wishes for what he does not now have. The external critics of religion point to this truth and infer from it that religion is false and illusory.

It is true that religion is in some sense an expression of man's wishes. "Prayer is the soul's sincere desire." From this truth, does it follow, as the external critics of religion urge, that religious beliefs are erroneous? Are they necessarily "rationalizations" rather than reasonable and true interpretations of the meaning of desire?

To hold that whatever is wished for is necessarily false is to hold an absurdity; after all, we wish for food and health and friends and very often we find just the food and health and friends that we wish for. But to hold that whatever is wished for is necessarily true is even more absurd; our wishes are often contradictory, and in many cases utterly impossible of realization. The tendency to wish for the impossible and even for the undesirable is a notorious trait of human nature. One of Anatole France's characters in *The Crime of Sylvestre Bonnard* says: "Beware, my lord! Beware lest stern Heaven hate you enough to hear your prayers!" A world in accordance with all actual human wishes would be a chaos, with no stable order in nature or society, no sense in inner or outer life. As a protest against trusting our uncriticized desires, the work of Feuerbach, Freud, and Pareto is a most useful warning. It teaches critical examination of all the hidden forces which influence belief and of the relations between our desires and our other experiences of reality.

When external critics infer from this warning that religion is false because based on desire, they become involved in internal contradictions. If all beliefs which originate in desire are false, science is as false as religion. Science doubtless originated in and is sustained by a desire for an ordered world of law in which prediction and control are possible. The desire for control is at least as dubious as the desire for goodness. The desire for truth is itself a desire. Without that desire, no experiment would ever be carried on and no discovery made. Hence, if an argument against religion is based on the fallaciousness of all beliefs initiated by desire, and religion collapses, the same argument would drag all science and all truth to destruction. The only truth that could be believed would be a truth that sprang up in the mind without effort, investigation, or curiosity; even the desire to test such a truth would fall under the ban. All such systems as those of Feuerbach, Freud, and Pareto, founded as they are on an earnest desire to solve problems, would have to be rejected, and nothing would be left but a mind not merely disinterested but utterly uninterested and uninteresting.

It is therefore far from self-evident that religion is false because it is an outgrowth of desire. The route of the external critics, which seemed a short and easy way of delivering a *coup de grâce* to religion, turned out to be a suicide lane in which all criticism, all science, and all thought destroys itself. Yet the walk down that lane was profitable, for it revealed the folly of judging religion or science on the basis of one isolated factor, such as desire. To say that we desire an object or an experience is to say nothing at all for or against the reality of the desired object or experience, until we examine the relations of the desire to further evidence.

Nevertheless, this argument has had an influence far beyond its logical merits; and if one asks why this is true one finds it hard to avoid the suggestion that for many people Freudianism and other antireligious views, such as Watsonian behaviorism, may with some plausibility be said to be rationalizations of the desire that religion be not true. But this sort of treatment of a great problem reduces to the childish level of seeing who can wish the harder. The task of philosophy is not to condemn wishes as unreal, or to trust them as divine revelations; it is rather to interpret their meaning for our total experience and for objective reality.

If such interpretation be undertaken, the first step is to note the conflict among human wishes. It is very difficult for anyone to say honestly what his wishes are until he has disciplined his life of desire by self-control and rational idealism. What are man's deepest wishes? Some say power, or self-preservation, or competition, or ambition; some say sex; some say beauty, some imitation; some say that expression of hatred is man's most potent desire; [10] some say race and blood; some say conflict, some peace; some say altruism; some say goodness; some say truth, and some God.[11] In almost every human being all of these desires have been felt at one time or another and many of the most incompatible of them have been felt at the same time. The chief problem of practical living is that of finding some principle of selection among these clashing desires. It is clear that a rational attitude toward desire would not mean the extinction of all desire (unless one is a Buddhist), but rather the choice of a system of coherent desires which support and

[10] In this connection, see W. B. Pillsbury, *The Psychology of Nationalism and Internationalism* (New York: D. Appleton and Company, 1919).

[11] For a good survey of man's complex desires, see M. K. Thomson, *The Springs of Human Action* (New York: D. Appleton and Company, 1927).

sustain each other instead of warring against each other. Such a system [12] must also contain only such desires as are in harmony with the real world, that is, desires which it is reasonable to suppose can be actually realized. The person who finds such a system of desires has not only learned the art of living, but has also solved the central problem of the philosophy of value, which is the heart of philosophy of religion.

To condemn religion as "rationalization of desire" is superficial unless the condemnation of religion is based on an adequate philosophy of desire. One fact alone should give pause to hasty external criticism at this point, namely, the fact that religion lays great stress on the vast difference between the will of God and the will of man. If religion is merely wishful thinking, it is a peculiar form of wishful thinking which disciplines "lower" wishes in the interests of "higher" wishes.

The external critic may still persist with a final argument that even higher wishes are wishes, and that a mere wish is no evidence of truth, be the wish high or low. This argument is valid. But the answer to it is also valid: wishing is not self-evidently erroneous any more than it is self-evidently true. Hence all partial arguments must be referred to the Supreme Court for decision, which in such matters is reason. By reason is meant the coherent interpretation of all experience—a view of experience which is not only self-consistent and inclusive, but also systematic and interrelated. Such desires as belong in the type of system described in the paragraph above are not only coherent with each other but are also coherent with the facts of experience which are there, regardless of our desires. The aim of philosophy of religion is to find such a rational interpretation of our desires as will afford a coherent interpretation of their place in the cosmos.

[12] See the treatment of the dialectic of desire in Chap. VIII.

This book as a whole has attempted to show the chief issues involved in such interpretation. The treatment of the "dialectic of desire" in Chapter VIII, § 7, is especially relevant. In order to clarify the issue, a concluding word is necessary. Throughout the literature of this problem the word rationalization occurs. The word is unfortunate because it seems to identify an irrational procedure with the rational, but it is fixed in usage and will probably survive. It is defined in H. C. Warren's *Dictionary of Psychology* as follows:

The mental process of devising ostensible reasons, to justify an act or opinion which is actually based on other motives or grounds, although this may not be apparent to the rationalizer.

That rationalizing as defined actually takes place is a well-established fact. It is obviously a form of overt or tacit self-deception which is unworthy of any mature person. In so far as psychologists can devise means for the discovery and cure of rationalization they are doing a needed service. Valuable as that service is, it has given rise to a serious abuse, namely, the practice of attempting to discredit any position with which one does not happen to agree, by calling it a rationalization. This procedure has a holy, scientific air; yet it is simply a "scientific" substitute for calling one's opponent by the unholy name of liar. A rationalizer is simply a more or less unconscious liar.

Now, even if a belief uttered by X or Y may be a rationalization of X's or Y's desires, possibly it may be true. The truth of the belief can never be determined merely by examining its relations to the desires of the one who holds it. It can be determined only by examining its relation to established truth and to facts of experience. To try to dispose of religion as a rationalization of desire is at once a manifestation of bad manners and of logical irrelevance. The real test is not rationalization, but rationality. No psychoanalysis will determine whether Plato or Jesus, Saint Augustine or Martin Luther were or were not discoverers of truth. That can be determined only by inspection of the rationality of their beliefs.[13]

§ 4.   RELIGION AS A DEVICE IN THE CLASS STRUGGLE

Some external critics of religion, as we have seen, judge it solely from the standpoint of its relation to fear or desire; others, from that of its relation to the struggle of social classes for power.

According to these last-named critics, it is of subordinate importance to examine religion from within or to consider its claims to truth on rational or empirical grounds. The only vital question centers about its social function, which (so these critics allege) has always been that of a device for keeping the ruling classes in power, and for pacifying the oppressed. This view was hinted at by the poet Lucretius, when he wrote of being "overcome by the terrific utterances of priests" (I, 102). The *terriloqua dicta*—the terrific utterances—were supposedly made terrific for the sake of perpetuating the power of the priests. In most developed ancient religions, the temples were magnificent structures, the sacrifices abundant and of excellent quality, the taxes (tithes) and freewill offerings extensive—all were owned and administered by the priestly class. As a rule the priests were close to the kings and the nobility. What was true of ancient religions has continued to be true of the history of Christianity to a large extent.[14]

For centuries, society was organized about Saint Paul's dictum that "the powers that be are ordained of God" (Ro-

[13] See the brilliant presidential address of Ralph Barton Perry, "The Appeal to Reason." *Phil. Rev.*, 30(1921), 131–169.

[14] David Hume had much the same idea in mind when he spoke of "priestly dogmas, invented on purpose to tame and subdue the rebellious reason of man," in *An Enquiry Concerning Human Understanding*, Sec. XII, Pt. II.

mans 13 1).   The feudal system was devised to give religious sanctions to a social order.   The doctrine of the divine right of kings allied church with state and made the established church sometimes hardly more than an organ of the ruling classes in the state.   The spiritual power of popes did not lead them to abate their temporal power.   Churches became wealthy, made investments, acquired endowments which gave them a vested interest in the perpetuation of the economic order, and welcomed prominent citizens and men of wealth more cordially than ordinary laborers.[15]   In time of war, the church has usually supported the government; in labor troubles, only the exceptional religious leader has taken the part of the exploited laborer against his exploiters.   "Religion is the opium of the people."   The rise of the oppressed classes has often been accompanied by attacks on the prevailing religion.   The Jews in Egypt rejected the religion of their conquerors and sought a new one.   The French Revolution, and the National Socialist and Communist Revolutions of recent times, were all antireligious.   One would be biased if one found in this a proof that revolutions are evil. It might be a sign that religions have often been on the wrong side in the social struggle.

Marx and Engels and the Communists of Soviet Russia have developed most radically the line of thought indicated in the previous paragraph.[16]   The following phrases from

---

[15] This phenomenon began to manifest itself in the first century and aroused the indignation of an early writer. "Ye have regard to him that weareth the fine clothing, and say, Sit thou here in a good place; and ye say to the poor man, Stand thou there, or sit under my footstool. . . . Ye have dishonored the poor man." (See James 2:1–13.)

[16] For a collection of most of the utterances of Marx and Engels against religion see Karl Marx, Friedrich Engels, *Religion ist das Opium des Volks* (Zürich: Ring-Verlag, 1934) (ROV). F. Yaroslavsky, *Religion in the U.S.S.R.* (London: Modern Books, Ltd., 1932) (REL), gives the recent Communist program. Other very informing books are Julius F. Hecker, *Religion and Communism* (London: Chapman and Hall, Ltd., 1933) (RAC), and his *Religion* (London: John Lane the Bodley Head, 1935) (REL). Dr. Hecker had the ad-

Marx-Engels, ROV,[17] will serve to illustrate the view. Since "being determines consciousness" (22), religion is a result of "the means of production of material life." (25) "Changes in religious ideas arise from the class distinctions." (38) "Religion is a cloak for the system of the exploiters." (42) "Religion is a means of stupefying the masses." (44) "The parson is the anointed bloodhound of the earthly police." (47) Yaroslavsky makes "Slaves obey your masters" (REL, 31), the burden of religion. It is not necessary to heap up further illustrations of the view of "dialectical materialism" about religion. The position is clear: religion is a reactionary force, intended to hold the people in submission to their economic and political masters.

What is to be said about the truth of this external criticism of religion? The objective student will admit that most of the charges are founded in fact, but that the view of religion as an instrument in the class struggle, although a partial truth, is so incomplete a picture as to be a distortion of the essential spirit and aim of religion at its best. The greatest religious personalities have almost without exception been on the side of the oppressed and the downtrodden. The Hebrew prophets repeatedly rebuked kings and nobles and men of wealth—"they that pant after the dust of the earth on the head of the poor." (Amos 2:7) When Jesus began his ministry, he read from the prophet Isaiah: "The Spirit of the Lord is upon me because he anointed me to preach good tidings to the poor." (Lk. 4:18) The gospel of Luke

vantage of a combined experience with American Christianity and Russian Communism. The best presentation of the Marxist view for American readers is V. F. Calverton, *The Passing of the Gods* (New York: Charles Scribner's Sons, 1934) (POG). Ex-Bishop William Montgomery Brown's *Communism and Christianism* (Galion: The Bradford-Brown Educational Company, n.d.) is a striking document. An interesting interpretation of Communism itself as a religion is found in E. R. Embree, "Rebirth of Religion in Russia," *Int. Jour. Eth.*, 45(1935), 422-430.

[17] Translated by the author.

is so full of denunciations of the rich and praise of the poor
that it is distressing to some modern Christians. Reference
has already been made to James's plea for the poor man.
Buddha's revolt against the caste system is far more typical
of the true spirit of religion than was the social system
against which he revolted. In Laidler's *A History of Socialist Thought,* the first six chapters deal entirely with religious socialism. The slavery reform was largely a result of
religious protests; and such social evils as war have been attacked more often by Christian and Jewish believers than by
the irreligious.

It is true that those who profess religion have rarely prac-
ticed its loftiest ideals, and that ecclesiastics, statesmen, and
industrialists have often prostituted religion to irreligious
ends. Many who today are bewailing the atheism of the
Soviets have no sincere regard for God; their whole scheme
of life would be utterly disorganized if they were to live
even for one day as if the will of God were a matter of real
concern to them. Despite these abuses and perversions, the
essential teaching of religion in its more developed forms has
been almost invariably on the side of the oppressed. Religion, and especially the Judaeo-Christian religion, has taught
social justice, social coöperation, and respect for every human
personality. The Communist criticism derives its chief force
from ignoring the best forms of religion and the internal
criticisms which religion has directed against its own abuses.
It must be admitted, however, that many antireligious Communists have more regard for social justice than do many
followers of the God of Justice. But the disloyalty of Soviet
Russia to its own best ideals, like the disloyalty of religious
believers, is a tragic fact with which we must reckon. It is
at least possible that the good that there is in Communism
will survive permanently only in so far as it is seen to be part
of the goal toward which God's cosmic will is inviting all

men to strive. At any rate, both Communism and religion should be judged by their best forms, not by their abuses. It is no more just for a Communist to say that religion is merely an instrument in the class struggle than it is for a religious believer to say that Communism is merely an instrument in Russia's struggle for power and imperialist domination. Truth is often betrayed by false friends; but truth cannot be judged by the company she keeps.

§ 5. Origin as Determining Meaning and Value

The three external criticisms just examined have in common the assumption that if the origin of religion can be shown to be unworthy, religion itself is unworthy. If religion comes from fear, it is no better than fear; if from desire, it is a mere empty wish; if from the class struggle, it is a sort of bomb or barricade.

It will be worth our while to assess this principle of criticism briefly. It does not need to be done in great detail, because Borden Parker Bowne has covered the ground repeatedly and adequately in his writings.[18] Two main points break the whole logical force of the theory that the origin of anything determines its meaning and value.

(1) *No developing process* (like our organism, an institution, or a religion) *can possibly be understood by considering its earliest stages.* No study of a life cell would reveal the slightest trace of what that life cell would do, until its behavior and function in the total life of the body is seen. The earliest stages of every process are always elementary and often quite dissimilar to what will grow out of those stages. If religion is to be condemned by humble origin, so too must astronomy be condemned for its growth out of astrology; chemistry for its growth from alchemy; and every human being for his origin in the womb of his mother. The

[18] See especially his *Theism*. His argument really goes back to Hegel.

logic of evaluating a process by its primitive stages is a repudiation of the evolutionary principle. (2) *No living process can be traced to any single and simple origin.* It may be that a single event initiates a long process of development, as planting a seed initiates the growth of the flower. But you cannot explain the flower from the single fact of planting a seed. The growth of a seed into a flower is a constant process of interaction with soil and moisture and sunshine. All of the forces which contribute to the growth of the flower are equally necessary to understanding it. So it is with the growth of religion. Religion is a long process of development, engaging the whole personality of men as individual and social beings in their interaction with their whole environment. It would be quite arbitrary to select one early factor, such as fear, or one constant factor, such as desire or social function, and explain religion in terms of it. But the external criticisms of religion which we have been considering are just such arbitrary selections of single factors out of a living whole. Unless all the factors are considered and the direction of their development investigated, a just understanding cannot be expected to emerge.

§ 6. Religion as Free Play of Imagination

There is a totally different approach to the external criticism of religion which many have felt vaguely, but which George Santayana has expressed most clearly.[19] In a sense, it is unjust to speak of Santayana as an external critic of

---

[19] The writings of Santayana in which his views on religion come best to expression are his *Poems* (New York: Charles Scribner's Sons, 1901) (POE); his *Reason in Religion* (New York: Charles Scribner's Sons, 1905) (RR); his *Scepticism and Animal Faith* (New York: Charles Scribner's Sons, 1923) (SAF); his "Brief History of My Opinions" in Adams and Montague (eds.), *Contemporary American Philosophy* (New York: The Macmillan Company, 1930), II, 239–257, and finally his novel, *The Last Puritan* (New York: Charles Scribner's Sons, 1936) (LP). *The Realm of Essence* (New York: Charles Scribner's Sons, 1927) (RE) should also be consulted.

religion. In his autobiographical note he says that he always sets himself down as a Catholic, and he speaks of religion as "the head and front of everything." (242) Yet his parents "regarded all religion as a work of human imagination" (243), and neither they nor he ever entered into religion either as a true believer or as a genuinely internal critic. In RR, Santayana makes his parental teaching the clue to an appreciative, yet external, criticism of religion. Religion, he there says, "pursues rationality through the imagination." (10) Religion, then, should not be regarded as literal truth. It is not real commerce with a real God; nor has it any insight into the destiny of human souls or societies. It is pure poetry "which never pretends to literal validity." (RR, 11) Viewed as imagination, religion is a supreme value. For Santayana, as he says in his autobiographical sketch, there is no implication "that the works of human imagination are bad. No, I said to myself even as a boy; they are good, they alone are good; and the rest—the whole real world—is ashes in the mouth."

Santayana's is the philosophy of a divided self. His world of existence is utterly severed from his world of value. The real world in which he believes by "animal faith," since he cannot prove it, is the world of matter (SAF). The materialistic world of existence is never "given" in experience; only essences are given, and the joy and meaning of life consist in the manipulation of these essences on the surface of consciousness by the imagination (RE). Religion is thus a magnificent play, which has no bearing on reality but which at least affords escape from its evils.

This criticism, as we have said, is external, in spite of its joy in religious feelings and symbols, for no religion could or should survive which supposed its faith to be pure imagination. There is something realistic about all true religion, something vitally concerned with the actual destiny of values and persons in the cosmos. This entirely escapes Santayana's purely aesthetic mind.

A curious property of Santayana's view is that it is supported by no arguments against the truth of religious beliefs. It consists simply in the setting up of an alternative possibility. It is as though he said, "I have no reason to reject faith in God, yet I cannot believe that he is. But even if he is not, the delight of thinking what life would be if he were is enough for me." The strength of Santayana's view is its honesty. There is no pretense and no ambiguity about it. It appeals to the aesthetic side of man's nature. Religion is a drama. Who must believe a drama to be literal history or biography in order to enjoy it?

Nevertheless, Santayana's view is a most difficult one to think through. If coherence means the rational understanding of systematic connections, then Santayana's is one of the most incoherent of philosophies. For him the realm of essence, revealed in immediate experience, stands in no intelligible relation to the real world of matter. There is nothing about matter, as he conceives it, to make clear its bearing on the pageant of essences. There is no connection between poetry and truth, no relation between values and existence. He grants that experience reveals values; he believes that there is an underlying existence which produces experience. But his whole philosophy depends on maintaining the position that there is no reason for supposing that values reveal any truth about existence, or that existence can offer any understanding of values. In short, he has to maintain that reality cannot be what experience indicates it is—a home of values.

Why does he maintain such a view? His answer is that he trusts to "animal faith," that is, such faith as the animals have when they assume the existence of a material world. He seems to forget that the animals lack the rich experience of values which men have and which leads them to art and to religion. Once, and once only, Santayana speaks of moral faith: ". . . when a man believes in another man's thoughts and feelings, his faith is moral, not animal." (SAF, 221) If Santayana had pursued this clue, moral faith might have led him to a real God and to a coherent philosophy. Animal faith is faith based on our physical experiences; moral faith is faith based on our ideal experiences. Santayana has chosen to enjoy his ideal experiences without faith in them as clues to reality and without even giving a coherent account of their relations to physical experience or the real world.

§ 7. RELIGION AS INCONSISTENT WITH SCIENCE

Socrates was condemned to drink the hemlock in 399 B.C. on charges of "not holding to the gods to which the state holds, and introducing new divinities, and corrupting the youth." [20] Ever since then there has been more or less continuous warfare between the defenders of the *status quo* in religion and the proponents of scientific method. The works of the first great scientific atomist, Democritus (460–370 B.C.), were so thoroughly destroyed by his contemporaries that only a few fragments remain; Plato, the defender of the free scientific method of Socrates, contributed to the censorship which suppressed Democritus by never mentioning his name. In the *Laws,* which represented Plato's mature thought in his old age, Plato advocates the punishment of death for especially incorrigible atheists (909A), although he tolerates those atheists who possess a just character (908B). Some 300 years before Plato's day, a Hebrew reformer, the Deuteronomist (650 B.C.), prescribed the death penalty for all who sought to dissuade Israelites from the worship of Jehovah (Dt. 13:1–

---

[20] Xenophon, *Memorabilia,* I, i, 1. See also Plato's *Apology,* 24BC, which is apparently a less precise wording of the indictment.

18). Neither Plato nor the Deuteronomist took into account the reasons which may have led men to atheism. The legislation contemplated by both the Hebrew and the Greek boded ill for any coming scientific thinker whose conclusions might veer away from orthodoxy.

For many centuries after the great period of the prophetic movement, science was in a state of prolonged infancy and offered no great challenge to religion, although here and there physicians, like Sextus Empiricus (about 200 A.D.) were philosophical skeptics. Meanwhile, Christianity was developing, sometimes in sharp opposition to Greek philosophy and science (Tertullian, the Montanists), sometimes in friendly appreciation of Greek thought (Justin Martyr, Clement, Origen). Greek science had long before become standardized in the writings of Aristotle (384–322 B.C.), and Aristotle had reconciled science with philosophy and theology. The greatest Roman Catholic philosopher and theologian, Thomas Aquinas (1225–1274), created a magnificent system of thought which related Christian doctrine to the teachings of "the philosopher," Aristotle. The conflict of science and religion, so sharp in the Athens of 399 B.C., appeared to have been settled and finally succeeded by an era of good feeling.

Like some other treaties of peace, this one turned out to be only a means to further war. The rise of modern inductive science found religion not only dogmatically formulated, but also officially wedded to the physics, biology, and psychology of Aristotle, and to the astronomy of Ptolemy (150 A.D.), in a unified and sacrosanct system. It is true that certain differences of opinion existed and were tolerated in the Schools, but in the main points agreement was rigidly enforced by the Church. The result is that apologists for religion have for centuries deluded themselves into thinking that they were defending **good** religion when really they were only defending the bad science that had become attached to it. Andrew Dickson White's famous work, *History of the Warfare of Theology with Science* (New York: D. Appleton and Company, 1896), is largely concerned with futile and irrelevant attacks of misguided theologians on science. Hardly any advance in science has failed to meet theological opposition. The Copernican view of astronomy, Harvey's theory of the circulation of the blood, Darwin's evolutionary hypothesis—to mention only a few—were at first bitterly opposed by many, if not by all theologians. Eventually, however, religious leaders have accepted all of these theories and now look back with shame on the past record of religion.

All that has been said thus far seems to indicate that the warfare between science and religion has been a sham battle, and it cannot be denied that much of it has been of that nature. Nevertheless, there are much deeper issues involved than appear on the surface. Two of these are most important.

(1) The progress of *science inevitably undermines the literal authority of the religious scriptures* of all faiths (except perhaps those of Buddhism, which were impregnated with the spirit of scientific positivism), in two ways. On the one hand, science recognizes no authority other than that of experience and reason, and no scripture is immune. On the other hand, all scriptures are influenced by the science of the day in which they were written, and consequently hold as a rule to special creation instead of evolution, to a flat earth instead of a round one, to demonic rather than pathological theories of insanity. When biology, astronomy, geology, and psychology challenge the science of scriptural writers, the religious believer faces the alternative either of rejecting the "cover-to-cover" theory of literal scriptural authority or of rejecting science. The compromise of asserting both and

regarding the contradiction as inexplicable to man but explicable to God is so fatal to the foundations of a rational faith that almost no responsible thinker has the hardihood to defend it.

(2) The deepest clash between science and religion lies in a quite different sphere. The issue of scriptural literalism is serious for some, but has no relation to any really fundamental problem of philosophy. The truly serious issue lies in the *prima facie contradiction between the scientific and the religious view of the world.* Religious believers view reality as expressing or embodying an order of spiritual values. Men of science tend to view reality as a physical system conforming to mechanistic laws. Even when they recognize the presence of consciousness as something nonphysical, they emphasize the dependence of mind on matter and the presence of mechanistic laws in mind. If science is man's only way of knowing truth, and if science proves the real to be physical rather than spiritual, and mechanistic rather than teleological, then science refutes religion.

Since the issue of mechanism as opposed to teleology was discussed in Chapter XII, "The Problem of Human Purpose," it is not necessary at this point to repeat the arguments for and against a purely mechanistic view, or the other arguments for and against the objectivity of spiritual ideals.

It is, however, desirable to make a few remarks about the present state of the problem. There is coming to be fairly general agreement about one central point, namely, that natural science has nothing to say about values. The agreement on this point is well illustrated by two little books which may be selected as representative of the extensive literature on the subject. Professor Michael Pupin edited a book called *Science and Religion* (New York: Charles Scribner's Sons, 1931) which consists of radio talks given by leading British scholars of varying points of view, including

Julian Huxley and Bronislaw Malinowski as religious agnostics, the Rev. C. W. O'Hara, S. J., Samuel Alexander, the realist, the "gloomy" Dean Inge, Sir Arthur S. Eddington (of course), and others. These men all agree in finding that science sheds no light on values, while values are the field of religion. The second book, written by Bertrand Russell, is his *Religion and Science* (New York: Henry Holt and Company, 1935). Lord Russell is definitely hostile to religion, an external critic if ever there was one, who devotes considerable space to attacking views advanced in the Pupin volume. But he, like the writers of that work, agrees that science has "nothing to do with values." (223) [21]

There is, however, less agreement in the inferences drawn from this division of labor. Some, including many practical-minded, unphilosophical scientists, argue that eternal peace henceforth obtains between science and religion, with science confining itself to knowledge of facts and religion to appreciation of values. Others, more tough-minded and assertive, hold with Bertrand Russell that science alone gives truth and that therefore there is no truth about values; values are purely a matter of taste and there is therefore no meaning at all in talking about the truth of religion. A third group, consisting of substantially all philosophers except the positivists and the materialists, holds that there is scientific truth and also truth about values; and that, since both types of truth arise in the same mind and apply to the same uni-

[21] The statement that science has nothing to do with values needs some qualification. On the one hand, scientific knowledge itself is a value, both intrinsic and instrumental. On the other hand, psychology, sociology, and economics, for example, are sciences which describe certain of man's value experiences. All this being granted, it remains true that within its area of scientific description, no science tries to tell whether the facts it describes are good or bad, beautiful or ugly, reverent or irreverent, holy or unholy. The ideal of science is to describe the facts. Strictly speaking, science gives no guidance at all in the evaluation of intrinsic value. It tells us what is, what has been, what can be; it does not tell us what ought to be. Further discussion of the problem is found in Burtt, RAS, and in Koehler, PVWF.

verse, it is necessary to take both religion and science into account in determining our philosophical definition of reality.

Thus the real conflict is not between science and religion, but between a philosophy that excludes religion and one that includes it. The present volume as a whole deals with this conflict.

§ 8. Religious Beliefs as Unverifiable

Closely related to the view that religion is false because inconsistent with science is the view that religious beliefs are false because they are unverifiable. Scientific propositions are based on experiments which are public operations, publicly verifiable. Religious propositions, about God, or prayer, or worship, or immortality, are not similarly verifiable and arrive at no publicly compelling results. Hence, the external critic of religion argues, religious propositions are pure fancy, yielding no truth. This view is held chiefly by philosophers called logical positivists.[22]

The difference in kind between scientific and religious propositions is obvious. The former refer either to purely logical truths or to the phenomena of sense. The latter refer to the experience of ideal values, and to man's relations to other human persons and to God. It is at once evident that if verification means the appearance in consciousness of sense data predicted by the hypothesis under consideration, then verification of religious ideas is impossible. It is also evident that religious phenomena do not behave in accordance with mathematical formulae, as sense data do under experimental conditions.

[22] A clear statement of the logical positivist's position is found in Ayer's chapter on "Critique of Ethics and Theology" in LTL, 149–183. Chap. VI of Russell's RS on "Science and Ethics" presents similar ideas, but less analytically stated. In Dewey's operational method and demand for public verification there is a related conception, although far more friendly to values.

From this shall we infer that religious propositions are entirely unverifiable? The answer to this question is one with which contemporary philosophy is wrestling.[23] The problem of the nature of verification is one of the most important in philosophy, and one of the most fundamental for religion. It is one to which dogmatic answers are especially inappropriate. A few suggestions, however, may shed some light on the problem. (1) *Scientific verification* is more than observation of a sense datum; it *is insight into the coherence between the hypothesis with which the experimenter starts and the results of his experiment.* No observation is a verification unless it is related to the hypothesis which it verifies. In short, a verification is an experience system, containing intellectual and empirical factors. Religious verification is likewise an experience system, with more emphasis on the experience of values and less on the properties of the sense data. Verification, therefore, consists of membership in a coherent experience system, rather than in restriction to sensory data. (2) **All verification rests on postulates which themselves cannot be verified in the positivistic sense,** that is, as sense data. Unless memory, reason, the personal identity of the experimenter, and the purpose of the experiment are granted, no verification can occur. Precisely these presuppositions are also essential to religion, and support its fundamental concepts of personality and purpose. (3) *Scientific hypotheses presuppose objective realities which can be guaranteed by coherent thought but not by sense observation alone.* The existence of the world when we do not perceive it could never be verified by perception, although it is required if science is not to be nonsense, and it is verified by coherent thought. (4) Likewise, *public verification presupposes the existence of many investigators,* all of them observers and

[23] An important work in the field is Reichenbach, *Experience and Prediction.*

thinkers. No sense experience of any one investigator could establish the existence of another investigator, unless his coherent thought interpreted his sense data as signs of the presence of other minds than his own. Verification viewed positivistically leads to solipsism; viewed as coherent interpretation, it leads to a social world.

If these suggestions point to truth, then religious propositions may be verified, although with less certainty than scientific ones. There is no reason why a coherent interpretation which includes both our value experiences and our sense experiences should not be true. Thus, unless verification be reduced to mere awareness of sense data, it is possible to approximate progressively the verification of the idea of God and other value-concepts, such as the religious ideal for society. If any values are regarded as verifiable and if the existence of society is granted, the same principles of verification which established them will, if thought through, render the idea of God tenable. In fact, that idea is better established than the idea of any single value, for it is the idea which coherently systematizes all values and on which lesser values depend.

§ 9. Religion as Providing no Positive Value

A final external criticism of religion remains to be stated. Religion rests on the experience of value, and in particular on the intrinsic value of personality. Bertrand Russell, however, finds human personality of so little worth that he can understand it far better as "a curious accident in a backwater" than as the work of omnipotence (RS, 221–222). If it be true that personality is not a value, or at least not a value worthy of a God, then this argument is devastating. It may be granted that an omnipotent God could do better than he has done in making humanity. In fact, it may be that a finite God could do, and will do, far better than he has yet done. In setting up such a standard as he has, Russell confuses the issue. The issue is not whether man is the highest and noblest creature that a God could ever create. The issue is whether there are signs in man of a reality far better than he is. Do his slight experiences of beauty, his few glimpses of truth, his feeble character and his tragedies, his hopes and his worship, afford evidence of a superhuman source of value? When the question is once put thus, as an internal rather than an external criticism of personality, the answer falls out more favorably to religion. And when Russell is not reminding himself that he is committed to the denial of religion, he, too, is devoted to values which lie beyond the actual achievement of man— values such as freedom, and justice, and social intelligence. The truth of religion is not to be judged by the present moment of man's achievement, but by the direction of his best aspirations.

Bibliographical Note

The greatest external criticism of religion is undoubtedly the classic poem by Lucretius (99 B.C.–A.D. 55), *De rerum natura,* which is best used in the edition of the Loeb Classical Library (Harvard University Press). David Hume's (1711–1776) *Dialogues Concerning Natural Religion* (published posthumously, 1779) are of great importance, and, in the opinion of their latest editor, Norman Kemp Smith, "much more sheerly negative than has generally been held."

In the nineteenth century, Ludwig Feuerbach (1804–1872), a left-wing Hegelian who became a materialist, has expressed acute criticisms in his *Das Wesen der Religion* (1849). George Santayana (1863–   ) is one of the most penetrating recent critics; his fundamental work is in *Reason in Religion* (1905).

Among more recent writings, Freud, FI(1928), has had considerable influence. The best concise statement of external criticism is found in Russell, RS(1935), which is especially interesting because it discusses in some detail the internal criticisms found in Pupin (ed.), SR(1931). Communist external criticism comes to rather mild expression in Hecker, RAC(1933). See also Calverton, PG(1934).

For background reading on the scientific criticism of religion, Koehler, PVWF(1938), is stimulating, although not directly concerned with religion. See also Titius, NUG(1926), an excellent monograph on the relations of science and religion, which unfortunately has not been translated. Barnes, STR(1933), is its analogue in English.

HISTORICAL BIBLIOGRAPHY

This bibliography is a list, in chronological order, of important works in the field of the philosophy of religion. The great classics are here followed by a list of modern writings which are representative of the best that has been written in recent years. The date (or estimated date where exact knowledge is lacking) is that of the first edition of the work mentioned. When an author has written more than one important book in the field, his first work appears under its date, and his later writings follow immediately. Ordinary bibliographical details are here dispensed with. Loeb means the Loeb Classical Library (now published by the Harvard University Press). The abbreviation "ca." means "circa," that is, about or approximately.

Ca. 400 B.C.	Plato, *Euthyphro*. (Loeb.)
	———— (355), *Timaeus*. (Loeb.)
	———— (350), *Laws*. Especially Book X. (Loeb.)
Ca. 330 B.C.	Aristotle, *Metaphysics*. (Oxford or Loeb.)
Ca. 45 B.C.	Cicero, *De natura deorum*. (Loeb.)
	(All dates following are A.D.)
Ca. 55	Lucretius, *De rerum natura*. (Loeb.)
————	St. Paul, Epistle to the Romans.
Ca. 426	St. Augustine, *De civitate dei*.
Ca. 1070	St. Anselm, *Monologium*. (Open Court.)
	———— (Before 1109), *Proslogion*. (Open Court.)
1264	St. Thomas Aquinas, *Summa contra gentiles*.
1534	John Calvin, *Institutes of the Christian Religion*.
1621	Jakob Boehme, *The Signature of all Things*. (Tr., Everyman.)
1641	René Descartes, *Meditationes de prima philosophia*. (Tr., Open Court.)

1677 (posthumous)   Benedictus Spinoza, *Ethica ordine geometrico demonstrata*. (Tr., Bohn Library, Everyman.)

1755   David Hume, *The Natural History of Religion*.

———— (1779, posthumous), *Dialogues concerning Natural Religion*.

1781   Immanuel Kant, *Kritik der reinen Vernunft*. (Tr., N. K. Smith.)

———— (1788), *Kritik der praktischen Vernunft*. (Tr., Abbott.)

———— (1790), *Kritik der Urteilskraft*. (Tr., Meredith.)

———— (1793), *Die Religion innerhalb der Grenzen der blossen Vernunft*. (Tr., Greene and Hudson.)

1799   Friedrich Ernst Daniel Schleiermacher, *Reden über die Religion an die Gebildeten unter ihren Verächtern*.

1832   Georg Wilhelm Friedrich Hegel, *Vorlesungen über die Philosophie der Religion*. (Tr., Speirs and Sanderson.)

1840-1850   Friedrich Wilhelm Joseph von Schelling, *Philosophie der Mythologie und Offenbarung*.

1874   Paul Janet, *Les causes finales*. (Tr., Affleck.)

———— John Stuart Mill, *Three Essays on Religion*. (Posthumous.)

1876   G. J. Romanes (pseud. Physicus), *A Candid Examination of Theism*. (Antitheistic.)

———— (1895, posthumous), *Thoughts on Religion*. (Theistic.)

1878   R. Flint, *Theism*.

1879   B. P. Bowne, *Studies in Theism*.

———— (1887), *Philosophy of Theism*.

———— (1902), *Theism*.

———— A. J. Balfour, *A Defence of Philosophic Doubt*.

——————— (1894), *The Foundations of Belief.*

—— O. Pfleiderer, *Religionsphilosophie.* (Tr., Stewart and Menzies.)

1880 J. Caird, *An Introduction to the Philosophy of Religion.*

1882 Rudolf Hermann Lotze, *Grundzüge der Religionsphilosophie.* (Tr., Ladd.)

1888 J. Martineau, *A Study of Religion.* 2 vols.

—— E. von Hartmann, *Religionsphilosophie.*

1891 F. C. S. Schiller, *Riddles of the Sphinx.*

1893 E. Caird, *The Evolution of Religion.*

—— H. Siebeck, *Lehrbuch der Religionsphilosophie.*

1897 A. Sabatier, *Esquisse d'une philosophie de la religion d'après la psychologie et l'histoire.*

1899 J. Ward, *Naturalism and Agnosticism.* 2 vols.

J. Royce, *The World and the Individual.* 2 vols. (Vol. 2, 1901.)

——————— (1913), *The Problem of Christianity.* 2 vols.

——————— (1911), *The Realm of Ends.*

1901 J. M. E. McTaggart, *Studies in Hegelian Cosmology.*

——————— (1906), *Some Dogmas of Religion.*

—— R. Eucken, *Der Wahrheitsgehalt der Religion.* (Tr., *Truth of Religion.*)

—— H. Höffding, *Religionsphilosophie.* (Tr., 1906.)

1902 W. James, *The Varieties of Religious Experience.*

1905 G. T. Ladd, *Philosophy of Religion.*

1907 E. Troeltsch, "Religionsphilosophie." In *Die Philosophie im Beginn des 20. Jahrhunderts* (ed. Windelband), 423–486.

——————— (1913), *Gesammelte Schriften.* Vol. II.

1908   E. Boutroux, *Science et la religion*. (Tr.)
1912   W. E. Hocking, *The Meaning of God in Human Experience.*
        ———— (1918), *Human Nature and its Remaking.*
——   É. Durkheim, *Les formes élémentaires de la vie religieuse.* (Tr.)
1914   G. Galloway, *Philosophy of Religion.*
1917   R. Otto, *Das Heilige.* (Tr.)
        ———— (1920), *West-östliche Mystik.* (Tr.)
——   A. S. Pringle-Pattison, *The Idea of God in Recent Philosophy.*
1918   W. R. Sorley, *Moral Values and the Idea of God.*
1919   C. C. J. Webb, *God and Personality.*
        ———— (1920), *Divine Personality and Human Life.*
——   D. C. Macintosh, *Theology as an Empirical Science.*
——   B. H. Streeter, and others, *The Spirit.*
        ———— (1926), *Reality.*
1920   S. Alexander, *Space, Time and Deity.* 2 vols.
——   J. B. Pratt, *The Religious Consciousness.*
        ———— (1937), *Personal Realism.*
1921   M. Scheler, *Vom Ewigen im Menschen.*
1923   C. A. Bennett, *A Philosophical Study of Mysticism.*
——   G. H. Joyce, *Principles of Natural Theology.*
1926   J. S. Bixler, *Religion in the Philosophy of William James.*
        ———— (1939), *Religion for Free Minds.*
——   A. Titius, *Natur und Gott.*
——   A. N. Whitehead, *Religion in the Making.*
        ———— (1929), *Process and Reality.*
1927   A. C. Knudson, *The Philosophy of Personalism.*
        ———— (1930), *The Doctrine of God.*

———————— (1933), *The Doctrine of Redemption.*

— H. N. Wieman, *The Wrestle of Religion with Truth.*

————, and W. M. Horton (1938), *The Growth of Religion.*

1928 A. S. Eddington, *The Nature of the Physical World.*

— F. R. Tennant, *Philosophical Theology.* 2 vols.

1929 J. Dewey, *The Quest for Certainty.*

———————— (1934), *A Common Faith.*

1930 A. E. Taylor, *The Faith of a Moralist.* 2 vols.

— E. Brunner, *Gott und Mensch.*

1931 J. Oman, *The Natural and the Supernatural.*

1932 K. Barth, *Die kirchliche Dogmatik.* Vol. I.

— H. Bergson, *Les deux sources de la morale et de la religion.* (Tr.)

1933 E. W. Lyman, *The Meaning and Truth of Religion.*

1934 J. E. Boodin, *God.*

— W. Temple, *Nature, Man, and God.*

— V. F. Calverton, *The Passing of the Gods.*

1935 R. L. Calhoun, *God and the Common Life.*

1938 P. A. Bertocci, *The Empirical Argument for God in Late British Thought.*

1939 H. A. Bosley, *The Quest for Religious Certainty.*

GENERAL BIBLIOGRAPHY

The purpose of this bibliography is twofold. In the first place, it serves as a key to the abbreviations in the text, where books and articles are often referred to by the author's last name, followed by the standard abbreviation, with or without date of publication. For example, the first item below may appear as Allers, PC, or Allers, PC(1931). In the second place, it is a selected list of mostly modern works and articles in the field of the philosophy of religion, many of which are not cited in the text, but are added here to encourage further reading. An alphabetical form is preferred to a classification by subjects. The latter is already available with annotations at the end of each chapter. Under each writer, his works are arranged chronologically.

Note that the abbreviation "tr." means either "translator" or "translated by"; while "ed." means either "edition," "editor," or "edited by." Undesignated Roman numerals refer to volumes, Arabic numerals to pages. Other abbreviations are self-explanatory. Where two dates appear, the one in parentheses is that of the first edition, and the other is the edition referred to.

Allers, Rudolf.—PC
  The Psychology of Character. New York: The Macmillan Company, 1931.
Allport, Gordon W.—PER
  Personality. New York: Henry Holt and Company, 1937.
Ames, Edward Scribner.—Art.(1922)
  "Religious Values and the Practical Absolute." *Int. Jour. Eth.,* 32(1922), 347–366.
———— Art.(1928)
  "Religion and Morality." *Int. Jour. Eth.,* 38(1928), 295–306.
Ayer, Alfred J.—LTL
  Language, Truth and Logic. New York: Oxford University Press, 1936.

Baillie, John.—IR
The Interpretation of Religion. New York: Charles Scribner's Sons, 1928.
————— LE
And the Life Everlasting. New York: Charles' Scribner's Sons, 1933.
————— KG
Knowledge of God. New York: Charles Scribner's Sons, 1939.
—————, and Hugh Martin (eds.).—REV
Revelation. London: Macmillan and Company, Ltd., 1937.
Baker, Rannie Belle.—CLG
The Concept of a Limited God. Washington: Shenandoah Publishing House, 1934.
Ballou, Robert O., Friedrich Spiegelberg, and Horace L. Friess.—BOW
The Bible of the World. New York: The Viking Press, 1939.
Barnes, Ernest William.—STR
Scientific Theory and Religion. New York: The Macmillan Company, 1933.
Barrett, Clifford (ed.).—CIA
Contemporary Idealism in America. New York: The Macmillan Company, 1932.
Barry, William.—TL
The Triumph of Life. New York: Longmans, Green and Co., 1928.
Barton, George A.—AB
Archeology and the Bible. 6th ed. Philadelphia: American Sunday-School·Union, 1933.
————— RW
The Religions of the World. 3d. ed. Chicago: University of Chicago Press, 1929.
Bastide, Roger.—ESR
Eléments de sociologie religieuse. Paris: A. Colin, 1935.
Beck, Lewis W.—Art.(1939)
"The Synoptic Method." *Jour. Phil.*, 36(1939), 337-345.
Bennett, Charles A.—DRK
The Dilemma of Religious Knowledge. New Haven: Yale University Press, 1931.

Bentwich, Norman.—RFI
The Religious Foundations of Internationalism. London:
George Allen and Unwin, Ltd., 1933.
Bergson, Henri.—CE
Creative Evolution. New York: Henry Holt and Company,
1913.
———— TSMR
The Two Sources of Morality and Religion. New York:
Henry Holt and Company, 1935.
Bertocci, Peter Anthony.—EAG
The Empirical Argument for God in Late British Thought.
Cambridge: Harvard University Press, 1938.
Beth, Karl.—EvR
Einführung in die vergleichende Religionsgeschichte. Leip-
zig: B. S. Teubner, 1920.
Bevan, Edwyn.—HWC
The Hope of a World to Come. London: George Allen and
Unwin, Ltd., 1930.
———— SAB
Symbolism and Belief. New York: The Macmillan Company,
1938.
Bixler, Julius Seelye.—Art.(1925)
"Mysticism and the Philosophy of William James." *Int. Jour.
Eth.,* 36(1925), 71–86.
———— RPWJ
Religion in the Philosophy of William James. Boston: Mar-
shall Jones Company, 1926.
———— IPM
Immortality and the Present Mood. Cambridge: Harvard
University Press, 1931.
———— RFM
Religion for Free Minds. New York: Harper and Brothers,
1939.
————, and others.—NRE
The Nature of Religious Experience. New York: Harper and
Brothers, 1937.
Boodin, John Elof.—TR
Truth and Reality. New York: The Macmillan Company,
1911.

—————— GOD
God. New York: The Macmillan Company, 1934.
Boring, Edwin G.—HEP
A History of Experimental Psychology. New York: The Century Co., 1929.
Bosanquet, Bernard.—PIV
The Principle of Individuality and Value. London: Macmillan and Company, Ltd., (1912)1927.
—————— VDI
The Value and Destiny of the Individual. London: Macmillan and Company, Ltd., 1913.
Bowne, Borden Parker.—ST
Studies in Theism. New York: Phillips and Hunt, 1880.
—————— THE
Theism. New York: The American Book Company, 1902.
—————— PER
Personalism. Boston: Houghton Mifflin Company, 1908.
—————— SC
Studies in Christianity. Boston: Houghton Mifflin Company, 1909.
—————— KS
Kant and Spencer. Boston: Houghton Mifflin Company, 1912.
Braden, Charles S.—MTWR
Modern Tendencies in World Religions. New York: The Macmillan Company, 1933.
—————— (ed.).—VAR
Varieties of American Religion. Chicago: Willett, Clark and Company, 1936.
Bradley, F. H.—AR
Appearance and Reality. London: Swan, Sonnenschein & Co., Lim., (1893)1906.
—————— ETR
Essays on Truth and Reality. Oxford: At the Clarendon Press, 1914.
Bridgman, Percy Williams.—LMP
The Logic of Modern Physics. New York: The Macmillan Company, 1927.
Brightman, Edgar Sheffield.—SH
The Sources of the Hexateuch. New York: The Abingdon Press, 1918.

———— Art.(1919)
"The Lisbon Earthquake: A Study in Religious Valuation."
Am. Jour. Theol., 23(1919), 500–518.
———— ITP
An Introduction to Philosophy. New York: Henry Holt and
Co., 1925.
———— RV
Religious Values. New York: The Abingdon Press, 1925.
———— IPKI
Immortality in Post-Kantian Idealism. Cambridge: Harvard
University Press, 1925.
———— PG
The Problem of God. New York: The Abingdon Press, 1930.
———— Art.(1931)
"The Dialectical Unity of Consciousness and the Metaphysics
of Religion." In Ryle (ed.), P7IC, 70–77.
———— Art.(1932) [1]
"A Temporalist View of God." *Jour. Rel.*, 12(1932),
545–555.
———— Art.(1932) [2]
"The Given and its Critics." *Religion in Life*, 1(1932), 134–
145.
———— Art.(1932) [3]
"The Finite Self." In Barrett (ed.), CIA, 171–195.
———— ML
Moral Laws. New York: The Abingdon Press, 1933.
———— Art.(1933)
"Dogma, Dogma, Who's Got the Dogma?" *Religion in Life*,
2(1933), 553–562.
———— PR
Personality and Religion. New York: The Abingdon Press,
1934.
———— Art.(1937)
"An Empirical Approach to God." *Phil. Rev.*, 46(1937), 147–
169.
———— Art.(1938)
"The Presuppositions of Experiment." *Personalist*, 19(1938),
136–143.
———— Art.(1939)
"What is Personality?" *Personalist*, 20(1939), 129–138.

————— (ed.).—P6IC
Proceedings of the Sixth International Congress of Philosophy.
New York: Longmans, Green and Co., 1927.
Brown, Charles R.—LA
Living Again. Cambridge: Harvard University Press,
1922.
Brunner, Emil.—PR
The Philosophy of Religion. New York: Charles Scribner's
Sons, (Ger. 1927)1937.
Burnet, John.—EGP
Early Greek Philosophy. London: A. & C. Black, Ltd., (1892)
1920.
Burnham, James, and P. E. Wheelwright.—IPA
Introduction to Philosophical Analysis. New York: Henry
Holt and Company, 1932.
Burton, Marion LeRoy.—POE
The Problem of Evil. Chicago: The Open Court Publishing
Company, 1909.
Burtt, Edwin A.—RAS
Religion in an Age of Science. New York: Frederick A.
Stokes Co., 1929.
————— TRP
Types of Religious Philosophy. New York: Harper and
Brothers, 1939.

Calkins, Mary Whiton.—ITP
An Introduction to Psychology. New York: The Macmillan
Company, (1901)1908.
————— FBP
A First Book in Psychology. 4th rev. ed. New York: The
Macmillan Company, (1909)1921.
————— PPP
Persistent Problems of Philosophy. 5th ed. New York: The
Macmillan Company, (1907)1925.
Calverton, V. F.—PG
The Passing of the Gods. New York: Charles Scribner's
Sons, 1934.
Carpenter, Edward.—PCC
Pagan and Christian Creeds. New York: Harcourt, Brace,
and Howe, 1920.

Carpenter, J. Estil.—CR
Comparative Religion. New York: Henry Holt and Company, n.d.

Carus, Paul.—GB
Gospel of Buddha. Chicago: Open Court Publishing Company, 1904.

Cave, Sydney.—LRE
An Introduction to the Study of Some Living Religions of the East. London: Duckworth, 1921.

Cell, George Croft.—RJW
The Rediscovery of John Wesley. New York: Henry Holt and Company, 1935.

Chase, Stuart.—TW
The Tyranny of Words. New York: Harcourt Brace and Company, 1938.

Clark, Elmer T.—PRA
The Psychology of Religious Awakening. New York: The Macmillan Company, 1929.

Clemen, Carl.—RE
Religionsgeschichte Europas. Heidelberg: C. Winter, 1926.

Clutton-Brock, A.—UB
The Ultimate Belief. London: Constable and Company, Ltd., 1920.

Coe, George Albert.—PR
The Psychology of Religion. Chicago: The University of Chicago Press, 1916.

Cohen, Morris R.—RAN
Reason and Nature. New York: Harcourt, Brace and Company, 1931.

Cohn, Jonas.—WW
Wertwissenschaft. 3 vols. Stuttgart: Fr. Frommanns Verlag, 1932.

Cohon, Beryl D.—PRO
The Prophets. New York: Charles Scribner's Sons, 1939.

Commager, Henry Steele.—TP
Theodore Parker. Boston: Little, Brown, and Company, 1936.

Conklin, Edmund S.—PRA
The Psychology of Religious Adjustment. New York: The Macmillan Company, 1929.

C.O.P.E.C. Commission.—HIS
Historical Illustrations of the Social Effects of Christianity.
London: Longmans, Green and Co., Ltd., 1924.
Coulter, John M. and Merle C.—WERM
Where Evolution and Religion Meet. New York: The Macmillan Company, 1924.
Creighton, James Edwin.—SSP
Studies in Speculative Philosophy. New York: The Macmillan Company, 1925.
Cross, F. Leslie.—RRS
Religion and the Reign of Science. New York: Longmans, Green and Co., 1930.

Demos, Raphael.—POP
The Philosophy of Plato. New York: Charles Scribner's Sons, 1939.
Dessoir, Max (ed.).—PEG
Die Philosophie in ihren Einzelgebieten. Berlin: Verlag Ullstein, 1925.
Dewey, John.—EN
Experience and Nature. Chicago: Open Court Publishing Company, 1925.
————— QC
The Quest for Certainty. New York: Minton Balch and Company, 1929.
————— CF
A Common Faith. New Haven: Yale University Press, 1934.
————— Art.(1936)
"Our Current Religious Problems." *Jour. Phil.,* 33(1936), 324–327.
————— LOG
Logic. New York: Henry Holt and Company, 1938.
Dinsmore, George Allen.—RCAS
Religious Certitude in the Age of Science. Chapel Hill: University of North Carolina Press, 1924.
Dittrich, Ottmar.—LE
Luthers Ethik. Leipzig: Felix Meiner, 1930.
Dixon, W. Macneile.—HS
The Human Situation. New York: Longmans, Green and Co., 1937.

Drake, Durant.—Art.(1916)
"May Belief Outstrip Evidence?" *Int. Jour. Eth.,* 26(1916),
414–419.

———— PR
Problems of Religion. Boston: Houghton Mifflin Company,
1916.

Dresser, Horatio W.—PR
Outlines of the Psychology of Religion. New York: Thomas
Y. Crowell Company, 1929.

Durkheim, Emile.—EFRL
The Elementary Forms of the Religious Life. London:
George Allen & Unwin, Ltd., 1915.

Eddington, Arthur Stanley.—SUW
Science and the Unseen World. New York: The Macmillan
Company, 1929.

———— PPS
The Philosophy of Physical Science. New York: The Macmillan Company, 1939.

Einstein, Albert, and Leopold Infeld.—EOP
The Evolution of Physics. New York: Simon and Schuster,
1938.

Ellis, Havelock.—DL
The Dance of Life. Boston: Houghton Mifflin Company, 1923.

Embree, Edwin R.—Art.(1935)
"Rebirth of Religion in Russia." *Int. Jour. Eth.,* 45(1935),
422–430.

Encyclopaedia Britannica.—EB
The 14th ed. 23 vols. and Index Vol. London: The Encyclopaedia Britannica Company, 1937.

Encyclopaedia of Religion and Ethics (ed., J. Hastings).—ERE
12 vols. and Index Vol. New York: Charles Scribner's Sons,
1908–1927.

Encyclopaedia of the Social Sciences (ed., Edwin R. A. Seligman).—ESS
15 vols. and Index Vol. New York: The Macmillan Company, 1935.

England, F.E.—VRE
The Validity of Religious Experience. New York: Harper
and Brothers, 1938.

Everett, Walter Goodnow.—MV
Moral Values. New York: Henry Holt and Company, 1918.

Fadiman, Clifton (ed.).—IB
I Believe. New York: Simon and Schuster, 1939.
Ferm, Vergilius.—FCRP
First Chapters in Religious Philosophy. New York: Round
Table Press, Inc., 1937.
Ferré, Nels F.S.—SCMT
Swedish Contributions to Modern Theology. New York:
Harper and Brothers, 1939.
Feuerbach, Ludwig.—WdC
Das Wesen des Christentums. Leipzig: Druck und Verlag
von Philipp Reclam jun., (1841)1904.
————— WR
Das Wesen der Religion. Stuttgart, A. Kröner, (1845)1938.
Fichte, Johann Gottlieb.—SW
Sämmtliche Werke (ed., J.H. Fichte). 8 vols. Berlin: Verlag
von Veit und Comp., 1845-6.
————— RS
Religionsphilosophische Schriften, in Fichte, SW, V.
Flewelling, Ralph Tyler.—PPP
Personalism and the Problems of Philosophy. New York:
The Methodist Book Concern, 1915.
————— RIF
The Reason in Faith. New York: The Abingdon Press, 1924.
————— CP
Creative Personality. New York: The Macmillan Company,
1926.
Flower, J. Cyril.—PR
An Approach to the Psychology of Religion. New York:
Harcourt, Brace and Company, 1927.
Foster, M.B.—Art.(1934)
"The Christian Doctrine of Creation and the Rise of Modern
Natural Science." *Mind,* 43(1934), 446-468.
————— Art.(1935)
"Christian Theology and Modern Science of Nature." *Mind,*
44(1935), 439-466.
Frazer, J. G.—BI
The Belief in Immortality. London: Macmillan and Com-
pany, Ltd., 1913.

Freud, Sigmund.—FI
The Future of an Illusion. New York: Horace Liveright Co.,
1928.
Fries, Jakob Friedrich.—WGA
Wissen, Glaube und Ahndung (ed. Leonard Nelson). Göt-
tingen: Vandenhoeck & Ruprecht, (1865)1905.
———— SM
System der Metaphysik. Heidelberg: bei Christian Friedrich
Winter, 1824.
Friess, Horace L., and Herbert W. Schneider.—RVC
Religion in Various Cultures. New York: Henry Holt and
Company, 1932.
Fuller, B.A.G.—HP
A History of Philosophy. 2 vols. New York: Henry Holt
and Company, 1938.

Galloway, George.—PR
The Philosophy of Religion. New York: Charles Scribner's
Sons, 1914.
———— II
The Idea of Immortality. Edinburgh: T. and T. Clark, 1919.
Garnett, A. Campbell.—IP
Instinct and Personality. London: George Allen and Unwin,
Ltd., 1928.
Geiger, Joseph R.—Art.(1932)
"The Religious Faith and the Will to Know." *Int. Jour. Eth.,*
42(1932), 193–200.
Gilson, Étienne.—RRMA
Reason and Revelation in the Middle Ages. New York:
Charles Scribner's Sons, 1938.
Glasenapp, Helmut von.—Art.(1927)
"Pragmatische Tendenzen in der Religion und Philosophie der
Inder." In Brightman (ed.), P6IC, 102–107.
Gordon, Ruth M.—Art.(1928)
"Has Mysticism a Moral Value?" *Int. Jour. Eth.,* 31(1920),
66–83.
Gottschalk, D.W.—SR
Structure and Reality. New York: The Dial Press, 1937.
Grensted, L.W.—PG
Psychology and God. New York: Longmans, Green and Co.,
1931.

Groos, Karl.—Art.(1931)
"The Problem of Relativism." *Forum Philosophicum,* 1
(1931), 468-473.
Gunn, J. Alexander.—PT
The Problem of Time. London: George Allen and Unwin,
Ltd., 1929.

Halliday, W. F.—PRE
Psychology and Religious Experience. New York: Richard
R. Smith, Inc., 1930.
Harkness, Georgia.—CRT
Conflicts in Religious Thought. New York: Henry Holt and
Company, 1929.
——————— JC
John Calvin: The Man and his Work. New York: Henry
Holt and Company, 1931.
——————— RI
The Recovery of Ideals. New York: Charles Scribner's Sons,
1937.
Hartmann, Eduard von.—AW
Ausgewählte Werke. 13 vols. Leipzig: H. Haacke, 1885–
1901.
——————— KGTR
*Kritische Grundlegung des transcendentalen Realismus: eine
Sichtung und Fortbildung der erkenntnisstheoretischen Prin-
cipien Kant's.* AW, I.
Hartmann, Nicolai.—ETH
Ethics. 3 vols. New York: The Macmillan Company, (Ger.
1926)1932.
Hastings, J.—HDB
Dictionary of the Bible. 4 vols. and Extra Vol. New York:
Charles Scribner's Sons, 1903-1904.
Haydon, Albert Eustace.—MTWR
Modern Trends in World Religions. Chicago: University of
Chicago Press, 1934.
Hecker, Julius F.—RAC
Religion and Communism. London: Chapman and Hall,
Ltd., 1933.
——————— REL
Religion. London: John Lane, 1935.

Hegel, Georg W. Fr.—SW
Sämtliche Werke (ed. Hermann Glockner). Jubiläumsausgabe, 20 vols. Stuttgart: Fr. Frommanns Verlag, 1928.
——— VPR
Vorlesungen über die Philosophie der Religion. Vol. I. In Hegel, SW, XV.
Hegner, Robert.—BFLF
Big Fleas have Little Fleas. Baltimore: Williams & Wilkins Co., 1938.
Heiler, Friedrich.—PRA
Prayer (tr. S. McComb and J. Edgar Park). London: Oxford University Press, (Ger. 1919)1932.
Hickman, Frank S.—IPR
Introduction to the Psychology of Religion. New York: The Abingdon Press, 1926.
Hicks, G. Dawes.—HPFL
Human Personality and Future Life. London: The Lindsey Press, 1934.
Hill, Mabel.—WMW
Wise Men Worship. New York: E. P. Dutton and Company, Inc., 1931.
Hinton, James.—MP
The Mystery of Pain. New York: Michael Kennerley, (1866) 1914.
Hocking, William Ernest.—MGHE
The Meaning of God in Human Experience. New Haven: Yale University Press, 1912.
——— HNR
Human Nature and its Remaking. New Haven: Yale University Press, (1918)1923.
——— Art.(1927)
"Mind and Near-Mind." In Brightman (ed.), P6IC, 203–215.
——— TP
Types of Philosophy. New York: Charles Scribner's Sons, 1929.
Hoernlé, R.F.A.—SCM
Studies in Contemporary Metaphysics. New York: Harcourt, Brace and Howe, 1920.
——— Art.(1927)
" 'Existence' and 'Subsistence' in Contemporary Logic and Epistemology." In Brightman (ed.), P6IC, 261–271.

Höffding, Harald.—PR
The Philosophy of Religion. London: Macmillan and Company, Ltd., (1901)1906.

Holmes, John Haynes.—RR
Rethinking Religion. New York: The Macmillan Company, 1938.

Holt, Edwin B., and others.—NR
The New Realism. New York: The Macmillan Company, 1912.

Hopkins, Edward Washburn.—OER
The Origin and Evolution of Religion. New Haven: Yale University Press, 1923.

Hopkins, Mark.—SR
Science and Religion. Albany: Van Benthuysen, 1856.

Hughes, Percy.—Art.(1936)
"Current Philosophical Problems." *Jour. Phil.,* 33(1936), 212–217.

Hume, Robert Ernest.—WLR
The World's Living Religions. Rev. ed. New York: Charles Scribner's Sons, 1928.

Jacobi, Friedrich Heinrich.—WER
Werke. 6 vols. Leipzig: Gerhard Fleischer d. Jüng., 1812–25.

Jaeger, Werner.—ARI
Aristotle. Oxford: Clarendon Press, (Ger. 1923)1934.

James, William.—VRE
The Varieties of Religious Experience. New York: Longmans, Green and Co., 1902.

———— PRA
Pragmatism. New York: Longmans, Green and Co., 1907.

———— ERE
Essays in Radical Empiricism. London: Longmans, Green and Co., Ltd., 1912.

Jones, E. Stanley.—CHS
Christ and Human Suffering. New York: The Abingdon Press, 1933.

Josey, Charles Conant.—PS
The Psychology of Religion. New York: The Macmillan Company, 1927.

Joyce, George Hayward, S.J.—PNT
Principles of Natural Theology. London: Longmans, Green and Co., Ltd., 1923.

Jung, Carl G.—PT
Psychological Types. New York: Harcourt, Brace and Co., 1926.

————— MMSS
Modern Man in Search of a Soul. New York: Harcourt, Brace and Co., 1934.

————— PR
Psychology and Religion. New Haven: Yale University Press, 1938.

Kant, Immanuel.—CPR (Ger. KrV)
Critique of Pure Reason (tr. N. K. Smith). New York: The Macmillan Company, (A1781, B1787) 1929.

————— MVT
Über das Misslingen aller philosophischen Versuche in der Theodicee. In any edition of Kant's Complete Works. (1791)

————— RLR
Religion within the Limits of Reason Alone (tr. T. M. Greene and H. H. Hudson). Chicago: The Open Court Publishing Company, (Ger. 1793) 1934.

————— OP
Opus Postumum (ed. Artur Buchenau). 2 vols. Berlin: Walter de Gruyter & Co., 1936, 1938.

Karpf, Fay Berger.—ASP
American Social Psychology. New York: McGraw-Hill Book Company, Inc., 1932.

Kaye, Martin.—Art.(1926)
"Is Theism a Help to Social Service?" *Int. Jour. Eth.,* 36 (1926), 290–304.

Kirkpatrick, C.—RHA
Religion in Human Affairs. New York: Wiley and Sons, 1929.

Klein, D.B.—Art.(1930)
"The Psychology of Conscience." *Int. Jour. Eth.,* 40(1930), 246–262.

Knudson, Albert Cornelius.—BLP
The Beacon Lights of Prophecy. New York: Eaton and Mains, 1914.
————— POP
The Philosophy of Personalism. New York: The Abingdon Press, 1927.
————— DG
The Doctrine of God. New York: The Abingdon Press, 1930.
————— DR
The Doctrine of Redemption. New York: The Abingdon Press, 1933.
————— VRE
The Validity of Religious Experience. New York: The Abingdon Press, 1937.
Koehler, Wolfgang.—PVWF
The Place of Value in a World of Facts. New York: The Liveright Corporation, 1938.

Laird, John.—IV
The Idea of Value. Cambridge: Cambridge University Press, 1929.
Lamont, Corliss.—II
Issues of Immortality. New York: Henry Holt and Company, 1932.
————— IOI
The Illusion of Immortality. New York: G.P. Putnam's Sons, 1935.
Laurie, S. S.—SYN
Synthetica: being Meditations Epistemological and Ontological. 2 vols. London: Longmans, Green and Co., Ltd., 1906.
Leighton, Joseph Alexander.—Art.(1918)
"Temporalism and the Christian Doctrine of God." *The Chronicle*, 18(1918), 283–288, 339–344.
————— MC
Man and the Cosmos. New York: D. Appleton and Company, 1922.
Lempp, Otto.—PT
Das Problem der Theodicee. Leipzig: Dürr, 1910.
Leslie, Elmer A.—PTS
The Prophets Tell their Own Story. New York: The Abingdon Press, 1939.

Leuba, James H.—PSR
A Psychological Study of Religion. New York: The Macmillan Company, 1912.
———— BGI
The Belief in God and Immortality. Chicago: The Open Court Publishing Company, 1921.
———— PSM
The Psychology of Religious Mysticism. New York: Harcourt, Brace and Company, 1925.
Lewis, Edwin.—GO
God and Ourselves. New York: The Abingdon Press, 1931.
Lighthall, W. D.—Art.(1926)
"Is Superpersonality the Looked-For Principle?" *Phil. Rev.,* 35(1926), 360–365.
Lippmann, Walter.—PM
A Preface to Morals. New York: The Macmillan Company, 1929.
Lotze, Rudolf Hermann.—MIC
Microcosmus (tr. Hamilton and Jones). 4th ed. New York: Scribner and Welford, 1890.
Lovejoy, Arthur Oncken.—RAD
The Revolt Against Dualism. New York: W. W. Norton and Co., 1930.
———— GCB
The Great Chain of Being. Cambridge: Harvard University Press, 1936.
Lupton, Dilworth.—RSC
Religion Says You Can. Boston: Beacon Press, 1938.
Lyman, Eugene William.—MTR
The Meaning and Truth of Religion. New York: Charles Scribner's Sons, 1933.

MacArthur, Kathleen Walker.—EEJW
The Economic Ethics of John Wesley. New York: The Abingdon Press, 1936.
Macintosh, Douglas Clyde.—PK
The Problem of Knowledge. New York: The Macmillan Company, 1915.
———— TES
Theology as an Empirical Science. New York: The Macmillan Company, 1919.

————— RC
The Reasonableness of Christianity. New York: Charles Scribner's Sons, 1926.
————— and others.—RR
Religious Realism. New York: The Macmillan Company, 1931.
Mackintosh, Hugh Ross.—TMT
Types of Modern Theology. New York: Charles Scribner's Sons, 1937.
MacMurray, John.—SRE
The Structure of Religious Experience. New Haven: Yale University Press, 1936.
Mahoney, C. K.—RM
The Religious Mind. New York: The Macmillan Company, 1927.
Malinowski, Bronislaw.—CCS
Crime and Custom in Savage Society. Harcourt, Brace and Company, 1926.
————— AWP
Argonauts of the Western Pacific. London: George Routledge and Sons, 1932.
Martin, Everett Dean.—MR
The Mystery of Religion. New York: Harper and Brothers, 1924.
Marx, Karl, and Friedrich Engels.—ROV
Religion ist das Opium des Volks. Zürich: Ring-Verlag, 1934.
McConnell, Francis J.—RC
Religious Certainty. New York: Eaton and Mains, 1910.
————— BPB
Borden Parker Bowne. New York: The Abingdon Press, 1929.
————— JW
John Wesley. New York: The Abingdon Press, 1939
McDonald, Duncan Black.—HPG
Hebrew Philosophic Genius. Princeton: Princeton University Press, 1936.
McTaggart, J. M. E.—SDR
Some Dogmas of Religion. London: Edward Arnold, 1906.
Mehring, Franz.—KM
Karl Marx (tr. Fitzgerald). New York: Covici Friede, (Ger., 2nd ed., 1933) 1935.

Menzies, Allan.—HR
History of Religion. New York: Charles Scribner's Sons, 1927.
Montague, William Pepperell.—WK
The Ways of Knowing. New York: The Macmillan Company, 1925.
————— BU
Belief Unbound. New Haven: Yale University Press, 1930.
Moore, George Edward.—PE
Principia Ethica. Cambridge: University Press, (1903)1922.
Moore, George Foot.—HR
History of Religions. 2 vols. New York: Charles Scribner's Sons, 1913, 1919.
————— BGR
The Birth and Growth of Religion. New York: Charles Scribner's Sons, 1930.
Moore, Jared Sparks.—RIU
Rifts in the Universe. New Haven: Yale University Press, 1927.
————— and Herbert Gurnee.—FP
The Foundations of Psychology. Princeton: Princeton University Press, 1933.
Moore, John Morrison.—TRE
Theories of Religious Experience. New York: Round Table Press, Inc., 1939.
More, Paul Elmer.—POD
Pages from an Oxford Diary. Princeton: Princeton University Press, 1937.
Münsterberg, Hugo.—EV
The Eternal Values. Boston: Houghton Mifflin Company, 1909.
Murdock, George Peter.—OPC
Our Primitive Contemporaries. New York: The Macmillan Company, 1934.

Nall, T. Otto (ed.)—VR
Vital Religion. New York: The Methodist Book Concern, 1938.
Needham, Joseph (ed.)—SRR
Science, Religion, and Reality. New York · The Macmillan Company, 1925.

Newton, Joseph Fort (ed.)—MIG
My Idea of God. Boston: Little, Brown, and Company, 1926.
Niebuhr, Helmut Richard.—SSD
The Social Sources of Denominationalism. New York: Henry
Holt and Company, 1929.
Niebuhr, Reinhold.—MMIS
Moral Man and Immoral Society. New York: Charles Scrib-
ner's Sons, 1932.
Nock, Arthur Darby.—CON
Conversion. London: Oxford University Press, 1933.
Oakeley, Hilda D.—Art.(1926)
"The Religious Element in Plato's Philosophy." *Int. Jour. Eth.,*
37(1926), 67–80.
Otto, Rudolf.—IH   [1926.]
The Idea of the Holy. New York: Oxford University Press,

Pareto, Vilfredo.—MS
The Mind and Society (tr. Arthur Livingston). 4 vols.
New York: Harcourt, Brace and Company, 1935.
Patrick, George Thomas White.—ITP
Introduction to Philosophy. Boston: Houghton Mifflin Com-
pany, 1924.
Perry, Ralph Barton.—AP
The Approach to Philosophy. New York: Charles Scribner's
Sons, 1905.
———————— PPT
Present Philosophical Tendencies. New York: Longmans,
Green and Co., 1912.
———————— PCI
Present Conflict of Ideals. New York: Longmans, Green and
Co., 1918.
———————— GTV
General Theory of Value. New York: Longmans, Green and
Co., 1926.
———————— Art.(1932)
"Religion versus Morality According to the Elder Henry
James." *Int. Jour. Eth.,* 42 (1932), 289–303.
———————— TCWJ
The Thought and Character of William James. 2 vols. Bos-
ton: Little, Brown, and Company, 1935.

Pfleiderer, Otto.—GRP
Geschichte der Religionsphilosophie von Spinoza bis auf die Gegenwart. 3d ed. Berlin: Reimer, 1893.
Picard, Maurice.—VIC
Values, Immediate and Contributory. New York: New York University Press, 1920.
Poincaré, Henri.—FS
The Foundations of Science. New York: The Science Press, 1913.
Potter, Charles Francis.—SR
The Story of Religion. New York: Simon and Schuster, 1929.
Pratt, Carroll C.—LMP
The Logic of Modern Psychology. New York: The Macmillan Company, 1939.
Pratt, James Bissett.—RC
The Religious Consciousness. New York: The Macmillan Company, 1923.
———— MS
Matter and Spirit. New York: The Macmillan Company, 1922.
———— PR
Personal Realism. New York: The Macmillan Company, 1937.
Pringle-Pattison, A. S.—IGRP
The Idea of God in the Light of Recent Philosophy. New York: Oxford University Press, 1917.
———— II
The Idea of Immortality. Oxford: Clarendon Press, 1922.
Pupin, Michael (ed.).—SR
Science and Religion. New York: Charles Scribner's Sons, 1931.

Radin, Paul.—PR
Primitive Religions. New York: Viking Press, 1937.
Rauschenbusch, Walter.—TSG
A Theology for the Social Gospel. New York: The Macmillan Company, 1917.
Read, Carveth.—OMS
The Origin of Man and of His Superstitions. Cambridge: University Press, 1920.

Reeman, Edmund H.—NIG
Do We Need a New Idea of God? Philadelphia: Geo. W. Jacobs and Co., 1917.

Reichenbach, Hans.—EAP
Experience and Prediction. Chicago: The University of Chicago Press, 1938.

Reid, John R.—TOV
A Theory of Value. New York: Charles Scribner's Sons, 1938.

Reid, Louis Arnaud.—Art.(1925)
"Religion, Metaphysics, and Practice." *Mind,* 34(1925), 204–216.

Reinach, Salomon.—ORP
Orpheus, a History of Religions (tr. by Florence Simmonds). New York: Liveright, 1932.

Roback, A. A.—BCP
A Bibliography of Character and Personality. Cambridge (Mass.): Sci-Art Publishers, 1927.

Robertson, H. M.—REI
Aspects of the Rise of Economic Individualism. Cambridge: University Press, 1933.

Robinson, D. S.—ILP
An Introduction to Living Philosophy. New York: Thomas Y. Crowell Company, 1932.

Roelofs, Howard Dykema.—Art.(1929)
"The Experimental Method and Religious Beliefs." *Mind,* 38(1929), 184–206.

Rogers, Arthur Kenyon.—EAP
English and American Philosophy since 1800. New York: The Macmillan Company, 1922.

Rowe, Henry Kalloch.—HCP
History of the Christian People. New York: The Macmillan Company, 1931.

Royce, Josiah.—WI
The World and the Individual. 2 vols. New York: The Macmillan Company, 1904.

——————— SRI
The Sources of Religious Insight. New York: Charles Scribner's Sons, 1912.

———— and others.—CG
The Conception of God. New York: The Macmillan Company, 1902.

Rueff, Jacques.—PSS
From the Physical to the Social Sciences. Baltimore: The Johns Hopkins Press, 1929.

Russell, Bertrand.—IMP.
Introduction to Mathematical Philosophy. New York: The Macmillan Company, n.d. (1919?).

———— RS
Religion and Science. New York: Henry Holt and Company, 1935.

Ryle, Gilbert (ed.).—P7IC
Proceedings of the Seventh International Congress of Philosophy. London: Humphrey Milford, 1931.

Santayana, George.—RR
Reason in Religion. New York: Charles Scribner's Sons, (1905)1930.

———— SAF
Scepticism and Animal Faith. New York: Charles Scribner's Sons, 1923.

Schaub, Edward L.—Art.(1927)
"The Psychology of Religion in America." In Smith (ed.), RTLQC, 116–139.

Schelling, Friedrich W. J.—SW
Sämmtliche Werke. 14 vols. Stuttgart und Augsburg: J. G. Cotta'scher Verlag, 1856.

Schiller, F. C. S.—ROS
Riddles of the Sphinx. 3d ed. London: Swan, Sonnenschein and Co., Lim., (1891)1910.

Schilpp, Paul A. (ed.)—PJD
The Philosophy of John Dewey. Evanston: Northwestern University, 1939.

Schleiermacher, Friedrich.—ÜR
Über die Religion. Reden an die Gebildeten unter ihren Verächtern. Berlin: Johann Friedrich Unger, 1799.

———— CG
Der christliche Glaube. 5th ed. 2 vols. Berlin: Georg Reimer, (1821–22)1861.

Schlick, Moritz.—GA
Gesammelte Aufsätze: 1926–1936. Wien: Gerold & Co., 1938.
Schneider, Herbert Wallace.—MS
Meditations in Season. New York: Oxford University Press, 1938.
Selbie, W. B.—PR
The Psychology of Religion. Oxford: Clarendon Press, 1924.
Sellars, Roy Wood.——PR
The Philosophy of Physical Realism. New York: The Macmillan Company, 1938.
Smith, Gerald Birney (ed.).—RTLQC
Religious Thought in the last Quarter-Century. Chicago: The University of Chicago Press, 1927.
Smith, Norman Kemp.—DNR
Hume's Dialogues Concerning Natural Religion. Oxford: Clarendon Press, 1935.
Sneath, Elias Hershey (ed.).—ERR
The Evolution of Ethics as Revealed in the Great Religions. New Haven: Yale University Press, 1927.
Söderblom, Nathan.—ER
Einführung in die Religionsgeschichte. Leipzig: Quelle und Meyer, 1928.
Soper, Edmund Davison.—RM
Religions of Mankind. New York: The Abingdon Press, 1921.
Sorley, W. R.—MVIG
Moral Values and the Idea of God, 2nd ed. Cambridge: University Press, (1918)1921.
Spaulding, E. G.—WOC
A World of Chance. New York: The Macmillan Company, 1936.
Starbuck, Edwin Diller.—PR
The Psychology of Religion. London: Charles Scribner's Sons, 1900.
Stern, William.—WP
Wertphilosophie. Leipzig: Johann Ambrosius Barth, 1924.
Stolz, Karl R.—PRL
The Psychology of Religious Living. Nashville: The Cokesbury Press, 1937.

Strong, Charles Augustus.—ENOM
Essays on the Natural Origin of the Mind. London:
Macmillan and Company, Ltd., 1930.
Strickland, Francis L.—PRE
Psychology of Religious Experience. New York: The Abing-
don Press, 1924,
Swisher, Walter Samuel.—RNP
Religion and the New Psychology. Boston: Marshall Jones
Company, 1920.

Tennant, F. R.—PT
Philosophical Theology. 2 vols. Cambridge: University Press,
1928, 1930.
Thouless, Robert H.—IPR
An Introduction to the Psychology of Religion. New York:
The Macmillan Company, 1923.
Tillich, Paul.—RP
Religionsphilosophie. In Dessoir, PEG(1925), 765–835.
Titius, Arthur.—NUG
Natur und Gott. Göttingen: Vandenhoek und Ruprecht,
1926.
Toy, Crawford Howell.—IHR
Introduction to the History of Religions. Boston: Ginn and
Company, 1913.
Trout, David M.—RB
Religious Behavior. New York: The Macmillan Company,
1931.
Trueblood, D. Elton.—TRE
The Trustworthiness of Religious Experience. London:
George Allen and Unwin, Ltd., 1939.
Tsanoff, Radoslav A.—PI
The Problem of Immortality. New York: The Macmillan
Company, 1924.
——— NE
The Nature of Evil. New York: The Macmillan Company,
1931.

Ulrici, Hermann.—GN
Gott und die Natur. Leipzig: T. O. Weigel, 1875.

Urban, Wilbur Marshall.—VAL
Valuation. New York: The Macmillan Company, 1909.
——— Art.(1938)
"Elements of Unintelligibility in Whitehead's Metaphysics."
Jour. Phil., 35(1938), 617–637.
——— LAR
Language and Reality. London: George Allen and Unwin,
Ltd., 1939.
Vaughan, Wayland F.—GP
General Psychology. Rev. ed. New York: Doubleday, Doran
and Co., (1936)1939.
Wach, Joachim.—ERS
Einführung in die Religionssoziologie. Tübingen: J. C. B.
Mohr, 1931.
Warren, Howard C.—DP
Dictionary of Psychology. Boston: Houghton Mifflin Com-
pany, 1934.
Waterhouse, Eric S.—PRE
The Philosophy of Religious Experience. London: The Ep-
worth Press, 1923.
Webb, C. C. J.—GP
God and Personality. London: Macmillan and Company,
Ltd., 1919.
——— RT
Religion and Theism. New York: Charles Scribner's Sons,
1934.
Weber, Max.—PESC
The Protestant Ethic and the Spirit of Capitalism (tr.
Talcott Parsons). New York: Charles Scribner's Sons, (1905)
1920.
Wells, Herbert George.—GIK
God the Invisible King. New York: M. A. Donohue and Co.,
1917.
——— UF
The Undying Fire. New York: The Macmillan Company,
1919.
Westermarck, Edward.—CM
Christianity and Morals. New York: The Macmillan Com-
pany, 1939.

Whitehead, Alfred North.—SMW
Science and the Modern World. New York: The Macmillan Company, 1925.
———— RM
Religion in the Making. New York: The Macmillan Company, 1926.
———— PR
Process and Reality. New York: The Macmillan Company, 1929.
———— AI
Adventures of Ideas. New York: The Macmillan Company, 1933.
———— MT
Modes of Thought. New York: The Macmillan Company, 1938.
Wieman, Henry Nelson, and Walter Marshall Horton.—GOR
The Growth of Religion. Chicago: Willett, Clark and Company, 1938.
————, Douglas Clyde Macintosh, and Max Carl Otto.—ITG
Is There a God? Chicago: Willett, Clark and Company, 1932.
————, and Bernard Eugene Meland.—APR
American Philosophies of Religion. Chicago: Willett, Clark and Company, 1936.
————, and Regina Westcott-Wieman.—NPR
Normative Psychology of Religion. New York: Thomas Y. Crowell Company, 1935.
Wilm, Emil Carl (ed.).—SPT
Studies in Philosophy and Theology. New York: The Abingdon Press, 1922.
Wilson, John Cook.—SAI
Statement and Inference. 2 vols. Oxford: The Clarendon Press, 1926.
———— Art.(1926)
"Rational Grounds of Belief in God." In Wilson, SAI, II, 835–867.
Wisdom, John.—Art. (1935)
"God and Evil." *Mind*, 44(1935), 1–20.
Woodburne, Angus Stewart.—RA
The Religious Attitude. New York: The Macmillan Company, 1927.

Wright, H. W.—Art.(1928)
"Does the Objective System of Values Imply a Cosmic Intelligence?" *Int. Jour. Eth.*, 38(1928), 284–294.
Wright, William Kelley.—SPR
A Student's Philosophy of Religion. New York: The Macmillan Company, (1922)1935.

Xenophon.—*Mem*.
Memorabilia (tr. E. C. Marchant in Loeb Classical Library). London: William Heinemann, 1922. (Now published by Harvard University Press.)

INDEX

INDEX AND LEXICON

Note: Items in the general Bibliography are omitted from this Index and Lexicon. In general, page references are listed in numerical sequence for each entry. References to sub-items are set off by semicolons.

Abelard, 66

Absolutism: The belief that the universe is an individual whole; also (and usually in the text) the belief that the power of the divine will is unlimited. 147, 219–220; appeal to ignorance, 309–310; argument against, 307–313; argument for, 305–307; ascription of surd evils to divine will, 310–311; cutting of the nerve of moral endeavor, 312; historical sketch of, 283–284; ideas common with theistic finitism, 301–303; tendency to make good and evil indistinguishable, 311–312; theistic, 274, 276–304, 325; versus theistic finitism, 280–283; unempirical character, 313. The Absolute, 122, 220, 236, 267, 297–298, 328

Action, as way of knowing God (pragmatism), 186–189, 192

Adams, G. P., 477 n.

Adler, A., 73

Aesthetics, as a normative science, 12; philosophical science, 20

Agnosticism, 366

Ahriman, 63, 80, 135, 248, 292

Ahura-Mazda, 61, 63, 248

Ainus, of Japan, 32

Alexander the Great, 464

Alexander, H. B., 299

Alexander, S., *Space, Time, and Deity*, 151–153, 214; 198, 211, 271 n., 297 n., 484

Al-Ghazali, 67

"All-Father," 39, 40

Allport, G. W., 72 n., 225 n., 240 and n., 349 n., 353 n., 369 n.

Ambiverts: Those interested in others and in things as well as in themselves and in thought processes. 72

Ames, E. S., 75, 211

Animism, 42–43, 64 n.

Anselm, 207–209

Anthropology, as descriptive science, 11; 19; evolutionary, 39; 465

Anthropomorphism: The tendency to view objective reality as resembling man. 138, 226; argument against a finite God, 328–330; 368

Antinomians: Those who believe themselves justified in disregarding all law. 433 and n.

A priori principle: A principle which is necessary if a specific class of experiences (or objects) in a given universe of discourse is to be possible. 182–186, 191, 416. A priori, 1–7

Apriorism, 1–3; rationalistic, 5; religious, 184–186, 416

Aquinas, Thomas, Saint, 66, 221 n.; *Summa contra Gentiles*, 283–285 n.; 286–287, 325, 451, 481

Aristides, 203

Aristotle, 23, 60, 62; *Metaphysics*, 63 n.; 99, 135, 183 n., 192 n.; *De coelo*, 193; *Physics*, 210 and n., 252 n., 284–286, 294, 299; Pure Form, 306, 325; 308, 314 n., 355, 374, 375, 451, 481

Arius, 66

Arnold, Matthew, definition of God, 136; 185

Aruntas, of Australia, 32, 44–45

Astrology, 11, 37, 153, 476

525

Astronomy, 18; and empirical science, 19, 37; 376, 377, 476, 481
Athanasius, 66
Atheism, 197, 199, 202–203
Auer, J. A. C. Fagginger, 144
Augustine, Saint, 66–67, 69, 110, 179, 255, 275 n., 291, 293; *Confessions*, 312; 420, 421, 447, 472
Aurelius, M., 140 and n.
Avicenna, 451
Axiology: Investigation of values and their relation to existence. 21, 22, 106
Axiogenesis: The development or production of value. 204 n., 217, 230, 372
Axiogenetic: That which develops or produces value. 204 n., 205, 216, 232, 372
Axiosoteria: The preserving of values. 209 n., 217, 230, 372
Ayer, A. J., 29 n., 121 n., 179 n., 271 n., 273 n., 323 n.; *Language, Truth, and Logic,* 396 and n., 485 n.

Babylonians, 46, 50, 449; *Epic of Creation,* 53; *Epic of Gilgamesh,* 53
Bacon, F., 311 and n., 374, 375
Baillie, J., 195 n., 410 n., 416 n., 437 n.
Baker, R. B., 324 n.
Bakewell, C. M., 458 n.
Ballou, R. O., 80 n.
Banning, A., 324 n.
Barnes, E. W., 386 n., 489 n.
Barrett, C., 208 n.
Barth, Karl, 6, 25, 132 n., 145–148; conception of God, 146; 150, 156 n., 162, 173–174, 176, 178, 301, 328, 420, 453, 454. Barthian deity, 256. Barthians, 1, 2, 6, 7, 172, 180, 383, 416
Barton, G. A., 46, 47 n., 49 n., 50 n., 61, 80 n.
Bayle, P., *Dictionaire historique et critique,* 292–293
Beck, L. W., 132 n.
Behana, K. T., 340 n.
Behaviorism, methodological and metaphysical, 212–214; Watsonian, 346, 469; 347
Bennett, J., 24, 195 n., 300
Bentwich, N., 80 n.
Bergson, Henri, 28; as modern theist, 159; *The Two Sources of Morality*

Bergson, Henri (*Cont.*):
and Religion, 159; 198, 297 n., 298–299, 317 n., 386 n.
Berkeley, G., 451
Bertocci, P. A., 29 n., 106 n., 159, 239 n., 300, 323 n., 416 n.
Bevan, E., 80 n., 156 n., 410 n.
Bhagavad Gita, 69, 87, 423, 436 n., 454–456, 463
Bible, criticism of, 23, 24; Code of the Covenant, 436 n.; Decalogue, 436 n., 449; as divine revelation, 23; New Testament, 53, 387, 445–446, 457, 480–481; Old Testament, 48, 66, 402, 420, 462; Sermon on the Mount, 436 n., 445–446, 449, 451; 53, 421, 423, 452, 458 n.
Bibliography, historical, 490–494; general, 495–522
Biology, and empirical science, 19; 409, 481, 482
Bixler, J. S., 29, 148, 195 n.
Blake, W., 170, 434
Boehme, J., 170, 292, 328
Boethius, *De Consolatione Philosophiae,* 292 and n.
Boodin, J. E., 160 and n., 195 n.; definition of God, 299 n.
Boring, E. G., 369 n.
Bosanquet, B., 27, 236, 260 and n., 452 n.
Bowne, B. P., 23, 27, 32 n., 142 n., 159, 161 n., 184–186, 195 n., 206 n., 208 n., 227 n., 231 n., 278 n., 281, 285, 307 and n., 314 n., 317 n., 320, 334 and n.; *Studies in Theism,* 338 n.; 398 n., 437 n., 452, 476 and n.
Bradford, R., 140 n.
Bradley, F. H., 27; *Appearance and Reality,* 236–237; "God and the absolute," 297 and n.–298; 327 and n.
Brahmanism, 58, 110, 112, 135
Breasted, J. H., 54
Bridgman, P. W., 187 n., 213 and n., 414 n.
Brightman, E. S., 12 n., 29 n., 71 n., 90 n., 92 n., 97 n., 107 n., 120 n., 123 n., 127 n., 132 n., 161 n., 164 n., 165 n., 175 n., 186 n., 197 n., 212 n., 215 n., 224 n., 227 n., 231 n., 254 n., 266 n., 269 n., 295 n., 297 n., 299 n.; *The Problem of God,* 300 and n.; 314 n., 322 n., 324 n., 335 n., 337 n., 345 n., 349 n., 355 n., 359 n., 369 n.,

Brightman, E. S. (*Cont.*):
370 n., 379 n., 386 n., 410 n., 413 n.,
422 n., 434 n., 437 n., 447 n., 458 n.,
466 n.
Brown, Bishop W. M., 155 n., 156 n.,
474 n.
Brown, C. R., 401 n., 410
Brown, W. A., 24
Browne, T., 373 n.–374
Browning, R., 262, 389, 405
Brunner, E., 25, 30 n., 132 n., 173–
174 and n., 420, 422 n.
Buddha, rejection of caste system, 54,
58, 79, 446, 475; 59, 60–61, 63,
87, 115, 266, 282, 444, 447, 458 n.,
464. Buddhism, 16, 60, 64 n., 81,
110, 135, 144, 172, 180, 452, 458 n.,
469; Bhakti Marga, 182; Hinayana,
17, 103, 387, 393
Budge, E. A. W., 52 n.
Burnet, J., 458 n.
Burns, C. D., 259 and n.
Burton, M. L., 275 n.
Burtt, E. A., 132 n., 161 n., 484 n.
Bushnell, H., 67
Butler, Bishop, 392

Caird, Edward and John, 27
Calhoun, R. L., 24, 287 n., 300
Calkins, M. W., 220 and n.
Calverton, V. F., definition of religion,
16 n.; 29, 36, 239 n., 474 n., 489 n.
Calvin, John, 6, 145; *Institutes of the
Christian Religion,* 221–222, 281
and n.; 293, 420. Calvinism, 25,
79, 172, 180, 221, 274, 312, 383
Cannibalism, 45
Carpenter, E., 42 n.
Carus, P., 458 n.
Catholicism: The beliefs and practices
of the Roman Catholic Church.
79, 115, 127, 169, 172, 180, 325,
432–433, 445, 449
Cell, G. C., 79 n.
Chemistry: A description of the laws
of the composition and transforma-
tions of substances. 11. An empirical science, 19; 376, 409, 476
Christ, death of, 52, 64; 115, 449
Christian Fathers, 23
Christian Science: The beliefs of Mary
Baker Eddy and her followers. 11,
25, 80, 115; mysticism of, 170; view
of revelation. 172 and n.; 81, 221,
270, 277, 312

Christianity, experimental, 127; as living religion, 64–66; sacred dances
of, 51; 16, 17, 24, 44, 79, 80, 112,
172, 179, 290, 325, 393, 394 n.,
432–433, 435 n., 441–442, 446, 448,
454, 456–457, 472, 475
Church of the Latter Day Saints, 448
Clark, E. T., 68 and n.
Cleanthes, 293 and n., 294
Clement of Alexandria, *Stromata,*
290 n; 451, 457, 481
Clutton-Brock, A., 94
Coe, G. A., 35, 36, 68, 80 n.
Cohen, M. R., 239 n.
Coherence: Systematic consistency of
judgments with each other and with
all the facts of experience. A criterion of religious truth, 126–129, 190;
principle of, 421; as way of knowing
God, 189–193; 353
Cohon, B. D., 56 n.
Commager, H. S., 106 n.
Communism: Social ownership of the
means of production and distribution,
especially as applied in Soviet Russia. 81, 103, 144, 149, 197, 447,
473 and n., 475–476
Comte, A., 36, 75, 76–77; founder of
modern sociology, 143; as positivist,
143–144
Conation, 351–352
Council of Nice, 66
Confucius, 58, 60, 63, 447; Confucianism, 16, 64 n., 115, 393
Consciousness: Awareness of any objects, processes, or relations; synonymous with experience. 232 and n.,
265, 346–353, 355–356, 367, 371–
372, 395, 403
Conversion, psychology of, 67–68; 422–
423
Coöperation, as development of religious experience, 435–436
Cosmology: Investigation of the universe as a whole. 21. Cosmological argument for God, 222, 227
Creighton, J. E., 163 n.
Criterion, of religious truth, 122–129
Criticism, external, of religion, 459–
489; fear, 461–464; history of religion as process of internal, 440–
442; internal, 116–122; internal and
external, 439–440; internal, of religion, 438–458, 459–460; of immoral practices, 445–447; of mere

Criticism (*Cont.*):
traditionalism, 444–445; of the tendency of religion to extremes, 452–458; protest against religious materialism, type of, 447–450; religions of the present as disloyal to the past, 443–444; religions of the present and past as disloyal to the ideal, 444–450; religions of the present as disloyal to spiritual growth, 450–452; value and meaning of external, 459–461

Dance, religious, 51
Darwin, C., 315, 482
Deism: Belief in a God totally other than the world, and not immanent in it. Supernaturalistic, 221–222
Demiurge: Artisan; God who shapes the world out of pre-existing matter, rather than creating it out of nothing. 291 n. Platonic, 291, 299, 339
Democritus, 14, 149–150, 375, 480
Demos, R., 275 n., 287 n., 327 and n.; *The Philosophy of Plato,* 338 and n.–339 and n.
Descartes, 149, 207, 347 n., 451
Desire, for activity (doing), 253; dialectic of, 251–259, 272–273; dissatisfaction with the dialectic of, 257–259; for ideals (planning), 254–255; for other persons (sharing), 253–254; for physical things (having), 253; for pleasure (enjoying), 252–253; for the Supreme Person (worshiping and coöperating), 256–257
Dessoir, M., 174
Dewey, John, 8; definition of religion, 16 n.; 28, 30 n., 77 and n., 79 n., 80 n., 89 n., 126 and n.; *The Quest for Certainty,* 130; *A Common Faith,* 144 and n.; 151, 164 and n., 172 and n., 186 n., 188 and n., 198, 211, 213 n., 214, 254, 271 n., 348 n., 410 n., 413 and n.
Dialectic: The mind's search for completeness and coherence. 251–252. Of desire, 251–259
Dingle, H., 120 n. ·
Diogenes Laertius, 258 n.
Disvalue, 89; evidence against God, 199; 241, 251, 276
Dittrich, O., 311 n.
Dixon, W. M., 330 and n.

Dotterer, R. H., 300 n.
Drake, D., 42 n., 132 n., 386 n.
Dresser, H. W., 71 n.
Driesch, H., 353, 381
Dualism, 332, 366; epistemological, 414 n.
Durkheim, É., *The Elementary Forms of the Religious Life,* 28, 36, 44 n., 76–78

Eddington, A. S., as modern theist, 159 and n.; 484
Edwards, J., 35, 67
Egypt, religion, 46, 49–51, 140, 393, 449; *Egyptian Book of the Dead,* 52
Einstein, A., 14, 386 n.
Élan vital, 298, 318
Embree, E. R., 474 n.
Emergents, 149; emergent evolution, 317 and n.
Emerson, R. W., 419 and n.
Empirical method, 1; justification of, 6–7; objections to, 1–6
Empiricism. "Saving the appearances." 314 n.; 2–4, 7, 193, 349
Engels, F., 143 and n.
England, F. E., 29 n., 163 n., 195 n., 416 n.
Enlightenment, the, 33
Environment, 347 and n.; biological, 359; logical and ideal, 359–360; metaphysical, 359–360; physical, 359; response to, 351–352; social, 359; subconscious, 359 and n.
Epicurus, 193, 289 and n., 290, 294, 461–464
Epiphenomenalism: Consciousness regarded solely as effect, never as cause. 354. 355–356, 360–361
Epistemology: That branch of philosophy which deals with the nature and limits of knowledge. 60 n., 21. Epistemological immediacy, 169; 197, 413
Erigena, 66
Eternity, purpose and, 385–386; 404
Ethics, as a normative science, 12; philosophical science, 20
Everett, W. G., 100, 150, 214; *Moral Values,* 94–95, 107 n.
Evil, 89; analysis of, 244–246; current solutions of problem of, 259–272; as incomplete good, 264–265; as contrast to good, 265–266; empirical argument against belief in a

Evil (*Cont.*):

personal God, 232, 239; instrumental, 241–248; intrinsic, 241–246; moral, 260–261, 266, 279 n.; nonmoral, 261–264, 266, 279 n.; as unknown good, 269–270; unreal, 270–271; really good, 278–279; 276–277, 405–406

Evolution, biological, 332; creative, 317 and n.; emergent, 213, 317 and n.; 315–318, 367

Evolutionism, 335

Experience: Synonymous with consciousness, q. v. Religious experience is any experience of any person taken in its relation to his God. 415. Scientific: As described and explained by the sciences. Nonscientific: All human experience which is not science. 9. *Or,* Field of consciousness. 164. *Or,* Frequent observation and testing, particularly personal observation and testing. 413. *Versus* knowledge, 315 n, 1–7, 163–171; as activity, rational form, and brute fact, 319–321; conscious, 227–228, 403; development of religious, 423–436; foundations of religious, 417–423; immediate, of God, 168–171, 182; James's mystical, 69; meaning of, 412–415; meaning of religious, 415–416; nonscientific and scientific, 8–15; problem of religious, 411–437; religion as, 411–412; sense, 4–5, 124–125, 179; self-, 351–352; validity of religious, 436–437; value, 230–231, 418

Experient: synonym of self, q. v. 346, 348, 414

Exogamy: A practice of totemists forbidding marriage between persons of the same totem. 44

Extroverts: Those especially interested in other persons and in things. 72

Fadiman, C., 161 n.

Faith: (1) Acceptance of revelation; (2) a gift of God; (3) trust or obedience, 179. "Animal," 315–352, 397, 403; as foundation of religious experience, 417; "moral," 404 and n., 480; Santayana's doctrine of animal, 349 n., 414, 479; as way of knowing God, 167, 178–

Faith (*Cont.*):

183; 186, 191, 194, 342, 418, 422–423, 439 n.

Faust, C. H., 35 n.

Ferm, V., 15; definition of religion, 16 n.; 132 n., 300, 304 n., 325 n., 386 n.

Finitism: The belief that the power of God is limited. Argument against, 324–336; argument for, 313–324; in common with theistic absolutism, 301–303; empirical, 314–315; historical sketch of, 286–301; personalistic, 332–333; theistic, 274, 276–304; 366

Feuerbach, L., definition of religion, 16 n.; 76–77, 143–144 and n., 372 n., 466–468; *Das Wesen der Religion,* 465 and n., 487 n.

Fiske, J., 452

Flewelling, R. T., 159, 192 n., 195 n.

Foster, F. H., 299 and n.

Fowler, H. N., 287 n.

France, A., 467

Frazer, J. G., 34, 36, 41 and n., 387 n., 410 n.

Freedom: The experience of choice as self-determined. As emergent trait of personality, 353; moral and nonmoral evils result of, 266–267; problem of, 381–382; 403

Freud, S., 73–75, 464; *The Future of an Illusion,* 465 and n.–466 and n., 487 n.; *Totem and Tabu,* 466; 467–469

Friends, 169, 170; mysticism of, 434

Fries, J. F., 2 n., 94; definition of God, 136 and n.

Friess, H. L., 41 n., 46, 80 n.

Fuller, B. A. G., 63 n.

Fullerton, G. S., 20

Fundamentalism, 25, 175, 178, 412, 422

Galloway, G., 41 n., 42 n., 56, 132 n., 208 n., 227 n., 410 n.

Gandhi, 69, 449

Geisteswissenschaften (sciences of spirit or mind), 211

Gestalt psychology, 357, 376

Gedankenexperiment (experiment of thought), 117

Geology, an empirical science, 19; 482

Gibbon, E., 115

Gillen, F. J., 45

Gilson, É., 123 n., 154 n., 173, 192 n., 195 n., 422 n.

Given, The: Eternal experiences of God not produced by his will. 300, 332–334, 336–339; Controller of, 338, 360; 341, 364–367, 382, 385, 404–405, 407, 423

Glasenapp, H., 127 n.

Gnostics, heresies, 66; 290–291; Gnosticism, 298, 308, 457

God: In general, any object of religious worship. Viewed by the author as a personal consciousness of eternal duration; an eternally active will, which eternally finds and controls The Given within every moment of his eternal experience. 336. All that there is? 218–220; attempts to define, 281–282; conception of, 133–161; conceptions of as revolutionary or evolutionary, 153–157; as cosmic mathematician, 372 and n.–373; definitions of, 136; empirical adequacy of belief in a finite, 321–324; empirical facts as evidence for, 231; evolutionary conception: as conscious mind, immanent both in nature and in values (theism), 157–161; Conserver of persons, 400–404; Conserver of values, 401; fact of evil argument against a personal, 232; faith as way of knowing, 178–182; finite? 305–341; Finite-Infinite Controller of The Given, 336; goodness as argument for immortality, 400–404; as human aspiration for ideal values (humanism), 143–145; human experience only? 207–209; immediate experience of, 168–171; is nature a part of? 216–218; neural basis of consciousness argument against belief in, 232; as objective source and conserver of values, 134–137; one or many? 203–207; a person? 224–236, 362–369; as personified national spirit (henotheism), 138–140; as personified particular value (polytheism), 137–138; problem of belief in, 196–239; as responsible for creation, 331–334; as superhuman and supernatural revealer of values (deistic supernaturalism), 145–147; a superperson? 236–237; as supreme per-

God (Cont.):
sonal creator (monotheism), 140–141; as system of ideal values (impersonal idealism), 147–148; as the tendency of nature to support or produce values (religious naturalism), 148–153; unconscious axiogenesis? 223–224; as the unknowable source of being (agnostic realism), 142–143; ways of knowing, 162–195; as the whole of reality (pantheism), 141–142; wholly other than nature? 220–222

Gods, 47, 55–56, 80, 139, 205, 447–448, 461–462, 465

Goethe, 344, 367

Good: Synonymous with value, except that the former is applied chiefly to moral values, while the latter applies to the moral, the aesthetic, the logical, and the religious alike. 88.   276–277

Good-and-evil, belief in God raises the problem, 240–241; confusion of, 269–270; to be explained away? 277–278; intrinsic and instrumental, 241–248; masterpiece on problem, 275 n.; outcome of processes or entities axiologically neutral, 271–273; philosophical problem of, 250–251; problem of, 240–275; religious problem of, 248–250; summary of possible solutions of problem, 276–277; 332, 343, 385, 417

Gottschalk, D. W., 311 and n.

Great Awakening, The, 35

Greeks, 49, 140; philosophers, 449; religion, 451, 453–454

Grey, R. M., 140 n.

Groos, K., "The Problem of Relativism," 130–131; 194

Halliday, W. F., 230 n.

Hammurabi, Code of, 49, 436 n.

Harkness, G., 145 n., 161 n., 225 n., 300, 325 n., 328 n.

Harnack, A., 65, 290 n.

Hartmann, E., 136, 137 n.

Hartmann, N., 268 n.

Harvey, W., 482

Hastings, J., 34, 49, 423

Heavenly Father, 290

Hebrew, see Jew and Judaism.

Hecker, J. E., 473 n., 489 n.

Hegel, as empiricist, 26–27; 29, 34,

Hegel (*Cont.*):
112, 141, 148, 163 n., 183 n., 184–185, 254, 258 and n., 264, 284, 294, 339, 347 n., 360 n., 440, 458
Hegner, R., 315 and n.
Heiler, F., 51 n.; *Prayer*, 70, 425 n.
Heisenberg, W., 215, 309, 376
Henderson, L. J., 373 n.
Henotheism: The belief that, although there are many gods, only one is to be worshipped, 55–56. Or, God as personified national spirit, 138. 139–140
Heresies, Gnostic, 66; Montanist, 66
Herodotus, 53
Herrmann, W., 176
Hicks, G. D., 410 n.
Hinduism, 16; caste system of, 49; 64 n., 65 n.; mysticism, 170; 172; Bhakti Marga, 182; 270, 325, 432, 445–446, 449, 454, 458 n., 464
Hinton, J., 275 n.
History, as descriptive science, 11; 19; of religion, 33, 36–45; as science of religion, 33
Hobbes, T., 150
Hocking, W. E., definition of religion, 16 n.; 23, 27, 28, 77, 78 n., 80 n., 107 n.; definition of God, 136 and n.; as modern theists, 160 and n.; *The Meaning of God in Human Experience*, 160; 163 n., 195 n., 198, 208 and n., 239 n., 326, 327 and n., 370 n., 416 n., 424
Hoernlé, R. F. A., 224 n., 314 n.
Höffding, H., definition of religion, 16 n.; 27, 42, 86, 106 n., 107 n., 240 n.
Holt, E. B., 164 n., 228 n.
Hook, S., 204 and n.
Hopkins, E. W., 46, 80 n.
Horton, W. M., 24, 29 n.
Howison, G. H., 300 n.
Hügel, Baron von, 432 n.
Humanism: A religious view which identifies God with human aspiration for ideal values. Also: Any emphasis on human values. 143. 103, 144–145, 150, 207–209; agnostic, 274; 383, 422, 454
Hume, David, 26, 33, 59 n., 67, 161, 164 n.; *Dialogues Concerning Natural Religion*, 293 and n.–294, 310; 355, 472 n., 487 n.
Hume, R. E., 46, 64 n.

Huxley, J., 484
Hypotheses, synoptic, 117–119

Ideal: A general concept of any type of experience which we value. 90. Antinomy of the, 255; desire for the, 254–255; functions of, 91; idea of God the highest, 207; as instrumental values, 90–91, 95; relations to existence, 105, 113–114; spiritual, 361–362
Idealism, impersonal: God as the system of ideal values. 147. 148, 232 n.; personal, 414 n.
Ignorance, appeal of theistic absolutism to, 309–310; irrelevance of, 269–270
Iliad, The, 53
Immortality, 17; belief in as extension of experience and purpose, 388–389; conditional, 406–408; crucial argument against: physiological psychology, 395–400; crucial argument for: the goodness of God, 400–404; and problem of good-and-evil, 404–406; problem of human, 387–410; religious belief in, 387–388; religious value of belief in, 409–410; 265, 354, 373, 434, 439 n.; and soul, 47, 54–55; weak arguments, 389–394
Incarnation, 65, 175
Individualism, 58–59
Inge, Dean, 484
Instrumental value: Any fact, whether in my experience or out of it, which tends to produce the experience of intrinsic value. 89. Ideals as, 90–91, 95
Interpretation, method of philosophical, 116–122
Intrinsic value: Whatever is desired or enjoyed for its own sake, as an end in itself. 89. 90, 93, 95–98; uniqueness and coalescence of, 100–102
Introverts: Those especially interested in themselves and in thought processes. 72
Intuition: Immediate insight, not dependent on argument or other experience. As criterion of religious truth, 125
Irenaeus, 457
Islam, 67, 112, 172, 393, 454

Jackson, A. V. Williams, 291 n.
Jacobi, F. H., definition of God, 136
Jaeger, W., 63 n.
Jainism, 58, 63, 81, 134
James, William, 8; definition of religion, 16 n.; 27, 29 n.; 35, 68, 69 and n., 72, 80 n., 102, 126 and n.; definition of God, 136 and n.; 163 n., 168, 169 and n., 171, 186 n., 195 n., 198; *Pragmatism*, 296; 297, 324, 345 n., 348 n., 372, 391, 416 n., 432
Jeans, J., 229, 372 n.
Jesus, 59, 64–65, 85, 87, 127 and n., 180, 182, 261, 282, 290, 325, 394 n., 402, 419, 428, 435, 442, 444–446, 449, 455–457, 464, 472, 474
Jews, 25, 46; Jewish orthodoxy, 325; 432, 441–442, 448, 455, 473, 475, 480
Jones, E. S., 275 n., 449
Jones, R. M., 432 n., 434, 449
Johnson, T. H., 35 n.
Joyce, G. H., 28; 239 n.
Judaism, 16, 17, 64 n., 66, 79, 80 n., 112, 115, 387, 441–442, 446–447, 452, 454, 464, 474
Jung, C. G., 72–75
Justin Martyr, 451, 481

Kagawa, T., 449
Kant, 3 n., 10 n.; definition of religion, 15 n; 23; as apriorist, 26; *Fundamental Principles of the Metaphysic of Morals*, 98; 103, 109, 117; definition of God, 136; 177, 181, 183 n., 189, 192 and n., 210–212, 297 n., 307 and n., 309, 353, 369 n., 373 n., 386 n., 410, 454 n.
Karpf, F. B., 74 n.
Kathenotheism (one-at-a-time-theism): Practice of treating each god in succession as the only one while it is being worshiped. 139 n. 56
Kierkegaard, S., 110, 132 n., 145 and n.
King, H. C., 361 and n.
King, W., *Concerning the Origin of Evil*, 286 n.
Knowledge: Belief (more or less well-grounded) that a referent is as described. 165–166. As certain or as heuristic, 194; knowledge-claims, 165–169, 182

Knudson, A. C., 2 n., 3 n., 24, 25 n., 28, 29 n., 56 n., 61 n., 132 n., 147 n., 159, 163 n., 168, 183 n.; *The Validity of Religious Experience*, 184–186 and n.; 195 n., 227 n., 239 n., 269 n., 274 n., 285 and n., 303 n., 304 n., 309 n., 314 n., 324 n., 326 and n., 331 n., 334 and n., 416 n., 437 n.
Koehler, W., 212 n., 373 n., 489 n.
Koran: The sacred scripture of Mohammedanism. As divine revelation, 23; 67, 436 n., 458 n.

Lactantius, 289 and n.
Ladd, G. T., 27
Laguna, T. de., 412 n.
Laidler, H. W., *A History of Socialist Thought*, 475
Laird, J., 107 n., 370 n.
Lamont, C., *The Illusion of Immortality*, 395 and n., 410 n.
Lamprecht, S. P., 323 and n.
Lang, A., 39 and n.
Lao-tse, 57, 59, 60, 62–63, 69
Laurie, S. S., *Synthetica*, 297
Lavater, J. C., 177
Leibniz, G. W., 260 n., 275 n., 285, 320, 360, 405, 452
Leighton, J. A., 297 n., 386 n.
Lempp, O., 275 n.
Leslie, E. A., 56 n.
Leuba, J. H., 15, 35, 36; *The Psychology of Religious Mysticism*, 69–70 and n.; 80 n., 387 and n.–388; definition of God, 388 n.; 391, 410 n.
Lévy-Bruhl, L., 41 n.
Lewis, C. I., 396 n., 397 n.
Lewis, C. T., 413 n.
Lewis, E., 129–131 and n.
Life, reality of the spiritual, 361–362
Lighthall, W. D., 236 n.
Lippmann, W., 197 n., 325 n.
Locke, J., Essay, Bk. IV, 177, 421.
Loewenberg, J., 117
Logic, as a normative science, 12; symbolic, 197; 409, 421
Lotze, R. H., 27, 159, 206 n., 208 n., 269 n., 288 and n.
Lovejoy, A. O., 164 n., 195 n., 414 n., 437 n.
Lucretius, 43; *De rerum natura*, 43 n., 462 and n.; 149–150, 461, 463–465, 472, 487 n.
Lupton, D., 300 n.

Luther, M., 66, 145, 310–311, 442, 445, 447, 472; Lutherans, 25
Lyman, E. W., 132 n., 161 n., 227 n., 324 n.

MacArthur, K. W., 79 n.
Macintosh, D. C., 29 n., 136 n., 159 n., 161 n., 195 n.; "What has Professor Brightman done to Personalism?" 266–267; 287 n.
Mackintosh, H. R., 132 n., 145 n., 146 n., 299 n., 328 n.
MacMurray, J., 416 n.
Magic, 40–45, 153, 232 n.
Mahavira, 58, 59, 63
Mahayana, 387
Malinowski, B., 41 n., 484
Mana: A name for the power or force by virtue of which it exerts its peculiar effects. 45. 42, 44, 447
Mani (or Manes), 291–292; Manichaeism, 291–294, 298, 308, 324, 328
Marcion, 290–293; Marcionites, 293
Maritain, J., 154 n.
Markham, Edwin, 300
Marvin, W. T., 300
Marx, Karl, 76, 78 and n., 95, 143, 473 and n.; Religion ist das Opium des Volks, 474 and n.
Materialism: The belief that everything is reducible to matter. 148. 149–150, 397–400; protest against religion as type of criticism, 447–450
Mathematics, 197, 342, 409
Matter, 226, 403
Maya, 143, 249, 270
McConnell, F. J., 130, 268 n., 418
McDonald, D. B., 56 n., 61 n.
McDougall, W., 43
McGiffert, A. C., Jr., 419 n.
McTaggart, J. M. E., 28, 198 n., 239 n., 267; Some Dogmas of Religion, 296 and n.; The Nature of Existence, 296–297; 327 and n., 402, 410 n.
Mechanism: A view which explains all events according to causal laws which are not guided or controlled by purpose. 375. Atomistic, 215; limits of, 377–379; problem and definition of, 373–375; relations between teleology and, 382–383; scientific and philosophical, 378–379; stages of thought about, 375–376; validity of, 376–377; 385
Meditation. as a development of reli-

gious experience, 423–424
Mehring, F., 79 n.
Meliorism: The belief that the universe is such that conditions may be improved. 276–277, 280, 340
Menzies, A., 46, 139 n.
Metaphysics: The attempt to give a coherent and rational description of the real. 60 n. Fichtean, 11; 21, 22; philosophy of religion as branch of, 398 n.; 413
Mikado-worship, 48
Mill, J. S., 252; Three Essays on Religion, 295–296
Miller, D. S., 121
Modernism, 175, 178, 412, 422
Moffatt, J., 445
Mohammed, 66, 458 n. Mohammedanism, 16; as living religion, 64, 66–67; 127, 135, 172, 175, 180, 325, 383, 432, 441–442, 447, 452
Monism, epistemological: The view that objects and the experience of them are somehow identical. 414, 415. Outcome of mysticism, 169–171; value, 205
Monotheism: God as supreme personal creator. 140. Empirical fact of monotheistic faith, 140 n.; first case in history, 63 n.; primitive revelation of, 40, 55–56, 137, 140–141, 157, 204, 375, 442
Montague, W. P., 126 n., 168 n., 174 n., 186 n., 195 n.; Belief Unbound, 300
Montanism: A Christian sect of the second century which claimed special experiences of the Holy Spirit. Heresies, 66; 451, 457
Moore, G. E., Principia Ethica, 113, 118 n.
Moore, G. F., 34, 41 n., 45, 49 n., 51 n., 56 and n., 80 n.
Moore, J. M., 29 n., 228 n., 369 n., 416 n.
More, P. E., 327 and n.
Mores: The established customs of any social group. And morality, 47, 53–54
Morgan, L., 149, 317 n., 349 n., 452
Morgan, W., 179 and n., 180
Mormon, Book of, as divine revelation, 23
Mozley, J. K., 285
Müller, F. M., 34, 139 n.

Münsterberg, H., 195 n.
Murdock, G. P., 41 n., 45 n.
Mysticism: Immediate experience of the divine. 61–62. As a development of religious experience, 432–434; James's traits of mystical experience, 69; psychology of, 69–70; theistic, 170–171; 168–171, 363

Nall, T. O., 314 n.
National Socialism, 47, 58, 473
Naturalism, religious: The definition of God as the tendency of nature to support or produce values. 148. Chief traits of naturalism, 149; impersonalistic, 231; metaphysical, 213–214; methodological, 212–213; 150–153, 232 n., 330
Natur and *Geist* (nature and spirit), 212
Nature, Aristotle's definition of, 210; God's relation to, 209–218; a part of God? 216–218; God wholly other than? 220–222
Nature-worship, 48
Naturwissenschaften (natural sciences), 211
Neo-Hegelians, 27
Neo-Platonists: Followers of Plotinus. 23, 289
Nervous system, 232, 346 n., 349, 354 and n., 360, 366–367
Neumann, H., 291 n.
Neutralism: The view that objective reality is neutral as regards value, being neither good nor evil. 273 n. 273–274, 276–278, 280
Newton, Sir Isaac, 309
Newton, J. F., 161 n.
Nietzsche, F., 462
Nirvana, 87, 110–111, 371 n.–372 n., 393
Niven, W. D., 241 n.
Norm: An ideal which is the concept of a true value. 91. As emergent trait of personality, 353; imperative, 352–353; variety of, 205; 363
Norris, C. G., 225 n.

Odyssey, The, 53
O'Hara, C. W., 484
Ontology: Investigation of the nature of being. 21. Ontological argument for God, 208, 227, 295, 306
Optimism, outcome of mysticism, 169–171; 276–277, 279–280, 340

Oracles, Sibylline, 49
Orientation, 1–30
Origen, 451, 457, 481
Orphics, 57
Otto, M. C., 144, 161, 415 n., 416 n.
Otto, R., 2 n., 28, 94 n., 103, 107 n., 141 n., 170 and n.

Pantheism: God as the whole of reality. 141. 147, 157, 204, 218–220, 222, 433
Pareto, V., 465; *The Mind and Society,* 466; 467–468
Parmenides, 141
Particularism, 47–48
Pascal, B., 181
Patterson, R. L., 285
Paul, Saint, 65–67, 80, 113, 140, 166, 180, 260, 290, 362 n., 408 n., 420, 421, 442, 446, 456, 472
Peirce, C. S., 186 n.–187
Pelagius, 66
Perfectibility, 340–341
Perfection, 340–341
Perry, R. B., 88 n., 107 n., 126 n., 228, 271 n., 272 n., 300 n., 311 n., 472 n.
Person: A self that is potentially self-conscious, rational, and ideal. 350. 346, 348; characteristics of, 352–353; divine, 365–369; as purposers, 371–372
Personalism, 231, 314 n., 399
Personality: Sometimes used as synonym of person (q.v.), but more accurately, the essence or quality of being a person. Analytic theory of, 355; definition of, 346–353; and its environment, 358–361; human and divine: differences, 364–369; human and divine: likenesses, 362–364; organic theory of, 357–358; "personalistics," 357; problem of human, 342–369; unity and identity of, 354–358; 407
Pessimism, 276–277, 280, 362
Petronius, 41 and n.
Philo, 293–294
Philosophy: An attempt to discover a coherent and unified definition of the real; *or* an attempt to give a reasoned account of experience as a whole; *or* an attempt to discover the whole truth. 21. Differs from religion, 22; Platonic, 338–339; religion as a problem of, 108–132, 197–201; 344–345, 378–380

Philosophy of religion: An attempt to discover, by rational interpretation of religion and its relations to other types of experience, the truth of religious beliefs and the value of religious attitudes and practices. 22. Or, The experience of interpreting those experiences which we call religious and of relating them to other experiences, as well as to our conception of experience as a whole. 1. As a branch of metaphysics, 22, 398 n.; history of, 26–29; importance of purpose for, 383; as investigation of experience, 198; normative laws of, 12; problem of, 1; 283, 394 n.

Physics: A description of the laws of matter in motion. 11. An empirical science, 19; 342–343, 376, 409, 481

Physiology, 376, 377

Picard, M., 89 n., 107 n.

Pillsbury, W. B., 469 n.

Planck, M., 14

Plato, *Laws*, 228, 480; 230, 275 n., 278, 286; *Phaedo*, 375, 386 n., 410 n.; 442, 451, 464, 472, 480 n., 481; *Philebus*, 287 and n., 288, 338–339; 294, 299, 301, 314 n., 321 n., 327, 341; *Republic*, 53, 288 n.; 59, 60, 62, 99, 106–107 n., 118, 150, 165; *Timaeus*, 23, 288–289, 338–339; 33, 49; "faith," 182 and n.; Forms or Ideas, 136, 147, 320, 337; Platonic Demiurge, 291, 299, 339

Poincaré, H., 194

Plotinus, 141

Polytheism: Belief in many gods. 138. 55–56, 62–63, 137–138, 203–204, 325, 442

Pope, A., 291

Positivism: The theory that knowledge is restricted to scientific observations; usually, rejection of all aspects of experience except sensation. 396. Logical, 1, 4–6, 322 n., 323, 365, 396–397; 143, 400

Pragmatism: The theory that an idea is true if it works or has practical consequences. 127. Pragmatic movement, 186 and n.–189; 126–128

Pratt, J. B., 9, 35, 36; *The Religious Consciousness*, 71; 72, 80 n., 126 n., 131, 227 and n., 325 n., 338 n., 360 n., 368, 369 n.–370 n.

Prayer: A conscious appeal of the soul to God. Of adoration, 427–428; not answered as we desire, 431–432; appeal to natural law, 430–431; as a development of religious experience, 424–432; inconsistent with the goodness of God? 429–430; intercessory, 428–429; petition for forgiveness, 427; petition for personal spiritual values, 426–427; petition for physical things, 425–426; philosophy of, 425; psychology of, 70–71; of thanksgiving and praise, 429; theistic view of, 425

Price, H. H., 120 n., 346 n.

Priests, 49; priestly movement, 46–56

Primitivism, fallacy of, 37–39

Pringle-Pattison, A. S., 27, 161 n., 410 n.

Prophetic movement, 56–58, 62; table of, 57

Prophets, Hebrew, 79, 445, 446, 449, 464, 474

Protestantism, 79, 180

Psychoanalysis, 73–74

Psychology, rational: Investigation of the ultimate nature of human consciousness and its relations to body and world. 21. Associationist, 355; comparative, 350; of conversion, 67–68; as descriptive science, 11; *Gestalt*, 357, 376; individual, 72, 350; of mysticism, 69–70; physiological, 346 and n., 347, 355; physiological as argument against immortality, 395–400; of prayer and worship, 70–72; purposive, 357; of religion, evidence of, 229–230; a science of religion, 33; self, 357–358; social, 74–76; of the subconscious, 73–74; treatment of personality, 225–226; 19, 344, 376–377, 403, 481, 482

Ptolemy, 481

Pupin, M., *Science and Religion*, 483–484, 488 n.

Purpose, and community, 383–384; and eternity, 385–386; problem of human, 371–386; and time, 384–385

Pythagoras, 61

Qualia: Distinguishable qualities, whether of sense, of pleasure, of liking, or of any other sort. 351–352, 363

Racialism, 46
Radhakrishnan, S., 141 n.
Radin, P., 41 n.
Ramanuja, theistic mystic, 170–171
Rashdall, H., 300 n.
Rationalization: The mental process of devising ostensible reasons to justify an act or opinion which is actually based on other motives or grounds. 471. 470–472
Read, C., 41 n., 42 and n.
Realism, agnostic: The theory that reality, although unknown, is of a different kind from consciousness. 142–143; 365; critical, 414 n.
Reason: A logically consistent and coherent method of interpreting experience. Aristotelian-Kantian conception of, 183–184, 189, 192; coherent, 191, 353; as emergent trait of personality, 353; Platonic-Hegelian conception of, 183–185, 189, 192; "pure," 179; supreme source of religious insight, 192; way of knowing God, 183; 2, 364, 403, 421
Reeman, E. H., 300 n.
Reformation, 66
Regula fidei (rule of faith), 179
Reichenbach, H., 486 n.
Reid, J. R., 107 n.
Reinach, S., definition of religion, 16 n.; 17
Relativism, Groos's theory of theoretical, 194
Religion: Concern about experiences which are regarded as of supreme value; devotion toward a power or powers believed to originate, increase and conserve these values; and some suitable expression of this concern and devotion, whether through symbolic rites or through other individual or social conduct. 17. Or Coöperation with God and man for the realization of individual and of shared values. 435. (See Kant, Schleiermacher, Feuerbach, Reinach, Höffding, James, Whitehead, Calverton, Dewey, Hocking, Ferm, 15–16 n.) Atheistic, 56; attempts to define, 13–18; beginning of, 39–45; beliefs, 80–84, 111, 114–116; beliefs as unverifiable, 485–487; central beliefs of, 131; as concern about purpose, 372–373; as a device in the class struggle,

Religion (*Cont.*):
472–476; and economic forces, 78–79; essence of, 249; ethical, 59–61; evidence of, 229–230; as experience, 411–412; as experience of value, 85–88; external criticisms of, 459–489; as a fact, 31–60; as free play of imagination, 477–480; history of: primitive, 36–45; tribal, 45–46; national (priestly), 46–56; universal (prophetic), 56–63; importance of man for, 342–344; as inconsistent with science, 480–485; individualistic, 58–59; internal criticism of, 438–458; living, 63–67; monotheistic, 56, 62–63; Mystery, 44, 393; mystical, 61–62; origin of as determining meaning and value, 476–477; as outgrowth of fear, 461–464; philosophy of, 22; as a philosophical problem, 108–132; philosophy of religion as critical interpretation of, 438–439; of the present and past as disloyal to the ideal, 444–449; of the present as disloyal to spiritual growth, 450–452; a problem for history, psychology and sociology of, 111–112; problem of religious experience, 411–437; as providing no positive value, 487–488; psychology of, 35–36, 74–76; as rationalization of desire, 464–472; reasons for treating it as philosophical problem, 112–115; religious certainty, problem of, 129–131; religious criticism: of the present as disloyal to the past, 443–444; religious problem of good-and-evil, 248–250; religious protest against religious materialism, 447–450; sciences of, 18–20, 33–36; scientific and philosophical investigation of, 31–33; and social groups and institutions, 76–78; and social reforms, 79–80; sociology of, 36, 76–80; tendency of to extremes, criticism of, 452–458; and theory, 237–239; trilemma of, 272–274
Religions, living, 63–67; Mystery, Greek, 393; Mystery, Oriental, 44; table of, 64 n.
Revelation, as argument for immortality, 393–394; doctrinal theory of, 422; dogmatic or intellectualistic view, 175–179; as foundation of religious experience, 417–423; functional theory of, 422; revelation-

Revelation (*Cont.*):
claims, 173–178, 191, 222, 394; teleological or dynamic view, 175–179; way of knowing God, 167–178, 182–183; 23–24, 194, 423
Riehl, A., 225 n.
Rilke, R. M., 300
Rites, religious, 50–51
Ritschl, A., 108, 132 n.
Ritual and sacrifice, 47, 51–52
Roback, A. A., 369 n.
Robertson, H. M., 79 n.
Robinson, H., 293 n.
Rock Veddahs, 48
Rogers, A. K., 186 n.
Roman Catholic Church, theology of, 25. *See* Catholicism.
Rosenberg, A., 29
Rouse, W. H. D., 462 n.
Rousseau, 295 and n., 420
Royce, J., 23, 27, 28, 141, 161 n., 183, 192 n., 195 n., 198, 220, 310, 348 n.
Rueff, J., 19 n.
Russell, B., 4, 168 n., 198, 273 n.; *Religion and Science,* 336, 484, 485 n., 487–488 and n.

Sacraments, 51
Sacred writings, 47, 52–53
Sacrifice, 51–52, 54; human, 52, 54
Sankara, 141 and n.
Santayana, G., 144 n., 198, 477 n.; "animal faith," 349 n., 414, 478–480; "moral faith," 404 n., 480; *The Realm of Essence,* 478–480; *Reason in Religion,* 478–480, 487 n.; *Scepticism and Animal Faith,* 478–480
Satan, 80, 135, 248–249, 264
Schaub, E. L., 132 n.
Schiller, F. C. S., 132 n., 186 n., 188–189, 296
Schilpp, P. A., 132 n.
Schleiermacher, F., definition of religion, 16 n.; 29 n., 222, 419 and n., 434
Schlick, M., 373 n., 396 n., 397 n.
Schneider, H. W., 41 n., 46
Scholastics, 23, 154, 355, 395
Schopenhauer, 40–42, 248
Science: A description of the laws of the behavior of objects disclosed by some particular field of experience. 11, 18. Descriptive, 12, 197; formal and empirical, 18, 19; growth of, 8; normative, 12; problem created

Science (*Cont.*):
by moderns for traditional belief in God, 190–191; of religion, 33–36
Scriptures, Homeric, 33; Oriental, 34; 419–420, 450
Scotus, Duns, 66
Sein and *Sollen* (fact and value), 199, 212
Selbie, W. B., 73 n.
Self: Any and every consciousness, however simple or complex it may be. 350. Analytic theory of, 355–356; characteristics of a minimum, 351–353; datum, 227–228, 358, 359, 360 n., 363, 414
Seligman, C. G., 39
Sellars, R. W., 118 n., 144, 211, 214 and n., 271 n.
Sense data, 179, 348, 363, 403
Shakespeare, 203, 344
Sheffer, H. M., 223 n.
Shintoism, 47–48, 64 n., 127; scriptures of, 53
Shrines and temples, 47, 50–51
Simplicius, 192–193, 314 n.
Simpson, J. Y., 408 n.
Situation: Any actual state of affairs, whether now experienced or not. Believed-in, 347–349 and n., 359, 360 n.; as datum self, 227–228, 348 n.; Disbelieved-in, 348; empirical, 227–228, 358; Experienced, 347–349 and n., 359, 360 n.
Smith, C. P., 312
Smith, N. K., 293 n., 307, 487 n.
Social organization, 47–50
Sociology, Comte as founder of modern, 143; as descriptive science, 11; of religion, evidence of, 229–230; as science of religion, 33
Socrates, appeal to reason, 59; 60–62, 84, 287, 375, 440, 444, 451, 464, 480
Solipsism: The view that there are no objects other than my present experiences. 414. 322, 415 n.
Sorley, W. R., 101 n., 208 n., 240 n.
Space-Time, 200, 214, 216–220, 223
Spaulding, E. G., 118 n., 148, 309 n.
Spencer, B., 45
Spencer, H., 110–111; *First Principles,* 142–143; 150, 155
Spinoza, 103; definition of God, 136 and n.; 210–211, 218, 310, 387, 404, 452

Spiritism: The belief that nature is animated by spirits. 42–43, 55
Starbuck, E. D., 35, 36, 68, 80 n.
Statius, 41 and n.
Stern, W., 351
Stevenson, B., 41 n.
Stoics, 23, 464
Stolz, K. R., 68 n., 80 n.
Stratton, G. M., 68 and n.
Strickland, F. L., 35, 80 n.
Studdert-Kennedy, G. A., 300
Subjectivism: Synonym of solipsism. 110
Subsistence, logical: The meaning of a concept, regardless of the existence of the object to which it refers. 235–236
Substance, spiritual: A permanent immaterial reality underlying consciousness. 356. Theory of, 355–357
Supernaturalism, deistic: God as superhuman and supernatural revealer of values. 145. 146–147, 157–158, 221–222; neo-, 420
Surd: An evil that is not reducible to good, no matter what operations are performed on it. 245 n. Coherent account of, 318–319; the dysteleological, a type of evil, 245, 382; 276–277, 297, 309–312, 314, 325 n., 327, 331–332, 334
Sutherland, 315

Tagore, R., 69, 423
Taoism, 64 n., 432
Tarde, G., 75
Telang, K. F., 455 n.
Teleology: The view that the cosmos, or at least some cosmic power beyond man, expresses purpose through the realization of ends. 374. Argument for God, 215–216, 227; evidence for, 379–380; and mechanism: problem and definition, 373–375; relations between mechanism and, 382–383; stages of thought about, 375–376; teleological view of revelation, 175–179; 204
Telepathy: Transmission of thought from mind to mind without a physical medium. 359
Temporalism: The view that time is irreducibly real. 335
Tennant, F. R., 28, 29 n., 132 n., 227 n., 370 n.

Tertullian, 420, 451, 481
Theism: The conception of God as conscious mind, immanent both in nature and in value. 157. Or, God the cosmic source of all nature and of all value experience. 166. 158–161, 199, 203; atheism as evidence for, 232; empirical, 212 n.; naturalistic, 212 n.; personalistic, 226–227; 231; 369, 383, 399, 403, 407, 423, 433
Theology: "Theory about God." 23. Feuerbach's, 465; in Middle Ages, 33; natural and revealed, 23–26; 394 n., 411
Theosophists, 261 and n.
Thomas à Kempis, 69, 237
Thomists: Scholastics, followers of Saint Thomas Aquinas. 208, 274
Thompson, F., 258 n.
Thomson, M. K., 469 n.
Thouless, R. H., 68 n., 71 n., 73 n., 76 n.
Tillich, Paul, 25, 132 n., 173–174, 328, 362 n.
Time, and space, 351–352; and purpose, 384–385; transcendence of, 351–352, 363–364
Titius, A., 489 n.
Totemism, 42–44
Toy, C. H., 34, 42, 46, 48, 52 n., 80 n.
Troeltsch, E., 3 n., 132 n.
Trueblood, D. E., 163 n., 195 n.
Truth, criterion of religious, 122–129
Tsanoff, R. A., 275 n.; The Nature of Evil, 300; 410 n.

Underhill, Evelyn, 432 n.
Universe, interaction of all parts, 206
Unknowable, The, 110–111, 143, 150, 223–224, 237
Urban, W. M., 107 n., 278 n., 346 n., 386 n.
Upanishads, 57, 60, 141

Value: Whatever is actually liked, prized, esteemed, desired, approved, or enjoyed by anyone at any time. 88. Prereligious value: Any experience of an empirical value (whether or not it be a true value) which is not yet "taken" as related to a cosmic source of value. n. 11, 417. Actual, 88; apparent, 91–92; coalescence of religious with other values, 104–

Value (*Cont.*):

105, 113; connection with interaction, 206; Continuer of, 194, 198, 200; Continuer and Source of, 202–203, 209 and n., 217, 221; empirical, 91; evidence for God, 199; experience, 198, 206–207, 230–232, 240 n.; God as conscious mind, immanent in, 157–161; God as human aspiration for ideal, 143–145; God as personified particular, 137–138; God as source and conserver of, 134–137; God as system of ideal, 147–148; God as the tendency of nature to support or produce, 148–153; ideal, 361–362; instrumental, 89–90, 241 and n.–248; intrinsic, 89–90, 93, 95–98, 244 n., 246; potential, 88; religious, 85–107, 111; source of, 203; spiritual, 361–362; symbolized in conceptions of the divine, 135; table of, 94–100; true or real, 92–93; value-claims, 91–92, 114–116, 206; uniqueness of religious, 102–104; unity in source of, 205–206; 401, 403

Vatke, J., 236, 260

Vaughan, W. F., 369 n.

Vedas, 47, 53

Verification: Insight into the coherence between the hypothesis with which the experimenter starts and the results of his experiment. 486. 119–121; problem of, 234; public, 486; scientific, 486; social, 321–322

Voltaire, *Candide,* 260 n.; 295 and n.

Wach, J., 36, 77–78, 80 n.

Walker, E. R., 30 n.

Ward, J., 452

Ward, W., *All Religions and Religious Ceremonies,* 34 n.

Warren, H. C., 471

Waterhouse, E. S., 76 n.

Watson, J. B., 213

Webb, C. C. J., 300 n.

Weber, M., 36, 77; *The Protestant Ethic and the Spirit of Capitalism,* 78; 79 n., 80 n.

Wells, H. G., 275 n.; *God the Invisible King,* 298; 301, 310 n., 324

Wertfrei (free from value), 33, 85 n., 276

Westermarck, E., 80 n.

Wheelwright, P. E., 165 n.

White, A. D., 482

Whitehead, A. N., definition of religion, 16 n.; 23, 28, 151; as modern theist, 160 and n.; 228 n., 236 n., 278 n., 299, 335, 337 n., 347 n., 348 n., 373 n., 383, 386 n.

Wieman, H. N., 24, 29 n., 30, 130–131, 132 n.; definition of God, 136 and n.; 146 n., 151–153, 161 n., 209 and n., 211, 212 n., 213 n., 214, 300–301, 325 n., 331 and n., 420

Wilde, O., 103

Williams, D. C., 314 n.

Wilm, E. C., 183 n.

Wilson, G. A., 159

Windelband, W., 94

Witchcraft, 41

Witnesses of Jehovah, 25

Woolman, J., 423

Worship, psychology of, 70–72; 249, 342, 434 n.

Wright, W. K., 42 n., 45 n., 54 and n.; *A Student's Philosophy of Religion,* 70 and n.; 132 n., 135 n., 227 n., 300, 386 n.

Writings, sacred, 52–53

Xenophanes, 63 and n., 292, 444, 449, 458 n.

Xenophon, *Memorabilia,* 62 n., 480 n.

Yahgans, 48

Yaroslavsky, F., 473 n.; *Religion in the U. S. S. R.,* 474

Yoga, 340

Zoroaster, 58, 59, 61, 63, 291–292, 464; Zoroastrianism, 172, 291

Zweig, S., 42